D1458133

Understanding the New Politics of ABORTION

To the women in my life who make life such a joy
Mary-Margaret, Jennifer, and Selena

Understanding the New Politics of ABORTION

Malcolm L. Goggin

editor

 SAGE Publications
International Educational and Professional Publisher
Newbury Park   London   New Delhi

For information address:

 SAGE Publications, Inc.
2455 Teller Road
Newbury Park, California 91320

SAGE Publications Ltd.
6 Bonhill Street
London EC2A 4PU
United Kingdom

SAGE Publications India Pvt. Ltd.
M-32 Market
Greater Kailash I
New Delhi 110 048 India

Printed in the United States of America

Library of Congress Cataloging-in-Publication Data

Main entry under title:

Understanding the new politics of abortion / edited by Malcolm L. Goggin.
   p.   cm.
  Includes bibliographical references and index.
  ISBN 0-8039-5240-6.—ISBN 0-8039-5241-4 (pbk.)
   1. Abortion—Political aspects—United States. 2. Abortion—Law and legislation—United States. 3. Abortion—Public opinion—United States. I. Goggin, Malcolm L., 1938- .
HQ767.5.U5U52 1993
363.4′6—dc20   93-17610

93 94 95 96 10 9 8 7 6 5 4 3 2 1

Sage Production Editor: Astrid Virding

Contents

Foreword

This book grew out of a happy coincidence of interests. During our editorship of the *American Political Quarterly,* we, along with the Editorial Board, decided that a special symposium on the politics of abortion would be a timely contribution to an issue of the journal. We hoped that such a symposium, announced well in advance, would both stimulate and report high quality research on this important issue.

At the same time, Sage Publications encouraged us to think about publishing edited collections of articles from *American Politics Quarterly.* The topic of abortion politics seemed exciting to them as well as to us.

Before long, we began to receive a steady flow of submissions for the special issue, many of very high quality. There were, in fact, 4 times as many as we could publish, and many good articles were rejected. With this in mind, we were delighted when Malcolm L. Goggin expressed an interest in writing an overview of the field of abortion politics for the special issue, and when, some time later, he accepted our invitation to edit this book.

Our special issue was published in January 1993 and reflected the best of up-to-date scholarship on public attitudes toward abortion, causes and consequences of state abortion policy, and abortion politics in the legislatures. In this volume, Malcolm L. Goggin has expanded the coverage to include substantially greater treatment of the context of the abortion debate, as well as additional chapters focusing on both public opinion and legislative politics. He has also revised and updated his own thinking on the framework for understanding the new politics of abortion.

Together, the chapters in this volume stand as an indication that political scientists have much to offer to our understanding of the nature of abortion politics. Given the likelihood that this issue will remain high on the public agenda for quite some time, we are sure these chapters will be widely cited by those laboring to understand this complex issue.

—SUSAN WELCH
Pennsylvania State University

—JOHN HIBBING
University of Nebraska-Lincoln

Preface

The seeds for this book were planted in 1988, when I spent the year at the Brookings Institution in Washington, DC, as a Guest Scholar. While interviewing members of the U.S. House of Representatives and Senate and their staff as well as several representatives of organized interests I soon learned that there was no "wall of separation" between abortion and family planning. It also was evident that abortion was a very complex issue when lawmakers were faced with tough policy—as opposed to moral or legal—choices. Moreover, many legislators in Washington hoped that they would not have to cast a vote on either the family planning or abortion issue during a Presidential election year, when party unity was so desirable.

On July 3, 1989, in its *Webster v. Reproductive Health Services* decision, the Supreme Court narrowly upheld a very restrictive anti-choice Missouri statute that prohibited public employees from performing abortions in public facilities, prohibited the use of public facilities to perform abortions, and required doctors to test to see if the fetus could survive outside the womb before performing an abortion. *Webster,* and *Planned Parenthood of Southeastern Pennsylvania v. Casey,* a second landmark Supreme Court decision on abortion restrictions that was decided 3 years later, applied an "undue burden" standard—permitting state restrictions as long as they did not substantially interfere with a woman's free choice to seek and acquire abortion services—that Justice Sandra Day O'Connor articulated in 1983 in *City of Akron v. Akron Center for Reproductive Health* and refined in 1986 in *Thornburgh v. American College of Obstetricians and Gynecologists.* Essentially, *Webster* and *Casey* redefined the political debate by giving states more leeway to adopt abortion restrictions and thus shifted the political venue to the states.

In a paper that I presented at the 1990 annual meeting of the American Political Science Association in San Francisco, I attempted to define the contours of post-*Webster* abortion politics and get down on paper some very preliminary thoughts about how one might make sense of this "new" politics of abortion. A vastly revised version of my APSA paper was published in the January 1993 special abortion politics issue of *American Politics Quarterly*. The Introduction to this volume represents another iteration of my theoretical argument. Seven other articles from *APQ*— most with additions and updates—appear as Chapters 2, 4, 6, 7, 9, 14, and 15 in this book.

I commissioned chapters for this edited volume that take into account shifts in the nature and scope of the conflict over abortion or changes in the institutional context within which the issue of abortion is being debated, changes that have been influenced by the *Webster* and *Casey* decisions. The aims of *Understanding the New Politics of Abortion* are to present a novel theoretical framework for understanding the "new" politics of abortion and serve as: (1) a vessel for the most current empirical and theoretical research on the issue; (2) an up-to-date assessment of the abortion controversy; (3) a stimulus for debate about what abortion policy is likely to be like in the future; and (4) a tool to teach students about abortion as a *political* issue—at all levels and in all branches of American government.

A project of this scope—15 chapters written under very tight deadlines by 28 different authors—could not have been possible without the help of many individuals. I am especially grateful to John Hibbing and Susan Welch, first, for encouraging me to submit an "agenda" piece to *APQ*, and, second, for suggesting that I work with Sage Publications to edit this volume. Others who deserve thanks are the score or so anonymous outside referees who critically reviewed at least some of the book chapters. Mary-Margaret Goggin selflessly put aside her own professional activities to nurse me through several weeks of pneumonia while helping me with the editing; and Peter Goggin prepared the index. Wanda Seguin, Deborah A. Orth, Ai-Ping Cai, Tiffany Quaranta, Robbie Strong, and German Espinoza helped with the administrative aspects of putting all the pieces of this rather complex writing project together. Finally, the book moved forward about as fast and as flawlessly as one could expect, thanks to the able nurturing of Carrie Mullen, editor at Sage Publications, and Mary Curtis, her editorial assistant.

—MALCOLM L. GOGGIN

Introduction

A *Framework for Understanding the New Politics of Abortion*

MALCOLM L. GOGGIN

As the United States entered the decade of the 1990s, battles over abortion were raging in all branches and at all levels of government. The U.S. Supreme Court's July 1989 *Webster v. Reproductive Health Services* decision granting states more freedom to place additional restrictions on abortions; the Court's June 1990 decision in *Hodgson v. Minnesota* that let stand a Minnesota law requiring teenagers seeking an abortion to get the consent of two parents as long as there is a judicial bypass option; the protracted struggle among the judicial, executive, and legislative branches of government over a controversial Department of Health & Human Services "gag" rule prohibiting workers in federally funded family planning clinics from giving advice about the availability of abortion services; as well as tough new state antiabortion laws like the ones in Idaho, Louisiana, and Utah have meant additional restrictions on a woman's already qualified right to have an abortion.[1] Together, these events also point to a new political climate surrounding the abortion issue.

What these rapid changes in the political landscape suggest is the emergence of a new, post-*Webster* politics of abortion. The parameters of this "new" politics of abortion are outlined in the first section of this introductory chapter. In the second section, a framework to aid understanding of the politics of abortion is explicated. This framework depends on an assessment of the nature and scope of the conflict over abortion and the institutional context within which that conflict takes place. In the concluding pages, the themes, purposes, and organization of this edited volume are briefly sketched.[2]

Contrasting the "Old" and "New" Politics of Abortion

What is different about the "new" politics of abortion? In the pre-*Webster* era, groups opposed to abortion directed much of their attention to the Supreme Court, where, between 1973 and 1989, approximately 50 abortion-related cases were decided (see Eisenstein 1988; Epstein and Kobylka 1992; Keyes, with Miller 1989; Mezey 1992; Rubin 1987).[3] The many court actions taken by the fetal-rights forces[4] were aimed at gradually chipping away at a woman's qualified right to have an abortion that was embedded in *Roe v. Wade*. Now, right-to-life forces are seeking nothing less than a reversal of *Roe*. Four developments since *Webster*—a shift in the composition of the Supreme Court, an increase in the percentage of the public who apparently now prefer to make abortion illegal, an expansion of activity in state legislatures, and an increase in public activities by members of fetal-rights groups—indicate that overturning *Roe* is much more likely.

The Political Context

Between January 1973, when *Roe v. Wade* was decided, and July 1989, when the *Webster* decision was handed down, the liberal 7-2 majority on the Supreme Court turned into a 5-4 conservative majority (see Table A.1). Since *Webster*, two more conservatives—Associate Justices David Souter and Clarence Thomas—have been added. There is now a solid 6-3 conservative majority.[5]

During the 1970s and 1980s, many Americans seemed ambivalent and uneasy about confronting the issue of abortion. But they appeared content with the status quo, preferring it to the two extremes of unrestricted access to abortion—abortion on demand—or making abortion illegal in all circumstances (see Table A.2).

Since *Webster*, a larger percentage of the public seems to think abortion "should not be permitted," increasing from 15% in November 1989 to 22% in June 1991 (*CBS News/New York Times* 1989-1991).[6] This recent, post-*Webster* shift in public opinion in the fetal-rights direction also makes it more likely that *Roe* will be overturned.

Webster effectively transferred authority over access to abortion services to state politicians, and the institutional forums quickly shifted to state legislatures and state political campaigns (Goggin and Wlezien 1992; Mezey 1992:262-63). States responded accordingly. In the months immediately following the July 1989 landmark decision, almost 40 bills were introduced in state legislatures around the country and in many states there were calls for special sessions to deal with the abortion issue (Alan

Table A.1 Major Abortion Cases 1973-Present

Case	Date	Issue(s)	Vote[a]	P/A[b]
Roe v. Wade	1973	Abortion criminalized	7-2	P
Doe v. Bolton	1973	Hospital/doctor restrictions; residency requirement	7-2	P
Planned Parenthood of Central Missouri v. Danforth	1976	Saline abortions; parental/spousal consent; recordkeeping/reporting; physician's duty to fetus; definition of viability	5-4	P
Beal v. Doe	1977	Medicaid funding limits under Social Security Act	6-3	A
Maher v. Roe	1977	Medicaid funding limits under equal protection clause	6-3	A
Poelker v. Doe	1977	Public hospital's refusal to perform abortions	6-3	A
Bellotti v. Baird	1979	Parental consent	8-1	P
Colautti v. Franklin	1979	Physician's duty to fetus	6-3	A
Harris v. McRae	1980	Constitutionality of Hyde amendment	5-4	A
M. L. v. Matheson	1981	Parental notice	6-3	A
Akron v. Akron Center for Reproductive Health	1983	Second-trimester hospitalization; parental consent; waiting period; risk/fetal development lecture	6-3	P
Planned Parenthood of Kansas City v. Ashcroft	1983	Second-trimester hospitalization; pathology report; second physician; parental consent	5-4[c]	A
Simopoulos v. Virginia	1983	Second-trimester abortions in licensed facilities	8-1	A
Thornburgh v. ACOG	1986	Risk-fetal development lecture; recordkeeping/reporting; physician's duty to fetus; second physician; waiting period	5-4	P
Zbaraz v. Hartigan	1987	Parental notice; waiting period	4-4[d]	P
Webster v. Reproductive Health Services	1989	Preamble defining life; public fund restrictions; viability testing	5-4	A
Hodgson v. Minnesota	1990	Two-parent notice	5-4[e]	A
Ohio v. Akron Center for Reproductive Health	1990	Parental notice	6-3	A
Planned Parenthood of Southeastern Pennsylvania v. Casey	1992	Spousal consent; informed consent; parental consent; waiting period	5-4[f]	A

SOURCE: Adapted from Susan Gluck Mezey, *In Pursuit of Equality: Women, Public Policy, and the Federal Courts*, New York: St. Martin's, 1992, p. 211.
NOTES: a. Because votes in abortion cases are often split on the specific regulation, the vote shown may not represent the votes on all issues decided.
b P = Pro-choice. A majority voted to strike all, or most of, the regulation under review; A = Antiabortion. A majority voted to uphold all, or most of, the regulation under review.
c. A 6-3 majority struck the hospitalization requirement; a different 5-4 majority voted to uphold the other provisions.
d. With an equally divided Court, the lower court ruling (striking the waiting period) was affirmed.
e. A 5-4 majority found the two-parent notice provision unconstitutional; a different 5-4 majority ruled that it was made constitutional by the judicial bypass procedure.
f. A 5-4 majority found the spousal consent provision unconstitutional; a different 5-4 majority voted to uphold the other provisions.

Table A.2 Attitudes Toward the Legality of Abortion, 1975-1988

Q. Do you think abortions should be legal under all circumstances, only certain
circumstances, or illegal in all circumstances?

	Legal in all circumstances (%)	Legal in certain circumstances (%)	Illegal in all circumstances (%)	No opinion (%)
1975 (1,500+)	21	54	22	3
1977 (1,500+)	22	55	19	4
1979 (1,500+)	22	54	19	5
1980 (1,500+)	25	53	18	4
1981 (1,500+)	23	52	21	4
1983 (1,558)	23	58	16	3
1988 (1,001)	24	57	17	2

SOURCE: The Gallup Poll.
NOTE: The results of the survey are based on telephone interviews with a national sample of adults, aged
18 and over. Number of respondents in each survey is in parentheses.

Guttmacher Institute 1990:3). Moreover, abortion quickly became a central issue in several state elections, for example, in the gubernatorial races in California, Virginia, and New Jersey, and the contest for mayor of New York City (see Dodson and Burnbauer 1990a; and Chapters 8 and 9, this volume). This increased attention to state politics is one of the characteristics of the "new" politics of abortion.

Perhaps because of the liberal majority on the Supreme Court, the "old" politics of abortion was also characterized by an abortion-rights coalition that was often on the defensive; especially after 1976, the movement became more reactive than proactive (Fried 1990:6; Staggenborg 1991:152). This posture changed in anticipation of *Webster* when, during the first half of 1989, pro-choice groups changed their tactics to become both more active and more confrontational (Goggin and Wlezien 1991, 1992). Right-to-life groups, on the other hand, waited until after *Webster* to step up their level of activity (see Table A.3); and during the summer of 1991, and again in the spring of 1992, fetal-rights groups such as Operation Rescue escalated the level of abortion clinic violence. For the pro-choice forces the "new" politics of abortion actually began in early 1989, whereas for right-to-life supporters it started in July 1989—with the *Webster* decision. Thus, one could read *Webster* as the midwife of a "new" politics of abortion.

These features of the shifting political landscape are conditions that favor enactment of the right-to-life agenda. Yet there are at least two recent developments—the Supreme Court's July 1992 *Planned Parenthood of Southeastern Pennsylvania v. Casey* decision to uphold the constitutionality

Table A.3 Abortion-Rights and Fetal-Rights Group Activities, by Year and by Type, 1985-1989

Activities	Year											
	1985		1986		1987		1988		1989		total	
Conventional Activities	AR	FR	AR	FR	AR	FR	AR	FR	AR	FR	AR	FR
Holding a Press Conference	3	0	1	0	3	1	0	0	1	0	8	1
Releasing Report/Poll	0	0	0	0	3	0	0	0	0	0	3	0
Commenting on Decision	1	0	0	0	0	0	0	0	1	1	2	1
Filing an Amicus Curiae Brief	0	0	0	0	0	0	0	0	1	0	1	0
Lobbying Congress	0	0	1	0	0	0	0	0	1	1	2	1
Sub-Total	4	0	2	0	6	1	0	0	4	2	16	3
	80%	0%	33%	0%	100%	33%	0%	0%	17%	13%	38%	8%
	1985		1986		1987		1988		1989		total	
Public Activities	AR	FR	AR	FR	AR	FR	AR	FR	AR	FR	AR	FR
Marching/Demonstrating	1	1	4	3	0	2	1	13	20	4	26	23
Boycotting	0	0	0	0	0	0	0	2	0	1	0	3
Civil Disobedience	0	0	0	1	0	0	0	0	0	9	0	10
Violent Protest	0	0	0	1	0	0	0	0	0	0	0	1
Sub-Total	1	1	4	5	0	2	1	15	20	14	26	37
	20%	100%	67%	100%	0%	67%	100%	100%	83%	87%	62%	92%
Grand-Total	5	1	6	5	6	3	1	15	24	16	42	40
	100%	100%	100%	100%	100%	100%	100%	100%	100%	100%	100%	100%

SOURCE: Adapted from Malcolm L. Goggin and Christopher Wlezien, "Interest Groups and the Socialization of Conflict." Paper Presented at the Midwest Political Science Association, Chicago, April, 1991, tables 1 and 2.
NOTE: AR = Abortion-Rights Group; FR = Fetal-Rights Group

of *Roe v. Wade* and the November 1992 presidential election of Bill Clinton, a committed pro-choice Democrat—as well as two countermobilization strategies that will make it more difficult to ban abortions and, at least in the short run, lead to stalemate, thus stalling any pro-life victory.

In July 1992 the Supreme Court decided to restrict access to abortion in the state of Pennsylvania by upholding all but one of the provisions in a statute that placed severe restrictions on choice. In *Casey,* the Court agreed with Planned Parenthood that spousal notification represented an undue burden for married women seeking an abortion. But the significance of the Court's decision also lay in its support for the state of Pennsylvania's ability to place further restrictions on abortion, for example, denying the use of public hospitals for the purpose of gender selection, and requiring a 24-hour notification period, parental notification, and a lecture from a physician.

But more important, the Court's narrow 5-4 vote to uphold *Roe* was a stunning upset for the Bush administration and fetal-rights forces who had seen the *Casey* decision as the first opportunity for the newly constituted Court to confront the constitutionality of *Roe* directly. The 1992 post-*Casey* decision by the Court to let stand *Ada v. Guam Society of Obstetricians/Gynecologists*—an outright ban on abortion—and a similar decision in early 1993 on Louisiana's tough antiabortion law underscore the point, and make it quite evident that the Court will probably refuse to use other state abortion rulings to overturn *Roe* as well.

On January 20, 1993, Bill Clinton, who was elected on an abortion-rights platform and supported by pro-choice interests, moved into the Oval Office, replacing a staunch fetal-rights President. During his campaign for the presidency, Clinton promised to appoint pro-choice supporters to the Supreme Court as vacancies occur, support the Freedom of Choice Act, overturn the "gag" rule, allow fetal tissue research, and consider the medical benefits of importing RU-486. These changes in executive branch policy will undoubtedly thwart the right-to-life agenda, especially the movement to reverse *Roe.*

Pro-choice organizations have also effectively mobilized their supporters, both in Congress and in the nation. Since *Webster,* pro-choice groups have worked hard to enact legislation that would put abortion rights beyond the reach of the Supreme Court. For example, they have supported the Title X Pregnancy Counseling Act (a direct response to the "gag" rule and the Supreme Court's decision in *Rust v. Sullivan*), the Reproductive Health Equity Act, and the Freedom of Choice Act.[7]

Indeed, it could easily be argued that *Webster* is already acting as a catalyst to mobilize pro-choice forces in the same way that *Roe v. Wade* served as the stimulant for a right-to-life single-issue countermovement in the early 1970s (Staggenborg 1991:57). In a sociological reconstruction of the development, maintenance, and growth of the pro-choice movement, both nationally and in the state of Illinois, Suzanne Staggenborg (1991:4-5) makes the argument that, "Despite its ups and downs, the pro-choice movement has remained continually mobilized since its 1973 victory," due in large part to its professional leadership and formalized organization. In short, an increasing threat from the Right helped create a pro-choice movement that became stronger and more institutionalized over time. Ironically, the very survival of the pro-choice movement is attributed to the right-to-life countermovement, beginning with its successful passage of the Hyde amendment banning federal funding for abortion in 1976. Staggenborg tells a fascinating story of escalating mobilization and countermobilization, and predicts that this cycle will eventually lead to a pro-choice victory.[8]

The essential characteristics of the "new" politics of abortion—expansion of activities to all levels and branches of government (especially the states); increased levels of public participation for fetal-rights groups, including an escalation of clinic violence; and pro-choice mobilization and countermobilization that certainly contributed to a Clinton victory in 1992—have implications for both sides of the abortion political controversy. Given a conservative public mood (Stimson 1991), a conservative majority on the Supreme Court, and a cadre of committed activists who now seem bent on changing abortion policy through the enactment of more restrictive state abortion laws, fetal-rights groups have good reason for thinking in terms of victory. On the other hand, abortion-rights groups have seen their cause advanced by the Clinton election victory and his choice of Janet Reno as Attorney General. Partly in response to escalating clinic violence, Reno cited in her confirmation hearings her intention to vigorously protect the right of access to abortion clinics.

Pro-choice forces, who sparred with fetal-rights groups in a cycle of escalating mobilization and countermobilization throughout the 1970s and 1980s, have once again gone on the offensive, targeting state legislatures, the U.S. Congress, and the White House. For example, the National Abortion Rights Action League (NARAL) worked hard to influence the outcomes of the 1992 Congressional and Presidential elections; and new techniques such as EMILY's List (Early Money is Like Yeast) and the Republican WISH List were used to fund successful campaigns of abortion-rights candidates in both political parties. In their choice of tactics, pro-choice groups seem to be trying to capture the middle ground, painting themselves as moderates while portraying pro-life groups as extremists.[9] Some within the ranks of pro-choice activists think that compromise will draw the "soft" supporters, that is, that compromise will move people from the "restrictions" position to the left of center.[10] Others adamantly oppose compromise (Fried 1990:7-8).[11]

Both groups have built networks and coalitions with other social, political, or religious movements and established linkages to other issues (Conover and Gray 1983; Gelb 1989:135). During the Reagan era, the right-to-life movement successfully tied abortion to the so-called social issues, and forged a link with political conservatives who favor the restoration of traditional family values (see Paige 1983). In seeking to go beyond the single issue of abortion, pro-choicers, on the other hand, couched their demands in terms of a wholesale transformation of society (Petchesky 1984), and in conjunction with a comprehensive reproductive health agenda that includes access to contraception and sex education, as well as an end to forced sterilization of poor and minority women (Bishop 1979; Freeman 1979; Fried 1990:9).

Understanding the Politics of Abortion

The conceptual framework that is used here to understand this "new" politics of abortion is constructed from two arguments: (1) E. E. Schattschneider's (1960) notion of "expanding the scope of the conflict"; and (2) David Greenstone and Paul Peterson's (1973) distinction between "ideological" and "pluralistic" bargaining. The politics of abortion can best be understood by examining—at various points in time—the nature and scope of the conflict over abortion and the institutional context within which that conflict takes place.

The Scope of Conflict

Consider Schattschneider's ideas about conflict. "The dynamics of politics," according to E. E. Schattschneider, "has its origin in strife" (Schattschneider 1960:35). In any strife, there are those who fight—the gladiators—and those who watch the fight—the spectators. Schattschneider's insight is that rather than the combatants, it is the spectators, especially the extent of their participation in the conflagration, who are the key to understanding politics. Schattschneider (1960:3) defines the outcome in terms of the degree to which conflict is contagious:

> At the nub of politics are, first, the way in which the public participates in the spread of the conflict and, second, the processes by which the unstable relation of the public to the conflict is controlled.

Strategically, it is in the best interest of the contestant who is losing a fight to bring more and more fence sitters into the conflict—socialize it—until the balance of forces changes. Thus, it is to the advantage of the one who is losing a contest to "expand the scope of the conflict" (Schattschneider 1960:2). Conversely, it is advantageous for the one who is winning to contain the scope of the conflict—to privatize it—so as not to upset the favorable balance of power. To summarize, fights are frequently won or lost over the combatants' success either at getting the spectators involved in or excluding them from the fight. A change in scope may lead to a new balance of power and a new result (Schattschneider 1960).

> If one side is too hard-pressed, the impulse to redress the balance by inviting in outsiders is almost irresistible. . . . It is the loser who calls for outside help. (Schattschneider 1960:15)

One tactic used by the faction that is not getting its way is to involve more and more people by making the issue more visible—by provoking those people who are sitting on the sidelines to take a stand on the issue. Getting fence-sitters to take a position or opponents to switch sides usually comes from raising consciousness by drawing attention to the issue via "public" strategies, for example, boycotts, demonstrations, riots, public hearings, and media coverage. Another goal for interest groups is to mobilize loyalists. Both sides are doing this: pro-choice groups by direct mail, by educating the public about the threat of losing the qualified right to an abortion, and by painting the opposition as extremists; and pro-life groups by direct mail and civil disobedience.[12]

This "winning/losing side" perspective depends upon major interventions or "shocks" such as the *Roe v. Wade* or *Webster v. Reproductive Health Services* that alter the status quo dramatically (Walsh 1988). Viewing abortion through this lens should shed new light on the ways in which events like *Roe* and *Webster* affect the mobilization and countermobilization tactics of groups on both sides of the issues (Zald and Useem 1987).

The Nature of Conflict Over Abortion

Schattschneider's ideas about the *scope* of conflict can shed light on the politics of abortion, but the *nature* of the conflict can be an aid to understanding abortion politics as well. Indeed, the questions driving much of the research on the issue of abortion are questions about conflict, whether that conflict be political, ideological, religious, moral, social, or about conflicting abortion attitudes among people with gender, racial, or social class differences. For many of those who hold the fetal-rights position, abortion is fundamentally a religious and moral conflict.

Religious Conflict

One of the basic themes of *Roe v. Wade* is that a woman's right to an abortion supersedes the rights, if any, of the fetus. One interpretation of this "clash of absolutes" (Tribe 1990) between the rights of a pregnant woman to the *liberty* to decide for herself and in privacy whether or not to have an abortion, and the rights of the fetus to *life* is that this is a religious rather than a legal conflict with its roots in two fundamentally different religious philosophies. One is Secular Humanism, which values life of the mother over the fetus. The other is the decidedly anti-woman Judeo-Christian religious tradition that presumes abortion to be murder—a clear case of a violation of natural law (Paige 1983:30-31, 34-5).

The pro-choice position is consistent with *Roe* on this clash between life and liberty. But because of the "terminal value" nature of the abortion issue, *Roe* is rejected by those who hold the right-to-life position. The religious conflict is over whether or not the fetus is human, and, if so, in what sense it is human, and in what ways the fetus is to enjoy a claim to life (Lotstra 1985:4). The Catholic Church is "unwilling to deprive one human being of its most fundamental right for the sake of another's less fundamental right" (Lotstra 1985:297). And for fundamentalists, only God can create a human being, and therefore only God has a right to destroy her or him (Merton 1981:6). For the Catholic Church and several Fundamentalist Christian denominations have taken the position that life begins at conception, and thus abortion is murder. The fetus is portrayed as a helpless victim. Fetal-rights organizations have rallied behind this idea of fetal innocence and have mobilized the faithful around the religious symbols of the "sanctity of human life" and "fetal personhood" (Petchesky 1984:332). For fetal-rights forces, abortion is a moral and religious issue, a symbol of America's moral decay and decline of traditional religious values; for pro-choicers, abortion is more a political and ideological issue.

Political Conflict

Abortion symbolizes a fundamental political struggle in the United States for control and power over the *ends* of government. Right-to-life groups and antifeminists are using politics—a method for resolving conflicts over what governments should or should not do—to maintain existing power arrangements and to restore patriarchal control over whether, how, and with whom women have children (Boneparth 1982; Petchesky

1984:16). Leaders of the reproductive-rights movement are working to alter the power structure not only to achieve equality of conditions for reproductive choice (Petchesky 1984:390) but also to create a society in which women are released from existing social and sexual roles of home-makers, wives, and mothers (Gelb and Palley 1987:6). The political argument of feminists (e.g., Fried 1990; Petchesky 1984) is that the women's movement has to move beyond the limited political goal of "choice" to the goal of greater equality between the sexes, races, and classes.

Abortion also has come to symbolize a struggle for control and power over the *means* of government, for example, the judiciary, the executive, and especially, the legislature. The success of the New Right in gaining control of the judiciary and the White House is well documented (Klatch 1987:204; Schwartz 1988; Tribe 1990:chap. 8). Furthermore, in an effort to punish women who express themselves sexually outside the "traditional" family, fetal-rights groups have also been able to convince the Congress to withhold funds that Medicaid had earmarked for those who may require medical assistance but cannot afford it.

The issue of how the power to make public policy should be shared among the levels and branches of government is also an area of conflict. In 1980, it surfaced when the Supreme Court upheld the Congressional prerogative to deny federal Medicaid funding for abortions (*Maher v. Roe,* 432 US 464, 479). And it emerged most recently in March 5, 1992 House Judiciary Subcommittee Hearings in connection with H.R. 25—the Freedom of Choice Act. Harvard Constitutional law professor Lawrence Tribe, testifying in support of H.R. 25, argued that passing this law would guarantee the protection of a woman's life and health and uphold the right to freedom of choice. He claimed that Section 5 of the 14th Amendment permits Congress to write a national abortion law in the event that the Supreme Court overturns *Roe v. Wade*. Timothy Flanigan, Acting Assistant Attorney General, a lawyer at the Justice Department and spokesperson for the Bush administration, argued that if H.R. 25 were enacted, the basic principle of federalism would be damaged. The Constitutional design of balancing state and federal interests would be seriously undermined. Moreover, Flanigan argued that Congress has no power under Section 5 of the Fourteenth Amendment to determine substantive Constitutional provisions. The arguments were repeated in the Senate Finance Committee Hearings of May 13, 1992. John Harrison, with the Office of Legal Council in the Department of Justice, countered that as a matter of law and a matter of policy *Roe* was wrong and should be overturned; abortion restrictions should be a matter for the individual states to decide. Harrison contended that Congress cannot use the authority of Section 5 to restrict individual rights.

Another dimension of political conflict is partisan politics. In terms of *national* party politics, abortion has become a major social issue on which the two major political parties disagree.[13] In the past several presidential campaigns, candidates clearly have squared off on this issue; and, as evidenced by the national party platforms and conventions, the 1992 campaign was no exception. In spite of recent efforts on the part of Republican Party leaders to define the party as the party of inclusion—a "big tent" capable of accommodating pro-choice as well as right-to-life members—the Republican party is having difficulty shedding its "anti-abortion" image.

Ideological Conflict

Ideological polarization between liberal feminists and conservative antifeminists is another type of conflict that characterizes the abortion issue. The conflict is essentially over the vision of what it means to be a woman (Conover and Gray 1983). On the one hand, the feminists' vision is of an emancipated or liberated woman taking control of her own body (Eisenstein 1988; Gordon 1977). The claim is for reproductive rights—a woman's right to limit her own reproduction. And feminists demand that these rights of sexual autonomy be respected; that is, women should be afforded the same rights and privileges that are available to men. Feminists seek to empower women by altering their political, economic, and social status (Mezey 1992:1).

As a political protest movement that was born as a countermobilization to the pro-choice victories of the early 1970s, antifeminists went well beyond Catholic dogma. Antifeminists not only have attacked the feminists' liberal agenda, but also aggressively pursued their own ideas of how the world should work. Rosalind Petchesky (1984:242) sees the antiabortion movement as a "battering ram" against "non-traditional families, feminism, teenage sexuality, welfare state, socialism, and every other target of the Right."

In a study of fetal-rights and abortion-rights protagonists in the state of California, Kristin Luker (1984) shows how activists clash—over world-views, life expectations, and life choices. Pro-choice and right-to-life activists—those people most heavily involved in the movements to affect abortion policy[14]—have conflicting ideologies that are manifested in their different views about sex roles, motherhood, family size, and careers.

Fetal-rights activists tend to define the fetus as a person and value motherhood as the most important role a woman can play in life; they are much more likely to accept traditional sex roles. Organized religion is a fixture in the pro-life activist's life and church attendance is high. As a result, the fetal-rights activist is more likely to rely on faith than reason, and more likely to accept gracefully the hand that life has dealt her, an unwanted pregnancy for example (Luker 1984:214). In contrast, pro-choice activists tend to deny the personhood of the fetus, and value career over motherhood. They are also less likely to accept traditional sex roles.

One thing is clear from Luker's and others' studies of activists: neither the Right nor the Left is monolithic (Boneparth 1982; Eisenstein 1984; Fried 1990; Frohock 1983; Gelb 1989; Ginsburg 1989; Klatch 1987; Luker 1984; Merton 1981; Paige 1983; Petchesky 1984; Staggenborg 1991). Ideological conflicts are found *within* each camp as well. A number of studies of leaders of the pro-choice movement note the distinction between the goals of "radical" and "reformist" feminists (Gelb 1989; see also Eisenstein 1984). And at least one detailed case study of New Right activists distinguishes the "social" from the "laissez faire" conservative (Klatch 1987). Nevertheless, the real conflict is not *within* the Left or the Right but *between* them (Boneparth 1982:305; Eisenstein 1984). Another real conflict is one between the sexes.

Gender Conflict

Indeed, there is a clear gender basis of the abortion issue. Those who are fighting to win and protect abortion rights for women are often motivated by the desire to remedy the dual problems of gender division of labor and gender hierarchy, or the subordination of women in society (MacKinnon 1987; Meyer 1987; Mezey 1992). Gender inequality and gender injustice are two organizing themes in the women and politics literature (Okin 1989; Young 1990); they help shape the abortion debate as well.

Luker found that about 20% of the activists in her sample were men. In contrast to fundamental differences between women activists on each side of the issue, she found that men in the abortion rights movement had background characteristics very similar to men in the fetal rights move-ment (Luker 1984:194). Luker's study of male and female activists and other studies comparing the abortion attitudes of males and females in the general public have concluded that men and women think differently about the abortion issue (Ebaugh and Haney 1985; Luker 1984; Scott and Schuman 1988; Wilcox 1990). Because the abortion debate is essentially about the lives of women, they have a greater vested interest in abortion. For career women with an unwanted pregnancy, a pregnancy to term usually means an interruption in career; for men it usually does not. The extent to which these differences in feelings about abortion between men and women are translated into differences in political action (Sapiro 1983) is debatable.

Gender is also an important predictor variable in the literature on women's representation in American politics and government. Attitudinal gender differences have, for some time, been found among state legislators (Diamond 1977; Diamond and Hartsock 1981; Sapiro 1981), with female policymakers more likely than male legislators to support liberal legislation (Dodson 1989; Welch 1985). Gender attitudinal differences have also been associated with differences in willingness to support women's issues, for example, abortion and the broader, related issue of reproductive health. Evidence from Saint-Germain's (1989) study of policy making in the Arizona legislature shows that gender affects both the choice of which policies to initiate and the degree of success in getting women's issues enacted. In a recent study of members of the lower houses in 12 states, Thomas and Welch (1991) examine priorities rather than votes. Nevertheless, they observe that female legislators are more likely than men to give priority to issues concerning women.

Class and Racial Conflict

Abortion presented a threat, not only to traditional gender and sexual relations but to traditional racial and class relations as well (Lipset and Raab 1970; Merton 1981:31). In addition to gender, Luker compared pro-choice and right-to-life activists according to class and race. They differed with respect to their socioeconomic status, that is, levels of education and income, and type of occupation. Indeed, in addition to valuing motherhood over a career, the typical fetal-rights activist is less well educated, less likely to be in the work force, and poorer than her counterpart on the pro-choice side. Studies relating racial differences to abortion attitudes among the public also document conflicting attitudes and behaviors across racial lines: Compared to whites, blacks are consistently less supportive of legal abortion (Arney and Trescher 1976; Combs and Welch 1982; Hall and Ferree 1986; Ransford and Miller 1983). When controls for the effects of extraneous variables are introduced, the differences by race are less pronounced but still statistically significant (Combs and Welch 1982).

The Institutional Context

David Greenstone and Paul Peterson's (1973) ideas about policy making provide the second dimension of the proposed analytical framework. For noncontroversial "valence" or "style" issues (Carmines and Stimson 1980; Goggin 1984; Key 1961), *pluralistic bargaining* leading to compromise is the rule. For contentious "position" issues such as abortion—where there are two identifiable sides—the principal means of making public policy is, and will continue to be, *ideological bargaining.* Pluralism may be a useful way of analyzing the politics of a large number of public, mostly distributive, policies; but it is not very helpful in understanding the politics of abortion. Abortion, as an issue, is largely redistributive.[15] The single-issue groups who are locked in the abortion struggle are doing everything they can to avoid compromising their principles. Indeed, each side is trying to defeat rather than persuade the other. These are some of the reasons that abortion politics is classified as a case of ideological bargaining.

In this context, pluralistic bargaining is characterized by multiple, disparate groups with cross-cutting membership and shifting alliances. Because no one faction has sufficient power to impose its will on the rest, fragile, temporary compromises among contestants are the rule. In contrast, in the case of ideological bargaining competing factions are neither interested in pleasing all parties to the dispute nor in reaching a compromise. Conflict is frequently more bipolar than multi-sided: One side usually wins at the expense of the other.

The analytical framework outlined above directs our attention away from questions of morality and legality and thus away from the two extremes—for example, stark choices between choice and life or life and liberty—to subtle nuances between the absolutes. The cognitive map that I have suggested above should help the reader chart the choppy waters of some recent dramatic changes in the political landscape, and thus should serve as a guide to educated guesses about the future. But it also raises a number of important questions:

- What is the basis of conflict?
- How is conflict likely to be resolved?
- How is state abortion policy likely to be made?
- What are the implications of *Casey?*
- What are the implications of the Clinton victory?

The chapters that follow provide answers to these and other related questions and thus should serve as an aid to predictions about the future of the new politics of abortion.

Plan of This Book

To begin to answer these questions, I invited 27 specialists in abortion politics—some well-established scholars and a few newcomers to the field—to write the 15 chapters that follow. I used a number of explicit criteria of scholarly merit when selecting and editing chapters for this volume. First, I wanted to include chapters that reported on original, up-to-date research. Second, I tried to find chapters that both had something new and important to say and employed methods of analysis that, together, showed the wide variety of approaches to studying abortion as a *political* phenomenon. Third, in addition to the 6 chapters that had previously gone through a rigorous peer review process at *American Politics Quarterly,* I tried to commission chapters that not only could meet similar academic standards, that is, that represented the highest calibre of recent, post-*Webster* and post-*Casey* scholarship, but also report on original and previously unpublished research. Finally, I looked for chapters that combined the advantage of being a source of the latest scholarship in the field *and* the benefit of being suitable for classroom use.

The chapters are organized into three sections, with a brief summary of each chapter preceding each section. The organization of the book is informed by the theoretical framework, with the first section concentrating on conflict. The first two chapters in this section describe and explain the sources of abortion opinion among individuals (Chapter 1) and political activists (Chapter 2). The remaining chapters in Part I use a variety of sophisticated statistical techniques to analyze abortion attitudes among the mass public, with special attention to the stability of abortion attitudes (Chapter 3), individual-level differences in opinion across generations (Chapter 4), and conflicting values and attitudes among both fetal-rights and abortion-rights supporters when an alternative to abortion—adoption—is considered (Chapter 5).

The four chapters in Part II explore conflict in a variety of institutional settings. Two of the chapters shed light on various aspects of abortion policy making in the legislative branch of government, with Chapter 6 focusing on roll call voting on the issue in the U.S. House of Representatives and Chapter 7 analyzing the legislative behavior of state politicians in Idaho. The other two chapters analyze gubernatorial elections, Chapter 8 from the perspective of media coverage of elections in New Jersey, Virginia, Texas, and California; and Chapter 9 in terms of the influence of voter abortion opinion on their vote for governor in the 1991 Louisiana election.

Because one of the underlying premises of this book is that the institutional setting within which abortion politics occurs has shifted to the states as a result of the 1989 *Webster* and 1992 *Casey* Supreme Court decisions, it is logical to include a number of chapters that focus on state abortion policy and politics. The first chapter in Part III provides an historical perspective on the role that the states have traditionally played in expanding the scope of the conflict and in keeping the issue of abortion on the political agenda. Two chapters (Chapters 11 and 12) shed light on the relationship between the abortion attitudes of state residents and the abortion policies of their states while Chapters 13 and 14 report on research that identifies the factors that influence state abortion policies. Chapter 15 examines the role that women state legislators play in shaping state abortion policy. Together, these chapters illuminate the politics of abortion in the post-*Webster* era and pave the way for promising new lines of inquiry.

Notes

1. See Halva-Neubauer (1989b, 1990, and Chapter 10, this volume) for a description of interstate differences in abortion laws and Goggin and Kim (1992) and Chapter 13 for results of a multivariate analyses of what accounts for these differences.

2. For a more detailed summary of each of the chapters in this book, see the introductory comments to each of its three parts.

3. This represents only a small fraction of the cases that were filed. Most proposed state restrictions on abortion were, in fact, struck down by the courts.

4. *Roe v. Wade,* 410 U.S. 113 (1973). One of the most basic conflicts pits a woman's claim to be left alone to make her own decision about abortion in private against claims on behalf of the fetus. This "clash of absolutes" (Tribe 1990) has informed the choice of terms to be used throughout this essay: "fetal-rights" and "abortion-rights" are the primary terms used to describe the two protagonists in the abortion conflict. However, I use "fetal-rights" and "right-to-life" interchangeably and "abortion-rights" and "pro-choice" interchangeably.

5. Based on her recent opinions in *Webster* and *Casey,* I am classifying Sandra Day O'Connor as neither conservative nor liberal on this issue. For an early assessment of the voting record of Associate Justices Souter and Thomas, see "Pennsylvania Case Portends New Attack on Abortion" in the January 25, 1992 issue of *Congressional Quarterly Weekly Report* (Biskupic 1992:169).

6. I wish to thank Michael Kagay, News Service Editor for *The New York Times,* for these survey results. The exact question wording in the four *CBS News/New York Times* surveys between November of 1989 and June of 1991 is: "Which of these comes CLOSEST to your view? (1) Abortion should be generally available to those who want it; or (2) Abortion should be available only under stricter limits than it is now; or (3) Abortion should not be permitted." Most Americans seem not only to want to keep abortion legal, but also to keep government out of what many see as essentially a woman's private decision (*CBS News/New York Times* poll, September 17-20, 1990). These data suggest that the abortion issue is multidimensional.

7. *Rust v. Sullivan,* 110 S.Ct.2559 (1990). Proponents of the Freedom of Choice Act (H.R. 25) are not suggesting that Congress should reverse or overrule the Court. Rather, they want Congress to perform its traditional lawmaking function. Opponents are worried that H.R. 25 would not protect important state interests, for example, the potentiality of life, maintenance of the family unit, and maintenance of parental authority.

8. Staggenborg (1991) is unequivocal in her predictions that the struggle will eventually end in a pro-choice victory. Despite the trends cited by Staggenborg, the severity of the problem, the saliency of the issue, and the intensity of preferences for people on both sides

of the issue are likely to lead to continued, indefinite stalemate. Of course, the issue may become moot if the abortifacient RU-486 is imported. Until that happens, however, I side with Zald and Useem (1987) when they write that the abortion-rights and fetal-rights groups' "victories" and "defeats" in one time period will limit group choices and tactical responses in the next period. Unless something dramatic happens, this "cycle of protest" will very likely continue.

9. This shift to a more moderate position could be seen in the abortion-rights-sponsored advertisements that were aired around the country in various 1992 political campaigns. The image of fetal-rights organizations as extremist was certainly supported by the March 1993 murder of Dr. David Gunn, a Pensacola, FL physician, who provided abortion services, by a Rescue America demonstrator at an abortion clinic.

10. This is precisely what happened between 1985 and 1989. *CBS News/New York Times* pollsters asked an identically worded three-pronged question, "Should abortion be legal as it is now, OR legal ONLY in such cases as rape, incest, or to save the life of the mother, OR should it not be permitted at all?" on eight different occasions between January 1985 and April 1989. The percentage of the public supporting the middle, "restrictions" position fell from 45% in January 1985 to 39% on the eve of *Webster.* The percentage of those supporting the position that comes closest to the pro-choice position ("legal as it is now") increased from 38% to 49% during that same period. The percentage of respondents who supported the fetal-rights position fell from 13% to 9% and the percentage of those responding "don't know" or "not sure" fell slightly from 5% to 3%. For a more detailed analysis of what moved public opinion, see Goggin and Wlezien (1991, 1992) and Wlezien and Goggin (1973).

11. The leadership of the pro-choice movement has apparently reached a compromise by running a two-tiered campaign. On the national level, a more moderate appeal is targeted to the "middle-of-the-road" person. On the local level, the message is more uncompromising, directed at committed supporters of abortion rights.

12. The most confrontational of the antiabortion activists, Randall Terry, and the Operation Rescue organization he heads, increased the number and intensity of acts of civil disobedience, building to a crescendo in the summer of 1991 in Wichita, KS.

As a countermobilization strategy, feminist organizations such as the National Organization for Women (NOW) responded by training thousands of volunteers around the country in clinic defense methods, filing court-ordered injunctions, and seeking court-imposed fines to neutralize Operation Rescue's attacks on abortion clinics.

13. Partisan differences are most clearly established at the national level. What is true of the nation, however, is not necessarily true of the states. Since the 1989 elections Republicans at many levels are indicating considerably more flexibility. In Illinois, for example, it is hard to differentiate a clear party difference on the abortion issue; and in Pennsylvania the Democratic Governor (Casey) was an outspoken critic of the pro-choice plank in the 1992 national Democratic party platform.

14. Luker's conclusions about active participants in the abortion debate are based on interviews with activists in California. These profiles, therefore, cannot be generalized to either the activist population in general or the general public.

15. Abortion, like many other policies, has elements of all three of the policy types suggested by Lowi (1964). It is distributive in the sense that funding is involved; and it is certainly regulatory. Besides the reasons mentioned in the text, I believe abortion is redistributive in the sense that (1) it pits one competing claim against another in a way that if one wins, the other cannot; (2) a means test is used to allocate funds when they are available; and (3) it is a large-scale contest over noneconomic issues, involving two class-based factions (Luker 1984; Tatalovich and Daynes 1981). For other views on how to classify abortion as an issue, see Smith (1975), Outshoorn (1986), and Chapters 3, 5, and 14 in this book.

PART I

THE NATURE AND
SCOPE OF CONFLICT

Conflict among individuals, political elites, and groups over the issue of abortion is at the heart of the abortion controversy and can manifest itself in a number of ways. The five chapters in this section seek to improve our understanding of the "new" politics of abortion by describing, analyzing, and interpreting the subtleties of conflicting values, attitudes, behavior.

Frauke Schnell's chapter attempts to further our theoretical and empirical understanding of the value basis of abortion attitudes. She argues that individual normative values are critical determinants of abortion attitudes: The morally complex and personally wrenching issue of abortion can activate different sets of values that often conflict with each other. Thus, the model she proposes in Chapter 1, which differentiates between firmly held or strong attitudes and merely superficially held expressions of an attitude, moves beyond a single value-attitude formulation to a consideration of the interrelationship among core values. The result of holding equally strong and conflicted values relevant to the issue is a decrease in the strength with which abortion attitudes are held.

Support for the theoretical framework developed in Chapter 1 comes from a survey of 437 students in political science classes at the State University of New York, Stony Brook. The survey results indicate that the

various components of attitude strength appear to be sufficiently independent dimensions of involvement with the abortion issue, and conflict
between relevant core values is associated with a decrease in attitude
strength for most of the attitude strength measures. Moreover, if the
concept of attitude strength is taken into account, then abortion attitudes
are robust predictors of political behavior.

In Chapter 2, James L. Guth, Corwin E. Smidt, Lyman A. Kellstedt, and
John C. Green also raise questions about the relationship between ideology, abortion attitudes, and political behavior. They use the results of a
survey of 4,995 activists from several large religious interest groups to
analyze the demographic, religious, and ideological influences on abortion
attitudes. The results of their statistical analysis show that detailed denominational, doctrinal, and religious practice items are powerful predictors of abortion attitudes among a demographically homogeneous sample
of activists. They also discuss the implications of their findings for the
future of abortion politics.

In Chapter 3, Matthew E. Wetstein uses a linear structural equation
(LISREL) model—a statistical method that is rarely used to analyze
abortion attitudes—to uncover the extent to which *individual* abortion
attitudes are stable over time. He uses panel study data from the 1972-1976
National Election Studies to demonstrate that abortion attitudes are as
stable as party identification. The LISREL model explains 45% of the
variance in responses to six abortion questions in the 1988-1989 General
Social Surveys. The chapter also discusses the impact that recent Supreme
Court decisions might have on the stability of abortion attitudes in the
American public.

Elizabeth Adell Cook, Ted G. Jelen, and Clyde Wilcox argue that
although scholars who focus on generational change generally portray the
youngest cohorts as most liberal, this need not be so. The authors of
Chapter 4 provide evidence that among whites but not blacks, those who
reached adulthood after the 1960s are less supportive of legal abortion than
those who came of age during that decade. Explanations for this result are
tested.

According to Ellen M. Dran and James R. Bowers, public opinion
research on abortion has tended to emphasize public attitudes toward
specific restrictions, ignoring an important question: What if abortions
were illegal, or at least highly restricted? Although there is little data that
examines alternatives to unwanted pregnancies, a 1989 *Los Angeles Times*
poll asked for opinion on adoption, which some public officials have
offered as a panacea for abortions. Dran and Bowers hypothesize that
adoption is an "easy" issue on which to hold an opinion, but that the policy
to realize it is not so facile. Using a typology of opinion from two survey

questions, they demonstrate the conflicting values and attitudes that individuals, both abortion-rights and fetal-rights adherents, would bring to the policy arena if adoption were seriously considered as an alternative. The analysis that is presented in Chapter 5 suggests that one reason public discussion on abortion generally focuses on its morality or legality is that this indeed is the easy dimension of the debate.

1

The Foundations of Abortion Attitudes
The Role of Values and Value Conflict

FRAUKE SCHNELL

During the past two decades abortion, one of the most controversial issues of our time, has received increasing scholarly attention. Inquiries have focused on the intricate web of abortion politics on the state and federal level (e.g., Halva-Neubauer 1991; Woliver 1991), on the impact of the abortion issue in national (e.g., Granberg and Burlison 1983) and state elections (e.g., Dodson and Burnbauer 1990a), as well as on the potential of the abortion issue to mobilize a single-issue public (e.g., Conover and Gray 1983). Less context-bound analyses have examined the vocabulary used and the values that come to bear in the highly charged abortion debate (e.g., Luker 1984, 1985). These analyses reveal that abortion is one of the most value-laden issues in contemporary American politics.

In line with this research, this chapter deals with the value basis of abortion attitudes, the potential for fundamental values to come into conflict, and the impact of individual value configurations on the strength of abortion attitudes and resulting political behavior.

I begin by outlining the relationship between values, value conflict, and public opinion and by specifying the opposing worldviews that influence abortion attitudes. Then, I describe the impact of value conflict on the strength with which abortion attitudes are held, which is the focus of subsequent empirical analysis. The analysis reveals that the experience of conflicting values diminishes the strength of abortion attitudes, and, in turn, decreases an individual's likelihood to engage in political behavior related to the issue. I conclude by attempting to integrate these findings into the broader context of abortion politics.

Values, Value Conflict, and Abortion Attitudes

In trying to explain the intellectual and emotional civil war that is fought over the abortion issue, core beliefs that influence abortion attitudes have to be taken into account (e.g., Falik 1983; Luker 1984, 1985; Scott 1989; Tatalovich and Daynes 1981; Tribe 1990). Advocates of choice believe that abortion is a fundamental right. For the pro-life movement, on the other hand, abortion is equivalent to murder (Luker 1984, 1985). Between these two positions there is little room for agreement—and, in fact, dialogue between the pro-choice and the pro-life movements is almost nonexistent (Dionne 1990). Luker's (1984) interviews with abortion activists clearly suggest that abortion attitudes are merely "the tip of the iceberg" (p. 158) and are a reflection of a set of underlying values.

Despite the marked influence of normative values on abortion attitudes, empirical research has not put its primary emphasis on the value structure underlying abortion attitudes.[1] A few studies investigate the impact of core values, most notably religiosity and sexual morality, on abortion attitudes (e.g., Harris and Mills 1985; Jelen 1988a; Johnson, Tamney, and Burton 1990; Sears and Huddy 1988). Yet, most of the research on the abortion issue focuses on sociodemographic and attitudinal determinants of abortion attitudes.[2]

The importance of normative values as determinants of abortion attitudes becomes apparent if we consider that, unlike attitudes, values are stable and enduring, and often serve as the basis for attitude judgments (Allport, 1954; Katz, Wackenhut, and Hass 1986; Kluckhohn 1965; Rokeach 1973). Rokeach (1973:5), for instance, defines the value concept as an "enduring belief that a specific mode of conduct or end state of existence is personally or socially preferable to an opposite or converse mode of conduct or end state of existence."

Such a reasoning is in accord with a long tradition of scholarship in American politics and public opinion that has attributed much of the distinctive character of American politics to basic values (e.g., Hartz 1955; Hofstaedter 1972; de Toqueville 1955). Unfortunately, this tradition had surprisingly little impact on empirical studies of political attitudes and behavior. As a result, the impact of normative values on political attitudes has not yet developed into a major research paradigm (for an exception, see Feldman 1983, 1988).

Values have been, at least partially, ignored in studies of public opinion for two reasons. First, unlike attitudes, values have been the subject of relatively little systematic assessment in psychological and political research due to operational problems in the measurement of the highly elusive value concept (Levitin 1973).[3] More important, the functional

interconnections between values, attitudes on a particular issue, and behavior are complex (McGuire 1969, 1985) and cannot be understood by
relying on the simplistic assumption that there is a one-to-one relationship
between values and attitudes. In order to understand the functional interconnections between values related to the abortion issue, mass attitudes
on abortion, and political behavior related to the issue, an exact specification of the value-attitude relationship is required.

As journalist Dionne (1990) argues, many Americans are unwilling to
express their preferences in "either/or" terms, but endorse both sides of
the issue. That is, the public resists simple "yes" or "no" answers to certain
policy choices and refuses to accept one value paradigm over the other.
Instead, it has a more nuanced view about the issue at stake.

Exactly this kind or reasoning about the public's sensitivity toward
complex issues of public policy is the core element of Tetlock's (1984,
1986) "value pluralism" argument. Tetlock's position emphasizes that the
effect of values on attitudes cannot be described by a simple one-to-one
relationship. Any issue can activate a multitude of values, or, in other
words, a single attitude is determined by one's whole system of attitude-
relevant values. Thus, policy preferences often embody clashes of abstract
values in concrete form (Tetlock 1986). As a result, arriving at an attitudinal position on any complex issue is inherently difficult because values
themselves are very often in conflict. This holds especially if the issue at
stake is a difficult one to straddle or to compromise.

Values, Worldviews, and Abortion Policy

Despite the fact that arguments for or against abortion are often stated
in simple moral terms, there is more at stake than the controversy over
fetal rights versus personal freedom. A comparison of the public's opposition to abortion for different reasons justifying the intervention—for
example, rape or incest versus consensual sexual behavior of a teenager—
suggests that the margins for opposition and support differ sharply. Although 40% of the public opposes abortion for teenage pregnancies,
opposition shrinks to 17% if the pregnancy occurred because of rape or
incest (Tribe 1990). This asymmetric pattern, according to Tribe (1990),
shows that attitudes of abortion opponents are based on more than the mere
desire to protect the sanctity of life. In fact, the abortion dispute involves
a whole array of broad values concerning sexual morality (Granberg 1978;
McCutcheon 1987), the role of men and women in American society (Sears
and Huddy 1988), and broad life-style questions involving social and
moral traditionalism (Luker 1984, 1985). Especially, aversion to abortion

rights seems to reflect a "deeply held sexual morality, in which pregnancy and childbirth are seen as punishment that women in particular must endure for engaging in consensual sex" (Tribe 1990:234). In addition, religious variables are among the most prominent predictors of abortion attitudes (Barnartt and Harris 1982; Harris and Mills 1985; Sears and Huddy 1988). The impact of religious variables can be further qualified by distinguishing between fundamentalist and nonfundamentalist denominations. Catholics and fundamentalist Protestants are least likely to give support to legalized abortions (Blake and del Pinal 1980; Johnson et al. 1990).

The investigation of the values' direct influence on abortion attitudes is a necessary but not sufficient criterion to understand abortion attitudes and their potential to generate political action. A complex attitude object such as abortion can activate several and sometimes competing values within a personal value system that can serve as standards in evaluating the attitude object. One specific individual, for example, may subscribe to religious beliefs and at the same time favor gender equality in all aspects of life. Therefore, abortion attitudes are not only a function of pro-life and pro-choice values, but also are based on a tug-of-war among multiple values.

Consequences of Value Conflict: Value Structure and Attitudinal Strength

In order to draw inferences about abortion attitudes and their potential to translate into politically relevant behavior such as issue voting, demonstrating, or donating money to pro-life or pro-choice causes, the consequences of value conflict have to be stipulated. The central hypothesis to be tested is that value conflict decreases the strength with which attitudes on abortion are held.

Assessing the strength of abortion attitudes is important because attitude strength moderates the attitude-behavior relationship (e.g., Petersen and Dutton 1975; Raden 1985; Sample and Warland 1973; Schuman and Presser 1981; Schwartz 1978) and is a diagnostic criterion differentiating attitudes from nonattitudes (see also Abelson 1988; Converse 1970; Krosnick 1988).[4]

Past research differentiating between firmly held or strong attitudes and merely superficial expressions of an attitude has produced a rather heterogeneous and eclectic list of strength-related attitude properties. This list includes concepts such as intensity (Suchman 1950), direct experience (e.g., Fazio and Zanna 1981; Regan and Fazio 1977), certainty (Sample and Warland 1973; Suchman 1950), importance (Krosnick 1988, 1989), vested interest (Sivacek and Crano 1982), crystallization (Schwartz 1978), and memory accessibility (e.g. Fazio, Powell, and Herr 1983).

In contrast to past research that conceptualized attitude strength as being unidimensional,[5] this research develops a multidimensional attitude strength concept. Such an assumption is warranted because previous unidimensional conceptualizations do not account for the fact that individuals not only vary in the level of strength attached to an attitude, but also in the way they are involved with an attitude object (Abelson 1988; Raden 1985).

Multidimensional conceptualizations of attitude strength are considered by Converse (1970) and Abelson (1988). Both Converse and Abelson define their strength-related constructs "centrality" and "conviction" as a collection of qualitatively different connections between a person and an issue. Converse (1970:181), for example, defines centrality as having the two facets of motivational and cognitive centrality. Motivational centrality "has to do with the degree to which the object gears into the primary goal or need structures of the individual." Cognitive centrality, on the other hand, refers to the sheer amount of thinking devoted to the attitude object.

In addition to these two dimensions, there are more distinct ways in which an attitude can be related to an individual's self-concept (Johnson and Eagly 1989). First, attitudes can be related to an individual's self-concept if the issue is of personal importance or associated with one's self-interest (e.g., Sivacek and Crano 1982). Second, a further aspect of attitude strength is the self-presentational consequence of holding a certain attitude. In other words, attitudes are strong if the individual is concerned about expressing an opinion that is socially acceptable to potential evaluators (e.g., Johnson and Eagly 1989; Leippe and Elkin 1987). This dimension will be referred to as *impression-relevant involvement* hereafter. In addition, an attitude can be related to an individual's self-concept by perceiving the attitude as important in leading to or blocking the attainment of personal values. Value-relevant involvement increases the more an attitude is perceived to be related to one's cherished values (e.g., Ostrom and Brock 1968; Sherif and Cantril 1947). Last, my conceptualization of attitude strength includes a stability component. The underlying assumption is that strong attitudes are stable over time (Schuman and Presser 1981).

These six components—thinking about the issue, relating the issue to one's primary goal and need structures, having a vested interest in the issue, perceiving it as relevant to important others, and perceiving the issue to be related to one's values over an extended period of time—capture the different psychological aspects of attitude strength.

Summary of Hypotheses

In sum, this research proposes that abortion attitudes are influenced by underlying core values. Yet, unlike prior research, the proposed model moves beyond a single value-attitude formulation to a consideration of the interrelationship among core values. It is argued that normative values can come easily into conflict. Holding conflicted values relevant to abortion is expected to diminish the strength of attitudes toward abortion. Attitude strength is a crucial component in this process because it moderates the attitude-behavior relationship. This research relies on a conceptual definition of attitude strength that encompasses multiple dimensions. Such a conceptualization has the advantage of taking into account that there are different ways in which an individual can be psychologically involved with an issue. The proposed dimensions include cognitive and motivational involvement, vested interest in the issue, impression-relevant involvement, value-relevant involvement, and attitude stability.

Thus, attitude strength is largely a function of the underlying value structure, and the degree of inter-value conflict is assumed to influence the multiple components of attitude strength. Because attitude strength moderates the attitude-behavior relationship, the link between holding an attitude on the abortion issue and political behavior can only be understood if the multiple components of attitude strength are taken into account.

Methods and Results

In order to investigate the relationship between core values, attitude strength, and political behavior related to the abortion issue, a survey was conducted to examine attitudes toward the abortion issue, the strength of these attitudes, and individual value structures. Between February and August 1991, 437 Stony Brook students from various political science undergraduate classes completed the abortion survey in partial fulfillment of class requirements. From an external validity point of view, subjects did not qualify as either a probability sample or as representative of any larger, national population. Also, it can be argued that college students differ systematically from the population at large. According to Sears (1986), college students tend to have a less than fully formulated sense of "self," which manifests itself in less crystallized attitudes. Indeed, this may hold for attitudes that do not bear on students' lives. In this research, however, it is asserted that the use of a narrow data base does not impact on the generalizability of the findings. Abortion is an issue that influences directly and indirectly the lives of female as well as male students and it can be argued that students' attitudes are as crystallized as those held by the population at large. Therefore, the reported findings are likely to be comparable to results generated from a representative sample drawn from the population at large. Thus, the study does provide an internally valid means through which the basic hypotheses can be tested.

The completion of the survey took approximately 20 to 30 minutes. The sample was approximately evenly split according to gender, and the average age of the survey respondent was 21 years.

Description of Key Measures

Attitudes toward abortion were assessed in two ways. First, a battery of standard abortion items were included, asking respondents whether they think abortions should be possible for a variety of reasons ranging from a serious threat to the mother's life, to abortion if simply desired by the woman.[6] This variable will be referred to as *abortion constraints* hereafter. In addition, attitudes toward abortion were measured by placing the issue into the policy domain of state regulation of abortion. Respondents were asked to indicate their support or opposition toward state laws (1) requiring parental consent for teenagers under 18, (2) prohibiting public spending on all abortions, (3) prohibiting public spending on abortions except to save a woman's life, (4) proscribing abortions in public facilities with the exception of a threat to the mother's health, and (5) prohibiting public employees from performing, assisting in, or advising on abortions. The five state-regulation-of-abortion items form a reliable scale, with Cronbach's alpha exceeding a .82 level. Not surprising for a Northern student population, 47.5% of the student sample supported abortion rights for all the specified circumstances, including abortion if desired by the woman for any reason. Support for legalized abortion seems to be somewhat less if the issue is put in the domain of state regulation than if the issue is portrayed as one of a woman's choice. The majority (58.8%) opposed or strongly opposed state regulation of abortion. Yet most of the respondents preferred the "oppose" over the "strongly oppose" option.

The specific abortion-relevant values assessed in this survey—the desirability of free choice, gender roles, gender equality, moral freedom, moral traditionalism, sexual morality, religiosity, and religious fundamentalism—were measured by relying on multiple-item scales. Moral traditionalism was measured by relying on a modified moral traditionalism measure first developed in Conover and Feldman (1986). This scale focuses on preferences for older and more traditional family values. Moral freedom, on the other hand, aims at assessing the extent to which individuals, and not society, can determine moral standards. The items used to construct this scale, the traditional gender-role scale, as well as the religious fundamentalism items were drawn from Feldman (1989). Items assessing gender equality were drawn from Sears and Huddy (1988). The four sexual morality scale items are similar to those used in the General Social Survey. Religiosity was assessed by using standard National Election Study items measuring respondents' religiosity, strength of religious affiliation, and frequency of church or synagogue attendance. Some guidance for the construction of the items measuring the desirability of free and independent choice was provided by the Philosophy of Human Nature Scale developed in Wrightsman (1973). Most of the items thought to measure specific values form reliable scales. Reliability coefficients are adequately high, with Cronbach's alpha exceeding a .7 or .8 level for most of the scales.

The concept of attitude strength was measured by greatly expanding upon a list of attitude-strength items proposed by Abelson (1988). As explained earlier, this study relies on a multidimensional conceptualization of attitude strength. Therefore, the survey questionnaire included items measuring cognitive involvement, motivational involvement with the abortion issue, impression-relevant involvement, value-relevant involvement, vested interest in the issue, and attitude stability.[7] This new conceptualization of attitude strength greatly improves upon previously used attitude strength measures in two respects. First, single dimensions are assessed by relying on multiple-item scales. Second, multidimensionality of the concept is taken into account.

Behavioral involvement, that is, the willingness to act upon the abortion issue, was measured by an additive scale composed of seven questions asking the respondents if they ever engaged in, might engage in the future, or never would engage in various kinds of issue-relevant behavior such as issue voting or demonstrating.[8]

The Value-Attitude Relationship

In line with Rokeach's (1968, 1973) argument that stable and enduring values serve as the basis for people's attitude judgments, the value-attitude relationship was tested by a series of bivariate correlations. As expected, fundamental values are strongly related to both dependent variables—the abortion constraints—as well as the state regulation of abortion dependent variables.

More specifically, the correlation between religious fundamentalism and abortion constraints amounts to .523 ($p < .01$). Correlation coefficients are somewhat lower for religiosity ($r = .415$, $p < .01$), sexual morality ($r = .437$, $p < .01$), moral traditionalism ($r = .416$, $p < .01$), moral freedom (r

Table 1.1 Value Determinants of Abortion Constraints and State Regulation of
Abortion Attitudes

| | Dependent Variable | |
	Abortion Constraints	State Regulation of Abortion
Individual Choice	.299 (.098)**	.056 (.031)+
Sexual Morality	.426 (.127)***	.074 (.077) n.s.
Gender Roles	.256 (.108)*	.051 (.031) n.s.
Moral Freedom	.269 (.118)*	.140 (.036)***
Religiosity	.313 (.150)*	.064 (.055) n.s.
Gender Equality	.166 (.114) n.s.	.030 (.035) n.s.
Moral Traditionalism	.020 (.124) n.s.	.076 (.04)+
Religious Fundamentalism	.496 (.132)***	.122 (.04)**
Constant	5.082 (.289)***	1.530 (.286)***
R^2	.336	.32

NOTE: (***) $p < .001$; (**) $p < .01$;, (*) $p < .05$; (+) $p < .1$. Entries are unstandardized regression coefficients. Standard errors are expressed in parentheses.

$= .395$, $p < .01$), gender roles ($r = .337$, $p < .01$), choice ($r = .259$, $p < .01$), and gender equality ($r = .247$, $p < .01$). These fundamental values do not only influence abortion attitudes when the issue is framed in a rather general way, but are of equal importance when abortion becomes translated into an active public policy issue concerned with the rights of the state to restrict public funding of abortion and to limit the access to abortion in various ways. Zero-order correlations between fundamental values and attitudes toward state regulation of abortion amount to .23 for the choice items, .412 for sexual morality, .260 for gender roles, .501 for moral freedom, .309 for religiosity, .228 for gender equality, .47 for religious fundamentalism, and .46 for moral traditionalism. All these correlations are significant at $p < .01$. The impact of one value on the dependent variables, if all the other values are controlled for, can be seen in Table 1.1.

Subscribing to value positions that endorse the pro-choice side of the abortion issue results in abortion attitudes that favor legalized abortion and oppose state regulation of abortion. The eight values explain a significant share of the variance, 33.6% for the abortion constraints variable, 32% for the state regulation of abortion dependent variable. All of the values, with the exception of moral traditionalism and gender equality, are highly significant and contribute to explaining the abortion constraints variable. Because these two values are highly correlated with all the others, the rather low beta coefficients may be caused by multicollinearity.

The Multidimensionality of Attitude Strength

Before the relationship between value structure and the strength of abortion attitudes can be explored, the assumption that attitude strength encompasses different dimensions requires further empirical refinement. In order to test the hypothesis that attitude strength is a multidimensional construct, the attitude strength items' intercorrelations were subjected to an exploratory factor analysis. The resulting five-factor solution corresponds closely to prior theorizing about the multiple dimensions of attitude strength.[9] Table 1.2 displays the five-factor solution of the attitude strength items.

As can be seen, the items thought to assess cognitive involvement with the issue load on a first factor; the motivational involvement variables load on a second factor. A closer look at the items' scoring on the second factor suggests that the term *motivational involvement* may be misleading. Items such as "I think my views about abortion are absolutely correct," or "I cannot imagine ever changing my mind about the abortion issue" express an individual's perception that his or her attitude on abortion is correct and incontestable. Thus these items are more adequately described by the term *certainty* than by the term *motivational involvement*. The term *motivational involvement* will be replaced by the term *certainty* hereafter.

The self-interest items load clearly on a third factor. Factor four closely represents the self-perceived value attitude consistency of one's abortion attitudes, and the fifth factor resembles the stability and length of holding one's attitude. While these distinct dimensions correspond to prior theorizing, the social identification items do not represent a singular dimension. In fact, most of the items assessing the frequency and importance of abortion discussions within the close circle of friends and family score with the cognitive involvement items. Nevertheless, if it is taken into account that the frequency with which friends and family members discuss the issue may represent an indicator of one's own interest in the issue, this does not come as a surprise.

Overall, however, the rather crystalline results of the exploratory factor model are close to theoretical expectations and indicate that attitude strength is not one master dimension but rather a multidimensional concept. Thus this investigation adds empirical support to prior theorizing about the multidimensionality of attitude strength (e.g., Abelson 1988; Converse 1970; Raden 1985).

The results also provide a guideline for the construction of the attitude strength scales. Cronbach's alpha for unweighted and congeneric measures provides a conservative estimate of a measure's reliability. It exceeds a .8 level for the measure of cognitive involvement (Factor 1) and vested

Table 1.2 Factor Analysis of All Attitude Strength Items (Principal Axis Factoring With Oblique Rotation)

	Factor 1 Cognitive Involvement	Factor 2 Certainty	Factor 3 Vested Interest	Factor 4 Value Attitude Consistency	Factor 5 Attitude Stability
DISCUSSION[a]	**.83**				
DISC./FRIENDS&FA	**.81**				
THINKING	**.72**		.57	.43	
IMPORTANCE/FRIENDS	**.63**				
FEELING STRONGLY	**.57**	.43	.53	.56	.40
ATTENDING	**.50**				
KNOWLEDGE	**.48**		.43		
IMP./FAMILY	**.45**				
CONNECTED	**.45**				
NEGATIVE	**.40**				
CORRECTNESS		**.69**		.44	
MIND		**.68**		.41	
HARD		**.66**			
SURE		**.65**			
EXPLAIN		**.53**			.48
WRONG		**.44**			
PERSONAL			**.88**		
EASY			**.73**		
LAW			**.73**		
IMPORTANT	.53		**.72**	.51	
DIRECT			**.55**		
MORAL				**.69**	
BELIEF				**.56**	
VALUES				**.56**	
STRONGER		.41		**.50**	
NO CHANGE		.43			**.69**
LONG			.46		**.61**
DISAPPOINTED				.40	
SIMILAR				.37	

NOTE: Factor Loadings < .40 were omitted.
a. For the exact wording of the attitude strength items, please refer to the list in the Appendix.

interest in the issue (Factor 3). Cronbach's alpha for the certainty scale (Factor 2) is .79; it amounts to .70 for the self-perceived stability of one's abortion attitudes (Factor 5), and to .65 for the dimension of value-relevant involvement. Not surprisingly, the measures of attitude strength are somewhat correlated and this was taken into account in the factor analysis that utilized oblique rotation. Although the correlations between most of the measures do not exceed a .3 level, the correlation between perceived self-interest and cognitive involvement is rather high ($r = .51$, $p < .01$). However, because the two scales represent theoretically distinct constructs, they remained separate.

Consequences of Value Conflict

As outlined above, the assumption of a one-to-one relationship between values and attitudinal measures is overly simple. In other words, an investigation of the main effects of values, in a statistical sense, as determinants of attitude importance is not sufficient because the presence of value conflict is not taken into account. However, the operationalization of value conflict is not without problems. Although the literature on values offers some guidance on how to operationalize value conflict on the basis of Rokeach's value survey (i.e., Liberman and Chaiken 1991; Tetlock 1986), it is not at all indicative as to how value conflict can be operationalized on the basis of multi-item scales similar to the ones utilized in this survey study.

This study operationalized value conflict as the product of two standardized value scores.[10] Specifically, the original value scores were recoded so that the first value supporting a pro-choice position received the highest negative score, the anti-choice position received the highest positive score. The second value was reverse coded; that is, the anti-choice position was assigned a negative score, the pro-choice position a positive score. Thus the highest level of conflict that can be experienced—cherishing one value that endorses a pro-choice position, and a second that inhibits exactly this position, coincides with the highest score on the newly created value conflict scale.[11]

In order to test the hypothesis of conflicting values and their impact on the different components of attitude strength, pairs of conflicting core values, as well as the value conflict measure, were regressed separately on the five attitude strength measures. In line with the theoretical framework, the mere direction of a value measure should not be related to the strength of abortion attitudes. That is, strongly favoring a traditional sexual morality or strongly opposing sexual morality should have similar effects on attitude strength. Accordingly, the absolute scores of the standardized value measures were utilized. The absolute scores thus reflect the degree to which one cherishes or opposes certain values and are independent of the directionality of one's value position.

The selected values were those that in a statistical sense were strongly correlated with abortion attitudes, and that provide from a theoretical

Table 1.3 Regressions: The Impact of Value and Value Conflict on Multiple Measures of Attitude Strength

| Conflicting Value Pair | Measures of Attitude Strength | | | |
	Cognitive Involvement	Certainty	Self-Interest	Stability Measure
GENDER ROLES vs. FUNDAMENTALISM				
Role	.004	.025	.142	.05
	(.07)	(.06)	(.08)	(.07)
Fundamentalism	.083	.143	.147	.062
	(.05)	(.05)**	(.056)**	(.05)
Value Conflict	−.151	−.067	−.164	−.15
	(.033)***	(.03)**	(.035)***	(.03)***
Constant	−.064	−.195	−.28	−.15
	(.09)	(.08)*	(.09)**	(.09)
R^2	.10	.06	.12	.08
GENDER ROLES vs. MORAL FREEDOM				
Role	−.07	−.016	.06	−.025
	(.06)	(.06)	(.07)	(.07)
Moral Freedom	.08	.09	.096	.05
	(.065)	(.06)	(.07)	(.06)
Value Conflict	−.132	−.071	−.133	−.072
	(.043)**	(.04)*	(.04)**	(.046)*
Constant	.007	−.078	−.138	−.022
	(.09)	(.08)	(.09)	(.09)
R^2	.07	.03	.05	.02
SEXUAL MORALITY vs. GENDER ROLES				
Sexual Morality	.08	.05	.02	.03
	(.06)	(.05)	(.07)	(.06)
Gender Roles	.05	.16	.12	.13
	(.07)	(.06)**	(.07)	(.07)
Value Conflict	−.14	−.11	−.13	−.13
	(.036)***	(.032)***	(.03)***	(.036)***
Constant	−.08	−.19	−.11	−.15
	(.09)	(.08)**	(.10)	(.09)
R^2	.08	.065	.055	.06

NOTE: Each column represents a separate regression equation. The entries are standardized regression coefficients with standard errors in parentheses.
* $p < .1$; ** $p < .05$; *** $p < .01$.

viewpoint support for the hypothesis of conflicting values. The value pairs included in the analyses are gender roles/religious fundamentalism, gender roles/moral freedom, and conflict between sexual morality and gender roles. The results of the regression equations can be seen in Table 1.3.

The results indicate support for the hypothesis specifying the value conflict/attitude strength relationship. For the value pair gender roles and religious fundamentalism, the regression results are clear and in line with prior expectations. The value conflict coefficients are significant for all strength measures but the value-attitude consistency dimension. The value conflict coefficients are negative, indicating that conflict between the respective values results in a significant decrease in attitude strength. An increase in value conflict results in a decrease in cognitive involvement with the attitude and it diminishes the certainty with which abortion attitudes are held. Value conflict has similar effects on the measure of perceived self-interest and on self-reported attitude stability.

The dynamics of these relationships can be exemplified by using the following three hypothetical cases. An individual who experiences extreme conflict, for example, who subscribes to religious fundamentalism and at the same time favors equal gender roles, or vice versa, serves, of course, as the extreme case of value conflict.[12] A respondent opposing religious fundamentalism and at the same time endorsing equal gender roles exemplifies the extreme case of a compatible value structure.[13] Respondents choosing the mean of the respective scales serve as a comparative baseline. For the first hypothetical case of extreme conflict between the two core values of fundamentalism and gender roles, a cognitive involvement score of -1.2 is obtained; for the case of no conflict a score of .33 can be calculated. These two hypothetical scores can be compared to a baseline, that is, to the mean response on both value scales of $-.064$. Albeit hypothetical, these numbers demonstrate the dynamics of value conflict.

Similar results were obtained for the other two value pairs. For the value pairs of gender roles and moral freedom, as well as sexual morality and gender roles, value conflict has similar consequences on the attitude-strength measures of cognitive involvement, certainty, vested interest, and self-perceived attitude stability.[14]

In sum, the regression results provide strong support for the hypothesis of conflicting values. Predicted results were obtained for all the three value pairs investigated and for four out of five attitude strength measures. Thus, value conflict matters; experiencing the "tug-of-war" among contradictory core values results in a decrease in the strength with which attitudes are held.

Attitude Strength and Behavioral Involvement

As noted earlier, attitude strength represents a desirable property because it moderates the attitude-behavior relationship and is expected to improve the predictive quality of attitudes. If attitude strength indeed enhances the usually weak attitude-behavior link, strong correlations between the strength indicators and the behavioral involvement measures ought to be expected.

The correlations between the cumulative behavioral involvement indicator (alpha .825) and the multiple measures of attitude strength amount to .59 ($p < .01$) for cognitive involvement, .36 ($p < .01$) for the certainty dimension, .41 ($p < .01$) for self-interest, .34 ($p < .01$) for self-perceived attitude stability, and .16 ($p < .01$) for self-perceived value-attitude consistency. These coefficients, in particular the cognitive involvement and the self-interest measure, are a remarkable improvement over more conventional attitude strength measures employed in attitude surveys. One of the measures usually relied upon to approximate attitude strength is *fold-over intensity*. Fold-over intensity is operationally defined as strongest at both ends of the attitudinal scale, and it decreases as one moves toward the midpoint of the scale (Suchman 1950). Pearson's correlation between the fold-over intensity measure of the abortion constraint attitude scale and the behavioral involvement indicators amount to only .13 ($p < .05$). Thus the measures employed in this survey greatly improve the predictability of political behavior.

The comparison of different attitude strength measures becomes even more apparent if the behavioral indicator of issue voting, that is, an individual's propensity to vote for or against a candidate solely because of the candidate's stand on the abortion issue, is considered. While the correlation between the fold-over intensity measure and issue voting fails to reach statistical significance ($r = .065$), the correlations between issue voting and the strength-related attitude dimensions amount to .34 ($p < .01$) for cognitive involvement, .30 ($p < .01$) for the certainty aspect of attitude strength, .28 ($p < .01$) for self-interest, and .24 ($p < .01$) for self-perceived attitude stability.

Discussion and Conclusion

First of all, the results reaffirm the importance of values as determinants of attitudes. Values such as gender roles, sexual morality, and religious fundamentalism undoubtedly shape abortion attitudes. More important, however, the results demonstrate that a one-to-one relationship between values and attitudes is too simplistic an assumption. Instead, the role of value conflict has to be taken into account. That is, thinking about complex policy choices such as abortion, involving two or more conflicting values, can be an extremely difficult task for the decision maker. As shown, the experience of conflicting values results in a decrease in the strength with which abortion attitudes are held.

The value conflict/attitude strength relationship has been demonstrated to hold for four out of the five strength dimensions investigated. Specifically, value conflict resulted in a decrease in cognitive involvement, certainty about one's position on the issue, self-interest, and self-perceived attitude stability. The hypothesized relationship between value conflict and attitude strength, however, did not hold for the dimension of value-relevant involvement. One likely explanation for the failure of this measure is that the items assessing the construct are not adequately reliable. That is, assessing the relatedness of one's values to one's attitudes is a rather complex task requiring knowledge about the importance of personal values, as well as information about the extent to which the values in question achieve or block one's position on a certain issue.

Overall, however, the obtained results reaffirm the notion that basic values cherished by the mass public do not always fit together into neat and coherent packages. Values are not necessarily ordered into a hierarchically organized system, but they can be contradictory, and still be valued at the same time.

It is because of these seemingly irreconcilable values that the abortion issue is at the forefront of the public debate. As Luker (1984, 1985) argues, the views of pro-choice and pro-life activists are based on radically different sets of values. If this line of reasoning is taken to a micro level of analysis, the same argument contributes to an explanation of public opinion about the abortion issue. Thus the conflict of absolute values not only characterizes the views of activists on either side of the issue, but also describes the clashes of values experienced by a single individual.

This implies that the mass public does not always share the choices offered by a small and rather extreme set of abortion activists who differ drastically in their basic frameworks, and in the vocabulary they use to discuss the issue (Fried 1988; see also Chapter 12, this volume). Instead, the electorate seems to subscribe to a more complex view on the issue that is based on equally important values that can come easily into conflict. The result of subscribing to equally important and conflicting values is a decrease in the strength with which abortion attitudes are held.

The different components of attitude strength are also crucial predictors of behavioral involvement with the abortion issue. In line with previous research on the moderating qualities of attitude strength (e.g., Krosnick 1988; Schuman and Presser 1981), the concept has been shown to impact upon behavioral predispositions to act upon the issue. The weaker the attitude, the less likely were the respondents to engage in any kind of political behavior related to the attitude object. Although traditional Likert-type attitude measurement techniques reflect the intensity as well as the directionality of a response, the measurement of attitude strength can be greatly improved by using properties other than intensity and direction.

These results suggest that the strength of abortion attitudes is a crucial variable that ought to be included in any research framework that attempts to predict the political consequences of abortion attitudes. As shown, the link between abortion attitudes, issue voting, and other forms of political behavior is better understood if the concept of attitude strength is incorporated. In other words, if we utilize measures of attitude directionality, we ignore important information contained in attitude strength measures. Attitudes vary in the strength with which they are held. Strength-related attitude dimensions distinguish attitudes from nonattitudes and therefore enhance the predictive power of attitudes.

These findings about the relationship between value conflict, attitude strength, and behavioral involvement with the abortion issue have important implications as far as the strategies and the success of pro-life and pro-choice groups are concerned.

Although pro-life and pro-choice arguments may seem to be diametrically opposite, pro-choice supporters do not reverse religious and moral arguments put forward by pro-life activists (Luker 1984; Scott 1989). In other words, pro-choice proponents do not argue that abortion is good and desirable, but rather assert that women should have the right to choose whether or not to have access to safe and legal abortions. By continuing to portray abortion as a matter of choice and by emphasizing public health concerns, pro-choice activists will continue to be able to accommodate the majority of the public that favors access to safe abortions.

Although *Webster* constituted a backlash to the struggle of the pro-choice movement, the pro-choice position still attracts more supporters than the idea of outlawing abortion under all circumstances. However, the dilemma faced by the pro-choice movement is that public sentiments toward abortion are often based on conflicting values. As demonstrated, the experience of the tug-of-war of opposing values decreases the strength with which abortion attitudes are held, and, in turn, diminishes the potential for these attitudes to translate into politically relevant behavior.

On the other hand, the minority pro-life position is an absolute one. Thus citizens who experience value conflict may feel less comfortable with pro-life than with pro-choice arguments. In contrast to public attitudes, the attitudes of activists are strong and the partial victory of the pro-life movement to change *Roe v. Wade* standards illustrates the success of an intense minority. Mansbridge (1986:34) remarks that the "attempt to ban legal abortion has remained a live issue only because its advocates feel so passionately about it, while many opponents are ambivalent" (see also

Luker 1984; Scott and Schuman 1988). Thus, numbers do not necessarily reflect the success or failure of a movement. However, an examination of the value structure underlying abortion attitudes suggests that the pro-life movement—because of the absolute values it appeals to—cannot easily expand the scope of conflict by appealing to formerly uninvolved individuals. Thus, by nature of the values appealed to by pro-life and pro-choice activists, only the pro-choice movement is in a position to gain substantially more supporters. Nevertheless, the success of pro-choice groups will depend upon their ability to mobilize those members of the public who hold ambivalent attitudes on the issue.

Notes

1. There are noteworthy exceptions. For instance, Kristin Luker's (1984) research on abortion activists has produced suggestive, rich data about the clash of fundamental values that come to bear in the abortion debate. Her insights are based on in-depth interviewing techniques, however, and do not allow one to test for particular hypotheses. Her respondents are California abortion activists; they neither represent the population of activists, nor the population at large.

2. For instance, Granberg and Granberg (1980) investigate sociodemographic determinants of abortion attitudes. Attitudinal determinants are examined by Jelen (1988a); changing distributions in public opinion toward abortion are monitored by Rossi and Sitaraman (1988) and Muldoon (1991).

3. Core beliefs or values can be reliably measured by utilizing multiple scale items. Such measures are strongly related to political and social attitudes (see Feldman 1983, 1988).

4. Although it is common wisdom that attitudinal responses, simply operationalized in terms of responses to some object along a bipolar evaluative dimensions are frequently poor predictors of behavior (McGuire 1969, 1985), the attitude strength concept has not been widely incorporated into political science and public opinion research. Some noteworthy exceptions, however, should be mentioned. Dahl (1956), for example, emphasizes the importance of estimating intensities in order to predict the stability of a democracy and the acceptance of a majority rule principle. The strength concept has been also utilized by Schuman and Presser (1981) and Krosnick (1988, 1989) to describe patterns of public opinions and to enhance behavioral prediction of attitudinal positions.

5. Although research on attitude strength utilized quite different conceptual and operational definitions to capture the attitude strength concept, the common denominator of this research is that attitude strength is a unidimensional concept that can be assessed by relying on one single indicator.

6. Abortion attitudes were measured by relying on a 7-item scale. These items are similar to the series of standard abortion items utilized by the General Social Survey. The scale assesses attitudes toward legalized abortions for the following reasons: (1) If the woman's health is endangered by the pregnancy, (2) if there is a strong chance of serious defect in the baby, (3) if the pregnancy occurred because of rape or incest, (4) if the woman is married and does not want any more children, (5) if the family has a low income and cannot afford any more children, (6) if the woman is unmarried and does not want to marry the man, and (7) if the woman does not desire the pregnancy for any reason. The scale was constructed by summing up affirmative responses to all seven items.

7. All together, 25 attitude strength items were assessed (see Appendix for the wording of the items). All items came after the attitude directionality questions, but preceded all the questions on individual value preferences. Because several items are intended to assess similar constructs, great care was taken to disperse these items across all attitude strength measures.

8. Political action related to the abortion issue assessed in this survey includes a wide variety of political behavior, such as issue voting, talking to people in order to influence their stand on abortion, participating in rallies, wearing buttons or displaying bumper stickers, writing or talking to elected officials about abortion, or writing to a newspaper, as well as contributing money to an organization whose major concern is abortion. These seven items were used to construct an additive scale indicating the respondents' willingness to engage in issue-relevant political behavior. The newly created behavioral involvement scale (Cronbach's alpha = .825) is adequately reliable.

9. Because a scree test did not provide an unambiguous answer as to how many major common factors ought to be extracted, a four-, five-, and six-factor solution was tried. The criteria used for evaluating the resulting factor solutions was to find the most parsimonious solution, that is, the smallest number of factors it takes to reproduce the correlation matrix, that is equally satisfying from a theoretical point of view. Only the five-factor solution was satisfying on the second criteria.

10. Operationalizing value conflict by using a multiplicative technique is superior to an operational measure that relies on an additive approach. Products are more influenced by the extremity of the scores than sums and create a more appropriate functional form with accelerating curvilinear relationships.

11. This coding procedure can be exemplified by using, for example, the value pair gender roles and sexual morality. The gender-role scale was recoded so that a negative score of −3 corresponds to a strong endorsement of equal gender roles; a value of +3, on the other hand, represents strong opposition to equal gender roles. Conversely, the sexual morality scale was recoded so that a value of −3 signifies a strong endorsement of a traditional sexual morality, and a value of +3 stands for opposition to a conservative sexual morality. Hence, the highest amount of conflict that can be experienced, for example, favoring equal gender roles but at the same time supporting traditional sexual values, or vice versa, results in a score of 9.

12. The purpose of using this rather extreme case is only illustrative. A cross-tabulation of the two value measures reveals that only 20 out of 437 respondents can be characterized as experiencing extreme value conflict. If less stringent criteria are used, however, 109 cases can be characterized as experiencing value conflict. These 109 respondents score high or moderately high on a pro-choice value, and at the same time subscribe to a contradictory pro-life value.

13. Similar to the extreme case of conflicting values, only 51 respondents display a completely hierarchical value structure; that is, they strongly endorse equal gender roles and strongly oppose religious fundamentalism, or vice versa. However, if we use a less stringent mode of categorization, 199 respondents can be characterized as holding compatible values.

14. R^2 for all the regression equations is rather low. However, as noted by King (1990), model performance and the value of R^2 are independent questions. Quite likely, the low R^2 can be attributed to measurement error in the dependent variable. As long as the error term is not correlated with any of the independent variables, the theoretical significance of the model is not endangered.

Exact Question Wording

DISCUSSION: "How often do you discuss the abortion issue with your friends or your family?"

DISC/FRIENDS&FA: "How often do your closest friends and your family members discuss the abortion issue?"

THINKING: "I think very often about the issue."

IMPORTANCE/FRIENDS: "How important is the abortion issue to your closest friends."

FEELING STRONGLY: "I feel strongly about the abortion issue."

ATTENDING: "How much attention do you pay to newspaper and television reports about the abortion issue."

KNOWLEDGE: "I consider myself more knowledgeable about the abortion issue than the average person."

IMP./FAMILY: "How important is the abortion issue to your family?"

CONNECTED: "Several issues could come up in a conversation about the abortion issue."

NEGATIVE: "Have other people ever reacted negatively to your views on abortion?"

CORRECTNESS: "I think my views about abortion are absolutely correct."

MIND: "I cannot imagine ever changing my mind about the abortion issue."

HARD: "Overall, how hard was it for you to answer the questions on abortion."*

SURE: "Overall, how sure or certain are you of your answers?"

EXPLAIN: "It is rather easy to explain my views on the abortion issue to other people."

WRONG: "People whose opinions about the abortion issue are different from mine are wrong or badly informed."

PERSONAL: "I think that the abortion issue affects me personally."

EASY: "It is very easy for me to think about ways the abortion issue might affect me personally."

LAW: "A state or federal law restricting legalized abortion would affect me personally."

IMPORTANT: "The abortion issue is extremely important to me."

DIRECT: "My views on abortion are based on the issue directly affecting me."

MORAL: "My beliefs about the abortion issue are based on my moral sense of how things should be."

BELIEF: "My attitudes on abortion are based on my general beliefs about what is good and bad in the world."

VALUES: "My opinions on abortion are related to my personal values."

STRONGER: "My views on abortion have gotten stronger over the years."

NO CHANGE: "My views about abortion have not changed during the last years."

LONG: "I've held my views about abortion for a long time."

DISAPPOINTED: "Would any of your friends or family members be disappointed if you changed your views about abortion?"

SIMILAR: "My views on abortion are similar to the opinions of people I care about."

Note

* This question, as well as the following one ("SURE") directly succeeds the standard 7-item scale asking respondents whether they think abortions should be possible for a variety of reasons.

2

The Sources of Antiabortion Attitudes

The Case of Religious Political Activists

JAMES L. GUTH

CORWIN E. SMIDT

LYMAN A. KELLSTEDT

JOHN C. GREEN

Since 1973 few issues have agitated Americans like abortion. Protagonists have staked out extreme positions that offer little room for compromise. To abortion supporters, personal choice is nonnegotiable, while their foes regard legal abortion as murder. Despite such polarization, public policy on abortion may ultimately be constructed upon some middle ground. Constitutional amendments to ban abortions have failed while, at the same time, the Supreme Court has recognized "legitimate state interests" in regulating access to abortion. Moreover, many Americans are deeply ambivalent, supporting neither a total ban nor an absolute right to an abortion.[1]

Abortion has also evoked passionate activity. Religious communities, especially the Catholic and evangelical Protestant churches, have provided armies of committed activists for the National Right to Life Committee,

AUTHORS' NOTE: The authors wish to acknowledge major financial support from the Pew Charitable Trusts, which made this study possible. Additional assistance was provided by the Institute for the Study of American Evangelicals at Wheaton College, the Research and Professional Growth Committee of Furman University, the Ray C. Bliss Institute for Applied Politics at the University of Akron, and the Calvin Center for Christian Scholarship.

Operation Rescue, and other pro-life groups. The pro-choice side draws more heavily from secular sources, but a variety of religious groups, including most mainline Protestant denominations, are officially—if not actively—in favor of abortion rights. No religious community is monolithic, however, and abortion remains a subject of controversy within American churches, with contending forces locked in bitter conflict and centrists trying to find common ground. Indeed, the prospects for détente in this policy area may depend on the strength and skills of activists in institutional settings who share the public's mixed sentiments.

This chapter analyzes views on abortion held by members of eight religious interest groups, drawn primarily from among Protestant evangelicals. The political importance of evangelicals has become obvious in recent decades: They are a sizable segment of the American electorate and have become increasingly active and cohesive (e.g., Smidt 1992). And, since the late 1970s, especially, evangelicals have been deeply involved in abortion controversies. Thus their views may push the politics of abortion in different directions: A hard-line, pro-life consensus would lend weight to attempts to restrict abortion, while moderation could shape a less restrictive compromise. Consequently, this chapter will address three questions: (a) What differences in abortion attitudes are evident among religious activists, (b) what factors account for variation in their attitudes, and (c) what do the findings portend for the future of abortion politics?

Abortion Attitudes:
Demographic, Religious, and Political Correlates

We assume that factors that predict abortion attitudes in the mass public will also be helpful in understanding the views of religious activists. Generally, three categories of variables influence abortion attitudes: demographic, religious, and political. Early studies focused largely on demographic differences between pro-life and pro-choice advocates, and suggested that only a few such variables have much influence. Of these, education was the strongest. Income, gender, age, family structure, occupation, and community of residence had less impact. Usually, better educated, upper income, young urban professionals are the most pro-choice demographic group (Granberg and Granberg 1980). Translating these findings into terms of the current sample, the demographic group most likely to be pro-choice has been dubbed "the coming generation" of evangelicals by sociologists of religion. The youngest, best educated, wealthiest, and most urbanized religious activists should hold the most liberal views, while those "furthest from modernity" may take more restrictive perspectives (see Hunter 1983, 1987).

Scholars have also investigated the impact of religion itself. For example, religious tradition has relevance: Catholics and evangelical Protestants more often oppose abortion than mainline Protestants or those with no affiliation. Likewise, very religious respondents (as measured by religious salience or church attendance) and those with high views of Scripture more often oppose abortion rights, regardless of affiliation (Cook, Jelen, and Wilcox 1992a). Much less attention has been paid, however, to specific components of religious beliefs and doctrine that may impact attitudes.

Other analysts have stressed the ideological context of abortion disputes (Fried 1988; Jelen 1988a; Leege 1983; Luker 1984). Attitudes toward abortion comport closely with other facets of an individual's social and political ideology. Many studies (e.g., Cook et al. 1992a; Himmelstein 1986) have found a strong nexus between abortion attitudes, sexual moralism, and social traditionalism, value systems deriving primarily, but not exclusively, from conservative religion. From this perspective, the demographic and even some religious differences between pro-choice and pro-life citizens pale in comparison with divergences over fundamental life-style values. Thus we have three competing, but partially overlapping, explanations for differences in abortion attitudes.

Just as both the social science literature and the press have dichotomized voters and ignored those with "mixed" opinions on abortion (McCutcheon 1987), most scholarly work has failed to explore religious differences over abortion, either with respect to their extent or sources. When evangelicals are the focus of inquiry, scholars emphasize their antiabortion sentiments, despite their political diversity on other issues (e.g., Guth and Green 1990; Jelen 1991; Smidt 1988; Wilcox 1986a). A few have noted, however, that evangelicals do differ on abortion, although not so much over its morality as over legitimate exceptions to an antiabortion rule, the wisdom of legal proscriptions, or the means to combat abortion on demand (Rothenberg and Newport 1984). Indeed, analyses of differences in attitudes among religious activists, whether evangelical or nonevangelical, are almost nonexistent. Little is known, therefore, about the range in abortion positions among religious activists. Nor is it clear whether factors that explain attitude variation across segments of the mass public (e.g., differences in religiosity) work among religious activists.

Data and Methods

This chapter is based on a national survey of religious activists taken in 1990-1991. A stratified random sample was drawn from the ranks of eight interest groups with strong evangelical ties, ranging roughly from left to right: Bread for the World, Just Life, Evangelicals for Social Action, the National Association of Evangelicals, Prison Fellowship, Focus on the Family, Concerned Women for America, and Americans for the Republic.[2] These groups were chosen because they represent a full range of predominantly evangelical interest groups, particularly those with a significant mass base,[3] and because their leaders offered some degree of cooperation.[4] Although our predominant focus was on evangelicals, the sample includes other kinds of religious activists, as these voluntary associations are open to anyone sharing their policy goals. Consequently, mainline Protestants from every major denominational and doctrinal tradition are present in large numbers, along with many Catholics, and a tiny percentage of nonreligious respondents.[5]

The questionnaire was 10 pages long and included almost 250 items. The survey elicited 4,995 completed questionnaires (a 56.9% response rate), providing the largest data set available on religious activists. Given the great variety of religious and political measures employed, we can provide a much more detailed picture of religious political activism than hitherto available.

Of central concern to the present inquiry, of course, are activists' views about abortion. Although we used several abortion items, here we will focus on one question—a scaled version of several General Social Survey (GSS) (Davis and Smith 1984) abortion items:

Choose ONE of the following opinions on abortion that comes CLOSEST to your own view.

a. Abortion should never be permitted.

b. Abortion should be permitted only in cases where the life of the mother is in danger.

c. Abortion should be permitted not only where the mother's life is in danger but in cases involving rape and incest.

d. Abortion should be permitted for the reasons listed above in b. and c. and also in cases involving serious birth defects.

e. Abortion should be permitted for the reasons above plus in circumstances where the family (or mother) is too poor to properly raise the child.

f. Abortion should be permitted for the reasons above plus in circumstances where the birth would interfere with a career.

g. A woman should always be able to obtain an abortion as a matter of personal choice.

Despite some dispute about dimensionality of the GSS questions when used with the mass public, the items invariably scale in activist surveys

(Granberg 1982); our respondents accepted this formulation with few dissents.

Religious Activists and Abortion

Not surprisingly, these activists generally take pro-life stances on abortion. Table 2.1 presents the distribution of abortion attitudes for the total sample, evangelical Protestants,[6] mainline Protestants, and Roman Catholics. (The three respondents choosing the "interfere with career" option were recoded "free choice.") Although a general consensus exists against abortion on demand (less than 10% stated that a woman should always be able to obtain an abortion), there is, at the same time, no agreement on banning all abortions. Only 18.6% stated that abortions should never be permitted, and only about one quarter of the activists expressed one of the two polar positions. Thus the overwhelming majority recognized situations in which abortion might be permitted—though they were far from unified on when this could occur.

The presence of mainline Protestants and Catholics in predominantly "evangelical" interest groups suggests the growth of traditionalist alliances across denominational lines, but even here, evangelicals themselves take more hard-line stances than mainline Protestants and Roman Catholics. Catholic activists were the most likely to oppose abortions under all circumstances, but they were also more likely than evangelicals to be pro-choice. Consequently, in this sample, evangelicals are the most pro-life, with Catholics close behind, and with mainline Protestants holding less restrictive views. Yet, even most mainline Protestants rejected abortion on demand, as a majority believed that abortion should be permitted, if at all, only when rape or incest had occurred or where a mother's life was in danger.

Evangelical activists appear less likely than evangelicals in the mass public to take either a "no exceptions" or "free choice" stance (see Rothenberg and Newport 1984:70-76).[7] At the same time, however, abortion appears to have a somewhat higher salience for activists than for the general public. When provided a open-ended question, 15% named abortion among the two or three "most important issues facing the country," whereas many others, no doubt, implicitly included it within more general responses on "family and social problems."[8] Recent National Election Study (NES) surveys, however, show far fewer evangelical voters preoccupied with abortion. Hence, the evangelical mass public is more willing to take an extreme position than our evangelical activists, who hold more nuanced views, while the issue is, nonetheless, more salient for activists.

Table 2.1 Distribution of Abortion Attitudes Among Religious Activists

Abortion View	Total Sample	Evangelical Protestants	Mainline Protestants	Roman Catholics
Should never be permitted	18.6%	21.2%	7.2%	25.4%
Permitted when mother's life in danger	41.5%	47.0%	26.2%	39.1%
Permitted in cases above plus cases involving rape & incest	21.3%	20.6%	24.8%	20.1%
Permitted in cases above plus cases involving serious birth defects	8.6%	7.1%	15.2%	4.3%
Permitted in cases above plus where the mother is poor	1.8%	1.0%	4.5%	1.1%
A woman should always be able to obtain an abortion	8.3%	3.0%	21.7%	10.0%
N =	(4,747)	(3,052)	(1,037)	(558)

Quite evidently, then, even among these predominantly "pro-life" activists, we have considerable variation in abortion attitudes. Predicting these gradations presents a challenge: The distribution of the dependent variable is skewed, and the respondents, like most activists, share elite demographic traits. As members of religious interest groups, they are quite observant by any religious measure, and are especially concerned with social and moral issues. Nevertheless, we can account for a good deal of the variation in opinion. In Table 2.2 we present our findings: The first column reports zero-level Pearson correlations between abortion attitudes and demographic, religious, and political variables; column 2 lists the beta coefficients, multiple Rs and variance explained from multiple regressions using variables in each of three categories in turn; and column 3 presents the results of a multiple regression with all significant variables from the three previous analyses.

Demography is only modestly related to abortion attitudes, even at the bivariate level. Among these activists, stronger antiabortion attitudes are linked with lower education, and weakly tied to youth (rather than age as in the mass public), female gender and homemaker status, lower income, and rural residence. The demographic variables, however, account for only 7% of the variance. Thus, although the relationships are usually in the expected direction, the sources of variation in opinion must be found elsewhere.

The religious variables are much more potent. Earlier studies have shown that salience of religion or church attendance is strongly linked to antiabortion attitudes, but such crude religiosity items are not likely to

Table 2.2 Correlation and Regression Coefficients of Demographic, Religious, and Ideological Variables and Abortion Attitudes

	Bivariate Correlation (Pearson's r)	Category Regression (beta)		Combined Regression (beta)
Demographic Variables				
Education	−.24	−.22	ns	
Gender Homemaker	.12	.04		ns
Income	−.10	−.07	−.08	
Age	−.09	−.11	−.11	
Community Size	−.07	.03		ns
Multiple *R*		.28		
Adjusted *R²*		.07		
Religious Variables				
Fundamentalism	.53	.41		.20
Orthodoxy	.45	.20		.14
Individualism	.41	.09		.03
Revivalism	.36	.05		.03
Mainline Affiliation	−.35	−.15	−.27	
Born-Again	.31	.05		.03
Evangelical Affiliation	.29	.07		.06
Spiritual Experience	.20	ns	ns	
Church Activity	.15	.05		.05
Salience of Religion	.14	.05		.03
Catholic Affiliation	.02	.27		.12
Multiple *R*		.65		
Adjusted *R²*		.42		
Ideological Variables				
General Conservatism	.54	.29		.19
Social Traditionalism	.54	.31		.20
Partisan Identification	.41	ns		ns
Social Welfare Conservatism	.40	ns	ns	
Multiple *R*		.58		.68
Adjusted *R²*		.34		.47

NOTE: The values for the abortion variable have been coded so that the greater the antiabortion sentiment, the higher the value.
ns = not significant at $p < .01$

discriminate within this highly religious sample. Consequently, we used more sophisticated religious measures, tapping doctrinal perspectives, religious worldviews, spiritual experiences, and ritual practice. After extensive analysis, we reduced most items to several factor scores with high reliability (see Appendix). The best predictor (second column of Table 2.2) taps core elements of Protestant fundamentalism: biblical literalism, religious separatism, and premillennial or dispensational theology (Marsden 1980). This finding dovetails nicely with the argument that "politicized fundamentalism" lies at the center of Christian Right politics (Jelen 1991; Wilcox 1989a). Second, religious tradition matters, with evangelical and mainline Protestants diverging in the expected direction. (The Pearson's r for Catholics is very small, signifying that Catholics do not differ significantly from the combined Protestant subsample.) Moreover, antiabortion attitudes are related to religious "individualism," a preoccupation with a private relationship to God rather than with "communal" concern for others (Benson and Williams 1982; Leege and Welch 1989), and to Christian orthodoxy and revivalism (see Appendix). Not surprisingly, given the sample's strong religious commitment, religious salience and church involvement have only a weak (although significant) association. Born-again status and spiritual experience also have fairly high bivariate correlations with abortion attitudes. The multiple regression shows fundamentalism, religious tradition (mainline and Catholic), and orthodoxy to be the best predictors, but several other religious measures retain some influence. Note that the influence of evangelical denominational affiliation is largely absorbed by other religious variables—unlike the impact of Catholic and mainline affiliation. In sum, religious variables alone explain an impressive 42% of the variance, 6 times as much as the demographic variables—and this in a uniformly "religious" sample.

We also anticipated that abortion attitudes would be clearly related to other social and political views and we were not disappointed. Previous studies have found that the strongest connection between abortion attitudes and ideology is with social and sexual traditionalism (see Himmelstein 1986). Other scholars have shown linkages between conservative political ideology, Republican partisanship, and antiabortion attitudes (Jelen 1988a; Wilcox and Gomez 1990). Along with the NES partisan identification question, we used a rich battery of items to tap political conservatism and social traditionalism. A principal components analysis of 21 questions produced one factor explaining 43% of the variance, along with two smaller ones. A varimax rotation identified three interpretable factors. The first is a "general conservatism" dimension with strong loadings for self-identified ideology, anti-Soviet attitudes, free enterprise, and several social issues. The second has high loadings for "social welfare" items. The third factor taps pure "moral traditionalism," incorporating items on discomfort with moral diversity (see Appendix). The very fact that social issues loaded on the same factor as older components of traditional conservatism hints that among many activists the integrated conservatism long sought by Christian Right leaders has been achieved. As Table 2.2 shows, all three ideological scales and Republican partisanship correlate strongly with abortion attitudes, but only general conservatism and social traditionalism survive the multivariate analysis. Overall, ideological variables account for slightly less variance than religious variables, but much more than the demographic package.

What is the relative power of demographic, religious, and political variables? We incorporated the statistically significant indicators from column 2 in a single regression analysis (column 3 of Table 2.2). This final exercise demonstrates the combined power of the religious and political variables. Several religious measures retain their importance—in particular, orthodoxy, fundamentalism, and religious tradition, especially mainline Protestant affiliation. Likewise, most other religious variables retain statistical significance despite multivariate controls, although the betas are quite modest. General conservatism and social traditionalism also exhibit considerable staying power. Finally, age and income also continue to be significantly related to abortion attitudes, while the education variable appears to be absorbed by religious and ideological measures. Overall, the model explains an impressive 47% of the variance in abortion attitudes.

Discussion and Conclusion

Differences over abortion among these religious political activists can be explained, in part, by factors that influence other Americans, but a full accounting requires more detailed religious and ideological measures, of the sort unavailable in NES or GSS surveys. The latter are quite successful in predicting abortion attitudes, even within this relatively homogeneous sample. At the same time, one should not conclude that most demographic variables are unimportant in producing attitudes on abortion and other public policy issues. In fact, as we shall demonstrate in future work, demographic factors, especially the extent and nature of education, work in complex ways to influence the theological beliefs of religious activists, which, in turn, have a powerful effect on political identifications and attitudes. And it is these religious and political attitudes that directly influence the extent to which religious activists would go in advocating restrictions on abortions.

Second, the strong association between political conservatism and abortion attitudes helps explain a transformation of the antiabortion movement in the 1980s. Beginning with a largely Catholic base, the early movement had a decidedly mixed ideological identity, as liberals and conservatives combined into single-issue organizations devoted to fighting abortion, while they avoided most other issues. As Protestant evangelicals entered the fray, however, the movement gravitated toward the New Right, with its program of social traditionalism, economic conservatism, and militant nationalism (cf. Himmelstein 1990), creating some distinct problems for movement strategies.

The implications of our findings for the future of antiabortion politics are several. First, insofar as evangelicals come to dominate the abortion debate—as some observers see as likely—there will be a powerful tendency for the antiabortion forces to be further absorbed into the Republican Right, perhaps alienating more moderate mainline Protestant and Roman Catholic allies, while simultaneously creating more problems for Republican strategists seeking the votes of traditional economic conservative who are also social liberals. Second, as the federal courts permit states wider latitude in regulating abortion, divisions within the antiabortion movement between fundamentalists and charismatics (who favor strict antiabortion positions) and other evangelicals (who advocate somewhat less restrictive policies) are likely to open wider, limiting the movement's influence. Third, growing involvement by fundamentalists may divide the antiabortion camp in another way. Although our results suggest a possible new divide in American politics, with evangelical protestants and conservative Catholics joining forces in a traditionalist alliance, this may be an uneasy coalition. Fundamentalists have historically been strongly anti-Catholic, as well as anti-mainline Protestant, thereby limiting cooperation among religious groups (see Wilcox and Gomez 1990). This tendency certainly appears here: The stronger a respondent's fundamentalism and antiabortion sentiment, the further the respondent felt from the Catholic Church (data not shown). Whether common participation by Catholics and fundamentalists in the antiabortion movement can break down these ancient barriers is not certain (Wills 1989). Thus the growing visibility of evangelical activists in the antiabortion movement is likely to add further complexity to the politics of abortion.

Notes

1. A 1991 Gallup Poll, for example, revealed that 73% of Americans support abortion rights, while 77% also view abortion as a form of killing.

2. Bread for the World, founded in 1973 and now claiming more than 40,000 members, is an advocacy group on hunger issues. Just Life, created in 1986 with 5,000 financial supporters, is a political action committee promoting a "consistent life ethic" on abortion, economic justice, and the arms race. Evangelicals for Social Action, formed in 1978, fosters "a holistic discipleship which actively pursues peace, justice and liberty in society according to biblical principles." The National Association of Evangelicals, founded in 1942, is the voice of the evangelical movement, the counterpart of the mainline National Council of Churches. The Prison Fellowship, with a staff of 170 and 15,000 volunteers in 1983, ministers

to prison inmates, educates the public, and lobbies public officials on behalf of prison reform. Focus on the Family, led by radio psychologist James Dobson, has several hundred thousand members and is headquartered in Colorado Springs; its Washington lobbying arm is the Family Research Council, led by Reagan White House staffer Gary Bauer. Concerned Women for America dates from 1978 and has 300,000 members who seek to "preserve, protect, and promote traditional and Judeo-Christian values through education, legal defense, legislative programs, humanitarian aid and related activities." Americans for the Republic (formerly the Committee for Freedom) was part of Pat Robertson's 1988 presidential bid. The committee is now run by the Christian Coalition, which boasts some 300,000 members.

3. Because we were interested in grass-roots activism, rather than Washington lobbying activity, our groups do not include all those analyzed by Hertzke (1988) and Moen (1989).

4. Five organizations provided random membership samples and a cover letter from the executive director asking for respondents' cooperation. Focus on the Family cooperated to the extent of sending one wave of questionnaires to a random membership sample, but no follow-ups were possible. The CWA sample was drawn from leadership lists printed in the monthly CWA magazine. Donors to Americans for the Republic were found in Federal Election Commission public records. As the number of respondents from the groups varied, we used an identical weighted N for each group to prevent respondents in any group from dominating the results. In fact, analyses using the unweighted sample produced almost identical results.

5. Only 28 respondents claimed no religious affiliation. Due to their small numbers, they are excluded from further analysis. They are overwhelmingly pro-choice.

6. How to define evangelicals operationally has been hotly debated by scholars favoring doctrinal, denominational, behavioral, and or self-identification criteria (e.g., Kellstedt and Smidt 1991; Smidt 1988; Welch and Leege 1991; Wilcox 1986b). In this study, with its detailed denomination data, we use a denominational criterion.

7. Some caution is warranted in making comparisons as different abortion questions with varying response options are used. In addition, activists are better educated and more willing to express an opinion, and more likely to exhibit opinion constraint, than voters generally.

8. Although several of these groups count antiabortion activity as part of their program, 12% of the respondents still report being involved in single-issue antiabortion groups.

APPENDIX

In this chapter we use numerous multi-item measures of religiosity and ideology. These are factor scores isolated and derived by a series of principal components analyses with varimax rotations. The lowest theta reliability score was .69 for the revivalism variable.

Fundamentalism. Belief in biblical authority, the historicity of Adam and Eve, the rapture of the Church, original sin, that Paul's teaching on women is still valid, that women's ordination is not permitted by Scripture, that Christians must separate from the world, that U.S. laws should be based on the Old Testament law, that the prophets of Israel predicted the future, and that Christ will return to earth before the millennium.

General Orthodoxy. Belief in the virgin birth of Jesus, the historicity of His resurrection, that only Jesus provides salvation, and that He was both God and man.

Individualism/Communalism. Individualists believe that only changing individual hearts changes society, that the church should concentrate on individual morality, that individuals are poor because of personal inadequacies, and that if enough people were saved, social ills would disappear.

Revivalism. Frequency of watching religious TV, attending revivals, listening to religious radio, and speaking in tongues.

Spiritual Experience. Frequency of feeling God's presence, having prayer answered, experiencing divine inspiration, receiving a biblical insight, and feeling deep peace.

Born Again. An index created from two items, one inquiring whether the respondent was "born again," and the second inquiring about the meaning of the experience. This places respondents on a continuum with those not born-again at one end, followed, in order, by those who claim a born-again status by virtue of nurture in church, those who are born-again by a gradual experience, those who claim the identity from making a commitment to Christ, and, finally, those who claim a dramatic experience at a specific moment.

Involvement. Levels of church attendance, involvement in church, having most friends attend same church, and holding formal church membership.

Salience. A single item: "How IMPORTANT is religion in your life?" (4-point scale: At center, very, somewhat, not too.)

Religious Tradition. Virtually all Christian respondents were classified as evangelical Protestants, mainline Protestants, or Roman Catholics, using a very detailed classificatory code modified from the new NES denomination code. Write the authors for further details.

General Conservatism. Conservative self-identification, strong traditional family values, approve the death penalty, distrust the USSR, agree that free enterprise is Christian, oppose gays teaching school, believe that new lifestyles are bad, reject affirmative action, support scientific creationism, and oppose pornography.

Social Welfare Conservatism. Oppose higher taxes to solve problems of world hunger, poverty, the budget deficit and the environment, and oppose national health insurance.

Social Traditionalism. Belief that diverse moralities hurt society, that only one moral philosophy is correct, and that morality shouldn't adjust to modern conditions.

3

A LISREL Model of Public Opinion on Abortion

MATTHEW E. WETSTEIN

In an era of renewed interest in attitude stability (see Krosnick 1991; Smith 1989), the stability of individual abortion attitudes has gone unnoticed in the political science literature. More attention has been paid to the factors that shape abortion attitudes in the American public and the stability of aggregate opinion on abortion questions in national data sets. Moreover, although a number of quantitative approaches have been applied to abortion attitude research, structural equation models have not been published. This chapter examines the aggregate and individual stability of abortion attitudes in the American public, and presents a linear structural equation (LISREL) model of attitudes on abortion. The chapter concludes with a discussion of the effects recent Supreme Court decisions and the election of President Bill Clinton might have on the stability of abortion attitudes.

Updating the Study of Abortion Attitudes

There is a need in the literature to characterize the individual-level stability of abortion attitudes. Because abortion is an issue of incredible

AUTHOR'S NOTE: Portions of the data utilized in this study were made available by the Inter-University Consortium for Political and Social Research. The data for the American National Election Studies, 1972 and 1976, were originally collected by the Center for Political Studies at the Institute for Social Research at the University of Michigan. The data for the General Social Surveys (1977-1989) were collected by the National Opinion Research Center, the University of Chicago. Neither the original collectors of the data, nor the consortium bear any responsibility for the analyses and interpretations presented here. This chapter is a revised version of a paper presented at the annual meeting of the Midwest Political Science Association, Chicago, April 1992. The author is grateful for helpful comments on earlier versions of this study from Robert Albritton, Ellen M. Dran, Malcolm L. Goggin, Ken Rasinski, and Christopher Wlezien.

symbolic importance, and a potentially divisive issue (Goggin 1993), it is argued in this chapter that abortion attitudes should remain stable over time. The hypothesis behind such an approach is that when a controversial issue like abortion is in the public eye for a long period of time, attitudes become easy to form and difficult to change (Carmines and Stimson 1980). To paraphrase James Stimson (1991:83), it is difficult to imagine an adult of child-rearing age who has not thought about abortion as a public issue. The debate and rancor that surrounds the issue of abortion makes it relatively easy for individuals to form attitudes and remember their position on it. As Converse and Markus (1979) put it, abortion is an issue

> which pits the cutting edge of new mores against an array of traditional values . . . it is not entirely surprising that such moral issues should have a deeper resonance among those not normally attentive to much political controversy. (Converse and Markus 1979:42)

Because the abortion issue is so evident in public discourse, a central hypothesis of this chapter is that abortion attitudes are one of the most stable attitudes in the American public. Because the abortion issue is so controversial, attitudes on it are bound to be more stable than other issues.

In Chapter 1, Frauke Schnell outlined the impact of a number of competing values on abortion attitudes. In Chapter 2, Guth et al. outlined the structure of abortion attitudes in abortion activists. It is important to keep in mind that abortion attitudes are not formed in a vacuum separate from other attitudes. Clearly, issues like sexual liberalism, strength of religion, and attitudes about the role of the state in private affairs have the potential to conflict or interact with abortion attitudes (see Chapter 1).

The customary approach to abortion attitude research is to identify a number of independent variables known to affect abortion views and regress them on abortion attitudes. For example, Granberg and Granberg (1980) used a set of demographic variables including education, income, age, race, sex, region, rurality, and occupational prestige to characterize support for abortion in the General Social Surveys of 1965, and 1972 through 1978. Their single equation model explained roughly 10% of the variance in the 6-point abortion support scale (Granberg and Granberg 1980:254). Combining these variables with indicators of conservatism toward matters of personal morality, they were able to boost their R^2 values to around .25 (Granberg and Granberg 1980).

Much has also been written about the changing impact of variables on abortion attitudes. For example, the denominational differences that once existed between Catholics and Protestants seem to have given way to a general consensus across denominational lines (see "Attitudes on Abortion"

1989; Gallup and Newport 1990; Hertel and Hughes 1987; Jelen 1988a). Differences between blacks and whites on abortion have been disputed, with no apparent resolution (see Arney and Trescher 1976; Baker, Epstein, and Forth 1981; Combs and Welch 1982; Hall and Feree 1986; Wilcox 1990, 1992 for differing opinions on the impact of race). Recent research by Clyde Wilcox (1992) suggests that the gap between blacks and nonblacks on abortion has narrowed, especially when controlling for religiosity.

Legge (1983) used discriminant analysis to highlight the importance of religion and attitudes toward women's equality as predictors of abortion attitudes. Yet Legge found that only 44% of the cases could be classified correctly by his analysis, leading him to conclude that views on abortion were not structured strongly, and not salient to the American public (Legge 1983:488-89).

Legge's conclusion points to the apparent ambivalence most Americans have toward the abortion issue. Only a small portion of the American public occupy the pro-choice and anti-choice extremes. Roger Rosenblatt (1992, chap. 1) maintains that abortion is one of the few issues Americans attempt to avoid in private conversation because of the nature of the dispute between the two extremes. Divisions between the two extremes have created a "muddled middle" (Rosenblatt 1992:27) that often casts a wary eye on public demonstrations by abortion supporters and opponents.[1]

What is needed now is a more sophisticated rendering of the relationships between abortion attitudes and the variables identified in previous research. Structural equation approaches to abortion attitudes have not been published in the political science literature. Quantitative methods beyond multiple regression have not been utilized on the data. This chapter will present a LISREL model of abortion attitudes, offering a methodological update to the study of the structure of abortion attitudes.

Measures of Aggregate Stability

Evidence for the aggregate stability of abortion opinions within the American public is abundant in the literature (Ebaugh and Haney 1980; Gallup and Newport 1990; Glazer 1987; Granberg and Granberg 1980; Legge 1983). The years between 1965 and 1972 were marked by the apparent liberalization of opinions on abortion in the United States (Rossi and Sitaraman 1988). Since the *Roe v. Wade* decision in 1973, however, aggregate positions on abortion have remained stable.

The General Social Survey in almost every year since 1972 has asked respondents whether they support abortion for six reasons: ranging from abortion to protect the life of the pregnant woman, to elective abortion.[2]

Table 3.1   Approval of Abortion Circumstances in 1977-1987 General Social Surveys

	1977	1978	1980	1982	1983	1984	1985	1987
				Year of Survey				
Mean	3.95	3.73	3.89	3.79	3.53	3.69	3.62	3.55
Percentage Supporting								
0 reasons	8	9	9	10	11	9	10	12
1 reason	6	6	6	5	8	8	8	7
2 reasons	9	10	10	10	12	11	12	11
3 reasons	21	24	21	23	22	23	23	23
4 reasons	11	12	10	10	10	8	9	9
5 reasons	11	9	9	9	8	6	7	7
6 reasons	35	30	37	34	29	35	32	31

SOURCE: National Opinion Research Center, General Social Survey, various years.

Over the years, there has been only a slight drop in the mean support level for these six reasons. For example, in 1972, the mean support stood at 3.9, indicating that on average, the American public supported four of the six reasons for abortion (Granberg and Granberg 1980:253). Carrying that kind of analysis forward into the 1980s, the stability of abortion support in the aggregate becomes clear. Table 3.1 provides the mean abortion support scores for the General Social Surveys in 1977, 1978, 1980, 1982, 1983, 1984, 1985, and 1987. The table also reports the percentage of the American public that supports each number of reasons for an abortion, ranging from zero (no abortions at all) to six (allowing abortions for all circumstances).

The first set of figures in Table 3.1 indicate that the mean level of support for abortion across the six questions has hovered between 3.5 and 4.0; with perhaps a slight decline in the mean level of support over the period. The bottom set of figures indicate the percentage of respondents supporting abortion for a specific number of reasons. The data demonstrate there is a core group of about 10% within the American public that would prohibit abortion for any reason. During the 1977-1987 period, roughly a third of the American public supported the right to an abortion for all six circumstances. In between those two extremes are the majority of Americans (about 60%) who have differing views about the legal circumstances for abortion.

What is important about Table 3.1 is the relative stability in the cell percentages across the number of years. The greatest gap for any change between the two endpoints in the period is 4 percentage points. Between 1977 and 1987 there was a 4-point increase in absolute opposition to abortion, and a 4-point decline in absolute support for abortion. Although some would contend this is evidence of remarkable stability, given the error-prone nature of public opinion measurement, others would point to the changes and make different arguments. For example, Goggin and Wlezien (1991, 1992) argue that there were significant changes in attitudes on abortion in the 1988-1989 period just prior to the *Webster* ruling by the Supreme Court. They contend that public opinion on abortion was merely responding to the increased interest group competition and court activity in the abortion arena (Goggin and Wlezien 1991, 1992).

Scholars have argued that any slight shift in aggregate opinion deserves some fanfare, especially when attitudes have appeared to be stable in the past (see Stimson 1991, chap. 1). Yet it would be unwise to attribute any significance to the decline of a few points in the support score. It may be attributable to changes in the order of questions in the General Social Survey over the years (see Bishop, Oldendick, and Tuchfarber 1985; Rossi and Sitaraman 1988). In short, the change in abortion support may be an artifact of the survey and question context, and not based in some inherent change in attitudes within the public.

With such evidence of aggregate stability, what implications do such findings have for attitudinal theories that suggest little stability within the American public? First a word of caution is in order. The relationships mentioned so far have focused on aggregate data at different points in time. The relationships do not follow an individual over time. In other words, though the data present several snapshots over time, the data do not present the same people in those snapshots. The most promising way to examine this issue is to use panel data from the American National Election Studies to catalog attitude stability over time at the individual level.

Measures of Individual Stability

The question of attitude stability has troubled the discipline since the early 1960s. One of the opening claims of instability was brought by Philip E. Converse (1964) in his now famous article, "The Nature of Mass Belief Systems in Mass Publics." In a three-pronged argument, Converse found no constraint or consistency in political attitudes among the American public. First, he argued that only a small minority (something like 2% to 4%) could be labeled ideologically sophisticated (Converse 1964:214-19). Second, he found little systematic continuity between issue areas, indicating that political attitudes often appeared to be set off in separate belief systems, rather than in one organized system (Converse 1964:229). Finally, Converse (1964:239-45) used panel study data to demonstrate that there was little correlation over time on specific issue positions within the mass public (except for party affiliation). That is, Americans had a strong tendency to respond differently in different years, indicating unstable attitude positions on political issues.

Since that time, Converse has withstood criticism and garnered support within the discipline. Nie, Verba, and Petrocik (1979), relying on data from the 1960s and 1970s, argued that the American electorate became more ideologically sophisticated during those trying political times. Unfortunately, their results were based on question formats that had been altered, biasing the data in their favor (Kinder 1983:395). Indeed, controlling for the question changes, other researchers found the electorate to be just as ideologically unsophisticated in the 1960s as in the 1950s (Kinder 1983; Smith 1989).

Even symbolic issues like attitudes toward race relations were found to be unstable over time in the early panel studies. Converse (1964) found only a .48 correlation over the 1958-1960 panel on a question dealing with the government's role in desegregating schools. Recently, Smith (1989) has argued that the low levels of attitude constraint and stability in the American electorate have gone unchanged: The American voter of the 1980s is as ideologically unsophisticated and unstable as the voter Converse described. Party identification still remained relatively stable, but specific issue correlations across time fell well below the stability of partisan identification.

Yet there are increasing claims to the contrary arguing for stable attitudes in the American electorate. Morris Fiorina's (1981) model of retrospective voting implies that party affiliation is as subject to change as other attitudes. Thus party affiliation is potentially as stable as other attitudes. More recently, Krosnick (1991:561) reexamined NES panel data (using stability coefficients) and found equal levels of stability for party identification, ideological orientations, racial issues, nonracial policy issues, and matters of political efficacy and trust. In other words, party identification's supreme role in the attitude stability debate may no longer be appropriate.

Two possible findings could emerge in an analysis of abortion attitudes in panel studies. Under the Converse scenario, abortion attitudes will be much less stable than party identification. Krosnick's recent findings contradict this claim, implying that abortion attitudes can be as stable as party identification.

For this study, the stability of abortion attitudes was tested using the 1972-1976 National Election Panel Study. Comparisons were made between party identification across the 4-year span, as well as responses to an abortion question that was asked in both years.[3] The test is to determine how closely abortion attitudes match across the 4-year time frame, and compare them to party identification correlations. Note that this 4-year gap represents a stringent test of the stability hypothesis for two reasons. First, 4 years is a significant span of time to test issue agreement for an individual. Second, the *Roe v. Wade* decision falls between the two survey periods. This was clearly an era of intense abortion debate, and if there were ever to be switching of attitude positions because of education on the issue, the 1972-1974 period stands out as the benchmark to examine.

Examining correlation coefficients, we see a verification of the claims by Krosnick (1991).[4] The Pearson correlation coefficient for party identification across the two surveys is .68. The correlation coefficient for the abortion question in 1972 and 1976 is .62. Thus the stability of the abortion question over time rivals the stability of party identification in the 1972-1976 panel study. The results are similar to party correlations reported by Converse (1964; Krosnick 1991) in the 1958-1960 panel study (.74), and the average correlation across a number of subgroups reported in the 1972-1976 panel study (.60).

Further analysis of attitude positions on abortion in the 1972-1976 panel study points even more directly to the stability of abortion attitudes at the individual level. Sixty percent of the individuals in the NES panel gave the same attitude response in 1976 that they gave in 1972 (Wetstein 1992a). Moreover, if the definition of stability is relaxed to allow individuals to move one issue position on the abortion scale, 90% of the individuals in the panel study could be said to have stable abortion attitudes (Wetstein 1992a).

Evidence presented in this study may add to the growing debate surrounding attitude stability. Clearly the divisive nature of the abortion issue and its long tenure on the public agenda have helped to solidify individual attitudes on abortion. Attitudes on abortion appear to be less vulnerable to change than other issues, and apparently as stable as party identification.

A LISREL Model of Abortion Attitudes

This section characterizes American public opinion on abortion in 1988 and 1989, as recorded in the General Social Survey. The dependent variable consists of responses to abortion circumstances in cases of danger to the woman's health, rape or incest, birth defect, a woman not wanting to marry, a poor woman who cannot afford another child, and a married woman who does not want more children. In the General Social Survey, and in this chapter, these variables are labeled ABHEALTH, ABRAPE, ABDEFECT, ABSINGLE, ABPOOR, and ABNOMORE. In a structural equation model, these six attitudes were modeled as tapping one latent construct that shapes abortion attitude responses.[5]

The independent variables are a core set of demographic and attitudinal variables that have often been used in abortion research. They include: PREMARSX, whether a respondent opposed premarital sex; TEENSEX, whether a respondent opposed teens having sex; ATTEND, frequency of church attendance; RELITEN, a measure of religious intensity based on self-reported strength of religious affiliation; XNORCSIZ, the expanded coding of city size; AGE, the age of the respondent; EDUC, the highest level of education completed by the respondent; and PRESTIGE, an occupational prestige score.[6]

City size has been infrequently used in models of abortion opinion, despite an apparent connection (Granberg and Granberg 1980; Mileti and Barnett 1972). In previous research, it has been easy to see the aggregate connection between city size and abortion utilization (Albritton and Wetstein 1991; Hansen 1980; Powell-Griner and Trent 1987; Tatalovich and Daynes 1989). Large cities have more abortion providers, making an urban/rural cultural cleavage important for abortion utilization research. Such a cleavage might shape abortion opinions as well. The hypothesis is that large metropolitan areas may induce more liberal approaches to abortion.

The independent variables listed above were used in a principal components analysis to identify underlying factors that might shape abortion attitudes.[7] Results of the factor analysis are presented in Table 3.2. The first factor seems to tap attitudes on religiosity and moralism. Attitudes on strength of religious feeling (RELITEN, .872) and church attendance (ATTEND, .873) load very strongly on this factor. Attitudes on premarital sex load moderately on this factor as well (PREMARSX, .416). A second factor taps attitudes on sexual liberalism, with premarital sex (PRE-MARSX, .640), teen sex (TEENSEX, .730), and age (AGE, −.747) all loading strongly. The third factor is clearly a socioeconomic factor, with high loadings for education level (EDUC, .847) and occupational prestige (PRESTIGE, .897). City size returned the only large loading on a fourth factor (XNORCSIZ, .975).[8]

Using the principal components analysis results as a guide, a LISREL structural equation model was developed to characterize the relationships between abortion attitudes and the other variables. The four factors (relig-ious/moral, sexual liberalism, socioeconomic, and urban/rural) suggested causal paths that would influence a latent abortion attitudes factor. This abortion factor would influence the various attitudes respondents have on the six abortion questions in the General Social Survey.

In the hypothesized LISREL model, age is designated as an exogenous variable that impacts the underlying factor for sexual liberalism. This

Table 3.2 Factor Loading on Six Abortion Questions in 1988-1989 General Social
Surveys

Factor Variable	Religious/Moral	Sexual Liberalism	Socio-Economic Status	City Size
ATTEND	.873			
RELITEN	.872			
PREMARSX	.416	.640		
TEENSEX		.730		
AGE		−.747		
EDUC			.847	
PRESTIGE			.897	
XNORCSIZ				.975

SOURCE: National Opinion Research Council, General Social Survey, 1988 and 1989.
NOTE: Factor loadings less than .3 are omitted from this table.

underlying factor on sexual permissiveness serves as the driving force for
the two endogenous variables dealing with sexuality (TEENSEX and
PREMARSX). The urban/rural factor is an unobserved factor that hypo-
thetically drives respondent answers on city size (XNORCSIZ). It is
hypothesized that this urban/rural factor influences the sexual liberalism
of a respondent, as well as attitudes on abortion. Similarly, the socioeconomic factor is unmeasured, but influences two observed endogenous
variables, education and occupational prestige (EDUC and PRESTIGE).
This socioeconomic factor is suggested to affect the sexual liberalism
factor and the abortion attitudes factor. Finally, the religious/moral factor
is hypothesized as having an impact on sexual liberalism and abortion
attitudes. The religious factor is tied to two measured endogenous variables of church attendance and religiosity (ATTEND and RELITEN). A
diagram of the hypothesized model is provided in Figure 3.1.

The estimated model allows for correlation of the error terms between the
three "hard" questions and the three "soft" questions. Additionally, a small
amount of error was established for the AGE and XNORCSIZ paths.[9] Simultaneous estimation indicates that the hypothesized model fits the data rather
well. The chi-square value of 151.37 for 63 degrees of freedom is a good
indication that the model is reproducing the covariance matrix (see Long
1983a:65; Long 1983b). The Goodness of Fit Index is .976, nearly approach-
ing the desired level of 1.0. These values inspire confidence that the specified
model fit the data well (see Asher 1983; Joreskog and Sorbom 1986).

Figure 3.2 provides the LISREL estimates for the measurement model.
The sexual liberalism factor has the greatest influence on the abortion

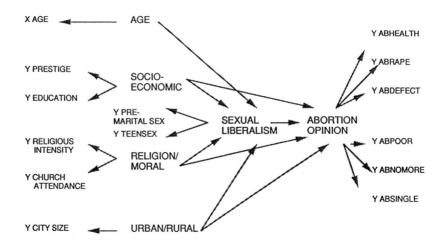

Figure 3.1. Hypothesized LISREL Model of Abortion Attitudes

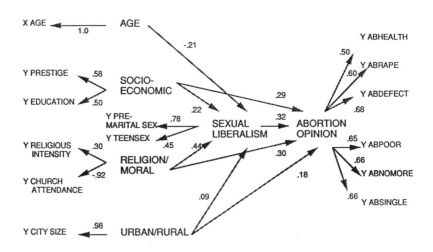

Figure 3.2. LISREL Model of Abortion Attitudes

NOTES: R^2 for abortion opinion = .448
R^2 for sexual liberalism = .292
χ^2 = 151.37 (63 degrees of freedom)
Adjusted goodness-of-fit index = .960

Table 3.3 Correlation of Abortion Error Terms in the LISREL Model

	ABDEFECT	ABRAPE		ABPOOR	ABSINGLE
ABHLTH	.248	.265	ABNOMORE	.333	.368
ABDEFECT		.187	ABPOOR		.330

NOTE: Values are theta epsilon estimates for the abortion question error terms not shown in Figure 3.2.

attitudes factor (beta = .32). Next in importance are the religious/moral factor (beta = .30) and the socioeconomic factor (.29), with the urban/rural factor having the smallest impact (.18). Moreover, the religious/moral factor plays an important role in shaping attitudes on sexual liberalism (beta = .44). Socioeconomic status (beta = .22) and age (gamma = −.21) also have significant impacts on the sexual liberalism factor.

The path coefficients indicate that all four of the hypothesized factors play some role in shaping the structure of abortion attitudes. Individuals with more liberal views on premarital and teen sex tend to have more liberal views on abortion. Respondents with little or no ties to strong religious practices tend to support abortion under more circumstances than strongly religious respondents. Higher socioeconomic respondents tend to have more liberal abortion attitudes. Residents of larger metropolitan areas also tend to be more supportive of abortion under various circumstances. Note that the negative sign for the path between age and sexual liberalism indicates that older respondents tend to be more conservative on issues of sexual liberalism.

The effect of the correlation among the six abortion questions can be seen in Table 3.3. There are moderate loadings from each of the error terms to the abortion questions, as well as moderate correlations between the error terms for the questions.

Overall, the factors and variables in the LISREL model explain nearly 45% of the variance in the abortion attitude factor, with 55% of the variance remaining unexplained. Moreover, simultaneous estimation allows us to see that 29% of the variance in the sexual liberalism factor is accounted for in the model.

The LISREL model produces higher levels of explanation than are found in previous multiple regression equation models. For example, Granberg and Granberg (1980) used 14 variables to explain 32% of the variance in the abortion support scale in the 1977 General Social Survey. The LISREL model presented in this chapter produces an R^2 value of .45 with only four latent factors and a total of eight observed indicators.

Conclusion

Several conclusions emerge from the foregoing analysis of abortion views. The stability and structure of abortion attitudes outlined here suggest that policymakers will face a relatively predictable mass public on the abortion issue in the next few years. Americans have come to hold stable attitudes on abortion, and the ideological polarization of the issue of abortion is likely to continue under a new presidential administration.

This chapter suggests that relatively stable attitudes on abortion were evident during the 4 years when abortion policy was in transformation in this country (1972-1976). It is remarkable that abortion attitudes remained so constant at the individual level during the era when *Roe v. Wade* was decided. Such a finding suggests that attitudes in the mass public are unlikely to be greatly swayed by recent or forthcoming court decisions. Although some scholars may debate this issue (see Goggin and Wlezien 1991, 1992), the *Webster* decision by the Supreme Court in 1989, and recent decisions are unlikely to have a marked impact on abortion attitudes in this country. The arguments in this chapter suggest that individuals in the United States have examined the abortion issue, and largely plan to retain the beliefs they have, despite changes in the political environment.

This is not to say, however, that interest groups will not attempt to sway abortion attitudes. As Goggin (1993) has argued, interest groups on both sides of the abortion dispute have used court decision "shocks" to either alter tactics or attempt to expand the scope of conflict by drawing in new supporters. Ostensibly, these supporters come from the ambivalent "muddled middle" in the mass public. The 1989 *Webster* ruling by the Supreme Court served as a catalyst for pro-choice activists to draw long-dormant pro-choice supporters into the streets for symbolic marches. Yet these shocks and changes in the abortion landscape have occurred periodically since 1973, and remarkably, attitudes on abortion have shown little movement.

The stability of abortion attitudes in the American public has important implications for policymakers. Such stability allows legislators and policymakers the luxury of working in a political environment that features relatively predictable mass opinions. State legislators, therefore, should be comforted by the notion that public opinion on abortion issues is likely to remain stable over the next few years. While that opinion often appears to be divisive and confrontational at the extremes, policymakers at least can be assured of stable attitudes in the mass public.

Finally, the agenda of abortion liberalization that appears to be on the horizon under the Clinton administration will only serve to fuel the battles between pro-choice and pro-life (anti-choice) advocates. Just as *Webster* and recent Supreme Court decisions have boosted membership and activities in abortion rights interest groups, legislative moves by a Democratic Congress and the Clinton administration are likely to mobilize pro-life (anti-choice) support. The Democratic party's dominance of national political institutions will counteract other trends in the abortion landscape that have led others to suggest that the overturning of *Roe* is more likely (Goggin, 1993). Thus the scope and nature of the abortion conflict that certainly changed in the wake of the *Webster* ruling is certain to change again in the wake of the 1992 election. The findings in this study suggest that the bulk of the mass public, however, will remain outside that conflict.

Notes

1. See Goggin and Wlezien (1992) for a discussion of the negative influence interest group activities can have on public attitudes on abortion.

2. The wording for the abortion questions in the General Social Surveys is: "Please tell me whether or not you think it should be possible for a pregnant woman to obtain a legal abortion if

1. there is a strong chance of serious defect in the baby?
2. she is married and does not want any more children?
3. the woman's own health is seriously endangered by the pregnancy?
4. the family has a very low income and cannot afford more children?
5. she became pregnant as a result of rape?
6. she is not married and does not want to marry the man?"

3. For information on the panel study, see the Center for Political Studies, *American National Election Series: 1972, 1974, and 1976,* volumes 1 through 5 (Ann Arbor: Center for Political Studies, University of Michigan, and the Inter-University Consortium for Political and Social Research, 1979). The exact wording for the abortion question in the panel study is: "There has been some discussion about abortion in recent years. Which one of the opinions on this card best agrees with your view? You can just tell me the number of the opinion you choose:

1. abortion should never be permitted.
2. abortion should be permitted only if the life and health of the woman is in danger.
3. abortion should be permitted if, due to personal reasons, the woman would have difficulty in caring for the child.
4. abortion should never be forbidden, since one should not require a woman to have a child she doesn't want."

4. See Converse and Markus (1979) for some discussion of abortion attitude stability in the 1972-1976 panels. Simple correlations are reported here because there is insufficient information (more unknowns than equations) to compute stability and reliability estimates through LISREL (see Asher 1983). Because there are only two waves in the panel, a multiple indicator model is needed to compute stability coefficients. This is not possible because there is only one abortion question in each of the panel waves. Had the abortion question been asked in the 1974 wave, stability and reliability coefficients could have been estimated.

5. An alternate model would have included two separate abortion factors: one dealing with the so-called hard abortion questions (ABRAPE, ABDEFECT, ABHEALTH), and one centering on the so-called soft abortion questions (ABNOMORE, ABSINGLE, and AB-POOR). Such a specification was impossible because of identification problems (see Asher 1983).

6. The General Social Survey cases were weighted to correct the sample for the number of adults in each household, as suggested in the cumulative codebook provided by the National Opinion Research Center (see Davis and Smith 1990).

7. A single multiple regression equation was also run to replicate prior research. The 6-point abortion scale served as the dependent variable. Variables were recoded to have the highest value represent the most liberal or most supportive abortion position. The equation explained 31% of the variance in the scale ($R^2 = .307$). Unstandardized regression coefficients and t values for the variables were:

Variable	b	t	Beta
PREMARSX	.515	11.4	.32
EDUC	.130	7.1	.20
AGE	.017	5.7	.14
XNORCSIZ	.095	5.7	.13
RELITEN	.259	4.6	.13
ATTEND	.086	3.8	.11
PRESTIGE	.010	2.6	.07
TEENSEX	.161	2.6	.06
CONSTANT	−1.487	−4.0	

8. Only the first two factors had eigenvalues in excess of 1.0. A four-factor solution was predetermined on theoretical grounds, based on an examination of the questions and previous research. The four factors explain 74% of the variance.

9. The value for the AGE theta delta was set at 1% error (under the assumption that there would be very little measurement error in reported age). The value for the XNORCSIZ theta epsilon was set at 10% error (under the assumption there would be slightly higher levels of error in reporting of size of city). Two additional paths were freed up for estimation in the measurement model: the theta epsilon path between education and teen sex (.19), and the lambda y path between socioeconomic status and teen sex (−.20).

4

Generational Differences in Attitudes Toward Abortion

ELIZABETH ADELL COOK

TED G. JELEN

CLYDE WILCOX

As social scientists have accumulated various time-series data on social and political attitudes, they have frequently found substantial generational differences that persist over time. Political scientists have reported generational differences on partisanship (Abramson 1976), electoral behavior (Butler and Stokes 1969), basic values (Inglehart 1977), and other attitudes. Most of these studies have reported that younger cohorts are more liberal than older ones, and that generational replacement is resulting in important changes in values and attitudes. Although there is evidence that adults are capable of sizable attitude change (Jennings and Niemi 1981), the studies above confirm the original suggestion of Mannheim (1972) that at least some cohorts share a common generational outlook and set of values.

Recently, Inglehart (1990) has marshaled an impressive array of data from a variety of societies to demonstrate that the process of generational replacement is resulting in a change in values in Western societies. Inglehart suggests that earlier generations experience privation during their formative years, and have subsequently centered their values on acquiring the

AUTHORS' NOTE: We would like to thank anonymous reviewers and the editors for helpful comments. The data were made available by the Inter-University Consortium for Political and Social Research. All interpretations are our own.

necessary resources to maintain economic security. The younger generations, however, raised after the Great Depression and World War II, have
generally taken material property for granted, and are consequently concerned with a different set of values, including expression and freedom.

Although attitudes toward moral and gender issues are not explicitly
part of Inglehart's materialist/postmaterialist typology, he reports that they
are closely related to these basic values, with postmaterialists more liberal
on issues such as abortion, homosexuality, and gender roles than materi-
alists. This liberalism is consistent with the postmaterialists' concern for
personal freedom and self-expression. The implication of this finding is
that the younger cohorts are more liberal on feminist issues than older
ones, and that generational replacement will result in more liberal mass
publics in Western nations.

Although early studies of the sources of support for feminist positions
in the United States generally found greater support among younger
citizens (Gurin 1985; Klein 1984; Miller, Hildreth, and Simmons 1986;
Sapiro 1980; Thornton and Freedman 1979), Cook (1993) reported that
those women who came of age during the Reagan era had lower levels of
feminist consciousness that those women who came of age in the 1960s
and 1970s. Cook's findings suggest that younger cohorts may not be more
supportive of feminist policies. Indeed, to the extent that younger citizens
take for granted the gains of the 1960s and 1970s, they may be somewhat
less supportive of feminist goals.

Of course, Cook's results on feminist consciousness may not be directly
applicable to abortion attitudes. Although legal abortion is an important
part of the feminist program, and gender equality an important symbolic
component of abortion attitudes (Fried 1988; Staggenborg 1987), other
attitudes are relevant as well. A number of writers (Baker et al. 1983;
Eckberg 1988; Findlay 1985; Granberg 1978; Hall and Ferree 1986; Jelen
1988a, 1988b; Legge 1987; Wilcox 1992) have found that gender role
attitudes, attitudes toward ideal family size, attitudes toward sexual morality, general political conservatism, attitudes toward the right to die, and
religious attitudes are all important predictors of abortion attitudes.

Recent studies on the determinants of abortion attitudes provide some
confirmation that there may be generational differences in abortion attitudes, however. Hall and Ferree (1986) and Wilcox (1990) both reported
that among whites, age was positively (although not significantly) related
to support for legal abortion after multivariate controls. In short, younger
white cohorts were less supportive of legal abortion that those who came
of age in earlier periods.

This chapter will examine cohort differences in support for legal abortion. Using primarily data from the General Social Survey (GSS) (Davis

and Smith 1972-1991), we will first explore cohort differences in attitudes toward abortion. The data suggest that in the youngest cohorts of whites (who came of age during and after the Reagan presidency) are somewhat less supportive of legal abortion that those who came of age during the formative years of the women's movement, but that this pattern does not hold for blacks.

We then posit and test four hypotheses for the lower levels of support among the Reagan/Bush cohort. First, it is possible that the right-to-life movement has succeeded in influencing these younger white citizens. Second, it is possible that the Reagan/Bush cohort is more conservative in general, and that abortion attitudes are merely part of this more general conservatism. Third, it is possible that Reagan and Bush have succeeded in persuading those young Republicans, who came of age during their presidencies, that their policies of opposing legal abortion are correct. Finally, it is possible that younger whites have been influenced by a media message that views abortion as morally problematic. We develop these hypotheses in more detail below.

Data

From the GSS we have constructed three additive indexes to measure attitudes toward abortion. The GSS has routinely asked respondents whether they favored legal abortion in cases of rape, fetal deformity, threat to the health of the woman, poverty, unmarried women, and when the woman wanted no more children. The first and most general index sums the number of positive responses to these six items. Factor analysis suggests that abortion attitudes may be conceived as constituting two related dimensions—support for abortion under traumatic circumstances (rape, fetal deformity, and mother's health) and elective abortion (poverty, unmarried mothers, and mothers who want no more children).[1] Two additional indexes were therefore constructed by summing the number of positive responses to these two sets of items. The general abortion scale therefore runs from 0 (abortion never legal) to 6 (abortion always legal), whereas both the traumatic and elective abortion scales have ranges of from 0 to 3.

Using GSS data, we constructed scales to measure attitudes toward women's roles in society, in politics, in the family, and in motherhood. An additional scale measured attitudes toward sexual morality. Details about these and other scales are in the Appendix. Additional independent variables from the GSS data include standard demographic variables such as education, income, sex, region (dichotomized in South/non-South), urbanization, and labor force attachment. As measures of religious involvement

and doctrine, we include the new GSS measure of denominational orthodoxy, a dummy variable that identified Catholics, a measure of religiosity
constructed from questions of frequency of prayer, subjective attachment
to denomination, and frequency of church attendance, and an item on the
interpretation of the Bible.

We restrict our analysis of GSS data to the period from 1987 to 1991.
This period allows us to identify sufficient numbers of respondents who
came of age during the 1980s to constitute a separate cohort. Moreover, it
includes 2 years before the *Webster* decision, and 2 years after.

In addition, we use data from the 1988 American National Election
Study to examine two hypotheses tested below. From these data we have
constructed two measures of affect—one toward antiabortionists and one
toward Ronald Reagan. In both cases we begin with the feeling thermometer, then subtract the individual's mean feeling thermometer score toward
all social groups.[2] We also use the American National Elections Study
(NES) item on abortion. These supplemental data permit us to evaluate
hypotheses not directly testable with the GSS data.

Cohort Differences in Abortion Attitudes

Our generations are adapted from the work of Sapiro (1980). Sapiro
defined seven coming-of-age cohorts by the historical events of women's
history. We define the cohorts according to when they reached age 18, and
include many of Sapiro's cohort, including those who came of age during
or before the Great Depression (prior to or during 1933), those who came
of age before or during World War II (1934-1944), a "feminine mystique"
cohort from the 1950s (who reached 18 between 1945 and 1960), a sixties
cohort (1961-1969), and a women's liberation cohort that came of age
during the early years of the women's movement in the 1970s (1970-1979),
as well as a Reagan/Bush cohort (not included in Sapiro's earlier work)
that reached age 18 after 1979.

Although Sapiro (1980) argued persuasively that each of these generations experienced different gender expectations and roles, it is possible
that this cohort classification may not be especially relevant to abortion
attitudes. Ideally a generational analysis of abortion attitudes should
identify cohorts whose experience of legal abortion differs in some way.
We think that the Sapiro generational categories (with the addition of a
Reagan/Bush Cohort) meets this criterion, especially for those who came
of age during or after the 1960s.

Luker (1984) characterized the period prior to 1960 as the "century of
silence," during which there was little organized challenge to the status of

abortion as regulated primarily by doctors. In the 1960s, however, abortion reform forces began to push for easier access to abortion. The claim that women had a "right to control their bodies" was made during this period, when advocates of legal abortion had the rhetorical field to themselves. After the *Roe v. Wade* (410 U.S. 113 [1973]) decision in 1973, however, antiabortion forces organized and began to publicize their position widely. Thus those who came of age during the 1970s experienced both the rise of the women's movement and that of the antiabortion movement. Sapiro's feminist cohort is also the cohort that was first exposed to the arguments and organizing of antiabortion activists. The 1980s saw the increasing politization of the abortion issue, with the national Republican Party officially adopting an antiabortion position and most national Democrats publicly endorsing legal abortion. Those who came of age in the 1980s saw two conservative presidents espouse an antiabortion position. After the 1989 *Webster* decision, pro-choice forces mobilized to protect abortion rights, and pro-choice candidates won election in a number of states (Cook, Jelen, and Wilcox, 1992a). Thus the 1960s, the women's liberation, and Reagan/Bush cohorts were socialized in eras with differing levels of abortion availability and elite debate.

We retain, therefore, the Sapiro (1980) cohort classifications with the addition of a Reagan/Bush cohort, although we do not expect cohort differences on abortion to be identical to those on gender roles and feminism. In particular, we expect smaller cohort differences between those cohort that came of age prior to 1960, for there were no notable changes in legal abortion during this period. Nonetheless, because part of the abortion debate concerns gender roles and these cohorts experienced differences in gender roles, we do expect some slight cohort differences among the older respondents. In addition, we are unable to predict the direction of the responses of those who came of age during the 1970s. This cohort was exposed to the efforts of the women's movement to build feminist consciousness, and also to those of the antiabortion forces to regulate abortion access.

Results

In the United States, our data show that the youngest cohorts of whites are less supportive of legal abortion than those who came of age during the 1960s and 1970s. This pattern does not hold for blacks: Among African Americans the youngest cohorts are the most supportive of legal abortion, whereas among whites they are less supportive than some other cohorts. Figure 4.1 shows the percentage of blacks and whites who approve of legal abortion in all or no circumstances by generation.

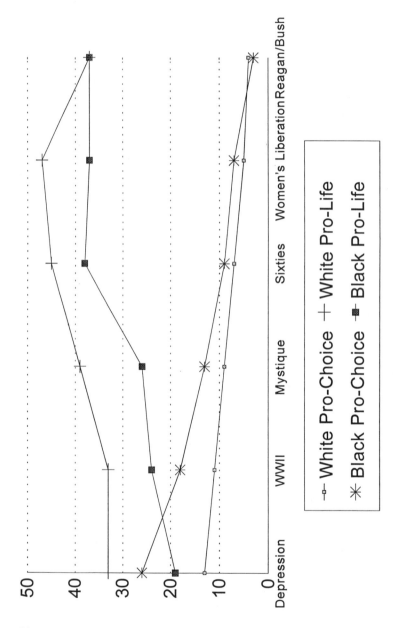

Figure 4.1. Support for Legal Abortion by Cohort
SOURCE: GSS 1987-1991

The data in Figure 4.1 suggest that these generational experiences mold the opinions of whites. Note that the youngest cohort of whites is markedly less supportive of legal abortion in all six circumstances than the sixties or women's liberation cohorts, but that they are not more likely to hold consistently antiabortion positions. Younger whites are more likely than their older counterparts to support legal abortion in some cases but not in others.

In contrast, among blacks the youngest cohorts are considerably more likely than older ones to take a consistent position in support of legal abortion. Indeed, although racial differences in abortion attitudes have been frequently documented (Combs and Welch 1982; Hall and Ferree 1986; Wilcox 1990, 1992), the data in Figure 4.1 suggest that these differences are largest among the oldest cohorts. Racial differences in the proportion of citizens who support legal abortion in all circumstances have disappeared by the Reagan/Bush cohort.[3]

The information in Figure 4.1 suggests that whites who came of age in the Reagan/Bush period are less likely to favor legal abortion consistently, but not more likely to take consistent antiabortion positions. The figure cannot tell us which specific circumstances receive less approval from the youngest cohorts. The data in Table 4.1 suggest that young whites are less likely than the sixties cohort to approve of abortion in elective circumstances, but are equally likely to approve of abortion under traumatic conditions. The decline in support for legal abortion in the youngest cohort is greatest for items concerning when the woman is unmarried or wants no more children. Note that the level of support for elective abortion for the Reagan/Bush cohort is similar to that for the "mystique" cohort, who were socialized during the 1950s.[4] We examined these patterns separately for white men and women. The results were similar, although the cohort differences were larger for women than for men.

Table 4.1 also shows similar information for blacks. Although the smaller number of cases makes estimates somewhat less reliable, the youngest cohort is as supportive of legal abortion on the traumatic and elective abortion scales as the women's liberation cohort, and more supportive than any other cohort. Note the substantial opposition to legal abortion among the oldest black cohort, suggesting that the process of generational replacement will greatly shift the average position of the black community on legal abortion.

That the youngest blacks are among the most supportive of legal abortion fits with the results of most earlier studies, which showed that the youngest respondents were the most feminist. The results for whites are more puzzling, and we devote the rest of the chapter to exploring cohort differences in white attitudes.

Table 4.1 Support for Legal Abortion by Cohort, Percentage of Each Cohort Falling Into Each Category

Era During Which Cohort Turned 18 Years Old	Trauma None	Trauma All	Elective None	Elective All	Health of Mother	Rape	Fetal Defect	Poverty	Single Mother	No More Children	N
Whites only, 1987-1991											
Depression	12	74	56	29	83	80	78	40	35	34	427
World War II	10	77	51	30	88	83	81	42	40	38	688
Feminine mystique	9	75	49	37	88	81	80	44	42	42	910
Sixties	7	79	44	43	91	83	83	50	49	49	838
Women's liberation	5	79	42	46	93	85	83	53	50	50	1,071
Reagan	4	81	44	37	94	89	85	49	43	44	726
Blacks only, 1987-1991											
Depression	20	41	65	18	82	55	54	33	22	22	47
World War II	16	56	57	24	82	65	63	35	30	34	96
Feminine mystique	12	65	56	24	86	75	69	38	0	34	164
Sixties	9	75	51	39	90	83	78	45	42	44	138
Women's liberation	5	76	42	34	93	83	82	47	0	49	248
Reagan	3	76	43	34	90	86	80	51	39	46	158

NOTE: N = number in each cohort. The Great Depression era is considered prior to or during 1933, the World War II era is considered 1934 to 1944, the feminine mystique era is considered 1945 to 1960, the sixties era is 1961 to 1969, the women's liberation era is 1970 to 1979, and the Reagan/Bush era is post-1979. African-American respondents include oversample.

Table 4.2 Cohort Differences in Abortion Attitudes: Longitudinal Trends, Whites Only, 1972-1991

Era During Which Cohort Turned 18 Years Old	1972-1976	1977-1980	1981-1985	1986-1991
Depression	3.99	3.94	3.72	3.57
World War II	4.17	4.18	3.78	3.74
Feminine mystique	4.12	3.97	3.93	3.85
Sixties	4.45	4.28	4.19	4.12
Women's liberation	4.30	4.25	4.19	4.24
Reagan/Bush			3.79	4.07

NOTE: Mean values for each cohort on 6-point legal abortion scale. High scores indicate greater support for legal abortion.
The Great Depression era is considered to be prior to or during 1933, the World War II era is considered 1934 to 1944, the feminine mystique era is considered 1945 to 1960, the sixties era is 1961 to 1969, the women's liberation era is 1970 to 1979, and the Reagan/Bush era is post-1979.

Explaining White Cohort Differences

The differences between white cohorts in support for legal abortion are clearly generational, not due to life-cycle forces. Table 4.2 shows cohort differences in support for legal abortion between 1972 and 1991. There is a steady decline in support among all cohorts through 1985 (evidence of a period effect), and an increase in support among the youngest cohorts in the last period (primarily after the *Webster* decision in 1989).[5] The relative ordering of the cohorts remains similar, except that the women's liberation cohort became more supportive of legal abortion than the sixties cohort in the final period. The relatively constant rank ordering of the cohorts is evidence of enduring generational differences.

Why are younger whites less supportive of legal abortion in the United States than those who came of age during the 1960s and 1970s? Several possible explanations come to mind. First, it is possible that the right-to-life movement has influenced their attitudes. The Reagan/Bush cohort was the first to grow up exposed to the arguments of a fully mobilized anti-abortion movement.

A second possibility is that the Reagan/Bush cohort is more conservative generally, and less supportive of feminism in particular, than those who were socialized in the more liberal climate of the 1960s. Others have reported that those socialized in the 1980s were less feminist than those who came of age during the 1960s (Boloton 1982; Cook 1993; Jacobson 1981; Komarovsky 1985; Renzetti 1987).

Table 4.3 Cohort Differences in Related Attitudes, Whites Only, 1987-1991

Era During Which Cohort Turned 18 Years Old	Mean	SD	N	Mean	SD	N
	Partisanship (GSS)			Affect, Reagan (1988 ANES)		
Depression	3.00	2.28	561	12.19	30.9	137
World War II	2.65	2.23	830	12.99	32.3	230
Feminine mystique	2.72	2.05	1,083	13.48	29.6	342
Sixties	2.98	1.92	980	13.97	28.1	303
Women's liberation	3.04	1.90	1,233	14.23	28.1	409
Reagan	3.28	1.84	596	15.99	25.8	233
Range	0-6, 6 = Strong Republican			−100 to 100, 100 = pro-Reagan		
	Ideology (GSS)			Affect, Antiabortionists (1988 ANES)		
Depression	4.37	1.28	785	−1.16	28.5	109
World War II	4.31	1.25	1,304	−8.51	27.5	205
Feminine mystique	4.29	1.29	1,714	−5.49	28.7	299
Sixties	4.09	1.37	1,592	−4.25	29.7	265
Women's liberation	4.05	1.31	2,113	−5.38	25.4	348
Reagan	3.99	1.29	1,205	−5.90	25.7	195
Range	1-7, 7 = conservative			−100 to 100, 100 = antiabortionists		

NOTE: Means and standard deviations for each item for each cohort. Items from GSS are PARTYID and POLVIEWS. Affect measures are feeling thermometers toward each item adjusted for individual differences as described in text.

The Great Depression era is considered to be prior to or during 1933, the World War II era is considered 1934 to 1944, the feminine mystique era is considered 1945 to 1960, the sixties era is 1961 to 1969, the women's liberation era is 1970 to 1979, and the Reagan/Bush era is post-1979.

A third potential explanation centers on the role of political leadership. As the Republican party became increasingly committed to the antiabortion position, it is possible that young Republicans became less supportive of legal abortion. The strong antiabortion rhetoric of Reagan (and later Bush) may have affected the attitudes of the strongest partisans, especially those who came of age during the 1980s. The GSS data show that the youngest white cohort is the most strongly Republican in partisanship, and the NES data suggest that they are the warmest toward Ronald Reagan. The details are presented in Table 4.3. Moreover, this explanation fits well the continued liberalization of black attitudes, for the youngest cohort of blacks would not have been swayed by Reagan, Bush, or other Republican leaders.

A fourth possibility is that the youngest white cohorts have been exposed to a media message that is supportive of the legality of abortion, but not of the morality of abortions in some circumstances. Condit (1990) reported that her content analysis of popular media coverage of the abortion issue suggested a consensus that developed in the late 1970s that abortion is a private matter, but should be viewed as a morally problematic step that is not to be taken lightly. Abortions as birth control or sex selection are generally condemned in media treatment. Abortions in other "elective" circumstances are viewed with some skepticism, particularly if the decision to abort seems to be made casually.

Finally, it is possible that those who came of age during the Reagan/Bush era take for granted their own access to legal abortion, which has been assured during their reproductive years, and are therefore less concerned about possible regulations of abortions in circumstances they find morally ambiguous. Those who came of age during the 1960s, however, recall the restrictive effects of some regulations, and are therefore more likely to favor no restrictions of abortions under any circumstances. In short, the 1960s generation may frame this question in terms of dangerous abortions and unwanted pregnancies, while the younger cohorts may focus instead on the frequency of abortion in circumstances that they do not find compelling.

Our data do not permit us to test each of these explanations fully, although we can indirectly test some of them. We believe that the lessened support for legal abortion among the youngest white cohorts is not due to the successes of the antiabortion movement, for two reasons. First, although this cohort is less likely to take consistent positions in favor of legal abortion, they are no more likely than the colder cohorts to take a consistent antiabortion position. Second, we examined cohort differences in affect toward antiabortion activists in the 1988 NES. Although the differences are not large, the youngest cohort of whites was the second most hostile toward antiabortion activists, cooler than any cohort except the World War II cohort. The details are in Table 4.3. The NES data confirm that the Reagan/Bush cohort is less supportive of legal abortion, but they are also less supportive of antiabortionists. The correlation between abortion attitudes and affect toward antiabortion activists is lowest among the Reagan/Bush cohort. Clearly this evidence is not conclusive, for it is possible that the antiabortion movement has not succeeded in persuading younger whites that abortion is murder, and has alienated them by its tactics, but has nonetheless succeeded in making abortion seem a morally ambiguous choice. Nonetheless, the available evidence suggests that the antiabortion movement has not had greater success with the white Reagan/Bush cohort than with older respondents.

We also conclude that generational differences are not due to a generalized antifeminism among younger whites. Figure 4.2 shows the percentage of

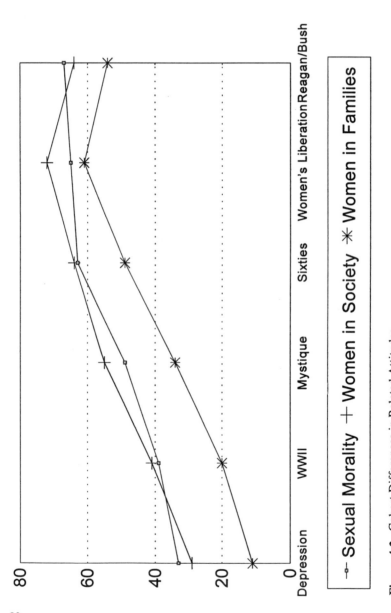

Figure 4.2. Cohort Differences in Related Attitudes
SOURCE: GSS 1987-1991

each cohort who take liberal positions on gender roles and on issues of sexual morality. The results show that the youngest cohort is indeed slightly less liberal than the women's liberation cohort on women's roles in society and the family. Yet the difference between the Reagan/Bush and the women's liberation cohorts in support for gender equality is far smaller than the difference in support for legal abortion. Moreover, the Reagan/Bush cohort is as liberal as any cohort on sexual morality issues, and they are the most liberal on ideological self-placement (see Table 4.3), suggesting that their lessened support for legal abortion is not part of a more generalized conservatism.

Although this suggests that the lower levels of support for legal abortion among the young are not due to a general conservatism on gender or moral issues, the evidence is not yet conclusive. It is possible that although the youngest respondents are not markedly more conservative on these issues, these attitudes may have a stronger influence on the attitudes of the Reagan/Bush cohort. Jelen (1984c) has shown that the determinants of abortion attitudes varies across religious subgroups, and it is possible that they vary across cohorts as well. To see if the determinants of the abortion attitudes of the youngest white respondents are different from older cohorts, we have regressed attitudes toward elective abortion (where the generation gap is largest) on demographic, religious, and attitudinal variables. Table 4.4 shows the differences in the determinants of attitudes toward elective abortion for four cohorts—the Reagan/Bush, women's liberation, and sixties cohorts, and for the other cohorts combined. The table shows the results of four separate ordinary least square (OLS) regression equations.

The sources of abortion attitudes are similar for each cohort. Religiosity and attitudes toward the Bible are significant predictors for all four groups, as are attitudes toward sexual morality.[6] The Reagan cohort differs from the others in only one way: Attitudes toward women's roles in the family are significant predictors of abortion attitudes for these youngest respondents, but are not related to abortion attitudes for the other three groups. Thus the Reagan cohort is slightly more conservative than the sixties and the women's liberation cohorts on women's roles in the family, and these attitudes are strongly related to their abortion attitudes. Yet when we measure the contribution of attitudes toward women's roles in the family toward explaining the greater conservatism of the Reagan cohort on abortion (see Gilens 1988 for a description of the methodology), we find that only a small proportion of the "generation gap" on abortion is due to this difference. We conclude, therefore, that the greater opposition to legal abortion among the Reagan cohort is not due to a more generalized antifeminism or conservatism.

Table 4.4 The Determinants of Attitudes by Cohort, Whites Only, 1987-1991

	Reagan		Women's Liberation		Sixties		Others	
	b^a	t^b	b	t	b	t	b	t
Sex	−.29	−1.33	−.05	−.25	−.18	−.79	−.08	−.49
Education	.07	1.48	.10	2.87***	.04	.99	.03	1.16
Income	−.00	−.57	.01	.78	.01	.65	−.00	.39
South	.10	.47	−.01	−.03	−.13	−.59	−.08	−.48
Urbanization	.13	.96	.06	.49	.09	.62	.17	1.70*
Labor force	.24	1.05	−.22	−.86	.47	1.55	−.07	−.40
Denominational orthodoxy	2.02	1.28	−.60	−.84	.80	.99	−1.77	−1.04
Catholic	−.19	−.84	−.22	−1.12	−.35	−1.50	−.77	−4.17
Bible	−.49	2.82***	−.42	−2.45	−.47	−2.54	−.41	−3.11
Religiosity	−.20	−3.67	−.23	−4.75	−.17	−3.09	−.20	−4.91
Ideology	.14	1.67*	.11	1.35	.17	2.01***	.20	3.28***
Party ID	−.03	−.51	−.00	−.09	−.05	−0.87	.04	1.07
Sexual morality	.44	2.48***	.65	4.21***	.59	3.34***	.59	4.69***
Women in society	.47	1.03	.19	.49	.64	1.36	−.49	−2.06
Women in family	.59	3.04***	.14	.83	.22	1.30	.03	.21
Constant	3.82	3.02***	2.87	2.67***	4.14	3.46***	4.82	5.92***
N	257		310		267		519	
Adjusted R^2	.31		.40		.36		.33	

NOTE: a. Unstandardized regression coefficients
b. *t* values for each cohort
* $p < .10$; ** $p < .05$; *** $p < .01$.

We also reject the notion that political leadership explains the lessened support for legal abortion among the young. The bivariate correlation between party identification and abortion attitudes is .00 for the Reagan/Bush cohort but significant and negative for the sixties and women's liberation cohorts. The strongest Republicans among the Reagan/Bush cohort are actually more supportive of legal abortion than the strongest Democrats. Moreover, the multivariate analysis in Table 4.4 suggests that there are no hidden effects of partisanship on the attitudes of the youngest cohorts that emerge after multivariate controls.

In addition, data from the 1988 NES show that for the Reagan/Bush cohort the correlation between affect for Reagan and support for legal abortion is nonsignificant and actually positive—that is, those who felt warmest toward Reagan were slightly more favorable toward legal abortion. For those of the sixties cohort, in contrast, the correlation was −.17, significant at .01 (the correlation was negative for all other cohorts).

Because research has shown abortion attitudes to be fairly stable over time, we interpret this correlation to indicate that the sixties cohort evaluated Reagan in part on his abortion stance. In contrast, the Reagan/Bush cohort like Reagan regardless of their position on abortion.[7] We see little evidence of the persuasive effects of Republican leadership on the youngest Republicans in these data.

We are unable to test the fourth and fifth potential explanations, although both explanations seem plausible and merit further investigation. We find especially compelling Condit's (1990) argument that the media consensus is that abortion is a private decision but it should not be taken lightly. The two items where whites of the Reagan/Bush cohort are markedly less supportive of legal abortion are when the woman is unmarried and does not want to marry the man, or where she is married but wants no more children. All citizens are less supportive of abortion in these circumstances, but it appears that those who grew up frequently exposed to this media consensus are even less supportive. Perhaps they are less supportive of legal abortion for married couples because they envision it as abortion as birth control. (Younger cohorts, who have had fewer years in which to experience contraceptive failure, may overestimate the reliability of available contraception.) They may be less supportive of abortion when an unmarried mother declines to marry the father because they view unwed motherhood as less objectionable, and therefore not a compelling reason to abort. Further research is needed to discover what these circumstances mean to younger citizens. Condit's explanations also fit the greater antipathy of the Reagan/Bush cohort for antiabortion activists, for Condit claims that the media consensus is that abortion is a private decision that does not warrant outside interference. Efforts at persuasion may be viewed as unhelpful.

Conclusions

Whites who came of age during the Reagan/Bush era are significantly less supportive of legal abortion than those who reached adulthood during the previous two decades. The decline in support is largest on items that focus on elective abortion, especially when married couples want no more children or unmarried women choose not to marry the potential father. The decline is not evident among blacks, however, and among the youngest cohorts the frequently observed racial gap has disappeared.

We suggested five possible explanations for the declining support for elective abortion among younger whites. First, it is possible that the exposure to the arguments of the antiabortion movement has led to a decreased support for legal abortion. There is some evidence for this explanation, for the decline in support begins with that cohort that first was exposed to organized antiabortion activity. But the younger cohorts are not more likely to take consistently antiabortion positions, and are actually more negative toward antiabortion activists. We tentatively reject this explanation, although it may deserve further research.

Second, we tested the hypothesis that the youngest cohorts opposed legal abortion as part of a general conservatism on gender matters, sexual morality, or political ideology. The data do not support this explanation, for the youngest cohorts of whites are not noticeably more conservative on these items, and controls for them do not erase the cohort differences.

Third, it is possible that the visible position of the Republican party and its presidents could have persuaded the youngest cohorts of Republicans to adopt the party position. In fact, however, the correlation between partisanship and abortion attitudes is lowest among the Reagan/Bush cohort, and strong Republicans in this cohort are more supportive of legal abortion than strong Democrats.

Fourth, we suggested that the media consensus documented by Condit (1990) may have shaped the attitudes of those exposed to that consensus in their formative years. That consensus holds that abortion is a private decision, but that abortion is especially morally problematic when there are no exceptional circumstances. We think that a promising line of inquiry lies in how the youngest cohorts view the two circumstances they disapprove of most frequently—that of unmarried mothers who do not want to marry the father, and married couples who want no more children. These are the types of circumstances that younger citizens may view as less compelling, and therefore outside the moral consensus.[8]

Finally, it is possible that the youngest cohorts take for granted the availability of legal abortion, and are more likely to favor restrictions on abortion in circumstances under which they disapprove abortion precisely because they do not recall the effects of regulation. They may frame the issue in terms of their moral objections to certain types of abortions, whereas those who personally experienced the regulation of abortion may frame the issue in terms of the difficulty in obtaining abortions in that era. We can offer no tests of this hypothesis with current data, but if some states move to restrict legal abortion in the aftermath of the *Webster* decision, then this explanation would predict a sharp change in attitudes among the youngest cohorts. The GSS data hint that this may already be occurring, for after 1990 the two youngest cohorts experienced a significant increase in support for legal abortion.

Notes

1. Others have referred to these different sets of conditions as "hard and "soft" conditions. We have used *elective* and *traumatic,* although we are aware that conditions such as poverty are in many ways traumatic. Clearly the public distinguishes between these two sets of issues, and finds the latter more compelling that the former.

2. See Wilcox, Sigelman, and Cook (1989) for a justification of this procedure.

3. We are unable to explain the racial difference in cohort patterns. Wilcox (1992) has shown that racial differences in abortion in recent years are entirely explainable in terms of demographic and especially religious differences between blacks and whites. In part, racial differences in cohort patterns may be due to the sharp decline in religiosity and doctrinal orthodoxy among younger blacks. In addition, younger blacks may associate antiabortion sentiments with the political Right and with Ronald Reagan, both negative referents in black America. Scott and Schuman (1988) show that blacks feel less intensely about abortion than whites. For a discussion of black attitudes toward legal abortion, see Petchesky (1984).

4. This pattern is not unique to the United States. Data from the World Values Survey (World Values Study Group 1990) conducted between 1981 and 1983 in a number of advanced industrial societies (not shown) show that in 12 of 17 countries, the youngest cohort is at least slightly less approving of abortion than one or more older cohorts. In nearly all countries, however, the youngest cohort is more supportive of abortion than the oldest cohorts, suggesting that generational replacement will continue to create a more supportive general climate for abortion.

5. There were only a few respondents in the Reagan/Bush cohort between 1981-1984, so estimates of their attitudes are somewhat unreliable.

6. Jelen (1989) has demonstrated that the two versions of the GSS Bible item can be combined. We have done so.

7. Jelen (1984a) showed that college students of the Reagan/Bush cohort projected their own positions of abortion onto their favored candidate. Although Reagan took an unambiguous position on abortion, then, it is possible that this message was not received among the youngest cohort.

8. This suggests the possibility of a life-cycle effect as well. As individuals age, they become increasingly likely to have experienced contraceptive failure or to know someone who has.

APPENDIX

Scale Construction

Elective Abortion: Count of circumstances abortion should be legal:
ABPOOR, ABSINGLE, ABNOMORE
Alpha = .92

Traumatic Abortion: Count of circumstances abortion should be legal:
ABRAPE, ABDEFECT, ABHLTH
Alpha = .81

Sexual Morality: Mean of:
PREMARSX, TEENSEX, XMARSEX, HOMOSEX
Alpha = .68

Women's Roles in Society: Mean of:
FEPOL, FEPRES, FEHOME, FEWORK
Alpha = .65

Women's Family Roles: Mean of:
FEFAM, FEPRESCH, FEHELP, FECHLD
Alpha = .79

Religiosity: Constructed from:
ATTEND, RELITEN, PRAY
Alpha = .85

5

What if Abortion Were Illegal?

Policy Alternatives Won't Be Easy

ELLEN M. DRAN

JAMES R. BOWERS

In the immediate aftermath of the 1989 Supreme Court decision of *Webster v. Reproductive Health Services,* the political climate in many states turned against maintaining general access to abortions. Some state legislatures began to push the new judicial leniency to the maximum. Idaho and Louisiana, for instance, enacted legislation criminalizing abortion except when the life of the woman is threatened. The Louisiana legislation made no exception for cases of rape or incest. The Idaho legislation was only slightly "kinder and gentler," allowing for abortion in cases of incest if the victim is less than 18 years old and in cases of rape if reported to the police within 7 days (Carlson 1990:22-26).

The Supreme Court's 1992 decision in *Planned Parenthood of South-eastern Pennsylvania v. Casey* reaffirmed its increasing tolerance of restrictive abortion statues. Justices O'Connor, Kennedy, and Souter, speaking for the Court, argued against overturning *Roe v. Wade.* Nevertheless, they upheld all the restrictions in the Pennsylvania law except the requirement of spousal notification. Thus the Court has yet to clear the way to make abortion illegal once again, but its tolerance of severely restrictive laws has the potential for producing effects similar to a reinstatement of illegality. Through its recent opinions in *Webster* and *Casey,* the Supreme Court has reinvigorated the abortion debate by allowing for an expansion of the scope of the conflict into state politics. In so doing, it has set the stage for a conflict between states pursuing more restrictive abortion laws and a new Congress and president supportive of a national Freedom of

Choice Act. This conflict directly affects the balance of power between the states and the national government and will determine whether abortion can be so severely restricted as to approximate an actual ban.

In light of the new politics of abortion, characterized by *Webster* and *Casey's* increased leniency toward restrictive abortion statutes, the predisposition among many states to pass such laws, and the election of a pro-choice Congress and president poised to do battle against the states, it is unsettling that public opinion research has not examined reaction to the possibility that abortion may still become illegal or access to it so highly restricted that the effect is similar to an actual ban. Instead, it has focused primarily on public attitudes toward specific restrictions, ignoring the important question: "What if abortions were illegal?" Little attention has been given to such issues as whether the public would be willing to spend government funds to provide alternative solutions to unwanted pregnancies.

At this point, the only public data set of which we are aware that addresses this question is the *Los Angeles Times* March 1989 poll on abortion opinion.[1] This poll is itself limited in that it does not examine all alternatives to abortion. It has two questions, however, pertaining to public support for adoption as an alternative to abortion. The first question asks: "Do you think the solution to abortion is adoption, or not?" The second question is: "If abortions were to become illegal, would you be in favor of using public funds to support the adoption of babies that would result from that policy, or would you be opposed to that?"

In recent years adoption has become a high-profile political alternative to abortion that many candidates and public officeholders embrace. According to one adoption expert:

> Pro-choice candidates have used it [adoption] to side-step the abortion issue. They do not say that they are for or against abortion; just that they prefer adoption. . . . More commonly, pro-life candidates use the phrase to demonstrate that while they are not in favor of abortion, they are sensitive to the needs of women with unplanned pregnancies. (Melina 1989:1)

One incarnation of the adoption solution to abortion was George Bush's often-stated 1988 presidential campaign slogan: "Adoption Not Abortion." During the early months of his presidency, adoption continued to be a preferred policy solution of his administration to the abortion issue. For example, in his November 1989 memo to Department of Justice employees encouraging them to consider adoption, Attorney General Dick Thornburgh wrote:

> The foundation of our Nation is the American Family, protector of our most valuable yet vulnerable resource—our children. . . . Each year nearly 25,000

babies are given life and the chance to be loved when their mothers choose adoption over abortion or unwanted parenthood; yet the opportunity to consider adoption is often denied the pregnant women. I am told that as much as 40 percent of pregnancy counseling does not even mention adoption. (Marcus 1989:A3)[2]

For our purpose, then, the focus of the *Los Angeles Times* survey on adoption is particularly useful. The questions were asked just a few months after the 1988 presidential campaign, a time when the public's exposure to the adoption alternative was particularly high. Also, the first question was asked in a form that closely paralleled the political rhetoric of candidates who embraced the adoption solution. In Bush's campaign slogan, adoption was proposed as *the* solution to the abortion controversy, with the implicit message that abortion should be illegal. By approximating the language of candidates who endorse adoption as the solution, the *Los Angeles Times* survey question provides us with an opportunity to evaluate public support for policy proposals in the manner in which public officials phrased the choices. The second question, on public funding, allows us to put the reactions in a concrete policy context.

We suspect that support for adoption as the alternative to abortion is a relatively "easy" issue on which to have an opinion (Carmines and Stimson 1980), but the support may be soft when its proponents are asked to follow through with financial support. To pursue this suspicion, we will look first at the structure of support for the two aspects individually; then we bring the two questions together with a four-part typology showing support for both the adoption solution and public funding of it, rejection of both options, and support for either one or the other but not both.

Analysis

Legge (1987) notes in his analysis of attitudes toward public funding of abortions that opinion can be expected to be complex because of the mixing of two emotional issues—abortion and public welfare. The issue of adoption as an alternative to abortion and its public funding is likely to be even more complex. Not only does it mix two emotional, symbolic issues—abortion and government spending—it also is likely to pull the pro-choice segment of the public in different directions because it provides help for women in need, but also concedes to government the restriction, and perhaps even the prohibition, of abortion. Individuals who are anti-abortion will also face conflict. Drawn disproportionately from the politically and socially conservative segments of the population, they will have to overcome their disdain for government activism and especially in-

Table 5.1 Support for Adoption as an Alternative to Abortion

Adoption as Alternative (%)		Funds for Adoption (%)		Typology (%)	
Yes	54	Favor	64	Favor Both	38
No	36	Oppose	28	Adopt Only	15
Not Sure	10	Not Sure	8	Funds Only	25
				Oppose Both	13
				Other	8

creased government spending. For both sides it forces contemplation of drastic change in the status quo—the worst-case scenario for the one and the goal of the other.

Although 54% of the respondents to the survey agreed that adoption is the solution to abortion, more than a fourth of these individuals were not also willing to expend public monies to support adoptions for births that would presumably result from a prohibition against abortion. Thus only 38% favor adoption as the alternative to abortion and are also willing to pay for it (see Table 5.1). The correlation of the two items is positive but only moderate (tau $b = .16$). Furthermore, there is more support for funding adoption than there is for the alternative itself (64% versus 54%), which suggests that "funding" provides a distinct response cue independent of "adoption." Individuals are probably bringing different attitudes to each dimension.

Although the nearly constant presence of abortion on the public agenda imbues almost any aspect of it with policy connotations, the wording of the adoption question makes no explicit reference to public policy. We suspect that it taps general attitudes about abortion and related moral issues and should be closely linked with the opinion of individuals on abortion itself, as well as personal and attitudinal characteristics that are usually associated with abortion opinion.

Legge (1987), however, has suggested that the structure of support for abortion as a policy issue differs from that as a moral or personal concern (see also Baker et al. 1981, and Casey 1984). The reference to public spending and to an altered context in which abortion is illegal in the second question about adoption puts the policy ramifications up front and we therefore expect that the structure of support will be more directly political.

Public Support for Adoption as the Solution to Abortion

One hypothesis is that support for adoption is a function of support for abortion itself: The more strongly individuals oppose abortion, the more likely they are to support adoption as its solution. We regressed support for adoption (no/not sure/yes) on a measure of abortion opinion, plus demographic and attitudinal variables that have been shown in the literature to be important for abortion attitudes. These include personal characteristics such as gender, race, education, income, age, and religious affiliation, but more strongly, attitudinal characteristics such as religiosity, political ideology, traditional values of morality and sexuality, and attitudes toward the role and place of women in society (e.g., Barnartt and Harris 1982; Blake 1971; Combs and Welch 1982; Deitch 1983; Ebaugh and Haney 1980; Granberg 1978; Granberg and Granberg 1981, 1985; Hall and Ferree 1986; Legge 1983; McIntosh, Alston, and Alston 1979).[3] Where appropriate, attitudinal characteristics are coded with higher codes given to the more conservative response.

The first heading in Table 5.2 shows the unstandardized regression coefficients (standard errors in parentheses), the standardized coefficients, and the significance levels for all the demographic and attitudinal variables. Neither of the political indicators (political party identification or ideology) is significant; nor is religious affiliation, attitudes toward homosexual rights, level of education, the female wage indicator of traditional roles, or income.

The strongest variables describing support for the adoption solution are all measures of basic values or attitudes, with that toward abortion the strongest. As expected, opposition to abortion correlates with support for adoption funding. Religiosity and conservative views on women's issues also have the expected effects. Opposition to greater availability of contraceptives is actually negatively associated with adoption when the other characteristics are controlled. This is contrary to an intuitive expectation that the more conservative response might be associated with support for the adoption alternative. Race (nonblack/black), gender, and age each add a significant but small amount to the explained variance, with blacks, males, and older individuals less supportive of adoption than their counterparts.

Majority support for the adoption solution to abortion thus comes primarily from socially conservative elements already predisposed against abortion. Attitudes of direct political relevance seem to play no role. The question remains of what happens when this sentiment goes into the political arena.

Public Support for Funding the Adoption Solution

Our expectation is that support for the funding of the adoption alternative is different from that for adoption itself. We base this hypothesis on

Table 5.2 Regression of Opinion on Adoption and Adoption Funding on Demographic, Political, and Attitudinal Characteristics

Characteristic	Adoption			Funding		
	b	Beta	Signif	b	Beta	Signif
Abortion Funds	—	—	—	.168	.174	.0000
	—			(.020)		
Abortion Attitude	.170	.258	.0000	.171	.165	.0000
	(.013)*			(.022)		
Religiosity	.087	.153	.0000	.027	.030	.1300
	(.011)			(.018)		
Women's Issues	.079	.081	.0000	.020	.013	.5185
	(.019)			(.031)		
Black	−.184	−.060	.0011	−.297	−.061	.0010
	(.056)			(.090)		
Contraceptives	.065	.059	.0016	.106	.061	.0014
	(.021)			(.033)		
Female	.078	.042	.0263	.252	.085	.0000
	(.035)			(.056)		
Age	−.002	−.039	.0498	−.012	−.149	.0000
	(.001)			(.002)		
Income	.010	.020	.3043	.014	.017	.3987
	(.010)			(.016)		
Homosexual Rights	.011	.017	.3998	.098	.099	.0000
	(.013)			(.202)		
Education	−.007	−.014	.4585	.073	.093	.0000
	(.010)			(.015)		
Ideology	.003	.003	.8596	.077	.049	.0117
	(.019)			(.031)		
Female Wage	−.001	−.002	.9243	.012	.012	.5107
	(.012)			(.019)		
Republican**	.057	.026	.2299	−.099	−.029	.1893
	(.048)			(.076)		
Independent**	.016	.008	.7030	.135	.041	.0512
	(.043)			(.069)		
Other Party**	−.079	−.031	.1252	−.145	−.036	.0778
	(.051)			(.082)		
Protestant***	−.027	−.014	.4653	−.080	−.023	.1800
	(.037)			(.060)		
Other Religion***	−.120	−.026	.1607	.086	.012	.5311
	(.086)			(.137)		
Adjusted R^2	.136			.104		
N =	2,903			2,914		

NOTE: * Standard errors in parentheses
** Dummy variables: Democrats left out
*** Dummy variables: Catholics left out

the previously described difference in attitudes toward abortion as a private/moral concern and as a public policy issue. In addition, there are large segments of the public who have attitudes on government spending that are not always issue specific. For instance, the elderly tend to oppose government spending, at least in part because their incomes often grow more slowly than increased taxes. On the other side, some groups tend to support government spending on social welfare almost regardless of the substantive area. Although the *Los Angeles Times* data set lacks indicators for attitudes toward government spending in general or on social welfare issues, there is a question on support for public funds for abortions for poor women. We added this variable to the regression on funding for adoption as an indicator of opinion on social welfare spending.

The second part of Table 5.2 shows the same variables from the first equation plus the abortion funding variable.[4] Both funding variables—for adoption and for abortion—are coded from strongly oppose to strongly favor. The strongest predictor of funding for adoptions is funding for abortion, and the relationship is positive, thus indicating that spending on social welfare, regardless of the content, is a factor. As a validation of this interpretation, we note that in a second data set for a representative sample of Illinois residents in 1990, we obtained a cleaner indication of the relationship between government spending in general and spending for adoption services as an alternative to abortion. We observed that support of funding for adoption correlates positively with support of increased spending for eight traditional areas of state activity.[5]

Abortion attitude is still strong, with its opponents most likely to support adoption funding (the abortion variable is coded from favor to oppose). Age, as expected, is negatively related and is almost as strong as opinions on funding and on abortion.

The conflict between socially or morally conservative attitudes and financing their consequences shows in the negative coefficients for contraceptives and homosexual rights. That is, individuals opposed to both are also less willing to fund adoption services. Also, the nonsignificance of both religiosity and the women's issues scale indicates that traditionalism, which leads to greater opposition to abortion and to support of an adoption alternative, does not also mean support for public funding of adoptions. On the other hand, less traditional locations on both these variables do not necessarily lead to opposition to funding for adoption, a further indication that the funding option is viewed differently from the general moral question.

There are small effects for three demographics, with educational level the strongest of these. It is interesting that education plays a role in opinion on the funding of adoption, but not on adoption itself. This may indicate

the different role education plays when there are explicit political implications. Also, women are more supportive than men, but blacks are less
favorable than others. Both these groups are thus consistent, with men and
blacks more opposed to both the adoption alternative and its funding than
are women and nonblacks.

The political variables—totally absent in the explanation of adoption
option—do have an effect on funding, but it is quite small. Political
conservatives are more supportive of funding than liberals and moderates;
the partisan effect, however, is minimal. Republicans appear not to differ
from Democrats, but independents may be somewhat more supportive.

Thus the concrete funding question is indeed more complex than that
about the more abstract (and "easier") adoption question. Several variables
are significant, but after opinion on abortion funding (a social welfare
perspective), on abortion itself (a personal value), and age (probably
economic self-interest), the other variables make only small additional
contributions to the explanation, and all together they explain less of the
variance than did fewer variables for the adoption question. There are thus
important differences in the individual attitudes that explain support for
an adoption alternative and its actual implementation through government
spending.

A Typology of Attitudes

To examine these differences, we look at the typology that brings the
two dimensions together. Of the respondents, 38% favor adoption as the
solution to abortion and support public funding for it if abortion were made
illegal (cell 1, $n = 1,373$; see Table 5.3); 15% say they favor the adoption
solution, but reject public funding of it (cell 2, $n = 545$). Just the opposite
position is taken by 25%; they reject adoption as the solution to abortion
but would favor public funding of adoptions if abortions were illegal (cell
3, $n = 897$). Finally, 13% of the respondents oppose both the adoption
solution and public funding of it (cell 4, $n = 452$).[6] Thus, although strong
support for adoption over abortion is the modal choice, it falls well short
of a majority.

As an explanation of the typology, our hypothesis is that cell 1 contains
a disproportionately high percentage of the more conservative segments
of the population who are antiabortion and willing to accept the public
funding consequences of prohibiting abortion. Individuals in cell 2, who
support the adoption solution but reject its public funding, are likewise
drawn disproportionately from conservative and antiabortion ranks. But
we speculate that their rejection of public funding for adoption is tied to
an equally strong sentiment against increases in government spending and

Table 5.3 Typology of Opinion on Adoption as an Alternative to Abortion and Public Funding

| | Cells | | | |
| | 1 | 2 | 3 | 4 |
	Favor Both	Adopt Only	Funds Only	Oppose Both
Total	38%	15%	25%	13%
Age				
18-24	20	14	21	17
25-50	54	41	52	46
51-89	26	45	27	36
Education				
Less than High School	26	31	26	31
High School	31	32	27	29
High School +	25	26	24	25
BA or more	18	12	23	15
Income				
Under $20,000	26	29	26	31
$20,000-$40,000	40	46	37	36
$40,000-$60,000	23	16	23	22
Over $60,000	11	9	14	10
Abortion Funds				
Oppose	61	69	28	56
Not Sure	6	10	10	10
Favor	32	21	62	34
Ideology				
Liberal	19	26	28	22
Moderate	45	44	45	44
Conservative	35	30	27	34
Women's Issues (Traditional Responses)				
0	32	27	48	40
1	36	29	32	37
2 or 3	32	35	20	23
Religiosity				
Low	9	6	21	18
Medium	43	41	51	52
High	48	53	28	30
Abortion Attitude				
Oppose	54	47	22	30
Not Sure	22	24	29	23
Favor	24	27	48	46

a belief that the economic responsibility associated with unwanted pregnancies rests with the individuals experiencing them. We would label their support of an adoption alternative as soft because they indicate an unwillingness to follow through financially. The individuals in cell 2 are also likely to be among the older segments of the population who are traditionally against increases in government spending.

The individuals in cell 3 appear to present a contradiction. On the one hand, they reject adoption as the solution to abortion, but they favor funding this alternative if abortion became illegal. We hypothesize that this position stems from their being from the more liberal elements of the population. Individuals in this cell are likely to be largely pro-choice and pro-spending and are willing to consider alternatives that are supportive of women in need if abortion were illegal once again.

Individuals in cell 4 reject both the adoption solution and public funding of it. We speculate that these individuals are the strongest pro-choice advocates, and are unwilling to accept a hypothetical scenario of no legal abortion.

Table 5.3 presents a profile of the membership in each cell of the typology, based on the personal characteristics of age, education, and income, plus opinion on abortion funding, and attitudinal characteristics represented by political ideology, the women's issues scale, religiosity, and opinion on abortion. These are the variables that most strongly distinguish among the parts of the typology.

Age has the effect we anticipated, as the two cells that oppose government funding of adoption both have disproportionate representation from the oldest age group. But this group shows its mixed reaction by showing up most strongly in the second cell (in favor of adoption but not of funding).

The general irrelevance of socioeconomic status for this issue shows in the education and income subtables. For the most part, each cell of the typology contains approximately the same proportions of each group. The only (small) exception for education is that the funding-only category (cell 3) has proportionately more college graduates than do the others, indicating the policy-relevance of education that we discussed earlier. Lower income levels are somewhat more prevalent in the second cell, and especially the fourth cell for the lowest income group, emphasizing the economic self-interest noted earlier for older individuals.

Supporters of abortion funding are clearly a disproportionate part of the third cell, indicating their propensity to take the social welfare stance in a given policy context, in this case the context of abortions being illegal. Although policy liberalism in the form of an inclination to support social welfare spending is a strong characteristic of the typology, self-identification as liberal, conservative, or moderate is much weaker. Political liberals, however, tend also to populate cell 3 more than the others, while conservative presence in this cell is somewhat less.

Traditionalism on women's roles and on religiosity splits cleanly on the adoption question alone. In other words, there is less interaction with

Table 5.4 Defining Characteristics of the Typology of Opinion on Adoption and its Funding

| | Cells | | | |
Characteristics	1 Favor Both	2 Adopt Only	3 Funds Only	4 Oppose Both
Age	Middle	Oldest	Middle	Oldest
Education	—	< HS	BA+	< HS
Income	—	< $40,000	> $60,000	< $20,000
Abortion Funds	Oppose	Oppose	Favor	Oppose
Ideology	Cons.	—	Liberal	Cons.
Women's Issues	Cons.	Cons.	Liberal	Liberal
Religiosity	High	High	Low/Med	Low/Med
Abortion	Oppose	Oppose	Favor	Favor

funding, especially for individuals at the ends of the scales. The most liberal on women's issues (no conservative responses) are much more likely to be in cells 3 or 4 than in the other two, and the most conservative tend toward cells 1 and 2. The same pattern holds for those individuals who rank lowest and highest on the religiosity scale. Finally, one's position on abortion shows up as a fairly clean split between the first two cells on the one hand and the second two on the other. Again, the pattern holds only for the ends of the scale.

Table 5.4 summarizes the distribution within the typology, showing the groups that characterize each cell.[7] Cell 1 is indeed home to the most traditional or conservative political and social groups. It is also the locale of the highest proportion of the middle-aged group, which tends to have the higher incomes that can support this policy perspective.

Cell 2 also contains disproportionate numbers of the traditional groups, but it is also characterized by larger proportions of the oldest age group and lower income individuals (who are often the same), indicating that age and income militate against pursuing one's potential social agenda. Cell 3 turns out to be the most liberal or nontraditional of the typology. The occupants of this cell will apparently support the funding of alternatives for women regardless of policy context. It has the largest proportion of self-identified liberals, as well as the largest percentage of individuals who reject all three of the traditional women's issues and support abortion rights, and by far the largest proportion who support public funding of abortions. This cell also has proportionately more individuals with low religiosity than other parts of the typology, as well as more higher income and highly educated individuals.

Finally, the last cell, containing those who oppose both aspects of the adoption solution, is characterized by two divergent kinds of individuals. There are those who tend to be liberal or nontraditional on abortion, women's issues, and religiosity, but also those who self-identify as conservatives, oppose public funding for abortion, are older, and lower in socioeconomic status. This cell appears to be home to individuals who oppose government intervention in any aspect of abortion, and come to this conclusion from both liberal and conservative perspectives.

Conclusions

This look at public opinion about one possible resolution of unwanted pregnancy, especially if abortion were to become illegal again or highly restricted, underscores Legge's (1987) suggestion about the complexity of abortion opinion once it is removed from the personal or moral basis underlying the conflict and put in a policy context. The two questions from the 1989 *Los Angeles Times* poll show that opinion on abortion as a reflection of personal or moral values does not easily translate into policy solutions. The analysis suggests that one reason public discussion on abortion generally focuses on its legality or morality is that this indeed is the easy dimension of the debate. When policy alternatives are on the agenda, the issue becomes much more complex, as individuals bring within themselves many competing values and attitudes.

In addition to the different personal characteristics that are important for the two dimensions of an adoption alternative to abortion, there are also different institutional contexts. As presented in Malcolm L. Goggin's Introduction, the context for the core moral dimension of abortion centers on ideological bargaining, which virtually precludes compromise. Given the structure of support for adoption (as noted in Table 5.2), especially the importance of abortion opinion itself, we can expect the debate over an adoption alternative to have a similar noncompromising institutional context. The funding dimension, however, is more amenable to pluralistic bargaining.

Prior to the *Casey* decision and the election of Bill Clinton as president in 1992, it appeared that abortion opponents could achieve their goal simply by the Supreme Court's overturning *Roe v. Wade*. Because of these events, however, they now confront an ascending pro-choice ideology in no mood for compromise, and this direct approach is not likely to occur. At the national level, one option for opponents of abortion, then, is to compromise some other value for the sake of the core value on abortion.

One such compromise could be support for public funding for alternatives to abortion. As discussed earlier, supporters of the adoption alternative come from the more conservative elements of American society and are thus generally opposed to public spending for social welfare purposes, as well as to abortion. Hard supporters of adoption (cell 1 of the typology), however, appear willing to lessen or temporarily to set aside their general opposition to government spending in order to pursue a favored alternative to abortion. They recognize that by supporting public funding of alternatives they may be able to incorporate their moral position into government policy. In addition, this apparent concern for lessening the impact of highly restrictive abortion laws may make their position more attractive to some individuals who could not otherwise accept a direct ban or restrictions that did not address the implications of this policy.

Some supporters of the adoption solution, though, will have more difficulty with the pluralistic bargaining over funding (individuals in cell 2). In effect, these easy supporters of an adoption alternative assign personal responsibility to unwanted pregnancies and are satisfied with imposing their moral positions upon others. They are not necessarily willing to back it up with government funds. Their attitudes on personal responsibility and funding may prevent a working majority on the adoption alternative.

In light of the new politics of abortion that is outlined in the Introduction, it appears that pro-choice advocates will dominate the ideological bargaining and not have to engage much in pluralistic bargaining—at the national level. With the larger pro-choice majority in Congress, a new pro-choice president, and probable passage of the national Freedom of Choice Act, the right to choose now appears secure. But the same may not be true for state-level politics. Here, in light of the *Webster* and *Casey* decisions, pro-choice advocates may still find the need to engage in pluralistic bargaining to minimize the impact of state regulations on their core value.

But there will be constraints on their ability to do this. For example, the funding dimension is not available to them in the same way that it is for abortion opponents. As the analysis indicates, these are individuals who tend to come from the more liberal segments of society and already support government spending for social welfare. They therefore have nothing to offer for compromise on this dimension of the debate. They may thus become (or appear) more intransigent than the other side because they have no other compromise to offer.

Also, because of their support of public welfare spending in general, many of these pro-choice individuals are inclined to respond positively when asked about a program that would help women in need, *if* abortion were illegal. But support of public funding of alternatives to abortion can be interpreted as acknowledgment of defeat of their core ideological position. They may be torn between rejecting even the suggestion of a no-abortion scenario (cell 4) and fashioning a response if their worst fears do come true (cell 3). The pro-choice individuals who oppose the adoption solution do so primarily because it represents too much of an ideological defeat of a position that favors a range of alternatives to unwanted pregnancies, including abortion. Subscribing to such a position can inhibit some of them from even the suggestion of a no-abortion scenario and from fashioning policy responses to it.

In summary, this analysis clearly indicates that policy alternatives to abortion will not be easy, at least not those that try to deal with the problem after the occurrence of an unwanted pregnancy. Compromise will probably fare better if it is used to deal with the prevention of these pregnancies. There is a need for data to be collected that will address that possibility, rather than continued emphasis on the analysis of who supports and who opposes abortion rights.

Notes

1. The *Los Angeles Times* poll consists of two samples—a national probability sample of 2,406 adults and an oversample of 1,177 women. The file is weighted to reflect the proportion of men and women in the population, correcting back to the original number of 3,583.

2. More recently, antiabortion groups have undertaken a media campaign, primarily through television, to promote adoption and other alternatives to abortion.

3. The abortion question is: "Generally speaking, are you in favor of abortion, or are you opposed to it, or are you indifferent on the subject—or haven't you heard enough about it yet to say?" (IF IN FAVOR OR OPPOSED): "Is that (in favor/opposed) strongly or (in favor/opposed) somewhat?" We used this variable because it most directly measures opinion on abortion itself, but an index of the six NORC circumstances for legal abortion gave the same results.

The demographics—gender, race, educational attainment, age, and income—are measured in standard ways. Religious affiliation is the religion in which the individual was raised and includes atheist as a volunteered response. For religiosity we used an additive scale combining the strength of religious importance, from very unimportant to very important, and church attendance, from low to high. Political ideology is a 5-point scale of self-description from very liberal to very conservative. Party identification classifies individuals as Democrat (30%), Republican (24%), Independent (29%), or nonpartisan, that is, they do not think of themselves that way (16%). We have two indicators of traditional values about women in society. One is a Women's Issues Scale constructed from responses to three agree-disagree statements: (1) "There has been much talk recently about changing women's status in society today. On the whole, do you favor or oppose most of the efforts to strengthen and change women's status in society today?" (Probe: "strongly or not so strongly?"). (2) "Do you agree or disagree with this statement: 'It is much better for everyone involved if the man is the achiever outside the home and the woman takes care of the home and the family' " (Probe: "strongly or somewhat?"). (3) "Do you believe that motherhood must always be a woman's most important and satisfying role, or do you believe that motherhood can sometimes keep

a woman from fulfilling her true potential in life?" (Probe: "strongly or not so strongly?").
The scale, from 0 to 3, reports the number of traditional responses. The other indicator of
traditional attitudes is the proportion of household income earned by a female wage earner.
Work force participation by women indicates a socialization—for themselves and perhaps
for their families—into the modern American economy, the social welfare state, and nontraditional economic and gender roles (Klein 1984; Plutzer 1988). Finally, as indicators of
traditional sexual values, we have: "Do you think the government should make contraceptives
more widely available, or not?" and, "Generally speaking, do you approve or disapprove of
homosexual rights—or haven't you heard enough about that yet to say?"

4. "Generally speaking, are you in favor of using public funds for abortions when the
mother cannot afford it, or are you opposed to that?" (Probe: "strongly or somewhat in
favor/opposed").

5. The question is: "Would you favor or oppose using state funds to support adoption as
an alternative to abortion." The data set is for the 1990 Illinois Policy Survey, an annual
policy poll conducted by the Center for Governmental Studies at Northern Illinois University.
Unfortunately, we could not use this data set for more extensive analysis because it does not
contain the other attitudinal variables.

6. Eight percent of the respondents could not be classified into any of the four cells and
are not included in analysis of the typology.

7. These groups are not necessarily the largest in each cell, but their members occupy the
indicated cells more than they do others. For example, conservatives are only the second
largest ideological group in cells 1 and 4, but there are proportionately more conservatives
in those two cells than in cells 2 and 3 (see Table 5.3).

PART II

INSTITUTIONAL

SETTING

Expansion of the scope of conflict and resolution of deep conflicts over the issue of abortion can been found in a number of political forums, from the courts to legislatures to elections. The four chapters in Part II illustrate the importance of the institutional setting to any understanding of the "new" politics of abortion. The framework that was advanced in the Introduction drew attention to the distinction between ideological and pluralistic bargaining. The authors of the four chapters in Part II begin to shed light on the nature and importance of this distinction, in terms of national and Idaho legislative politics, and in terms of statewide campaigns for Governor in New Jersey, Virginia, Texas, California, and Louisiana.

In Chapter 6, Raymond Tatalovich and David Schier examine the voting behavior of members of the U.S. House of Representatives. Their research on votes on abortion legislation identify the abortion-rights and fetal-rights supporters in the House. And by following votes on abortion bills across two decades, they evaluate the extent to which voting behavior on abortion legislation has been changing. Interestingly, Tatalovich and Schier find that Catholic Democrats in the House apparently have become more pro-choice over time. These Democrats may have realized that the preferences of their own constituents are decidedly more liberal than the preferences of the Church hierarchy and fetal-rights activists.

Chapter 7 examines the Idaho State Legislature's roll-call vote on the controversial abortion bill known as H625, which would have strictly limited abortion access in Idaho. Stephanie L. Witt and Gary Moncrief analyze the relative impact of personal and constituent characteristics on the vote of individual legislators on a nonroutine and salient issue. The results indicate that personal characteristics are strong predictors of the vote on this highly emotional issue, and point as well to the impact that highly organized and vocal religious groups can have on important legislative decisions.

The Supreme Court's *Webster v. Reproductive Health Services* decision marked the beginning of a new round of conflict over abortion. The first opportunity to witness the impact of abortion on statewide electoral campaigns came with ongoing elections in New Jersey and Virginia. The battle over abortion not only centered on state government, it also came to be centered on these campaigns. In Chapter 8, Marilyn A. Yale analyzes the press coverage given to these two gubernatorial campaigns as well as the California and Texas campaigns occurring one year later. Based on her analysis of newspaper articles about the campaigns, she draws conclusions about the nature of press coverage given to state-level campaigns and the role that abortion played in these contests. Support is found for previous studies at the presidential and congressional level reporting the press's preoccupation with contest-centered coverage. Though restricted to the coverage of abortion in these campaigns, support is also found for previous studies of the complexity of campaign press coverage. The majority of the coverage devoted to these campaigns featured simple reports of campaign statements with little added information or investigation. Additionally, Chapter 9 concludes that where a strategic advantage was anticipated, campaigners utilized the issue of abortion in attempting to generate favorable media coverage and build electoral support. In reaction to the campaign agenda of the candidates, the press responded with coverage. Where no advantage was predicted, the issue was not pursued, and received very little press coverage.

Research on the impact of the abortion issue on electoral outcomes has yielded mixed results. Although no such impact has been found at the national level, recent research indicates that abortion attitudes may be influential in state-level elections. Using survey data gathered in 1990 and 1991, Susan E. Howell and Robert T. Sims examine the influence of the abortion issue on the recent Louisiana gubernatorial race. Louisiana serves as an appropriate case for analysis due to the high visibility of controversial antiabortion legislation passed by the state legislature and the incumbent governor's veto of that legislation. The findings reported in Chapter 9 indicate that the abortion issue's effect on voting is conditioned by a number of factors, and that its impact is likely to be felt only under very specific circumstances.

6

The Persistence of Ideological Cleavage in Voting on Abortion Legislation in the House of Representatives, 1973-1988

RAYMOND TATALOVICH

DAVID SCHIER

A fter the Supreme Court constitutionalized the right to abortion in *Roe v. Wade* (1973), the pro-life opponents turned their political energies to getting Congress to enact laws restricting the impact of that decision. One example has been the Hyde Amendment, which limits the use of Medicaid funds to pay for abortions for women on welfare. Some version of the Hyde Amendment has been enacted by Congress since 1976, which suggests that the legislative branch has been receptive to the appeals from pro-lifers. The purpose of this chapter is to study votes on abortion legislation in the House of Representatives to determine which members are pro-choice and which members are pro-life in their voting behavior. By following votes on abortion bills across two decades, moreover, we can evaluate whether voting behavior on abortion legislation has been changing.

The Supreme Court generally has supported abortion rights in its cases; until, that is, *Webster v. Reproductive Health Services* (1989), which upheld certain state restrictions on abortion services. The Supreme Court under Chief Justice William Rehnquist is decidedly more conservative than during the period when *Roe* was decided, and since 1989 there have been other rulings where the high court has aligned itself with those states

AUTHORS' NOTE: This chapter was substantially improved by the suggestions of the anonymous reviewers and the editors, and thoughtful comments from two congressional scholars and friends, Professors L. Marvin Overby of Loyola and Michael Mezey of DePaul.

seeking greater regulation over abortions. Because the Supreme Court today is an uncertain ally for pro-choice advocates, they may have to lobby Congress to, in effect, overturn the most recent antiabortion rulings by statute.

During the 102nd Congress liberals were promoting the Freedom of Choice Act (H.R. 25) as a means of guaranteeing women in all states the right to abortion. Because of political infighting among liberals and shrewd parliamentary maneuvers by conservatives, that bill never cleared either house of Congress. What are the chances for passage of the Freedom of Choice Act during the early years of the Clinton Administration? The likelihood that a pro-choice majority can be sustained in the House of Representatives during the 103rd Congress is discussed in the Epilogue that concludes this chapter.

Abortion as Moral Conflict

Categorization of public policies gained popularity with the paradigm developed by Lowi (1964), though his policy types represented economic conflicts whereas other scholars have noted that policies can also provoke moral conflicts. Although abortion is the best known example of "symbolic-emotive" policies (Smith 1975) or "social regulations" (Tatalovich and Daynes 1988), this category includes such issues as school prayer, pornography, gun control, capital punishment, and gay rights. Where much research on voting behavior has focused on economic issues (Danielsen and Rubin 1977; Silberman and Durden 1976; Tosini and Tower 1987), rarely have scholars followed the lead of Peltzman (1984), whose analysis of two "social" issues—school prayer and abortion—found ideology to be the significant predictor of congressional voting. Our longitudinal analysis of House of Representatives voting will validate the same hypothesis: *Ideology is a more important predictor of congressional voting on moral issues like abortion than party affiliation or constituency makeup.*

Several studies document that legislative voting on a range of policies is characterized by a liberal-conservative dimension (Schneider 1979; Smith 1981). Ideology was the key predictor of Senate voting on the ABM issue (Bernstein and Anthony 1974), Panama Canal treaties (McCormick and Black 1983), and of House voting on national security issues (Moyer 1973; Russet 1970) including the nuclear freeze question (McCormick 1985; Overby 1991). Voting in the House on health policy was also found to be more ideological than partisan (Mueller 1986). Recently there has been criticism of this literature on methodological grounds, because many studies have employed interest group ratings of how legislators vote on key issues as a proxy for ideology, rather than directly measuring the attitudes that guide the behavior of members of Congress (Jackson and Kingdon 1992). To date, however, even the critics have not offered an alternative methodology for operationalizing ideology as a variable.

These studies elevate ideology at the expense of party and also question the significance of constituency opinion. Rather than search for positive constituent effects on legislative voting, this scholarship operates from a different assumption. The finding that House or Senate votes on strategic weapons systems were determined more by the members' ideology than the economic interests of their constituencies led Lindsay (1990:957) to conclude that "legislators operate subject to a constituency constraint, that is, they act on their policy preferences as long as the cost of doing so is not prohibitive."

By a similar logic, Congressional voting on moral conflicts should generate high ideological cleavage, low partisanship, and a weak relationship to constituency makeup. Morality radicalizes political discourse because the debate centers on the ends, not the means, of public policy and ends are defined in zero-sum terms (Lowi 1988). It is also questionable whether issues like abortion or school prayer are salient to most people most of the time. Problems of the economy and war mainly preoccupy our collective attention (*The Gallup Poll Monthly* 1991), and in recent presidential elections relatively few people mentioned abortion as a significant issue (Granberg 1987; Granberg and Burlison 1983).

The new voting research conceptualizes party as an artifact because "political parties per se are not the primary variable; rather, the fundamental dimensions of belief that give rise to the parties are the primary variables" (Poole 1988). Party in Congress is weakened mainly because "the Democratic party is much less homogeneous than the Republican party. The Republicans are concentrated at center right to far right. The bulk of the Democratic party is concentrated at center left to far left, but substantial numbers of Democrats are located at center right and far right" (Poole and Daniels 1985:381).

On abortion, pro-life votes among Democrats are likely to be cast by Catholics who presumably are under cross-pressures when voting on this issue. On the one hand, they might be constrained by their personal religious values, official Church teachings, and constituency pressure from lay Catholics to oppose abortion; on the other, Democratic platforms and the congressional party leadership strongly endorse the pro-choice position.

Existing Research

A 1977 study by Eccles observed that party affiliation did *not* seem to be an overriding factor in the Senate vote on abortion (Eccles 1978), while

the National Abortion Rights Action League [NARAL] (1979) percep-
tively argued that Representatives who opposed abortion also voted against
other liberal programs. Only one amendment to reverse *Roe v. Wade* has
been cleared in either chamber for a floor vote. On June 28, 1983, the
Senate defeated (49-50) the Hatch-Eagleton Amendment [HEA], and Granberg
(1985:127) found that the odds of a pro-HEA vote increased "if the Senator
was a *Catholic,* if the Senator was a *Republican,* if the Senator's state had
a relatively *low income,* and if the Senator represented a state *not* in the
New England, Pacific, or *Middle Atlantic* region" [emphasis in original].

This same vote was utilized by Medoff (1989) to predict restrictive state
legislation in the aftermath of the Supreme Court ruling in *Webster v.
Reproductive Health Services* (1989). In a replication of Medoff's study,
Gohmann and Ohsfeldt (1990) improved upon his model by accounting for
"shirking" by Senators who follow their own ideology and not the ideological disposition of their states. The Hatch-Eagleton amendment also
was subjected to a logistic regression analysis by Strickland and Whicker
(1986) who compared it to voting on a pro-life bill sponsored by Senator
Jesse Helms (R-NC). Social variables had more impact than political
variables and constituency makeup exerted more influence than the Senators' personal attributes. But no measure of ideology was used by Strickland
and Whicker, so we do not know if liberalism would have been a strong
predictor in their model.

Both ideology and party variables were used in the latest analysis of the
HEA by Chressanthis, Gilbert, and Grimes (1991), whose results closely
parallel the findings presented here. They found not only that party was
insignificant but that "ideological measures may be more important than
constituent interests in voting outcomes on abortion legislation" (p. 596).
The Senators' religious affiliation was also a key predictor variable.

The only analysis of voting in the House of Representatives was by
Vinovskis (1980b) on three votes taken in 1976 on the original Hyde
Amendment. After studying the effects of 11 variables on each vote,
Vinovskis also concluded that party was *not* a primary determinant. The
Americans for Democratic Action (ADA) rating was most important and
second ranked was religion.

Longitudinal Analysis

Fifty-four roll calls on abortion legislation in the House of Representatives during the eight Congresses of 1973-1988 were subjected to
regression analysis, using the same model, to assess whether the determi-

Table 6.1 Regression Analysis of Predictors of Voting on Abortion Legislation in the House of Representatives, 1973-1980

Independent Variable		93rd Congress	94th Congress	95th Congress	96th Congress
		(standardized and unstandardized regression coefficients)			
ADA Score	Beta	.469*	.525*	.529*	.725*
	(b)	.005	.007	.008	.010
Religion	Beta	.352*	.372*	.333*	.289*
	(b)	.135	.173	.152	.130
Nonwhite	Beta	.123*	.154*	.149*	.112*
	(b)	.003	.005	.005	.003
Income	Beta	−.086	−.011	.040	−.032
	(b)	−.014	−.002	.008	−.007
Gender	Beta	.057**	.019	−.011	−.011
	(b)	.108	.042	−.024	−.026
Party	Beta	−.003	−.020	.091*	−.013
	(b)	−.002	−.019	.083	−.012
Urban	Beta	.205*	.069	.017	−.004
	(b)	.003	.001	.000	−.000
Constant	(a)	−.340	−.492	−.433	−.284
Multiple R		.641	.647	.683	.754
Adjusted R²		.401	.407	.457	.562
Members (N)		412	357	425	421
Roll Calls (N)		4	4	18	10

SOURCE: Votes taken from *Congressional Quarterly Weekly Reports*.
NOTES: * Indicates statistical significance at least at the .01 level; ** indicates statistical significance at least at the .05 level.

nants of pro-choice voting have changed over two decades and which predictors have gained or lost explanatory power over these eight Houses.

The dependent variable is a form of Guttman Scale to measure the legislators' relative support for abortion. A Guttman Scale assures us that several votes, in fact, reflect a common policy dimension and, by amalgamating all abortion votes as one scale score, it provides a measure of consistency by legislators.[1] Because so few House roll calls (see Tables 6.1 and 6.2) were taken on abortion bills during 1973-1988 virtually all were included in this analysis.[2] But since there is variability from Congress to Congress (ranging from 4 to 18 votes taken), each Guttman scale score was divided by the number of votes to standardize the dependent variable on a continuum from 0.0 (pro-life) to 1.0 (pro-choice). This allows for comparisons across eight Houses.

Table 6.2   Regression Analysis of Predictors of Voting on Abortion Legislation in
the House of Representatives, 1981-1988

Independent Variable		97th Congress	98th Congress	99th Congress	100th Congress
		(standardized and unstandardized regression coefficients)			
ADA Score	Beta	.502*	.606*	.776*	.828*
	(b)	.007	.006	.010	.011
Religion	Beta	.252*	.247*	.223*	.209*
	(b)	.113	.086	.095	.094
Nonwhite	Beta	.212*	.196*	.127*	.180*
	(b)	.006	.004	.003	.005
Income	Beta	.096	.075	.043	.047
	(b)	.020	.007	.005	.005
Gender	Beta	.067	.055	.063**	.033
	(b)	.148	.091	.126	.063
Party	Beta	.084	−.120**	−.107**	−.181*
	(b)	.073	−.087	−.093	−.167
Urban	Beta	−.010	−.069	−.015	−.013
	(b)	−.000	−.001	−.000	−.000
Constant	(a)	−.402	−.188	−.288	.350
Multiple R		.657	.626	.759	.767
Adjusted R^2		.422	.382	.569	.581
Members (N)		431	418	428	419
Roll Calls (N)		4	4	5	5

SOURCE: Votes taken from *Congressional Quarterly Weekly Reports*.
NOTES: * Indicates statistical significance at least at the .01 level; ** Indicates statistical significance at
least at the .05 level.

Of the seven independent variables included, three are personal attributes of legislators: political party (Democrats coded 1, and Republicans as
0), religious affiliation (non-Catholics coded 1, and Catholics as 0), and
gender (women coded as 1, and men as 0). Three demographic characteristics of House districts assess constituency makeup: percentage nonwhite, percentage urban (meaning places above 2,500 population), and
median family income).[3] These demographics were drawn from the 1970
Census to analyze the 93rd through 96th Congresses and from the 1980
Census to analyze the 97th through 100th Congresses.

To measure ideology, we use the raw[4] ADA Score, as have others who
studied abortion voting (Chressanthis et al. 1991; Granberg 1985; Vinovskis
1980b), though methodological advances now seek to control constituency
makeup on ADA voting to isolate residual effects as reflecting a "personal"

ideology (Segal, Cameron, and Cover 1992). Here the ADA Score is simply an "output" measure to assess whether a pattern of legislative voting on various economic and social-welfare bills extends to abortion, which is a moral issue. The ADA Score ranges from most conservative (0) to most liberal (100).

Party should be relevant given the divergent platform positions on abortion by the Democratic and Republican parties and the rhetoric of their presidential candidates (Daynes and Tatalovich 1992). Vinovskis (1980b:240) found, after controlling for other variables, that the differences between Catholic and non-Catholic representatives "substantially increased," whereas a previous study affirms that Catholic Representatives were decidedly more pro-life in their voting behavior than most other religious denominations (Daynes and Tatalovich 1984).

Vinovskis (1980b:237) found that women were less likely to support the Hyde Amendment though, after imposing controls, "the differences between male and female representatives were considerably narrower." However, abortion has gained saliency in the years since 1976 and become a high priority issue on the political agenda of the women's movement, so possibly there has been a deepening of the gender cleavage on this issue.

Vinovskis employed the percentage of families below $3,000 to index economic need, assuming that the Hyde Amendment would hurt indigent women who seek abortions through the Medicaid system, although others have argued that support for restrictions on abortion is greater among the less affluent than among upper SES groups (Skerry 1978). The majority of votes in our analysis also pertained to the Hyde Amendment, though we substituted median family income (expressed in units of $1,000) as a measure of economic "class" in the congressional districts.

Although blacks have higher abortion rates than whites and would be disadvantaged by antiabortion restrictions, there is scholarly debate about how liberal the views of blacks are on abortion despite the firm pro-choice commitment of the Congressional Black Caucus (Combs and Welch 1982; Hall and Ferree 1986). As did Vinovskis, we measure the influence of race by the percentage nonwhite in each House district. Recent U.S. statistics show that 98% of all abortions occur in metropolitan areas whereas 93% of all nonmetropolitan counties had no abortion providers (Henshaw and Van Vort 1990). The impact of urbanism on abortion voting is measured by percentage urban in each congressional district.

The effect of these seven independent variables on abortion voting during 1973-1980 (Table 6.1) and 1981-1988 (Table 6.2) are analyzed through a regression model. The standardized regression coefficient (beta) indicates the relative importance of the variable *within* each regression model. Statistical significance for each variable and the regression model is shown as well as the amount of variance in legislative voting explained by the model. To assess whether a variable has gained predictive power *across* eight Congresses, the more appropriate comparison is between the unstandardized regression coefficients (b).

Findings

Our hypothesis is validated across all of the eight Congresses. Ideology is consistently the most important predictor of voting on abortion, as higher ADA scores yield greater pro-choice voting and lower ADA scores result in more pro-life voting. The betas show that the predictive power of ideology exerted a stronger effect on voting pro-choice in the last two Houses, particularly the 100th Congress.

The effect of party on abortion voting in the 93rd, 94th, 96th, and 97th Congresses is not statistically significant. And where party does exhibit a statistical association with voting on abortion, the relationship is negative in three instances. Only after taking account of the substantial effect of ideology on voting pro-choice is there a slight tendency for Republicans to be more supportive of abortion than Democrats.

Constituency variables have very little effect on abortion voting in the House of Representatives. Median family income was statistically insignificant in every case, as was urbanism with one exception (93rd Congress). In all eight Houses the nonwhite percentage exerted a significantly positive, though decidedly minor, influence on pro-choice voting.

The gender variable, barely significant in two models, is noteworthy given the small number of women in Congress. Both indicate that women Representatives vote more consistently pro-choice than men. However, religion is much more important than party affiliation or constituency makeup, and the positive betas mean that non-Catholics vote more pro-choice than Catholics. But religion was a decidedly weaker predictor during the last three Congresses relative to the 1973-1982 period, and voting for legalized abortion in the most recent House, consequently, was more ideological and less religious than at any time since *Roe*.

Party and Ideology

The following regression analysis on the four most recent Houses, done separately for Republicans and Democrats, shows that ideology has grown more important in *both* parties and that deviations from pro-choice voting among Democrats is due largely to religion (Table 6.3).

For the 100th Congress, the value for (b) shows that ideology had equal impact on both parties but religion had *twice* the effect on Democrats as

Table 6.3 Regression Analysis of Voting by Party on Abortion Legislation in the House of Representatives, 1981-1988

Independent Variable		97th Congress	98th Congress	99th Congress	100th Congress
		(standardized and unstandardized regression coefficients)			
REPUBLICANS					
ADA Score	Beta	.441*	.455*	.632*	.509*
	(b)	.008	.008	.012	.010
Religion	Beta	.239*	.065	.150*	.154*
	(b)	.097	.021	.055	.058
Nonwhite	Beta	.015	.143	−.047	.058
	(b)	.001	.005	−.002	.002
Income	Beta	−.079	−.087	.054	.059
	(b)	−.013	.006	.004	.005
Gender	Beta	.228*	.096	.176*	.218*
	(b)	.384	.143	.292	.320
Urban	Beta	.120	−.080	.012	−.029
	(b)	.002	−.001	.000	−.000
Constant	(a)	−.174	−.051	−.215	−.218
Multiple R		.573	.495	.712	.618
Adjusted R^2		.306	.215	.489	.358
Members (N)		187	160	174	165
DEMOCRATS					
ADA Score	Beta	.391*	.471*	.531*	.578*
	(b)	.006	.006	.008	.010
Religion	Beta	.298*	.353*	.313*	.295*
	(b)	.122	.116	.116	.114
Nonwhite	Beta	.331*	.229*	.211*	.257*
	(b)	.008	.004	.004	.005
Income	Beta	.200*	.095	.062	.072
	(b)	.039	.009	.007	.008
Gender	Beta	−.046	.023	−.016	−.066
	(b)	−.108	.036	−.028	−.117
Urban	Beta	−.026	−.081	.005	−.006
	(b)	−.000	−.001	.000	−.000
Constant	(a)	−.486	−.364	−.415	−.612
Multiple R		.592	.619	.665	.706
Adjusted R^2		.334	.369	.429	.487
Members (N)		244	258	254	254

SOURCE: Votes taken from *Congressional Quarterly Weekly Reports.*
NOTE: * Indicates statistical significance at least at the .01 level.

compared to Republicans. Non-Catholic Democrats are still more liberal on abortion than Catholic Democrats. But the important trend is that the unstandardized regression coefficients show that the causal relationship between ideology and pro-choice voting has been *strengthened* across the four Congresses with an accompanying *decline* in the importance of religion.

For Republicans, although the importance of religion has been stabilized during the 99th and 100th Congress, voting in those Houses became markedly *more* ideological as compared to the 97th and 98th Congresses. Given the small number of liberals among Republicans in the House, the long-term policy implications from greater ideological voting by the GOP would be limited. The election of more women Republicans to Congress, however, may advantage the pro-choice position. The three statistically significant relationships show that gender is more important than religion in predicting a pro-choice vote by Republicans. Among Republicans, women are far more liberal than men.

Conclusion

Research on congressional voting needs to focus more attention on policies with moral content, not only because such issues loom large on the political landscape but because they pose unique threats to Democratic Party unity and thus provide an opportunity to confront directly the intellectual question of whether party or ideology is the force driving legislative behavior. We suspect that Democrats from rural areas would resist gun control laws and that Southern Democrats would resist supporting gay rights just as they continue to dissent on policies affecting race.

A recent analysis of Senate voting on civil rights from 1963 to 1988 (Nye 1991) parallels ours in important ways. Statewide demographic variables did not perform well, "perhaps reflective of the declining salience of civil rights on the national agenda" (p. 984) but region was significant in almost all cases, "indicating Southern resistance to civil rights policies (p. 981). Though the party variable was significant and showed Democrats to be more liberal, its impact over the decades fluctuated greatly. Again no ideological measure was included so the relative importance of party and ideology cannot be determined.[5]

Epilogue: A New Pro-Choice Majority

Shifting political alignments during the 100th Congress became decidedly pro-choice through the presidency of George Bush. The *Congressional Quarterly Weekly Report* identified 17 key House votes on abortion

Table 6.4 Type of Roll Calls and Frequency of Pro-Life Victories, 1973-1988 and 1989-1991

Type of Roll Call*	Total Roll Calls 1973-1988 N	Total Roll Calls 1989-1991 N	Pro-Life Victories 1973-1988 N	Pro-Life Victories 1973-1988 %	Pro-Life Victories 1989-1991 N	Pro-Life Victories 1989-1991 %
Party Vote	26	14	18	48	4	29
Bipartisan Vote	6	1	5	83	0	0
Conservative Coalition	20	2	20	100	2	100
Unclassified	2	0	2	100	0	0
TOTALS	54	17	45	83	6	35

SOURCE: Votes taken from Congressional Quarterly Weekly Reports.
NOTE: *Party vote: majorities of Northern and Southern Democrats oppose a Republican majority; bipartisan vote: majorities of Northern and Southern Democrats and Republicans vote together; conservative coalition: majorities of Southern Democrats and Republicans oppose a majority of Northern Democrats.

during the 101st and 102nd Congresses (through 1991), but pro-lifers prevailed on only 6 (35%) of those roll calls.

These roll calls involved controversial abortion policies of the Bush Administration. Three were efforts to block enforcement of the "gag rule" that disallowed clinics that received (Public Health Service Act of 1970) Title X family planning grants from counseling patients about abortion. Seven were directed toward family planning policies abroad, such as overturning the Mexico City Policy to allow funding for the U.N. Population Fund and to lift the ban on moneys for distribution to China, which has compulsory abortion practices. Two roll calls were on whether the District of Columbia could use local tax revenues to pay for abortions, and three votes represented the annual battle waged in Congress over weakening the Hyde Amendment restrictions on Medicaid payments for abortions. Two final roll calls involved the question of permitting military personnel stationed abroad access to military hospitals in order to secure abortions.

The changing political alignment on abortion in the House of Representatives is indicated by a comparison of the voting outcomes on abortion bills during 1973-1988 versus the 1989-1991 period of the Bush presidency (Table 6.4). Two patterns are noteworthy.

First, there has been an increase in "party votes" (where majorities of Northern and Southern Democrats oppose a majority of Republicans) from 48% over the 1973-1988 period to 82% during the 101st and 102nd Congress. At the same time, the frequency of "conservative coalition" votes (where majorities of Republicans and Southern Democrats oppose a majority of Northern Democrats) has declined from 37% to 12% of the roll calls.

Second, and more important, there had been some relationship between the type of voting coalition and the winning ability of pro-lifers. Over the 1973-1988 period a pro-life majority had prevailed on 83% of the 54 roll calls analyzed in this chapter, but the odds of victory rose when a bill garnered bipartisan support and especially when the "conservative coalition" emerged. Pro-lifers even won 69% of the party votes despite the fact that Democrats held control of the House over the entire period.

Voting that unites the Southern and Northern wings of the Democratic Party should imply that the frequency of pro-choice victories would be higher, but abortion roll calls often resulted in a *slim* Democratic majority that, heretofore, was insufficient to guarantee victory. Too many Democrats were defecting, and our analysis indicated that they were Catholic Democrats. But since 1989, 35% of the abortion votes resulted in a pro-life victory, even fewer (29%) whenever a party vote was recorded. And if two other roll calls, where the House got the majority but not two-thirds to override presidential vetoes, are counted here, then the pro-choice side numerically prevailed on 76% of the 17 key abortion votes in the 101st and 102nd Congress.

All but one of the Bush vetoes were sustained by Congress's failure to muster the necessary two-thirds vote. Some involved shifts by Congress in long-standing abortion policy. In 1989, for the first time since 1981, Congress included rape and incest as qualifying for Medicaid payment for abortions, but the language was removed following a Bush veto. Two 1989 vetoes and another in 1991 forced Congress to retreat in its effort to allow the District of Columbia to use locally raised revenues to fund nontherapeutic abortions. A fifth veto of the FY92 Labor, HHS, and Education Appropriations was provoked by Congress's attempt to block enforcement of the gag rule on abortion counseling.

On abortion the dissenters have been Catholic Democrats, so more ideological voting by those legislators should bring about more pro-choice victories. In 1989, 26 Representatives reversed their votes on the Hyde Amendment from the year before, when the House failed to include the rape and incest provision (Toner 1989), to now allow those additional therapeutic reasons for abortion. Unnoticed by the press, however, was the fact that 9 of 20 Democrats who changed their votes to allow more liberal abortion funding under Medicaid were Catholics while only one Catholic was among the 6 Republicans who changed their positions.

Thus, according to our analysis, a pro-choice majority can be sustained in the House, but not because many Republicans are abandoning their pro-life orthodoxy. What seems to be happening is that Catholic Democrats are shifting votes on abortion policy consistent with their liberal voting behavior on other domestic issues. Their changed behavior may be linked to a realization that the saliency of abortion politics for the Church hierarchy and pro-life activists may not extend to their own grass-roots constituency. Catholic Democrats may be taking to heart what the polls have long shown, that abortion attitudes by lay Catholics are similar to lay non-Catholics, and are generally permissive (MacIntosh and Alston 1977) In the absence of strong counterpressures in the districts, they now perceive greater freedom *from* constituency when dealing with the abortion issue.

There is little doubt that President Clinton would have signed the legislation to ease restrictions on abortion funding under Medicaid and in the District of Columbia. Within weeks of his narrow win over George Bush, moreover, the President-Elect promised that he would issue an executive order eliminating the gag rule on abortion counseling. In sum, the prospects for liberalization of federal abortion policy looked very good when President Clinton convened the 103rd Congress. The Senate has long been dominated by liberals who support access to abortion services,[6] and what had been a tendency during the 100th Congress has materialized into a pro-choice majority in the House as well during the 101st and 102nd Congresses.

Notes

1. There was generally a high degree of consistency in the voting behavior across the eight Houses analyzed. The percentage with perfect pro-life (0) *or* pro-choice (1) scores ranged from 52% in the 93rd and 95th Congresses to 77% in the 98th Congress.

2. Any roll call where less than 25% of the representatives voted in opposition was omitted from the analysis. Scale scores were created for representatives who voted on a majority of the roll calls in each scale. The number of Guttman scaling "errors" ranged from 2% to 5% of the total responses in any House, which yielded coefficients of reproducibility exceeding .90 and coefficients of scalability above the .80 level.

3. The ADA rating may not be entirely untainted as a predictor of abortion voting if votes on abortion bills are included to construct the ADA rating. The degree of contamination is minimal since no more than 10% of the votes included in the ADA composite for any House were roll calls on abortion.

4. Although there are statewide indices of religious affiliation, comparable data for House districts are not provided by the Census. No proxy, such as ethnicity, would directly measure the presence of those religious groups—Catholics, Orthodox, Mormons, Fundamentalists who are most opposed to legalized abortions.

5. She did not include ideology because correlations between party and the Conservative Coalition Score ranged from −.49 to −.60 (Nye 1991:976), which by prevailing standards does not portend a serious multicollinearity problem. Our ADA variable consistently outperformed party across all eight Houses and the coefficients between ADA and party ranged from .403 to .604 in all cases except the 98th (.701) and 100th (.977) Houses. The data do not suggest that party was suppressed to exaggerate an ideological effect. Simple correlations

between ADA and the dependent variable averaged .231 *higher* than with party, and a comparison of betas for the 99th and 100th Congresses (Table 6.2) shows that party grew more important (−.107 to −.181) relative to ADA (.776 to .828) even though ADA and party were more strongly intercorrelated in the 100th (.977) than the 99th House (.604).

6. From the *Congressional Quarterly Weekly Report* we identified 71 nonconsensual roll calls in the Senate on abortion bills during 1973-1988. On 54 of those votes (76%) the majority voted a pro-choice position that contrasts sharply with pro-lifers winning 83% of the roll calls in the House during the same period (see Table 6.4).

7

Religion and Roll-Call Voting in Idaho

The 1990 Abortion Controversy

STEPHANIE L. WITT

GARY MONCRIEF

I'm amazed at the outpouring of the LDS Church. They have not lobbied on things in the past. But I've had women from Relief Societies who have called and asked what they can do.

— Barbara Dehl, Eastern Idaho Director of Right to Life

You look about as tired as I feel. . . . This was probably the toughest session any of us legislators have been in—both physically and mentally.

— State Senator Bruce Sweeney, 12-year legislative veteran

The bumper stickers read, "NO VETO, NO VOTE," and they appeared on Idaho automobiles almost before the state senate roll-call vote was recorded. The message of the bumper sticker was obviously aimed at Cecil Andrus, governor of the state of Idaho. The "pro-choice" advocates saw Governor Andrus as their last hope in stopping legislation that would have given Idaho the most restrictive abortion law in the nation. Governor Andrus became the focal point because the legislature, amid considerable lobbying and media attention, passed the bill known as H625 in March 1990. Eight days later, at a packed press conference, Andrus vetoed H625.

As Goggin relates in his introductory chapter to this volume, the U.S. Supreme Court in *Webster v. Reproductive Health Services* (1989) had opened the door for substantial regulation of abortion practices. The 1989 decision led to increased activity in state legislatures all across the country as fetal-rights groups pushed for more restrictive abortion laws. In the spring of 1990 Idaho's was one of the state legislatures in which the battle over new abortion laws was fought. Although the focus of this chapter is on the relative importance of legislators' personal and constituency characteristics to their vote on H625, this case study provides an excellent example of the type of heightened political activity in the states that characterizes the "new politics of abortion" (see Goggin 1993).

The abortion debate moved on to other states in 1991, but for awhile it mobilized citizens and focused the eyes of Idahoans on their state legislature and chief executive in a way rarely experienced. To say that this was a salient issue is to understate the situation.

This issue can be viewed from many different perspectives. In this chapter we view it as an issue of legislative voting behavior, in which one's vote is affected by one's personal background characteristics and the characteristics of one's legislative district. The unit of analysis is the individual legislator. The dependent variable is, of course, the vote on H625. We examine several characteristics of the individual legislator (gender, party affiliation, religion) and a measure of the legislative district characteristics (religious makeup) as independent variables. In the process of analyzing the vote on this bill we will also point to similarities with the emergent literature on abortion politics in the states. Specifically, we will note the manner in which the Idaho case corroborates other studies that pinpoint religion as a critical determinant of the policy choices involved in the abortion debate.

The Legislative Odyssey of H625

H625 was one of 14 proposals concerning abortion drafted and submitted to the Centennial Legislature in Idaho. If passed, it would become the most restrictive abortion legislation in any state (although it wasn't the most restrictive of the bills introduced. Bill H627, introduced by Representative Myron Jones of Malad, would have allowed even fewer exemptions from a ban on abortion, and stiffer fines and jail sentences for both the doctor and the pregnant woman).

It was clear to the legislators from the beginning of the session that they would have to deal with the abortion issue. In the wake of *Webster v. Reproductive Health Services,* Idaho's was one of several state legislatures selected by the national Right-to-Life organization as a possible vehicle for passage of a strict antiabortion law to test the tolerance of the U.S. Supreme Court. The bill that was eventually passed, H625, was the preferred bill of the right-to-life forces.

One of the unique features of the Idaho legislature is that almost all bills are introduced through the committees, rather than by individual legislators. On February 9, 14 abortion bills (including H625) were introduced through the House State Affairs Committee. Early in the session it was decided by the House and Senate Republican leadership that public testimony on the abortion bills would be strictly organized. First, the testimony would be delivered before a joint hearing of the senate and house committees on state affairs. Second, due to the inordinate number of people who requested to speak at the hearings, individual testimony was limited to 3 minutes per person. Third, in order to accommodate the size of the audience anticipated at the committee meeting, the hearings were moved to a large auditorium at Boise State University (BSU). On the evenings of February 19 and 20, the joint hearings were held at BSU. More than 700 people attended the hearings *each* evening, and more than 300 individuals testified. The public hearings lasted more than 10 hours over the span of 2 evenings.

On February 28, the House State Affairs Committee considered the issue again. After several hours of testimony by legal experts and the sponsors of the bills, the committee considered each bill. Only two bills were reported out of committee. One of these was H625. The bill was reported out with a recommendation that it be amended (an amendment offered by one of the co-sponsors during the hearings) and passed. The vote was 13-8. The Chair of the committee, Pam Bengson (R-Boise), voted against the favorable recommendation on H625, preferring her own bill, which would submit the issue to a public referendum. As Chair of the House State Affairs committee, Representative Bengson was the recipient of many contacts concerning abortion. One report states that she received 1,123 written communications from Idahoans, 682 (60.7%) of which were defined as "pro-choice" and 414 (36.9%) as "pro-life."

The bill, as amended, passed the Idaho House of Representatives on March 9. The vote was 47 ayes, 36 nays, 1 absent. After the bill passed the House, it moved relatively quickly through the Senate. The chair of the Senate State Affairs committee, Mark Ricks, was a staunch pro-life advocate. The bill was approved by the Senate committee on a 7-4 vote on March 16 (1 week after it passed the House). Six days later (March 22) it passed the full Senate 25-17. After a remarkable week in which hundreds of pro-life advocates demonstrated on the capitol steps, hundreds more pro-choice demonstrators held nightly candlelight vigils, and the national organizations on both sides threatened boycotts of Idaho products, Governor Andrus vetoed the bill. He did so on March 31, at a press conference crammed with supporters, opponents, and the national media.

The subject of all this angst and attention is a bill that would have severely restricted the availability of abortions in Idaho. H625 would outlaw abortion except:

a. when the life of the mother would be endangered
b. when "severe and long-lasting" physical health damage would result to the mother
c. when the pregnancy was the result of a rape, *and* the rape incident was reported to the proper authorities within 7 days of the incident.
d. when pregnancy is the result of incest
e. the child would be born with "profound and irremedial" physical or mental disabilities.

Conditions (a), (b), and (e) would require the formal opinion of at least two licensed physicians. It was estimated that about 90% of all present abortions would be outlawed if H625 went into effect.

Legislative Decision Making

Most studies of legislative decision making seek to explain the "normal" calculus of voting decisions. There are well-known studies of this type (e.g., Clausen 1973; Matthews and Stimson 1975) that have contributed greatly to our understanding of the normal legislative decision-making processes in voting. But not all legislative decisions are "normal." Collie (1985) identifies no less than six legislative decision-making models. She notes that "these models testify to the variety of actors and decision rules that have appeared relevant to the decision-making process" (1985:495). Or, to put it in the words of Keefe and Ogul (1989:225), "Voting is a contextual act—to be more precise, how a member decides to vote depends on the kind of issue presented." Collie, in citing the work of Kozak (1982), notes that a legislator's decision-making process is a "highly contingent phenomenon" (1985:496).

The critical component of that contingency appears to be the level of controversy generated by the voting issue. Although routine issues may be decided on the basis of party affiliation or some other normalized cue-taking procedure, controversial decisions are not. Jewell (1981:16) notes that party is likely becoming less a factor in legislative voting because of "the growing importance of 'social issues,' sometimes highly emotional, that cut across normal party alignments." Hurwitz (1986) makes a cogent argument for studying the "abnormal" decisions. Almost by definition, these "abnormal" decisions are those that are highly salient to a large segment of the public.

In this chapter we focus on just such an "abnormal" decision—the vote on the abortion bill in Idaho. There are few issues that mobilize, intensify, and polarize public opinion as does the abortion issue. Consequently, the legislative decision calculus is based on different factors than is normally the case. As Keefe and Ogul (1989:225) note, "On 'hot' issues, such as abortion or tax reform, members already have a high level of information; their votes may be based on personal values, ideology, campaign promises, or constituency opinion."

Here we view the decision as one in which the individual legislator's vote is affected by certain personal background characteristics and the characteristics of one's legislative district.[1] Specifically, we test for the relative effects of the individual legislators' party affiliation, gender, and religious affiliation on his or her vote. Because this was such a salient issue, we also examine the religious composition of the legislators' electoral constituency.

Attitudes on Abortion

Many studies have analyzed the correlations between attitudes on abortion and various personal characteristics and beliefs in the general public (see, e.g., Strickland and Whicker 1990b). Similar studies involving the attitudes of political elites on this issue are more difficult to find; thus for our hypotheses we must extrapolate from studies of non-elites. Here we concentrate on four relevant variables (three background variables, one constituency variable) and their possible effect on legislative decision making on this issue.

Gender

We might expect that female state legislators would be more resistant than men to proposals that would diminish a woman's freedom of choice on this issue. One early study suggests that men were more likely to support the right to an abortion (Baker et al. 1981), but a more recent work finds that pro-choice women feel more strongly about the issue than do pro-choice men (Scott and Schuman 1988).

Party

At the national level, the two major parties have adopted opposite stances in regard to abortion (Democrats pro-choice and Republicans pro-life), and some studies suggest that this issue is more polarized along partisan lines (Strickland and Whicker 1990b). The Republican party took a strong pro-life stand in Idaho during 1990, perhaps best exemplified by the fact that the Chairman of the Republican Party (since replaced) attempted to have a pro-life plank placed in the national Republican party platform.

Religion

Perhaps the most important determinant of an individual's attitude toward abortion is religion. In general, Catholics tend to be more opposed to abortion than Protestants (O'Hara 1990), but church attendance is an important intervening variable (Legge 1983; see also Baker et al. 1981; Jelen 1984b; McIntosh et al. 1979).

Of critical importance to this particular study is the Church of Jesus Christ of Latter Day Saints (LDS, also known as "Mormon"). Previous analyses of religious groups and their attitudes and actions toward abortion often include members of the LDS Church in the larger grouping of "Protestant," thus making it impossible to examine in detail the attitudes of this one religious sect. Given the expressed strong opposition of the Mormon Church to abortion and the generally high levels of attendance and salience of religion to the LDS community, they may represent a significant deviation from the rest of the Protestant community. In fact, there is evidence that the LDS religion represents a distinct political cultural component unique from other Protestant religions.[2]

Even though more than one third of the state legislators identify themselves as Mormons, only about 20% of all Idahoans are adherents to the LDS religion (Quinn, Anderson, Bradley, and Goetting 1982). They are not, however, dispersed equally throughout the state. Mormons are heavily concentrated in the southeastern part of the state (where they constitute 70%-90% of the population in some counties), and are found in much smaller proportions elsewhere in the state, especially in the North.

Religious Composition of Constituency

It is rare for legislators to face electoral retribution because of their vote on a single issue. The vote on H625 may, however, be one of those issues. The issue was extremely salient, garnering substantial media attention. Legislators received more constituent input, in the form of mail and telephone conversations, on this issue than any other issue in recent memory. Because of the saliency of this issue, and the hypothesized connection to religious affiliation, we include religious composition of the constituency in our analysis.

The Data

To assess the effect of background and constituency characteristics on the individual vote decision, we collected data for all 126 Idaho state legislators (84 House members, 42 Senators). The dependent variable, of course, is the individual legislator's actual roll-call vote on H625. Only one legislator did not vote on the bill.

Constituency characteristics include *percentage LDS, percentage Catholic,* and *percentage Protestant* in the legislative district. Information on party affiliation and gender were easily obtainable from the *Idaho Bluebook* and the *Legislative Directory.* Data on religion were obtained from the *Bluebook* and from a survey conducted and reported in the *Lewiston Tribune.*[3] Because legislative districts are composed of one or more whole counties in Idaho, computing legislative district characteristics is a simple matter of summing the data from relevant counties.[4] The percentages of the population for the three religious groupings are from Council of Churches data (Quinn et al. 1982).

Data Analysis

To summarize descriptive information about the vote on H625, LDS legislators voted overwhelmingly for H625 (the pro-life position), with 41 of 46 LDS members supporting the legislation. More Protestant legislators, on the other hand, voted against the bill (21 "ayes," 38 "nays"). The Catholic legislators were split evenly (10-10). A much higher percentage of female legislators supported the pro-choice position (65%, or 19 out of 30), than did male legislators (36%, or 34 out of 95 voting pro-choice). Twice as many Democrats voted "no" (the pro-choice position) on H625 than voted "yes" or pro-life (26 versus 13). Among the Republican legislators, 59 voted for H625, and 27 voted against the bill.

In order to assess the extent to which the several variables included in our analysis are related to the vote on H625 and to each other, a correlation matrix was prepared. Table 7.1 displays the zero-order Pearson's correlation coefficients for the interrelation of all the variables used in this analysis.

All of the independent variables except the percentage of Catholics in the legislator's district are significantly related to the vote on H625 (see Table 7.1). The strongest association holds between the religion of the legislator and the vote on H625. In this case religion is coded to reflect LDS versus all other religious affiliations (i.e., it is a dummy variable to reflect "LDS" or "non-LDS"). The direction of the relationships are as expected.

Table 7.1 Pearson's Correlation Coefficients for Selected Variables

	1	2	3	4	5	6	7
1. Vote	1.0						
2. Party	.3484**	1.0					
3. Gender	.2380**	.0459	1.0				
4. LDS/Else	−.5086**	−.3755**	−.2035**	1.0			
5. Percentage Catholic	.1105	.2086*	.0178	−.3972**	1.0		
6. Percentage Protestant	.3267**	.0072	.2485**	−.4876**	.4523**	1.0	
7. Percentage LDS	−.4622**	−.2911**	−.2180*	.6771**	−.55%**	−.7922**	1.0

NOTES: * significant at .05; ** significant at .01.
vote: 0 = pro-life; 1 = pro-choice
party: 0 = Republican; 1 = Democrat
gender: 0 = male; 1 = female
We examined the vote breakdown by party, religious affiliation, and gender. The vote for H625 (pro-life) according to different characteristics: Republican (59-26), Democrat (13-27); Non-LDS (31-48), LDS (41-5); Male (61-34), Female (11-19). All differences are significant at the $p < .01$ level for χ^2 tests.

An examination of the relationships among the independent variables in Table 7.1 indicates that there is significant intercorrelation among the variables. For example, strong relationships hold between the percentage of Protestants in the district and the percentage of LDS (−.79) and the religion of the legislator (LDS vs. others) and the percentage of LDS adherents in the district (.68). What Table 7.1 shows statistically is the *reinforcing nature* of religious and political cleavages in Idaho. This corroborates observations about political cultural cleavages in Idaho by Blank (1978:157) and regionalism by Moncrief (1987). Because of the strong relationships among the independent variables included in this analysis, multivariate procedures involving all of the variables (both personal characteristics and constituent characteristics) were deemed inappropriate.

Because the dependent variable of interest to us is a dichotomous variable (yes or no on H625), a logit analysis was conducted to ascertain the multiple impact of the several variables discussed above. Table 7.2 displays the logit regression coefficients and effects coefficients for the three personal characteristic variables: religion of the legislator, party of the legislator, and gender.

Religion is split into three dummy variables: Catholic/non-Catholic, Protestant/non-Protestant, and LDS/non-LDS. Interpreting the coefficient/standard error ratio as a *t* statistic indicates that all of the personal characteristic variables except being Catholic can be considered signifi-

Table 7.2 Logistic Regressions for Selected Variables

Logistic Regression on the Vote for H625 Using Legislator's Personal Characteristics

	Regression Coefficient	Standard Error	Coefficient/ Standard Error
Democrat	.66	.26	2.55
Female	.55	.26	2.08
LDS	−.56	.22	−2.55
Protestant	.74	.18	4.20
Catholic	−.02	.22	−.096
$\chi^2 = 124.89; p = .27$			

NOTE: The logistic regression model used to generate the data is the following: $(\text{Log}[p/1 - p])/2 + 5$

cant (see Table 7.2). The direction of the relationships is as expected, with being Democrat, female, and Protestant associated with voting pro-choice. The inverse relationship between being LDS and the vote on H625 reflects the fact that LDS members voted overwhelmingly pro-life. While Catholicism has been reported as an important correlate of attitudes toward abortion and legislative action in regard to this issue in previous studies (see, e.g., O'Hara 1990), in Idaho it was not a significant factor.

A second logit model that includes the independent variables measuring religious characteristics of legislative districts is displayed in Table 7.3.

In this model, only the percentage of LDS adherents in the legislator's district is significantly related to the vote on H625. Interpreting the regression coefficient for the percentage LDS in the district as an effects coefficient (i.e., taking the exponential of 2 times the regression coefficient), the value is calculated as 0.92. This seems small (a one unit increase in the percentage of LDS increases the odds of voting yes on H625 by 0.92), but a one unit increase in percentages is small as well. If one

Table 7.3 Logistic Regressions for Selected Variables

Logistic Regression on the Vote for H625 Using Legislator's Constituent Characteristics

	Regression Coefficient	Standard Error	Coefficient/ Standard Error
Percentage LDS	−.04	.01	−4.15
Percentage Catholic	−.11	.06	−1.87
Percentage Protestant	−.02	.02	−.69
$\chi^2 = 126.17; p = .36$			

NOTE: The logistic regression model used to generate the data is the following: $(\text{Log}[p/1 - p])/2 + 5$

considers a 10% increase in the number of LDS adherents, the odds of voting yes on H625 increase by a factor of 9.2.

Conclusions

What can we learn from an analysis of a single vote, on a single issue, in a single state? First, we must recognize that this is no ordinary issue. It is one of the most salient issues to appear in any statehouse in a generation. It is, in that sense, an "abnormal" situation, and "normal" decision-making processes are less likely to be followed. As Hurwitz (1986:155) explains, "Many of these abnormal issues are particularly important in a substantive or political sense. Although such occasions may be relatively rare, they are disproportionately important to the workings of the legislature." We have shown that on this highly emotional issue, personal characteristics of the legislator are strong predictors of his or her vote.

This particular case study also informs us about the occasional role of regional political cultures and religion in the policy process. The state of Idaho is characterized by an extreme form of sectionalism that separates the state into very distinct regions (see Moncrief 1987). The role that the LDS religion plays in that sectionalism is key to understanding its impact on statewide politics. The fact that the percentage of LDS adherents in the district, and not the percentages of the other religious groups, was the only significant constituent characteristic related to the abortion vote supports the influence that the concentrations of LDS adherents can have. The LDS presence in Idaho state politics is strongly felt on those few occasions when the Church takes a definitive position on public policy.

In the few cases where the legislator's vote was apparently out of step with his or her constituency (as measured by the percentage LDS in the district), the electoral results from 1990 are instructive. Among the leading proponents of H625, the primary sponsor and author in the Senate (Madsen, R-Boise) was defeated. The same fate befell the Senate Majority Leader (Beck, R-Boise). The primary sponsor in the House (Montgomery, R-Boise) narrowly won (51%-49%) reelection in a heavily Republican district. All three of these incumbents were LDS males in a predominantly (80%) *non-Mormon* county. All three were challenged by pro-choice women. The only leader of the pro-life bill to escape defeat was Senator Claire Wetherell (D-Mountain Home)—a woman.

The 1992 election featured a rematch between Roger Madsen, the sponsor of H625, and Cynthia Scanlin, the pro-choice candidate who had defeated him in 1990. This time Madsen was victorious, promising his constituents that he would not pursue legislation about abortion if elected.

In fact, no legislation addressing abortion has been introduced in the legislature since H625. Other issues, including a property tax initiative that was defeated, have instead dominated the Idaho political agenda.

Given that the 1992 Clinton victory has sealed off the presidency as an avenue for restricting abortion, we believe that future attempts will continue to focus on state legislatures. The Idaho legislature is likely to be in that spotlight again. Without abortion as a high visibility issue in 1992, Republicans easily swept large majorities into both houses. The silence on the abortion issue, therefore, may be temporary. The director of the state right-to-life organization has indicated that if a pro-life governor is elected in 1994, fetal-rights groups will seek legislation restricting abortion again.

Notes

1. Jackson and Kingdon (1992:808-9) argue that "relying on aggregate economic or demographic variables as indicators of constituency interest does violence to [the] actual constituency complexity." Although this may be true of the sort of economic votes Jackson and Kingdon have in mind, we are concerned with a single vote on a very salient, "public good" issue.

2. McCulloch and Reinward (1988) argue that the LDS religion has had a distinct influence on Idaho's political culture. Blank (1978) finds a significant relationship between issue differences and religious affiliation in Idaho. Specifically, he concludes that Mormons could be distinguished from other religious groups on the ERA issue and gun control. Another issue in which official church opposition to a policy and church membership seem to have had an impact is the vote of the citizens of Idaho on a lottery referendum. Our analysis indicates that the correlation between the percentage of LDS adherents in a district and a "yes" vote for the lottery was −.92, clearly reflecting LDS opposition to the lottery.

3. This information was graciously supplied by Marty Trillhaase of the *Lewiston Tribune*.

4. The exception is Ada County (Boise metropolitan area), where the county is divided into seven districts. Since we don't have constituency characteristics by precinct, we are unable to create legislative district-level data on religion. We use countywide figures, recognizing that there are likely to be some variations within the legislative districts within the counties. It is very unlikely that this will have an important biasing effect on the analysis.

8

Abortion, Elections, and the Media

MARILYN A. YALE

A bortion has become an important issue in American politics. It has received a great deal of attention from individuals, interest groups, political activists, lobbyists, governmental officials, political parties, candidates, scholars, and the media. Activity on behalf of abortion has included marches, demonstrations, sit-ins, blockades, boycotts, speech-making, prayer vigils, bombings, lobbying, and single-issue voting. The groups battling over this issue have appealed to public officials in every political arena for redress. As a result of these appeals by both pro-choice and pro-life groups, abortion has gained the attention of all three branches of government at both the state and national levels resulting in legislative proposals, gubernatorial vetoes, presidential pleas and litmus testing, and court rulings.

The Supreme Court has been at the center of this battle since its 1973 *Roe v. Wade*[1] decision declared abortion a constitutionally protected right. The decision touched off an active campaign by pro-life forces to appeal it. This campaign involved several fronts and made use of a variety of strategies. To appeal the loss they suffered with *Roe,* antiabortion groups began turning to the public, along with the electoral and policy arenas at both the state and national levels (see Hershey 1986; Paige 1983). Their goals included finding and mobilizing right-to-life voters and conservative sympathizers. Once found, these sympathizers were encouraged to become active in the fight against abortion by pressuring elected officials and holding them electorally accountable for their positions on abortion.

Just as pro-life forces responded to *Roe,* so pro-choice forces responded to the Supreme Court's 1989 *Webster v. Reproductive Health Services* decision.[2] The goals of anti-*Webster* groups were similar to those of their opponents: to appeal to and mobilize sympathetic bystanders, and express strength to officeholders. In the struggle over abortion each side has sought to appeal to the public and public officials in order to gain a new chance at victory.

The first opportunity to appeal the loss pro-choice suffered with *Webster,* and the first opportunity to witness the impact of abortion on state electoral campaigns following that decision came with elections in New Jersey and Virginia—elections that were ongoing when *Webster* was rendered. The importance of these state-level elections is clear in that these campaigns would set the stage for future struggles over abortion. If in the future the Court does return complete authority over abortion policy to the states, governmental officeholders at that level (including governors) will determine the fate of this issue. As a result, both pro-life and pro-choice supporters now struggle to gain control over state governments by electing officeholders sympathetic to their definition of the issue, and their solution to it. The Court's decision increased the significance of state officeholders as abortion policy makers and as targets of pro-choice and pro-life efforts.

These first two post-*Webster* gubernatorial campaigns were both nonincumbent campaigns matching Republican candidates with outspoken pro-life policy positions against pro-choice Democrats. In New Jersey pro-life Republican James Courter was matched with pro-choice Democrat Jim Florio, while in Virginia pro-life Republican Marshall Coleman battled pro-choice Democrat Douglas Wilder. As a result of the policy preferences of the individual campaigners, the Court's controversial decision in *Webster,* and the activities of pro-choice and pro-life groups, the potential for conflict over this issue was high.

Even in states where no gubernatorial election would be held until 1990, the abortion issue was raised. The combatants for governor in both Texas and California began to field questions about abortion and their possible strategies regarding the issue. In Texas pro-choice Democrat Ann Richards issued a statement following *Webster* promising to make abortion a major theme in her campaign against pro-life Republican Clayton Williams. In California both primary winners, Democrat Dianne Feinstein and Republican Pete Wilson, held pro-choice positions on abortion. In both these later states activists, political analysts, campaign consultants, and reporters began anxiously discussing and debating the likely impact of abortion on the primaries as well as the general election. As with the earlier elections, these nonincumbent campaigns would be a test of the importance of abortion for state campaigners. Could this issue continue to impact state politics and political campaigning one year after the Court's *Webster* decision?

The battle over abortion not only centered on state government, it also came to be centered on these campaigns. The remainder of this chapter focuses on the issue of abortion in these four gubernatorial campaigns using a content analysis of newspaper coverage. From this, conclusions can be drawn concerning the nature of press coverage give to state-level campaigns and this issue, as well as conclusions concerning the role abortion played in these contests.

Use of the Media

In the present cases, the press covered both state electoral campaigns, and the battle over abortion. The campaigners were tracked as they traveled the state in search of electoral support. Abortion was tracked as it moved from the agenda of the Court to that of the states following *Webster*. As is the case with most modern political struggles, the groups involved in the battle over abortion have relied on the media to pursue their goals. The media are useful as a vehicle through which to display strength to elected officials, transmit symbols, and pursue and recruit less passionate bystanders (see Elder and Cobb 1983). In an effort to secure the attention of the legislatures, the executive, and the Court, antiabortion forces reacted to *Roe* and anti-*Webster* groups reacted to that decision by employing strategies designed to capture the attention of the mass media and, therefore, the public. These tactics included releasing official statements, and engaging in demonstrations on the steps of Planned Parenthood, clinics, hospitals, Congress, state houses, and the White House. The groups involved in the abortion debate have accommodated the needs of the media by displaying a great deal of activity and emotion as they engage in direct confrontation with one another and attempt to label one another "uncaring," "immoral," and "un-American." People participating in marches, demonstrations, and sit-ins do so while animatedly carrying pictures of aborted fetuses, coat hangers, and pictures of "back alley" deaths from unsafe procedures. These strategies coupled with the use of high-order, condensation symbols by the combatants such as "life," "motherhood," "control," "privacy," "liberty," and "equality" often led to media coverage (see Elder and Cobb 1983). The news coverage that generally followed would not only transmit the message and the symbols of the organizers of these events, it would also bring a measure of credibility to the groups' efforts and opinions. The goal of these activities was, then, to generate continued media coverage, leading to increased awareness, concern, and mobilization. Having become aware, concerned, and mobilized regarding abortion, the public would then come to government with a demand for action. For pro-choice supporters, the demand would be for protection of the right to abortion. For pro-life supporters the appeal would be for restrictions or criminalization.

Still further, both pro-life and pro-choice supporters have used these rallies and demonstrations, and the media coverage that follows, to display committed electoral strength to elected officials. The intended message for this group was, anything less than full support for their side of this issue would be politically disadvantageous.

The attraction of abortion to the media is clear. Abortion is controversial, the subject of an actively contested, often violent conflict, and involves a dramatic, emotional, moral dilemma. Abortion allows journalists to write stories filled with the passion and emotion of those involved in this struggle. In addition, the fact that there are two distinguishable sides makes abortion fairly easy to cover and promotes additional stories in an action-reaction mode (see Barber 1978). The two-sided nature of abortion also provides the possibility of brief and recognizable summaries of the conflict, along with many available sources of quotes and information (Arterton 1978). The media respond to abortion with coverage because of the ease with which a story can be produced (easing the pressure to fill pages), the desire to sell newspapers (by appealing to readers with high emotion, drama, and confrontation), and the expectation of coverage by at least some portion of the public.

The media focused on these electoral contests for perhaps the same reasons they devote attention to abortion and other political struggles. Campaigners receive coverage because of the ease with which these stories can be produced and the assumption that electoral campaigns are inherently important. Political campaigns are, like other political struggles, generally easily covered, two-sided affairs filled with drama, conflict, and controversy. Just as the contestants in other struggles, the contestants in electoral campaigns are readily available to reporters and employ strategies designed to gain the attention of the press and promote positive coverage in the hopes of mobilizing supporters.

Data and Method

This chapter studies the coverage given to abortion in the specific context of four gubernatorial campaigns. The data for this project were taken from the press coverage of the New Jersey, Virginia, California, and Texas gubernatorial campaigns as reflected in *The New York Times, The Washington Post,* the *Los Angeles Times,* and *The Houston Post,* respectively. In order to examine the coverage given these campaigns during the entire general election period, the data began with the editions immediately following the party primaries in each state and ended with election day.[3] The initial summary data for each state were compiled from the index entries of the corresponding newspaper.[4] All index entries referencing the gubernatorial elections or the candidates were included.[5] A total of 64 articles were found referencing the New Jersey campaign, 139 concerned Virginia's race, 160 were devoted to California, and 178 focused on the gubernatorial contest in Texas.

Exclusive Coding

Initially each article was coded exclusively into one of three categories:

1. *contest:* including coverage of candidate public appearances, crowd size and response, polls, finances, fund-raising, advertising, endorsements, voter mood and turnout predictions, general campaign strategy, "insider" analyses of campaign, and campaign issues (controversies devoid of issue content);
2. *candidate characteristics:* including coverage of candidate's personality, family background, qualifications for office, past record, and career; and
3. *issues:* including coverage of public policy issues (Hale 1987:95; see also Goldenberg and Traugott 1984; Tidmarch and Karp 1983; Tidmarch, Hyman, and Sorkin 1984).

This type of coding forced the story to be labeled as predominantly issue oriented, candidate oriented, or contest oriented. This permitted some summary conclusions regarding the often asked question, Does the press coverage devoted to electoral campaigns focus on policy, personality, or contest? Following Patterson's (1980) and Hale's (1987) finding that the media overwhelmingly focus on game or contest elements of electoral campaigns rather than public policy issues, the first hypothesis to be tested is that, using exclusive categorization, contest coverage will surpass that devoted to issues or candidate factors.

Explicit Issue Content

A second coding scheme was used to investigate the relative amount of coverage given to abortion in these campaigns and the content of that coverage. Following Tidmarch et al. (1984), the purpose of this second round of coding was to present information about the extent of issue coverage; thus the issue coverage category here represented all stories "with explicit issue content" (1984:1228). This does not mean, as it did above with exclusive coding, that these stories are exclusively or predominantly issue oriented. It means, rather, that there is some explicit issue

content. Following statements made by activists and supporters concluding that the media focused on abortion to the exclusion of other issues in
the campaign, the second hypothesis to be tested is that coverage of
abortion will surpass that given any other single issue.

Abortion Coverage

To determine the level or complexity of abortion coverage, articles
concerning this issue were examined for content and placed exclusively
into one of the following categories:

1. *peripheral:* articles containing passing mentions of issues or candidate's
   positions on the issue without any extra information or explanation provided
   by the reporter;
2. *reportorial:* articles containing reporter's quotes or paraphrases of what a
   candidate or his supporters said about issues without any extra information
   or explanation of the issues provided by the reporter;
3. *explanatory:* articles containing extra information provided by the reporter
   that supplies context for understanding the issue, by explaining either the
   issue or the candidate's position on the issue; and,
4. *analytic:* articles containing analysis provided by the reporter on issues, either
   by discussing the implications of issue positions for public policy, for the
   voters, or for the campaign, or by comparing the positions of candidates in
   such a manner as to give a clear understanding of the similarities or differences in their positions. (Hale 1987:98)

The third hypothesis, following Hale's (1987) conclusion that election
coverage is most often simplistic reporting, assumes that the coverage of
abortion will be dominated by the peripheral and reportorial levels. Abortion is expected to receive attention by the press because it is easily
covered, two-sided, and controversial. Based on past studies of issue
coverage during electoral campaigns, the focus of press coverage given to
abortion is expected to be surface rather than explanatory or analytic.

Virginia and New Jersey

Exclusive Coding

The gubernatorial contest in Virginia received much more coverage in
The Washington Post than the New Jersey campaign did in *The New York
Times* (Table 8.1). Perhaps the news coverage devoted to politics in the

Table 8.1 Contest, Candidate, and Issue References

	Contest		Candidate Characteristics		Issues		Total	
	N	%	N	%	N	%	N	%
NJ	45	70.3	7	10.9	12	18.8	64	100
VA	93	66.9	19	13.7	27	19.4	139	100
CA	111	69.4	7	4.4	42	26.3	160	100.1[a]
TX	143	80.3	6	3.4	29	16.3	178	100.0
Total	392	72.5	39	7.2	110	20.3	541	100

SOURCE: Computed by author.
NOTE: a. Percentage total exceeds 100 due to rounding.

Times was diverted to the mayoral race in New York City. Hypothesis one, reporting the expectation that contest centered coverage would exceed that given to issues or candidate characteristics, is supported. An overwhelming majority of all articles in both states centered on game or contest elements such as the latest poll results, campaign appearances, debates, endorsements, fund raisers, and strategies. These news stories also reported the content and likely impact of newspaper and television ads as well as reports of success or failure in image making, coalition building, and differentiating oneself from and attacking the opposition. Assessing the candidates' likelihood of electoral success as a result of these events and strategies was most often the purpose of the story.

The issue category of Table 8.1 reflects the traditionally poor showing of policy issues in news coverage of electoral campaigns. When exclusively coded based on predominant theme (either contest, issues, or candidate characteristics) less than one fifth of all articles dealing with these first two races were predominantly issue oriented.[6] The articles fitting the issues criteria were not presented as ordinary election coverage, but were often instead presented as special, "the candidates on the issues" stories. The average daily story focused instead on the candidates appearances, strategies, and poll standings.

The candidate characteristics category of Table 8.1 contains items such as profiles of the candidate including discussions of personality, family background, qualifications for office, and past performance. The findings in this category for Virginia were inflated by a racial focus. Nearly one half (9) of the stories referencing the characteristics of the candidates centered on the race of then Lt. Governor Douglas Wilder, who would go on to become the first black governor in the history of Virginia, and the United States. Race was treated as a candidate factor or contest element

Table 8.2 Frequency of Issues Referenced

	NJ		VA		CA		TX	
	N	%	N	%	N	%	N	%
Abortion	10	25.0	21	38.2	9	10.7	5	8.3
Crime	6	15.0	6	10.9	11	13.1	5	8.3
Environment	3	7.5	1	1.8	12	14.3	5	8.3
Taxes	2	5.0	4	7.3	10	11.9	14	23.3
Economy	3	7.5	4	7.3	6	7.1	3	5.0
Insurance	6	15.0	0	0	0	0	3	5.0
Education	0	0	5	9.1	5	6.0	11	18.3
Infrastructure	1	2.5	7	12.7	1	1.2	0	0
Drugs	2	5.0	3	5.5	7	8.3	4	6.7
Social Services	2	5.0	1	1.8	4	4.8	0	0
Death Penalty	1	2.5	1	1.8	2	2.4	3	5.0
Budget	4	10.0	2	3.6	16	19.0	4	6.7
Homosexual/Aids	0	0	0	0	0	0	2	3.3
Flag Burning	0	0	0	0	1	1.2	1	1.7
Total	40	100	55	100	84	100	60	99.9
		(62.5)[a]		(39.6)		(52.5)		(33.7)

SOURCE: Computed by author.
NOTE: a. This row represents the percentage of total articles in each state with issue content.

rather than a policy issue because these stories focused on the political impact of Wilder's race on strategy, fund-raising, and coalition building, rather than a matter of public policy.

Explicit Issue Mentioning

Exclusive categorization reveals a tremendous reliance on the physicality of campaigning by the news media. To discuss the coverage given these campaigns more closely, the data were recoded in search of stories with explicit issue content rather than stories that were *exclusively* or *predominantly* issue oriented. Once recoded, public policy issues did appear in the press's coverage of these campaigns (Table 8.2). The most striking feature of Table 8.2 for these early states is the impact of abortion. Fully one quarter of articles making some reference to issues with respect to the New Jersey gubernatorial campaign discussed abortion. In Virginia an even more impressive 38.2% of articles referencing issues reported on abortion. For each of these newspapers the coverage concerning abortion exceeded that given any other single issue including more traditional issues such as taxes, crime, and education. In fact, in Virginia abortion outscored any other single issue by a margin of three to one.

The focus of the stories dealing with abortion in both the early states centered on the gubernatorial campaigns including the following: interest group activity directed toward these contests; issue positions of the candidates; charges of insincerity, "waffling," or "flip-flopping"; and the strategies employed by the candidates or the strategic importance of this issue for the ongoing campaign. Interest group activity included attempts by both pro-choice and pro-life groups to focus attention on abortion as a critical policy issue and attempts to affect the candidates' levels of support. The introduction of abortion onto the state-level agenda by the Court was also discussed in terms of an event or happening that would likely impact the candidates' campaign strategies.

Like the overall coverage given these races, the majority of the coverage surrounding abortion in both these gubernatorial campaigns centered on the contest. In Virginia the candidates' positions and the apparent movement of the Republican were each the primary subject of three stories. The candidates' positions were the primary subject of only one story in New Jersey while the "waffling" of Courter added another candidate-centered story. Interest group activity was reported five times in Virginia and three times in New Jersey reflecting the added effort by pro-choice groups in Virginia. The contest-centered coverage of abortion included press stories reporting the latest television ad focusing on the issue, travel appearances where the candidate spoke about abortion, and discussions of the strategic importance of abortion. In New Jersey, half of those articles referencing abortion framed the issue in these terms while the contest element of abortion in Virginia was reported 10 times.

Complexity of Abortion Coverage

To begin discussing the content of this coverage, Table 8.3 categorizes the complexity of articles referencing abortion. This distinction was made in an effort to determine the degree to which the stories about abortion went beyond simply reporting what the candidate said in a press release, campaign stop, or advertisement. The level of complexity rose if the story included contextual information that helped the reader understand the candidate's statements and the implications of the issue. The raw numbers again show more coverage of the issue in Virginia than in New Jersey. Supporting previous research (Hale 1987), more complex explanatory and analytic reports of abortion appeared much less frequently than more simplistic accounts. More than three fourths of the articles discussing abortion in each campaign were either peripheral or reportorial discussions relaying statements made concerning abortion by the candidates, supporters, or opponents. Explanatory and analytic articles added another level of

Table 8.3 Complexity of Abortion Articles

	Peripheral		Reportorial		Explanatory		Analytic		Total
	N	%	N	%	N	%	N	%	N
New Jersey	6	60.0	2	20.0	1	10.0	1	10.0	10
Virginia	8	38.1	6	28.6	5	23.8	2	9.5	21
California	2	25.0	3	37.5	2	25.0	1	12.5	8
Texas	1	25.0	2	50.0	1	25.0	0	0	4
Total	17	39.5	13	30.2	9	20.9	4	9.3	43

SOURCE: Computed by author.

complexity by providing explanation and analysis of the issue and its importance to the campaigners and the voters. The content of the coverage devoted to abortion in both states can be characterized as simple and reactionary rather than explanatory and investigative. Rather than actively pursuing the issue, the press mirrored the agenda of the candidates by reporting the latest statement or charge concerning abortion. Once again the coverage given these early campaigns focused on contest elements.

Figure 8.1 tracks the number of stories referencing abortion in both races. The number of stories referencing abortion in the Virginia race peaked in July following the release of *Webster,* and again in the weeks prior to election day. The coverage in New Jersey, however, registered one mild peak in October. The stories occurring in July marked the appearance of *Webster* and were followed by reports of its possible importance for these ongoing campaigns. The question to be answered is, what drove the coverage of abortion? Did reporters put abortion on the campaign agenda for the candidates, or did the candidates put abortion on the campaign agenda, leading the press to respond with coverage?

During the campaigns in Virginia and New Jersey the Court's decision became part of the environment to which the candidates responded. The coverage of abortion in both campaigns was dominated by reports of the statements, activities, reactions, and advertisements of campaigners and interest. The Democrats in each state benefited from the introduction of abortion into the campaigns, the news coverage of that issue, and their strategies in dealing with it. The Democrats in both these states concluded that a political advantage could be created using this issue. Therefore, both Wilder and Florio responded to the introduction of abortion by staking claim to pro-choice symbols and attacking their Republicans' stated pro-life positions. In both states the strategy was aggressive pursuit of the issue in an attempt to differentiate themselves from their opponents.

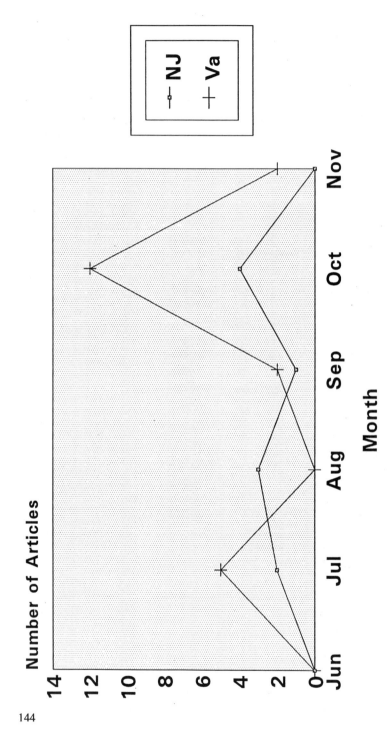

Figure 8.1. Abortion by Month: New Jersey and Virginia

NOTE: June 1, 1989, to November 11, 1989

The advantage the Democrats in these early races found with abortion was ammunition with which to attack their opponents' image and character. Though Wilder used abortion more aggressively, the goal of each was to take advantage of the issue by: displaying a policy connection with voters; portraying themselves as candidates concerned with women's issues and champions of individual rights; and painting their opponents as both extremists ready to impose governmental regulation in matters of personal privacy, and political opportunists whose convictions changed depending on the audience to whom they were speaking. Florio brought this image to life by equating abortion restrictions with governmental "intrusion, governmental growth, [and] domination of people's private lives" (Kerr 1989). Abortion allowed Wilder and Florio to link favorable symbols to themselves and unfavorable symbols to the opposition. In these races the Democrats wanted to fasten the symbols of responsiveness, caring, freedom, and choice to themselves, and inconsistency, insincerity, and unresponsiveness to their opponents.

Both Wilder and Florio were successful in bringing the advantages of this issue to their campaigns. Each was also successful at avoiding the disadvantage of being associated with "abortion on demand" and "radical feminism" while benefiting from the efforts of NOW and other "feminist" groups to keep abortion before the news media and the public. To do this, the Democrats sought to avoid the debate over abortion per se, the issue of life, and the question of *why* someone might want to have the procedure. They focused instead on *who* would make that decision, leading both candidates to emphasize the right to choose, and the right to be free from governmental interference, rather than merely the right to abortion.

The Republican gubernatorial candidates in Virginia and New Jersey apparently saw no strategic advantage in the issue of abortion or the Court's decision. In fact it was politically disadvantageous for Coleman and Courter to defend their previous pro-life positions following *Webster*. In an effort to moderate their positions during the campaigns to minimize the damage their pro-life positions could bring, they were accused of political opportunism and insincerity.

The New Jersey Republican, Courter, was accused of "flip-flopping" on abortion rather than supporting his previously stated pro-life position. In Virginia, Coleman softened his antiabortion stance as well by pledging that though he believed "we ought to protect the life of the pre-born," he would not propose such legislation as governor (Baker 1989:B5). Coleman was unable to escape criticism for altering his stance from favoring the prohibition of abortion in all cases except when the life of the mother is endangered, to a willingness not to act on that conviction. In addition to using abortion to accuse Coleman of shifting his convictions and playing politics, Wilder also continually stressed the more emotionally charged cases involving rape and incest in order to paint Coleman as an extremist who would take the state backward and jeopardize women's lives.

Florio and Wilder were successful in their attempts to frame the issue as privacy and freedom from governmental intrusion while avoiding connection with abortion on demand and "militant feminists." The Democrats focused overwhelmingly on abortion in the shocking and sympathetic cases of rape and incest. In fact, some leading Republicans, including several in Coleman's inner circle, said that of all the issues available to Wilder, abortion was potentially the most damaging because it operates on so many levels, not only because it affects huge numbers of women, but also because it raises concerns among other voters about government intervention and individual liberties. The Democrats in Virginia and New Jersey took advantage of this issue and punished the Republicans for their long-held but recently shaky pro-life positions.

Like the groups battling over abortion, the Democratic campaigners here made use of symbolic appeals and attempted to label their opponents as enemies of liberty and un-American. Like combatants in a political struggle, these candidates used the media to attract attention, fasten these labels, and mobilize support. The media responded to the continued abortion-centered offerings of Florio and Wilder both as they reported the daily comings, goings, statements, and accusations of the candidates for governor, and as they searched the news day for an easily covered, dramatic, controversial story. Without *Webster,* this issue would likely not have become important to the campaigners. Had they not actively pursued strategies designed to maximize the newsworthiness of this issue, abortion would not have received news coverage as a campaign issue.

California and Texas

Like the contests in Virginia and New Jersey, the gubernatorial campaigns in California and Texas were nonincumbent races. Unlike the contests in Virginia and New Jersey, however, the general election candidates for governor in California and Texas had the benefit of time, and the opportunity to watch the events unfold and to learn from the previous mistakes and strategies of the campaigners in Virginia and New Jersey. Analysis of *The Houston Post* and the *Los Angeles Times* will provide insight into the coverage given this issue and the strategies used by the campaigners in Texas and California, respectively.

The gubernatorial campaign in Texas matched pro-life Republican Clayton Williams with pro-choice Democrat Ann Richards. Richards opposed further restrictions on abortions, whereas Williams favored restricting access to abortion except in cases of incest, rape, and when the mother's life is endangered. The campaign in California matched two pro-choice candidates, Republican Pete Wilson and Democrat Dianne Feinstein. These races were unique because both Democratic challengers were women. California was additionally unique because both candidates held pro-choice positions on abortion. The lack of disagreement in California would initially lead to the expectation of little coverage of abortion given the press's usual reliance of conflict and controversy.

Pro-choice groups were newly energized and motivated to compete in Virginia and New Jersey because of the wake-up call issued following the threat to abortion rights created by *Webster*. One year later, in Texas, activist groups from both camps attempted to generate interest and concern. NARAL, joined by the Texas Abortion Rights Action League (TARAL), Texans United for Life, and Life Advocates worked on the grass-roots level by identifying and registering sympathetic voters, delivering literature, and working phone banks. These groups did not, however, provide a great deal of money, advertising, or media coverage as was the case in New Jersey and even more so in Virginia.

Exclusive Coding

The gubernatorial contests in California and Texas received roughly equal coverage as reflected in the total number of stories referencing each race. As was the case in Virginia and New Jersey, the results shown for the late races in Table 8.1 are based on exclusive placement of newspaper stories into three categories: contest, candidate characteristics, and policy issues. These were computed in an effort to compare these findings with other analyses of press reportage. These results again support the charge that the media most often cover the strategic element of political campaigning. In both Texas and California an overwhelming majority of the election coverage dealt with the contest between the candidates. Winning and losing, strategy and logistics, appearances and hoopla were the dominant themes. In Texas this category also included continuing coverage given to Williams's unfortunate gaffes. In California this category was boosted by coverage of a scandal involving Feinstein's husband.[7]

The candidate characteristics category contained stories focusing on the candidates' personalities, qualifications for office, past performance, business experience, and family status. Reminiscent of the race factor in Virginia, gender appeared in these campaigns as both Democratic contenders were women. It did not, however, inflate the frequencies in the candidate characteristics categories as race did in Virginia.[8] This characteristic did receive greater coverage in California as a result of Feinstein's attempt to create a strategic advantage by emphasizing gender and urging voters, particularly women, to elect the first female governor of California. Gender did not receive a great deal of coverage in Texas. Richards did not use her gender as a rallying point.

Explicit Issue Mention

Following the method applied to Virginia and New Jersey, the coverage of these late races was recoded allowing "issue articles" to be redefined as those stories with explicit issue content rather than only those that are exclusively or predominantly issue oriented. Based on this method, 84 articles covering the California race and 60 articles covering Texas mentioned issues such as taxes, the economy, crime, and abortion (see Table 8.2). In both California and Texas economic concerns such as taxes, the economy, and the state budget received a plurality of the issue coverage. Crime and the environment were also the focus of attention in California as each candidate struggled to appear sensitive to the environment and tough on crime. In Texas, education was a primary topic of concern with both candidates promising to bring about improvements.

Abortion did not dominate the issue coverage in California and Texas as it did in Virginia and New Jersey. It did, however, receive a somewhat surprising amount of coverage in California given that the candidates did not fundamentally differ on the issue. Because Feinstein made abortion an important issue in her campaign, it appeared in press reports. Feinstein herself was the focus of the majority of this coverage, again reflecting the fact that she sought to use the issue strategically to rally support and to distinguish herself from her opponent. The coverage of abortion in Texas was much less than in California. Abortion was not pursued by either candidate nor key to either campaign. The potential for controversy and conflict in Texas never emerged. As shown in the Virginia case, coverage of abortion occurs most impressively when a candidate actively used the issue to distinguish him- or herself from the opposition.

Complexity of Abortion Coverage

Table 8.3 reflects the extent of issue coverage by categorizing articles dealing with abortion according to their level complexity. As was found in both Virginia and New Jersey, issue articles regarding abortion presented peripheral and reportorial discussions rather than in-depth reports filled with explanation or analysis. When treating abortion in news stories, reporters tended to report only what a candidate or a spokesperson or supporter said about the issue. This reportorial mode "requires the reporter only to be a 'scribe' or a chronicler of the day's events" (Hale 1987:100).

The *Los Angeles Times's* coverage of the California race for governor reflected Feinstein's frequent efforts to keep abortion in the news in order to mobilize sympathizers and rally the female vote by insisting that she would be a better protector of a woman's right to choose. As did the Democrats in the early races, Feinstein sought to gain strategic advantage by attacking Wilson with charges of inconsistency. The accusation came not from charges of flip-flopping on a previously held pro-life policy position, but rather as a result of votes cast as a Senator denying federal funding for abortions and supporting two anti-*Roe* Republican appointees to the Supreme Court.

Wilson responded to *Webster* with a strategy designed to limit any disadvantage that might be brought by his Republican party affiliation. Immediately following his win in the Republican party primary Wilson sought to allay any fears held by pro-choice supporters and counter the chant by Feinstein supporters declaring "it's time we had a woman governor." To do this, Wilson surrounded himself with female choice supporters and notables (such as Norma McCorvey, Jane Roe in *Roe v. Wade*) who praised his long-time support for women's issues.

The retirement of Supreme Court Justice William Brennan and the opportunity to assign a replacement whose views on abortion were unknown, permitted Feinstein to raise the question of abortion again during the campaign. Souter represented a potentially decisive antiabortion vote on the Court that could result in the overturning of *Roe*. Feinstein continued to push the issue hard:

> Demanding that Wilson quiz Supreme Court nominee David Souter on abortion Feinstein equated abortion rights for women with civil rights for minorities saying that "Americans would not stand for the appointment of a segregationist to the Court and should not stand for the confirmation of an abortion-rights opponent." (Decker 1990:A3)

Attempting to associate Wilson with the traditional Republican party line on abortion, Feinstein declared that "abortion rights will be the definitive issue in the gubernatorial campaign" because "no single issue more clearly defines the difference between Republicans and Democrats this year than abortion rights" (Decker 1989:A3).

A disadvantage was created by Feinstein's quest for female solidarity when she promised, if elected, to fill half of the appointive offices with women. This led her opponent to criticize her for the use of quotas rather than competence. Framing abortion as a women's issue and pursuing a feminist platform proved politically disadvantageous for Feinstein. Richards, on the other hand, chose not to play up the gender issue or abortion.

In Texas, perhaps surprisingly, abortion was not actively pursued by the Democrat, even though early in the campaign Richards "pledged to make her pro-choice views on abortion a centerpiece of her campaign" (Grandolfo and Hailey 1990:A1). By late October, however, Richards had totally abandoned abortion, telling reporters that the top issues for the remainder of her campaign would be education, environment, and insurance reform. As evidenced by a poll conducted by Rice University, "the issue of abortion may not be *the* issue in the gubernatorial campaign because by that time it was not *the* issue for most voters" (Roberts 1990:A13).

What may explain Richards's hesitance to use abortion aggressively was her opponent's strategy along with his ability to outspend her. By June, Williams, following the lead of the Republican party, shifted attention to the specific question of parental consent for minors seeking an abortion and away from the broad pro-choice/antiabortion conflict. It appears that Richards did not want to push the abortion issue and risk appearing to support abortion on demand for minors (which is opposed by 70% of Texans, according to a June poll). She was perhaps also fearful that aggressively pursuing a pro-choice campaign would have fueled Williams's ongoing portrayal of Richards as a "hard-core liberal feminist" who was out of touch with Texas voters.

The attention given to abortion in California and the lack of attention given to this issue in Texas are at first surprising. The potential for conflict and drama were much higher in Texas, given the candidates' opposing views and Richards's early commitment to make abortion rights a major part of her campaign. Unlike the Republicans in the early races, Williams was not attacked during the general election campaign for his pro-life position. Richards did not use abortion to differentiate herself from him; or attack his character or consistency. Because the issue was not pursued by the candidates, the potential conflict was not realized and abortion received little press coverage in Texas.

In California the initial potential for conflict and drama were low. Both general election candidates made their pro-choice positions clear during the primary campaigns. In fact, both Wilson and Feinstein were quick to respond to the *Webster* ruling with statements declaring their disapproval of the decision. Even though both candidates shared the same policy position, abortion received some attention because Feinstein sought to keep abortion on the campaign agenda. Abortion was a useful issue for the Democrats in the earlier campaigns; it allowed Florio and Wilder to label their opponents as uncaring, unresponsive, and inconsistent. Feinstein wanted to use abortion to label herself as the champion of women and choice, and her opponent as an insincere political opportunist, but her campaign proved unsuccessful.

Conclusion

The summary findings of the content analysis in all four newspapers support the hypothesis that press coverage tends to focus on the game elements of electoral campaigns more than on the elements of candidate characteristics or policy issues. In fact, the Virginia contest was given far greater coverage than its counterpart in New Jersey. The added coverage did not, however, substantially boost the proportion of issue coverage (see Tables 8.1 and 8.2). Only 15 additional stories referenced issues in Virginia than New Jersey, and the Virginia campaign was the focus of 75 more stories than was New Jersey's. Thus the added stories devoted to Virginia focused overwhelmingly on the contest, not issues.

This game-centered coverage supports similar findings at the presidential and congressional level (Patterson 1980; Tidmarch and Karp 1983). The campaign itself is often the focus of media coverage because reporters seek events that are clear-cut, controversial, and dramatic. Horse-race coverage, gaffes, attacks, and conflict more often fulfill this need than does continuing coverage of the candidates' stance on education or crime.

The expectation that the complexity of the press coverage devoted to abortion during these campaigns would be low is also supported. The majority of the coverage devoted to abortion in all four cases featured either peripheral mentions or reportorial coverage without any added information or explanation by the reporter. Though restricted to the coverage of abortion, this supports Hale's findings in which this type of coverage is compared to that of "scribes who report 'just the facts' as provided by the competing campaigns" (Hale 1987:100).

The expectation that the states in which the contestants held opposing positions on abortion would receive the greatest amount of abortion coverage is only partially supported. This expectation follows from the idea that the press, given its taste for conflict and controversy, will more likely cover this issue when the campaigners are in conflict rather than in agreement. The findings in California do not support this. Both gubernatorial candidates stated pro-life positions, leading to the expectation of minimal coverage. The results however, show that abortion was the fifth most referenced issue in that race.

The immediate goal of candidates and campaigners is to devise messages that will motivate citizens to vote for them. Toward this end, campaigners develop communication strategies, themes, and specific messages, and attempt to convey them to the citizenry. As the focus of attention during election campaigns, candidates make the primary active contribution to the flow of communication (Joslyn 1984). Journalists make an important contribution to the flow of electoral communication by influencing a candidate's choice of campaign issues and strategy. The initial reports of abortion in the early campaigns in Virginia and New Jersey were event-driven as the Court's decision put the issue onto the agenda of state government. The press initially contributed to the campaign agenda by covering *Webster.*

It is clear that observations of and assumptions about public opinion as well as the needs of the media were important elements in the formation of the overall communication strategy in these states. While abortion was firmly in the hands of the Court, state-level officeholders and campaigners heard from (and felt the electoral pressure of) the mobilized pro-life forces. Once *Webster,* to some degree, put the issue back in the hands of the voters in the states, public officials and aspirants began to become aware that the majority is not anti-choice. Pursuing a pro-choice strategy was politically advantageous because abortion meets the needs of the media and could generate media coverage that could then allow the candidate to differentiate him- or herself from the opposition and build electoral support.

The winning candidates in New Jersey and Virginia concluded that political advantage could be created using abortion. The strategies they pursued emphasized the issue of abortion and a "choice" and "freedom" symbolization of it. The winning candidate in Texas saw no advantage in the issue and did not pursue it. Both candidates in California determined that a clearly stated pro-choice policy preference would be advantageous. The Democrat tried to create an additional advantage by stressing the issue using abortion as part of a "feminist" theme.

Gaining future political advantage from the issue of abortion following the Supreme Court's *Webster* and *Casey* rulings will likely depend in large measure on the symbols invoked. The newly elected administration has shown support for the right to choose while avoiding the term "abortion." In his debate with Vice President Quayle, Vice President-elect Gore tried to put his opponent on the defensive and create a connection with viewers by repeatedly asking Quayle to commit to supporting a woman's right to choose. Focusing on freedom from governmental intrusion and the general right to choose while avoiding abortion per se, "abortion on demand," and the issue of minors will likely be the symbolization used by future candidates who anticipate that a strategic advantage can be gained by expressing a pro-choice policy preference. Candidates predicting disadvantage from a strong pro-life stance may follow the Texas Republican's strategy by focusing on the cases of abortion involving minors. Emphasizing parental notification and consent may dilute any backlash from a public fearful of governmental intrusion.

Notes

1. 93 S. Ct. 705, 1973.

2. 109 S.Ct. 340, 1989.

3. The beginning dates were as follows: June 10, 1989 in Virginia; June 7, 1989 in New Jersey; June 7, 1990 in California; and April 11, 1990 in Texas.

4. For all states except New Jersey the index entries were taken from the state name under the broader heading "Elections-State." The data for New Jersey were compiled from index entries under the heading "New Jersey" rather than a subheading under a broader "Elections" heading.

5. Editorials were not included.

6. It is important to note that the issues category here included only those stories where the predominant focus was on issues.

7. Following Hale (1987) these campaign issues were included as instances of contest rather than issues because they are "controversies devoid of issue content."

8. Following the coding decision made in the Virginia case, gender was not included in the issue category when it was not a discussion of a public policy matter. Most articles mentioning gender went on to discuss strategic considerations and were thus coded as instances of contest.

9

Abortion Attitudes and the Louisiana Governor's Election

SUSAN E. HOWELL

ROBERT T. SIMS

Researchers have found the impact of abortion on elections to be quite elusive. Following *Roe v. Wade,* the policy debate as well as the social science research centered on abortion effects at the national level. But in spite of the high visibility of this issue and its activists, survey-based research in the late 1970s and early 1980s failed to find effects of the abortion issue on presidential and congressional elections (Granberg and Burlison 1983; Jackson and Vinovskis 1983; Traugott and Vinovskis 1980; Vinovskis 1980a). The decision of the Supreme Court in *Webster v. Reproductive Health Services* gave the states greater authority to regulate abortion. Subsequently, the focus of the debate shifted to state legislatures and governors. Utah and Pennsylvania have now passed strict laws regulating abortion that will ultimately test the *Roe* decision. Preliminary research on the first two gubernatorial elections after *Webster,* Virginia and New Jersey, demonstrated an impact of the abortion issue that was independent of partisanship (Dodson and Burnbauer 1990a; Chapter 8 in this volume). Such a conclusion stands in sharp contrast to the earlier research on national elections. The gubernatorial research is preliminary, however, and prevents our concluding with any certainty that the abortion issue does indeed impact state elections. A thorough examination of abortion effects requires full multivariate models with controls for other variables known to affect gubernatorial elections, such as economic conditions and partisanship.

Another problem that must be addressed is that the impact of the abortion issue on electoral outcomes is likely to be conditional. The extent

154

to which abortion attitudes are influential is likely to vary not only across elections, but also across groups within the context of any given election. Dodson and Burnbauer (1990a) suggest that attitudes toward abortion are more likely to influence vote choice in elections where candidates differ sharply on the issue and where events occur that increase public interest in the matter. Furthermore, their findings indicate that certain groups are more likely than others to attach importance to the abortion issue. Specifically, women, respondents with a college education, and pro-lifers who frequently attend church were more likely than their counterparts to see the abortion issue as important with regard to the gubernatorial races studied.

Previous research indicates yet another reason why models specifying a linear relationship between abortion attitudes and vote might be inadequate. It has been shown that opinions on the pro-life side are more intense and therefore more likely to impact other political preferences (Schuman and Presser 1981). If this is the case, the slope describing the relationship to a dependent variable will change depending on the category of the abortion attitudes variable, thus creating a curvilinear shape. Research must separate the effects (slopes) of the two ends of the abortion issue.

This research continues state-centered abortion research by placing the abortion issue within a multivariate model of gubernatorial choice. The nonlinear, conditional nature of the influence of abortion attitudes is tested by examining a multivariate model with relevant interaction terms.

The 1991 Louisiana governor's race serves as the setting of the research. During the 1990 and 1991 state legislative sessions two antiabortion bills were passed that would have given Louisiana one of the most restrictive abortion regulations in the United States and Western Europe. Governor Roemer vetoed all of these bills, to the dismay of pro-life advocates, while at the same time voicing his personal opposition to abortion. The 1991 veto was overridden by the state legislature, mobilizing the pro-choice forces to support the incumbent governor in the upcoming election. As yet we do not know if or how abortion attitudes affected voter choice for governor; however, the high visibility of the stringent abortion bills and their vetoes make Louisiana an appropriate setting for the study of abortion effects. If we are unable to detect abortion effects under these circumstances, they may not show up in less dramatic cases.

The Data and Model

This research utilizes two telephone surveys of registered voters in Louisiana, conducted in September 1990 and in September 1991 by the University of New Orleans Survey Research Center. Both surveys were conducted shortly after the abortion battles in the legislature, and the second survey preceded the governor's election by only 4 weeks. (Details on the surveys are in the Appendix to this chapter). The two surveys provide a more reliable estimate of abortion effects than a single cross-section.

Opinion on abortion was measured in both surveys by the Center for Political Studies/American National Election Study question about whether abortions should be legal under any circumstances, some circumstances, or no circumstances. Our dependent variable is whether or not the respondent would vote for the incumbent governor if the election were held today.

The analysis begins with a simple bivariate look at abortion opinion and vote for governor in both years, then proceeds to a multivariate model of vote for governor that includes several other explanatory variables. Opinion on abortion must have independent effects in the model for us to conclude that it affects vote for governor. Elections for governor have been shown to be affected by party ID (Jewell and Olson 1987; Piereson 1977); and the economic condition of the state, with economic downturns working against incumbents (Howell and Vanderleeuw 1990). A third control variable is trust in government, which national research has demonstrated to be related to approval of the incumbent president (Citrin 1974). We suspect that trust in state government affects state executives in the same manner. We also control for racial attitudes, which are always important in Louisiana elections and are particularly important in the governor's race due to the candidacy of David Duke. Education is introduced because of the high level of support for the incumbent governor among educated white voters. This list of control variables is not exhaustive of determinants of support. Missing are judgments about the governor's leadership qualities and other image variables. The models should be viewed with this limitation in mind.

The analysis includes only whites on the recommendation of other researchers who have studied New Christian Right issues (Brudney and Copeland 1984; Miller and Wattenberg 1984; Wald and Lupfer 1983). Many blacks hold pro-life sentiments, yet are very liberal on other political issues. Their racial identity is a far better predictor of their political behavior than is their religious conservatism. Consistent with this argument, blacks in Louisiana have the lowest approval ratings of this governor for reasons other than abortion (Schuler 1990). Their inclusion would unnecessarily confound the results.

Abortion Attitudes and Vote for Governor

At the bivariate level, opinion on abortion is associated with vote for governor in both 1990 and 1991 (Table 9.1). Pro-life respondents are

Table 9.1 Abortion and Vote for Governor in Louisiana, 1990, 1991 (Whites Only)

Opinion on Abortion[a]	Percentage Saying They Would Vote for Incumbent Governor	
	1990	1991
Never Legal	18	27
Certain Circumstances	40	35
Always Legal	36	43
Gamma	.21*	.21*
Tau β	.10*	.13*

NOTE: a. Do you think abortions should be legal under any circumstance, legal under only certain circumstances, or never legal under any circumstance?
* Indicates statistical significance at .05 level

considerably less likely than pro-choice respondents to report an intention to vote for the incumbent, who vetoed the strict abortion bills. The curvilinear relationship is apparent in 1990. A sharp decline in support for the governor occurs between the middle category and the pro-life category but not between the pro-choice and the middle category. However, in 1991 the relationship becomes linear with a steady decline in support for the governor as one becomes more pro-life. The increased linearity is a function of pro-choice activists mobilizing for the incumbent that counterbalanced the already active pro-life forces.

Multivariate Analysis

In order to estimate the independent effects of opinion on abortion, we specified a model with seven other independent variables: party identification, education, gender, religion, evaluations of the Louisiana economy, racism, and trust in state government. To test for nonlinear effects of abortion attitudes, two dummy variables are created from the ordinal abortion variable, one representing pro-life responses and one representing pro-choice responses.

The model is also tested while introducing hypothesized interaction effects between opinion on abortion and three demographics: religion, gender, and education. Specifically, we suspect that abortion attitudes have a greater impact on the vote preferences of fundamentalist Protestants, due to religious beliefs; and on women, due to being directly affected. Abortion attitudes may also have greater effects among educated

voters, because they are typically more politically aware and would have
more information about events in the legislature.

Our major concern is to discover whether, and under what circumstances, attitudes on abortion exert a significant independent influence on
the vote and the relative magnitude of that influence. Table 9.2 presents
logistic regression coefficients for additive and interactive models of
choice for governor in both surveys. Goodness-of-fit chi-square statistics
and related significance levels indicate that the models tested do not differ
significantly from "perfectly" fitting models (Norusis 1990). The logistic
coefficients indicate that, ceteris paribus, abortion attitudes are influential,
though their influence varies across elections. In the additive model for
1990, pro-life respondents were significantly less likely than persons with
middle-of-the-road abortion attitudes to support the incumbent. The incumbent's veto of a strict antiabortion bill was apparently sufficient to
alienate pro-life advocates in 1990. That same year, however, support
among pro-choice respondents was not significantly different than that of
others. A different situation developed in 1991. The incumbent's second
veto of antiabortion legislation was overridden by the legislature, thus
mobilizing pro-choice respondents. As a result, the pro-choice position
had a positive, significant effect on preference.

To test the hypotheses about interaction effects, explicit interaction
terms were added to the models. For the sake of brevity, insignificant
independent variables are omitted from the interactive models. One exception is the inclusion of the pro-life term in 1991, which is necessary for
proper specification of the interactive model. The "improvement" chi-
square statistic and related significance level is comparable to the *F*-
change test in multiple regression (Norusis 1990) and indicates that the
interaction term significantly improves the fit of the model.

In both years, these models indicate that, as hypothesized, Protestants
(who in Louisiana are primarily fundamentalist) are more likely than
others to take their abortion attitudes into consideration in making their
vote decision. Contrary to the hypothesis, this did not hold true for either
women or persons of high education. The institutional environment of the
Protestant (fundamentalist) churches and the association of pro-life positions with these churches appear to raise the salience of the abortion issue
for these respondents. It should be noted that an examination of the
bivariate relationship between the interactive term and its constituent
elements disclosed no multicollinearity problem; all relevant correlation
coefficients were less than .7.

Examining the model using both the 1990 and 1991 data allows us to
investigate the relative influence of abortion attitudes across electoral
contexts. Although both surveys examined preferences for governor, the

Table 9.2 Multivariate Model of Vote for Incumbent Louisiana Governor: Logistic
Regression

Y = Support	1990		1991	
for Incumbent	Additive	Interactive	Additive	Interactive
Life	−1.0315*	−.2967	−.3718	.2775
	(.2989)	(.3858)	(.2743)	(.3690)
Choice	−.4020	—	.5265*	.4645*
	(.2452)		(.2324)	(.2292)
Protestant	.6221*	.7765*	−.0148	.2220
	(.2009)	(.2130)	(.1977)	(.2143)
Education	.2726*	.2734*	.1864*	.1714*
	(.0858)	(.0813)	(.0875)	(.0870)
Party I.D.	.0526	—	.1445*	.1431*
	(.0587)		(.0597)	(.0594)
Trust in Govt.	−.3187*	−.3170*	−.1407	—
	(.0988)	(.0986)	(.1000)	
Racism	−.1949*	−.2086*	−.3768*	−.3718*
	(.1016)	(.1004)	(.1015)	(.1019)
LA Economy	−.3299*	−.3338*	−.3713*	−.3639*
	(.0954)	(.0956)	(.1151)	(.1137)
Gender	.0590	—	.3671	—
	(.1973)		(.1976)	
Life × Prot.	—	−1.2816*	—	−1.2571*
		(.5935)		(.5417)
Constant	−.9339*	−.9260*	−.5406	.4215
	(.4834)	(.4678)	(.5372)	(.5249)
Goodness-of-fit index (χ^2)	523.05	527.035	480.162	485.643
Significance (χ^2)	.4420	.4302	.3507	.2993
Improvement	—	4.807	—	5.554
Significance	—	.0283	—	.0184
N	529	530	479	479

NOTE: * Indicates statistical significance at the .05 level.
Standard errors are in parentheses.

field of candidates was somewhat different at the time of the 1991 survey.
Most notably, ex-Klansman David Duke had entered the list of candidates.
This appears to have increased the prominence of racial attitudes relative
to abortion attitudes in the latter survey. Judging by the ratio of the
coefficients to their standard errors (additive models), pro-life attitudes
were the most important predictor of vote in the 1990 model, whereas
racial attitudes just barely reached statistical significance. In 1991, however, the ratio of coefficient to standard error for the racial attitudes

Table 9.3 Probabilities of Supporting Incumbent Governor

	1990	*1991*
Additive Model:		
If Neutral on Abortion	.395	.424
If Pro-Life	.189	.337
If Pro-Choice	.304	.525
If Protestant	.404	.441
If Catholic	.267	.445
Interactive Model:		
If Life & Protestant	.151	.238
If Life & Catholic	.227	.468
Comparative Probabilities		
Life/Neutral	−.206*	−.087
Choice/Neutral	−.091	.101*
Life & Prot/Prot	−.253*	−.203*
Life & Cath/Cath	−.040	.023

NOTE: * Differences significant at the .05 level. Probabilities are computed using the logistic regression equations from Table 9.2 and setting control variables at their means.

variable exceeds that for either the pro-choice or pro-life variables, and the pro-life variable fails even to achieve significance.

Although the logistic regression coefficients help us determine the significance of abortion attitudes on vote choice, we can get a clearer picture of the magnitude of these effects by examining the probability of voting for the incumbent among respondents who share relevant attitudes and characteristics (Table 9.3).

The most revealing results in Table 9.3 are the comparative probabilities. In 1990, for example, we can see that, with other factors controlled, holding a pro-life position, as opposed to being neutral on the abortion issue, reduces the probability of supporting the incumbent by nearly 21%. The reduction for those taking the pro-choice side is only 9% and statistically insignificant. As indicated above, the direction of the abortion-vote relationship changes in 1991, and in that year, holding a pro-choice position increases the probability of support for the incumbent 10% above that of those holding neutral positions. The pro-life influence is still negative, but much smaller than it was in the previous year. The reduced overall influence of abortion attitudes in 1991 clearly reflects the intrusion of racial attitudes in that year.

The conditional nature of the abortion-vote relationship is also indicated quite clearly in the contrast between the candidate preferences of Protestants and Catholics once the pro-life condition is entered into the equation. In 1990 the probability of support for the incumbent among Protestants, holding abortion attitudes and other factors constant, was 40%; the probability among Catholics was 27%. When the additional condition of pro-life attitudes is included, the probability among Protestants tumbles 25%, while it remains essentially unchanged for Catholics. The situation is similar for 1991 as well. This illustrates more graphically the earlier finding that Protestants were much more likely than Catholics to consider their abortion attitudes in making their candidate choice. Because pro-life attitudes worked to the detriment of the incumbent, he suffered most among those who were most likely to give consideration to those attitudes.

Conclusion

The major question addressed in this research was whether or not the abortion issue influences elections at the subnational level. Our findings indicate, as expected, that the answer depends on specific electoral and other contextual circumstances.

First, it is clear that effects of abortion attitudes are conditioned by religion. In our study, the influence of abortion attitudes on electoral choice was greater for Protestants than for Catholics. Although not directly tested, it would seem reasonable that Protestants, especially fundamentalists, might hold more intense abortion attitudes than others.

In addition, whether the pro-choice or the pro-life side of the abortion debate is currently "losing" has implications as well. Those most threatened seem more likely to take their abortion attitudes into account in making their vote decision, as indicated by the increased impact of the pro-choice position in 1991.

Finally, it is evident that election-specific circumstances also influence the extent to which abortion attitudes affect the vote. In the Louisiana case, when the field of candidates changed, the attitudes that influenced vote changed as well. When David Duke, a racially divisive candidate, became prominent among the gubernatorial contenders, abortion attitudes were subordinated to racial attitudes in terms of relative importance. It seems that candidates must not only take contrasting stands on the issue for abortion attitudes to become important, but other, more deeply held attitudes must remain in the background.

The impact of the abortion issue on elections was described at the outset as elusive. This elusiveness seems to reflect the high degree of specificity of the circumstances under which its impact is likely to be felt.

APPENDIX

Survey Design

The 1990 and 1991 Louisiana surveys were based on systematic random samples, one black and one white for each survey, drawn from a machine readable list of all registered voters in the state with listed phone numbers. We generated 10 times as many voters as the desired number of completed interviews to allow for refusals and difficulties with the phone numbers.

Interviewers were students at the University of New Orleans who were paid and trained by the Survey Research Center. The interviews were conducted from a central phone bank with constant supervision by graduate students in political science. We matched all respondents and interviewers with respect to race.

Interviewers had lists of sample names (10) with addresses and phone numbers. They were instructed to make two attempts to reach the first person before moving on to the next. Nonresponse (refusals, no answers, wrong numbers, and disconnected numbers) was 56% in the 1990 survey and 42% in 1991. The final ns for the white samples were 639 and 541. Sampling error in the white samples on a bivariate variable with 50% "yes" answers is 3.8% and 4.1% at the 95% confidence level. Specific question wording is available from the authors upon request.

PART III

STATE ABORTION
POLICY AND POLITICS

A s the Introduction and many of the chapters in this volume have
already demonstrated, *Webster* and *Casey* have invited increased
state legislative action on abortion access. In recognition of the shifting
political landscape that accompanied these two Supreme Court decisions,
the focus in Part III shifts to abortion politics and policy in the states.
According to many observers, it will be in state legislatures, state governors' offices, and in statewide elections that protagonists will fight new
battles over just how restrictive abortion laws and regulations will be.
Many of the chapters in this section describe and explain the parameters
of the debate over abortion policy in the states. Some chapters take a stab
at predicting the future.

Glen A. Halva-Neubauer's chapter is perhaps the most historical of
those in this volume. In Chapter 10, Halva-Neubauer adds an important
corrective to the emphasis on political bargaining in the *post-Webster*
period: Contrary to popular opinion, states played a significant role in
abortion policy making after the U.S. Supreme Court's 1973 *Roe* decision.
Rather than being inert bodies, state legislatures debated a wide array of
abortion restrictions and regulations between 1973 and 1989. Furthermore, they developed distinctive policy-making approaches. Fetal-rights

groups found state legislatures to be especially receptive to their demands. As a result, state legislatures assisted in expanding the scope of conflict and in keeping the issue on the national political agenda. Halva-Neubauer predicts that in light of *Casey* and President Clinton's 1992 election victory, state legislatures are likely to take on an even more important role in making abortion policy, because those controlling the policy agenda in Washington, DC, are hostile to the demands of the fetal-rights movement.

The second chapter in this section examines theories of representation by analyzing the relationships among the absolute and relative abortion preferences of state "publics" and state abortion policy. Using *CBS/New York Times* November 1990 exit poll data in 42 states, a 1989 *CBS/New York Times* time series, and an updated version of the Halva-Neubauer index that is discussed in Chapter 10, Christopher Wlezien and I show that state "publics" are attentive and responsive to the policy choices of state policymakers, and adjust their abortion preferences as a result of what these elected and appointed officials do. Our collaborative research shows that, with respect to abortion policy, state publics effectively behave like thermostats: In those states in which abortion policy is more (less) restrictive than the public wants, the public generally is less (more) supportive of further restrictions on the availability of abortion.

In Chapter 12, Jeffrey E. Cohen and Charles Barrilleaux compare the relative influence of public opinion and interest groups on state legislative action in the abortion issue. Using November 1990 *Washington Post* exit polls that were conducted in 41 states, Cohen and Barrilleaux construct direct measures of state-level public opinion toward abortion policy. They find that both public opinion and interest groups significantly affect state legislative abortion policy making, but that interest groups are slightly advantaged. Large public majorities in support of abortion rights are required to overcome a well-organized opposition interest group. The authors then use these results to simulate expected state action on abortion. Their simulation predicts that few states will outlaw abortion. This comes from the fact that the public opinion leans in an abortion-rights direction, but the interest group environment is often composed of competing interests, which have the effect of canceling each other out.

Susan B. Hansen's chapter examines a number of alternative explanations for state restrictions on access to abortion that states have imposed since 1973. Her research shows that religion, the proportion of hospital providers, and a history of policy liberalism or previous abortion restriction all predict recent state policies affecting women. Hansen also concludes that, on average, the states with the least restrictive abortion laws tend to have a higher percentages of women elected to the state legislature.

Abortion rates, however, reflect the availability of services in urban areas rather than funding cutoffs, legal restrictions, or levels of clinic violence.

In Chapter 14, Kenneth J. Meier and Deborah R. McFarlane examine the politics of funding abortions for low-income women in the American states in the years 1985, 1987, and 1990. Their data analysis shows that state policies on abortion funding reflected the relative strength of citizen groups on both sides of the issue and an array of partisan forces. By 1990 a four-variable model could correctly predict the abortion funding policy of 49 of the 50 states. After policy adoption, the number of government-funded abortions was determined by public policy and the relative demand for abortion services. Politics played only a secondary role in determining the number of abortions actually funded by the state.

The impact of women state legislators on state abortion policies is assessed in Chapter 15. In this chapter, Michael B. Berkman and Robert E. O'Connor identify two dimensions of state abortion policy. Their analysis of the data shows that women state legislators, once they reach a critical mass within the legislature, can affect state policies on regulations concerning parental notification of abortions, but not public funding. But women legislators, and especially women Democratic legislators, can affect state abortion policies in other ways that are less well understood. Through an analysis of post-*Webster* abortion bills the authors find that women representatives secure committee assignments that allow them to block pro-life legislation. This is especially pronounced in states with few women legislators and states most likely to support policies restricting choice.

10

The States After *Roe*

No *"Paper Tigers"*

GLEN A. HALVA-NEUBAUER

The sweeping nature of the U.S. Supreme Court's 1973 *Roe v. Wade* (410 U.S. 113 [1973]) ruling led journalists and scholars alike to conclude that states were inert policy-making entities at worst or largely inconsequential at best. Even though early scholars of abortion politics (Conover and Gray 1983; Rubin 1987; Tatalovich and Daynes 1981) acknowledged the role that state legislatures play in abortion policy making, subnational jurisdictions are not the primary focus of their work. The 1989 *Webster v. Reproductive Health Services* (492 U.S. 490 [1989]) ruling, in which the U.S. Supreme Court declared its willingness to give states greater authority to regulate abortion, spawned an interest in state abortion policy. Despite the conventional wisdom fashioned in light of *Webster,* state legislators played a significant role in making abortion policy throughout the post-*Roe* period (1973-1989). State lawmakers did not suddenly awake from a 16-year slumber to discover abortion policy in light of *Webster*—they had debated such policies since *Roe.*

To fruitfully analyze state-level abortion politics from 1973-1989, the following strategy is adopted. First, I chart significant legislative enactments, ballot initiatives, and state court decisions during this time. Second, interstate variations in abortion policies are summarized; a typology of post-*Roe* abortion policy-making approaches in the states also is presented. Section three employs the works of Baumgartner and Jones (1991) and Goggin (1993) to illustrate the importance of state legislatures in providing an institutional venue sympathetic to antiabortion partisans, expanding the scope of conflict, and promoting a pluralistic institutional context. Finally, I discuss state-level abortion activity since *Webster* and

167

speculate on the role states may play in abortion policy making in light of *Planned Parenthood of Southeastern Pennsylvania v. Casey* (112 S.Ct. 2791 [1992]) and the election of President Clinton.

State Abortion Policy, 1973-1989

In this section, I identify the major policy initiatives undertaken at the state level during the post-*Roe* period. Rather than treating the 16 years between *Roe* and *Webster* as a single unit, I follow Staggenborg's (1991) demarcation of the era into three phases: 1973-1976; 1977-1983; and 1984-1989. An examination of both the changing substance and the ebb and flow of abortion legislation, ballot initiatives, and state court decisions by era illustrates the continuities and changes in state-level abortion policy making better than an overview of the post-*Roe* period. Furthermore, dividing the 1973-1989 period into distinct phases highlights the changing scope and nature of the abortion conflict.

1973-1976: Limiting the Effect of *Roe*

In response to *Roe,* an avalanche of legislation restricting abortion was introduced. The bulk of these bills stringently regulated the abortion procedure, thus curbing the effect of the Supreme Court's decision to the greatest possible degree. While state legislators knew they could not proscribe abortion, they were uncertain of the precise parameters of permissible state regulation; hence, state lawmakers debated whether a particular bill could withstand constitutional scrutiny. Because *Roe's* jurisprudence offered little guidance, legislators were willing to enact laws that interpreted the decision narrowly, such as parental and spousal consent. Consequently, during the first 3 years following *Roe,* more state legislatures discussed the practice than in any other time during the post-*Roe* period. Moreover, pro-life activists formulated proposals and lobbied for legislation that regulated the procedure in the most restrictive manner. The broad-based attack on *Roe* also allowed antiabortion activists to define the issue as one pitting the rights of the fetus against those of the woman.

The Alan Guttmacher Institute grouped early abortion restrictions into five general categories: performance requirements; consent requirements; reporting and record-keeping regulations; conscience clauses; and provisions protecting the fetus (Alan Guttmacher Institute, 1974:88). Performance regulations defined by whom and under what conditions abortions could be performed, whereas consent laws required that women be given information about the procedure or secure permission of a third party, such as a parent or spouse. Reporting and recordkeeping mandates dictated that physicians keep detailed records on the abortions they performed and report this information to a state health agency. Among the most popular restrictions were "conscience clauses," which shielded physicians (and other health care providers) and/or hospitals from lawsuits if either refused to perform an abortion or allow its facilities to be used for abortions. To protect fetuses, states passed laws requiring physicians to save a viable fetus when possible and declare a live-born aborted child a ward of the state. In addition, legislators adopted resolutions asking Congress to send a human life amendment to the states.

A wide-ranging discussion of abortion regulations characterized the first 3 years of the post-*Roe* era. Until these laws were challenged in federal court and found unconstitutional, many state legislatures entertained discussions on an array of abortion restrictions. But as lower federal courts nullified early legislative responses to *Roe,* state lawmakers became more cautious about entering the abortion thicket. In its 1976 *Planned Parenthood of Central Missouri v. Danforth* (428 U.S. 52 [1976]) holding, the U.S. Supreme Court signaled the end to the first era of the post-*Roe* period. By striking down Missouri's parental and spousal consent requirements as well as its ban on saline abortions, while upholding relatively benign informed consent and recordkeeping requirements, the Court severely curbed the scope of the abortion debate. After 1976, fewer states would be actively involved in a broad-based assault on *Roe*. The nature of the conflict also would change: No longer would the debate center so directly on the rights of the fetus versus those of the woman, but on issues further removed from the core of the abortion controversy.

1977-1983: The Narrowing of
State Legislative Abortion Discussions

Between 1977 and 1983 the scope of state legislative abortion discussions narrowed, focusing on public funding in particular. In 1976, Congress approved the Hyde amendment, which cut off federal Medicaid monies for abortion except when the mother's life was endangered. During the summer of 1977, the U.S. Supreme Court held that states were not required to fund nontherapeutic abortions in *Maher v. Roe* (432 U.S. 464 [1977]) and *Beal v. Doe* (432 U.S. 438 [1977]). The Hyde amendment, coupled with the Court's 1977 funding decisions, set off a firestorm of activity. Although public funding was a much narrower issue than most of those discussed in the first period, the subject evolved into an explosive debate in several state legislatures, following much the same course as it did in Congress during the late 1970s. In Michigan, Illinois, and Massachusetts, for instance, public funding pitted pro-life legislatures against pro-choice governors, paralyzing government in Lansing and Boston (Nicholson and Stewart 1978).

Public funding battles were not the sole domain of state legislatures and the federal courts. Pro-choice organizations in Massachusetts turned to state courts, where they successfully forced the Bay State to fund abortions (*Moe v. Secretary of Administration and Finance,* 417 N.E.2d 387 [1981]). Similar rulings were made by state supreme courts in New Jersey and California. Antiabortion partisans traveled the initiative and referendum route to stop public funding. In 1978, Oregon voters rejected attempts to halt public funding; Alaska voters followed suit in 1982. Nevertheless, these defeats did not deter antiabortion organizations from employing ballot measures to limit abortion access.

The *Danforth* ruling provided the impetus for the era's other two major legislative initiatives. First, antiabortion lobbyists urged state lawmakers to consider parental involvement legislation; the Court's abortion holdings, including *Danforth,* were vague on the subject and, hence, elicited continued attempts to legislate in the area. However, efforts stalled in 1979 when the Court invalidated Massachusetts's parental consent statute allowing a minor to obtain a court order for an abortion if her parents refused to consent (*Bellotti v. Baird,* 443 U.S. 622 [1979]). In the aftermath of *Bellotti,* only those legislatures firmly committed to overturning *Roe* seriously considered parental consent legislation. Such was the case with Minnesota, where antiabortion supporters enacted a parental notification, rather than consent, law. Second, antiabortion partisans examined ways to strengthen informed consent requirements in light of *Danforth.* Several legislatures enacted informed consent laws requiring that women be given detailed information on fetal development prior to an abortion. In 1983, the U.S. Supreme Court ruled that detailed informed consent laws were unconstitutional (*Akron v. Akron Center for Reproductive Health,* 462 U.S. 416 [1983]).

Soon after *Roe,* state legislatures began calling for an Article V constitutional convention (Con-Con). The momentum for this activity, however, began in earnest during the mid-1970s, after congressional efforts to propose a constitutional amendment failed. Changing political fortunes brought about by the 1980 elections gave antiabortion partisans new hope that Congress would propose a human life amendment, thus quelling the Con-Con effort. Nineteen states called for a constitutional convention, none after 1980.

With the exception of Con-Con, direct efforts to restrict abortion were abandoned between 1977 and 1983. By concentrating on ancillary issues, the abortion conflict was transformed into questions more easily debated by state lawmakers: Was it fair to exclude public funding for abortions for the indigent? What interest did the state have in promoting family communication through parental involvement laws? What information should physicians be required to provide a woman prior to undergoing an abortion? Whereas state legislators were the principal abortion policymakers between 1973 and 1976, state judges, welfare department bureaucrats, and the electorate (through the initiative and referendum process) became more involved in setting abortion policy after 1977. Consequently, even as the abortion debate focused on narrower issues, the number of participants involved in the conflict increased.

1984-1989: Keeping the Abortion Issue Alive

The summer of 1983 brought the defeat of the human life amendment in the U.S. Senate and the Supreme Court's reaffirmation of *Roe* in its *Akron* holding. The antiabortion movement was in disarray following these losses, while a complacency associated with victory settled in among pro-choice activists (Staggenborg 1991:125-27). Yet, the abortion issue was not dead in state capitals. No uniform agenda, however, dominated state-level abortion politics during this period.

In states that had paid little attention to the issue, such as Virginia, Georgia, and Alabama, antiabortion supporters lobbied for parental involvement laws. These bills enjoyed overwhelming support in public opinion polls; in addition, the Court found Missouri's parental consent law constitutional in 1983 (*Planned Parenthood Association of Kansas City v. Ashcroft*, 462 U.S. 476 [1983]). This restriction was defined by antiabortion supporters as parental rights legislation, not an abortion regulation. Mississippi and Alabama enacted parental consent laws in the mid-1980s—the first substantive abortion restrictions passed in either state since *Roe*.

In many states providing public monies for abortion, heated debate over that policy continued. Legislators in California, Maryland, North Carolina, and New York grappled with this issue repeatedly. The most protracted legislative debate occurred in Michigan. After failing to override 17 gubernatorial vetoes, Michigan Right-to-Life successfully organized an initiative severely limiting abortion funding. Ballot box measures halting public funding also passed in Arkansas and Colorado, but failed in Washington, Massachusetts, Rhode Island, and Oregon. State court litigation also continued, with courts in Vermont and Connecticut ordering funding, while the Pennsylvania Supreme Court refused.

In states where parental involvement and public funding debates were dim memories, a different set of policies was addressed, such as legislation requiring sanitary and humane disposal of fetuses, fetal pain bills, and prohibitions on gender-selection abortions. States also considered forbidding wrongful life/wrongful birth suits and creating the crime of feticide. In Minnesota and Illinois these issues kept the abortion controversy before state legislatures, albeit indirectly. Finally, in states most committed to *Roe's* demise, legislatures discussed sophisticated bills to undermine the ruling: Pennsylvania, Missouri, North Dakota, and Idaho fall into this classification.

Pro-choice forces also assisted in keeping the issue alive by going on the offensive for the first time. Their legislative initiatives included proposals to outlaw harassment of those seeking and performing abortions, resolutions condemning clinic violence, and legislation designed to regulate antiabortion pregnancy counseling centers. New Hampshire lawmakers went even further by decriminalizing abortion, thus guaranteeing access to abortion regardless of future Supreme Court rulings, but the bill was vetoed.

Definitions employed during the 1984-1989 period moved the abortion debate further from the core issue. Parental involvement became defined as a parental-rights issue, not one that would reduce abortions. Ancillary issues of wrongful life/wrongful birth and feticide involved discussions of tort and criminal law far removed from the legality of abortion. Attaching abortion to these discussions, however, allowed antiabortion organizations to remind legislators that they remained opposed to legalized abortion. Meanwhile, pro-choice partisans attempted to define pro-life activists as trespassers who would stop at nothing to achieve their aims. Such a definition distanced pro-choice activists from portraying abortion as an issue of a woman's reproductive autonomy. And yet this new definition likely was a catalyst for legislative discussion.

Interstate Variations in Post-*Roe* Policy-Making Approaches

While states actively considered abortion legislation throughout the post-*Roe* period, variations existed in their approach to abortion policy making. In earlier work (Halva-Neubauer 1990), I categorized states by their policy-making approaches—challenger, codifier, acquiescer, or supporter—based on the number of restrictions each passed between 1973 and mid-1989 (prior to the *Webster* decision). This information is contained in Table 10.1. Challengers demonstrated the greatest hostility toward *Roe,* passing numerous constitutionally questionable statutes; codifiers were willing to pass restrictions deemed constitutional by the U.S. Supreme Court; acquiescers largely ignored the issue or engaged in a debate on a

Table 10.1 Post-*Roe* Policy-Making Approaches, 1973-1989

Challengers	Codifiers	Acquiescers	Supporters
Idaho (10)[a]	Arizona (8)	Alabama (2)	Alaska (0)
Illinois (15)	California (5)	Arkansas (4)	Colorado (1)
Indiana (9)	Florida (8)	Delaware (4)	Connecticut (0)
Kentucky (13)	Georgia (8)	Iowa (4)	Hawaii (1)
Louisiana (12)	Maine (6)	Maryland (4)	Kansas (1)
Massachusetts (11)	Montana (7)	Michigan (3)	New Hampshire (1)
Minnesota (11)	Ohio (5)	Mississippi (3)	Oregon (0)
Missouri (13)	Oklahoma (7)	New Jersey (4)	Vermont (1)
Nebraska (9)	South Dakota (8)	New Mexico (3)	Washington (1)
Nevada (9)	Virginia (5)	New York (3)	
North Dakota (16)	Wisconsin (5)	North Carolina (3)	
Pennsylvania (14)	Wyoming (7)	South Carolina (2)	
Rhode Island (9)		Texas (3)	
Tennessee (11)		West Virginia (2)	
Utah (14)			

SOURCE: Reprinted with permission from Glen A. Halva-Neubauer. 1990. Abortion policymaking in the post-Webster age. *Publius: The Journal of Federalism* 20:32.
NOTE: a. Numbers in parentheses represent enactments. Hence, the chart does not reflect abortion battles below the enactment stage such as close defeats, tabled bills, sustained vetoes, and so on.

limited scope of abortion restrictions; supporters embraced *Roe* and did little to disturb the abortion status quo. Readers interested in the specific policies passed by a particular state as well as a detailed explanation of post-*Roe* abortion policies should refer to the Appendix to this chapter.

The Halva-Neubauer typology illustrates how states began to institutionalize their approach to abortion policy making after 1973. Not all provided hospitable ground for launching antiabortion initiatives. When the Supreme Court invalidated abortion restrictions, challenger states responded by enacting new statutes or variations on previous regulations that stretched the latest ruling as far as possible. Hence, as the post-*Roe* period progressed, efforts to overturn *Roe* centered on these states. States employing other policy-making approaches were less enthusiastic than their challenger counterparts to enter the abortion fray after the Supreme Court had made its pronouncement on a particular abortion restriction. This was especially true with acquiescer and supporter states. Codifier and acquiescer legislatures battled over parental involvement legislation, whereas the antiabortion agenda focused on eliminating public funding in supporter states.

Although the Court may have envisioned a nationalized abortion policy in light of *Roe,* the data show that, over time, states took several approaches to making abortion policy. Utah lawmakers continued to write abortion restrictions, while Washington legislators rarely discussed abortion—preferring to keep its liberal policy intact (even when the Supreme Court deemed more conservative statutes constitutional). Other states were neither openly hostile nor supportive, assuming a cautious approach to post-*Roe* abortion policy making. Adopting distinctive approaches during a period in which states were thought to be largely inconsequential policy-making actors adds further credence to the chapter's thesis: States were no "paper tigers," but played significant roles in determining abortion policy. In the next section of this chapter, I explore why states played an important part in abortion policy making after 1973.

The Role of States in Abortion Policy Making

An examination of post-*Roe* debates at the state level also expands our understanding of abortion policy making. In this section, I employ two works to assess the importance of states in the larger abortion policy-making framework. Baumgartner and Jones (1991) write of the significance of institutional venues in developing alternative definitions of public policies, while Goggin (1993) analyzes abortion in terms of the nature and scope of conflict and its institutional context.

Seeking Hospitable Ground: States and the Antiabortion Agenda

Baumgartner and Jones (1991) found that the subgovernment dominating the nuclear power policy agenda collapsed in the 1970s due to the negative image of the nuclear power industry. This image was created in large part by those locked out of the subgovernment who took their case to government institutions more sympathetic to their cause. Although nuclear power policy differs markedly from abortion policy, Baumgartner and Jones contend that losers in a policy debate often seek more hospitable ground (different institutional venues). By gaining a foothold in these institutional venues, losers can help create a negative image of the policy status quo.

State legislatures provided hospitable terrains for the antiabortion movement when other institutional venues were closed, particularly Congress and the federal courts. Over time, the changing composition of federal courts and the receptivity of Congress to abortion restrictions became more pronounced. Indeed, the least antiabortion activity in state legislatures occurred in 1983 when the human life amendment reached its apogee in Congress. Nevertheless, neither the Congress nor the Supreme Court has been willing to grant the antiabortion movement either of its goals: sending a human life amendment to the states or reversing *Roe*. As a result, state legislatures—particularly in challenger states—played a critical role in giving voice to those arguing against the abortion status quo.

By gaining access to state legislatures, antiabortion activists were able to keep negative issue definitions before the public. For instance, if abortion is permissible, why does the state not fund it like other medical procedures (O'Steen and St. Martin 1985)? Continued discussion of abortion regulations assisted in painting the Supreme Court's position on abortion as one view, rather than the law of the land. Through parental involvement and informed consent legislation, pro-life supporters attempted to portray pro-choice organizations as supporters of unfettered abortion—groups who would exclude parents from the abortion decisions of their minor daughters and prevent information about abortion from being given to a woman prior to undergoing the procedure. By creating a more negative image of abortion, more state legislatures (as well as other governmental institutions) became involved in the discussion, especially in the public funding and parental involvement areas.

The Scope of the State-Level Abortion Conflict

Goggin (1992, 1993:13-14) considers the scope of conflict a useful concept in analyzing abortion politics. Essentially, losers in a policy debate seek to expand the scope of conflict, while winners try to limit discussion to its current participants. Goggin's framework shows that winners and losers are dictated by interventions that fundamentally change abortion policy. Among the most important are U.S. Supreme Court decisions that modify past policy. While Goggin notes the gravity of landmark decisions such as *Roe* and *Webster* in significantly changing which side is winning the abortion war, other decisions (including those made in Congress) also alter the balance of power.

Goggin's framework assists in understanding the pattern of state legislative activity following *Roe*. Decisions made by Congress and the Supreme Court opened and closed doors to the discussion of abortion and also dictated the specific subjects that would gain attention. Following *Roe*, pro-life groups mobilized and zealously pressed their agenda in state capitals, while pro-choice organizations were less successful in mobilizing their faithful, despite warnings that *Roe* was not the final victory (National Association for Repeal of Abortion Laws 1973).

In the mid-1970s, the contours of the abortion debate were reshaped due to the Hyde amendment and the Supreme Court's decision in the Connecticut and Pennsylvania funding cases (Staggenborg 1991:81-83). Both events represented important political successes for the antiabortion movement and led to the first substantial post-*Roe* mobilization of abortion-rights supporters. The mobilization following Hyde resulted in heated debates in state legislatures, protracted litigation in federal and state courts, and a plethora of ballot questions on public funding. While Hyde was a pro-life victory, *Danforth* was a defeat. Resolute pro-life strategists, however, continued their efforts to pass laws involving parental involvement and informed consent statutes, both of which offered hope of being deemed constitutional.

A different pattern evolved after 1983—a year that witnessed two major blows to the pro-life movement—the defeat of the Hatch-Eagleton human life amendment in the U.S. Senate and the Supreme Court's ruling in *Akron.* After initial disarray, the pro-life movement remobilized; *Akron,* however, had significantly limited the options available to state legislatures. Hence, pro-life supporters lobbied for more novel abortion restrictions, such as wrongful life/wrongful birth, fetal disposal, and fetal pain. Challenger states, such as Pennsylvania and Missouri, were undaunted by *Akron* and continued to consider fine-tuned proposals that cut away at *Roe.* Antiabortion supporters, impatient with conventional political activity, turned to picketing clinics and tried to persuade women seeking abortions to reconsider their decision. The violent nature of some of this activity spawned a pro-choice offensive in state legislatures as evidenced by anti-harassment laws and resolutions condemning abortion clinic violence.

Throughout the period, the right-to-life movement relied on state legislatures to expand the scope of conflict by continually challenging *Roe.* Without the efforts of pro-life forces at the state level, little post-*Roe* litigation would have resulted, hence, effectively killing the issue in the federal courts. Although Congress was more favorable to the pro-life position than the federal courts, it was unwilling to abandon *Roe* by proposing the human life amendment. Furthermore, the only significant piece of federal legislation that resulted in a U.S. Supreme Court case was *Harris v. McRae* (448 U.S. 297 [1980]), which upheld the Hyde amendment. Moreover, not all states had to participate in this assault to expand the scope of conflict. Necessary elements included a state legislature willing to pass a new abortion regulation, an abortion-rights organization willing to challenge that law in federal court, and an attorney general willing to provide a serious defense of the law. Missouri and Pennsylvania usually met all three criteria.

The Nature of Abortion Conflict at the State Level

Post-*Roe* policy-making studies add to the continuing discussion of the nature of the abortion debate. While Goggin (1993:14-20) considers myriad conflicts surrounding the issue, the multiplicity of conflicts offers no good reason why state legislators continued to entertain such an emotional, no-win topic. When viewed from the perspective of interest group activists, abortion is a debate about motherhood, "choice" versus "life," or traditional versus secularist values. From a policymaker's stance, however, abortion is a matter of regulating a controversial medical procedure. State legislators are uniquely situated to discuss many regulatory aspects of abortion: parental involvement, public funding, informed consent, and the standard of care required for post-viability abortions. Continued discussion of the subject did not require an up-or-down decision on the procedure's legality, but the conditions under which it could be performed safely. When viewed as a debate over the regulation of a medical practice, continued discussion of abortion policy beyond 1973 is accounted for more easily.

Antiabortion organizations also prompted legislative debate by linking a growing number of societal conditions with abortion. Activists became skilled at turning the latest developments in neonatal technology into a case for more restrictions on post-viability abortions. Moreover, because only a handful of state legislatures gave serious consideration to outright bans on abortions prior to *Webster*, antiabortion activists also became adept at defining their initiatives as having little to do with abortion. For instance, parental involvement legislation was not an attempt to restrict abortion, but rather an issue of parental rights (i.e., permitting a minor to secure an abortion without parental permission undercut her parents and compromised family integrity). Likewise, informed consent was not designed to limit abortion, but to ensure that a woman be fully informed about the act's consequences. Anti-funding tax initiatives stressed that taxpayers should not have to pay for a procedure they found abhorrent. In each case, abortion was defined in a way that removed its moral dimensions from central consideration. Such definitions made abortion easier for policymakers to debate; as a result, the issue was kept before the legislature and the public. Rather than arguing for restrictions along religious or moral lines, antiabortion activists now term abortion regulations such as those above "reasonable" and "rational."

Institutional Context: The Case for Pluralism

Goggin (1993:20-21) argues that abortion politics is characterized by ideological, rather than pluralistic, bargaining. In other words, abortion interest groups, who view policy outcomes in zero-sum terms, are unwilling to compromise; however, compromise is a hallmark of pluralism. An examination of post-*Roe* state legislative debates suggests some modifications are necessary in Goggin's framework. Pro-life organizations compromised their principles as soon as they chose to support regulation of abortion. Indeed, an important debate raged among pro-life partisans in the early years following *Roe* that those truly committed to the pro-life movement would not support passage of the bulk of state regulatory laws (Moen 1974; Morriss 1974; Rice 1974). Nevertheless, those willing to accept half a loaf prevailed at the state level. Even in Pennsylvania, where the tradition for writing tough abortion laws is legendary, antiabortion lawmakers were willing to compromise (Halva-Neubauer 1992).

On the pro-choice side, Staggenborg (1991:110-22) shows that the movement was divided between groups committed to a single-issue focus and those who saw abortion as part of a larger set of reproductive rights and health issues. The manifestation of these differences was not felt as acutely on the state level, where the groups united to oppose abortion regulations. In 1989, pro-choice lobbyists in Maine worked to enact a parental involvement law that required either the consent of a minor's parent or counseling by a qualified individual. Rather than oppose this law, pro-choice groups chose to shape legislation into a more acceptable form.

Though it is unorthodox to write of compromise on abortion and view its interest group politics in pluralistic terms, state legislative discussions during the post-*Roe* period make the best case for this perspective. Interest group leaders were not inclined to compromise, but the options available to state legislators during the bulk of the post-*Roe* period did not augur well for purists. The alternatives most legislatures were willing to consider conformed closely to the parameters of the latest Supreme Court decision.

Abortion Policy Since 1989

In 1989 the U.S. Supreme Court issued its most significant abortion ruling since *Roe* when it upheld a set of Missouri restrictions on second-trimester abortions and the involvement of public employees and facilities in performing abortions. The *Webster* case led political pundits to predict an onslaught of new abortion restrictions (Church 1989). These predictions were not realized, however. In the 3 years following *Webster,* there has been much abortion talk but little state legislative action.

State Abortion Policy Following Webster

Table 10.2 shows the pattern of state legislative enactments and sustained gubernatorial vetoes since *Webster.* The 1989-1992 period spawned few new abortion restrictions. Rather, restrictions discussed throughout the post-*Roe* period were brought up for reconsideration. The centerpiece of the antiabortion movement's post-*Webster* strategy—banning birth control abortions—was new, however (Balch 1989). Birth control abortions are defined by antiabortion activists as all abortions except those necessary to save the mother's life, and in cases of rape, incest, and gross fetal abnormality. Because the majority of abortions are performed for other reasons, this legislation outlaws all but 10% of abortions. While public opinion polls show only 6% of Americans consider abortion an acceptable form of birth control, these surveys also reveal that 40% of Americans favor laws that restrict abortion solely to cases of rape and incest (Apple 1989). As the name implies, "ban abortion" goes further than birth control bills by prohibiting all abortions, except those necessary to save the mother's life. Only the territory of Guam enacted a "ban abortion" statute after *Webster.* The Guam law, which permits abortion only to save the mother's life or to prevent grave danger to her health, was struck down by the Ninth Circuit Court of Appeals; in December 1992, the U.S. Supreme Court let this decision stand (*Ada v. Guam Society of Obstetricians/Gynecologists,* 962 F.2d. 1366 [1992]).

The post-*Webster* period has witnessed the introduction of many more bills favored by abortion-rights proponents, including resolutions asking that RU-486 (the French abortion pill) be brought into the United States for testing, that states enact special penalties on those who harass abortion clinic workers and clients (in light of Operation Rescue), and that *Roe's* principles be codified into state law. Furthermore, abortion-rights lobbyists have continued the effort begun in Maine by writing alternatives into parental involvement legislation. South Carolina, Maryland, and Wisconsin have opted for these kinds of parental involvement laws.

Initiative and referendum, a regular feature of the 1973-1989 period, has been used frequently since *Webster.* Abortion-rights supporters were successful in Nevada, Maryland, and Washington in codifying *Roe* into state law. Oregon voters rejected two initiatives—one requiring parental notification, the other limiting abortions to cases of rape, incest, and life endangerment. In Michigan, the legislature overwhelmingly approved a parental consent initiative.

Finally, abortion legislation has been the subject of several gubernatorial vetoes. New Hampshire Governor Judd Gregg (R) has vetoed two abortion-rights bills since 1989, both of which were sustained. Three restrictive abortion bills were vetoed by Louisiana Governor Buddy Roemer (R), the last of which was overridden by legislators. Bills banning birth control abortions were vetoed by Governors George Sinner (D) of North Dakota and Cecil Andrus (D) of Idaho (for details of the Idaho case, see Chapter 7). Finally, Governor Douglas Wilder (D) vetoed a parental

Table 10.2 Post-*Webster* State Legislative Enactments and Sustained Vetoes

Category	Enacted	Vetoed
Abortion Rights	CT (1990), NV (1990), MD (1991), WA (1991), KS (1992)[a]	NH (1990), NH (1992)
Informed Consent	PA (1989), MS (1991), ND (1991), OH (1991), KS (1992)	
Public Funding	CA (1990),[b] WV (1990)[c]	
Parental Consent	PA (1989), MI (1990), SC (1990), MI(1992),[d] WI (1992)	MI (1990)
Clinic Licensing[e]	FL (1991),[f] MS (1991)[g]	
Birth Control Abortions	LA (1991), UT (1991)	ID (1990), LA (1990), ND (1991)
Ban Abortion		LA (1990)
Ban Gender-Selection Abortions	PA (1989)	
Late-Term Abortion Restrictions	PA (1989)	
Reporting Requirements	PA (1989),[h] FL (1990),[i] NY (1991)[j]	
Spousal Notification	PA (1989)	
Parental Notification	MD (1991), NB (1991), KS (1992)	VA (1992)
Counseling Minors Prior to Abortion	CT (1990)	
Clinic Harassment	KS (1992)	
RU-486	CA (1991),[k] NH (1991)[l]	
Feticide	GA (1991), NH (1991)	
Miscellaneous	ID (1990),[m] CA (1991),[n] CA (1991),[o] IA (1991),[p] MD (1991)[q]	

SOURCES: 1989, "State Legislative Record on Fertility-Related Bills and Law"; January 1990-September 1992, *State Reproductive Health Monitor*. Both are publications of the Alan Guttmacher Institute.
NOTES: a. This law is a "compromise" piece of legislation. Early in the session, Kansas House members passed a stronger abortion-rights bill (similar to those enacted in Maryland and Connecticut). At session's end, however, the bill had been amended to include informed consent and parental notification provisions as well as guaranteeing the right to an abortion until viability. The bill also provides penalties for criminal trespass and harassment at abortion clinics. Governor Joan Finney (D), an abortion foe, signed the bill over the protest of Kansas antiabortion organizations.
b. After 13 years of cutting off funds for abortions under the Medi-Cal program and being ordered to provide them by the California courts (under the state constitution), the California legislature included full funding of abortion in its 1990 and 1991 budgets.
c. In 1990, the West Virginia legislature chose to stop public funding of abortions for indigent women, except in cases of rape, incest, when the fetus would be born with gross physical or mental abnormalities, or when the mother would suffer severe physical problems as a result of carrying the pregnancy to term. Prior to this time, the state funded all abortions. The law is not being enforced because the attorney general

continued

Table 10.2 Continued

---

declared that the funding decision was made as part of the appropriations process (the West Virginia constitution prohibits legislating on an appropriation). As a result, Governor Gasper Caperton (D) did not enforce the new provisions and the West Virginia Supreme Court refused to hear an appeal. A similar situation resulted following the 1991 legislative session; to date, public funds remain available for most abortions in West Virginia.

d. The Michigan legislature repealed a provision of its 1990 parental consent law requiring that public school officials inform all students in 6th grade and above that they could not seek an abortion without a parent's permission or a court order.

e. On the day *Webster* was announced, the Supreme Court also issued certiorari in *Turnock v. Ragsdale* 841 F.2d 1358 (1988), a case challenging Illinois's abortion clinic regulations and licensing requirements. Dr. Richard Ragsdale, a Rockford physician who performed abortions, argued successfully in federal court that the regulations served no useful public health purpose and were an attempt to put Illinois abortion clinics out of business. The regulations required abortion clinics to provide facilities similar to a hospital. The case was settled out of court 2 weeks prior to oral arguments to the satisfaction of abortion clinic operators; hence, the Supreme Court has not decided upon the constitutionality of such regulations.

f. Every abortion clinic in Florida is required to obtain a certificate of need under this statute.

g. Mississippi legislators overrode Governor Ray Mabus's (D) veto of a clinic licensing and regulation bill in early 1991. The legislation was so changed from its original version that the ACLU remained neutral on its passage.

h. As part of its 1989 Abortion Control Act, the Pennsylvania legislature required that physicians file a detailed report after each abortion and that abortion facilities make quarterly reports to the state health department. These reports are part of the public record.

i. Physicians performing abortions and abortion clinics were required to submit monthly reports to the state health department (which were kept confidential) on the number of abortions performed, the reason for the abortion, and the length of the woman's gestation.

j. No state health department report could contain the name or other identifying information about a woman who procured an abortion. Prior to this time, New York was the only state that allowed this information on its report and made the information part of the public record.

k. The California General Assembly asked President Bush and Congress to make RU-486 available in the United States for clinical testing and biomedical research.

l. The legislature passed a resolution telling the federal government that New Hampshire is available for clinical trials of RU-486, the French abortion pill.

m. Idaho repealed its trigger law in 1990. Trigger laws were designed to go into effect immediately if *Roe* were reversed. Idaho's law mandated prison terms for women who had illegal abortions as well as for the physicians who performed the procedure. Idaho Right-to-Life urged Idaho lawmakers to reject the proposal, but they failed.

n. California lawmakers approved a resolution asking Congress to repeal the federal ban on family planning clinics receiving Title X funds from referring their clients for abortions.

o. This resolution expressed the support of California lawmakers for the Reproductive Health Equity Act, which would remove abortion funding restrictions on all programs where they currently exist (e.g., Medicaid, federal employees and their dependents, etc.).

p. Iowa legislators sent a state ERA to its citizens that did not include abortion-neutral language. Antiabortion legislators believe that state ERAs will be interpreted by the courts to prohibit legislators from regulating abortion, although to date only one lower state court has rendered such an interpretation (which was overturned on appeal). Iowa voters rejected the ERA proposal in November 1992.

q. This 1991 Maryland law shields health care personnel opposed to abortion from civil and criminal penalties when they do not refer a woman for an abortion, unless the abortion is necessary to save the woman's life.

notification bill after the Virginia General Assembly refused to rewrite the bill to his specifications.

Table 10.2 also shows the 22 states that enacted abortion laws after *Webster* (between July 1989 and September 1992). More important, only a handful (Idaho, Louisiana, North Dakota, Utah, and Pennsylvania) attempted to curb abortion access severely. For the most part, state legislatures followed their post-*Roe* policy-making approach after *Webster.* The Texas legislature, for example, did not suddenly ban abortion after having taken a hands-off approach for 16 years. And no one should be surprised that the legislatures producing the most restrictive policies after 1989 (Utah, Louisiana, and Pennsylvania) were among the most consistently hostile toward *Roe* or that states such as Maryland and Connecticut (which passed few restrictions after 1973) enacted abortion-rights legislation. While *Webster* was important in producing more abortion-related proposals in 1990 state legislative sessions, the number of bills declined by 1992 (Alan Guttmacher Institute 1992b:i).

The *Webster* decision kept the subject before the American people by remobilizing the abortion-rights movement. The issue definition that accompanied the *Webster* decision has been most intriguing. Abortion advocates are downplaying the "woman's right to control her body" credo so often associated with the movement during the post-*Roe* period in favor of a "Who decides—you or the government?" approach. The latter tack is better suited for a limited government era and is intended to broaden the base for abortion rights. Abortion foes, too, have been busy redefining restrictions. The words most often associated with parental involvement, informed consent, clinic licensing, spousal notification, and banning birth control abortions are "reasonable," "rational," and "mainstream" (Balch 1989). The clear message is that abortion foes are not extremists intent on eliminating rights but ordinary people seeking reasonable regulation of a practice they detest. Both definitions make it easier for policymakers to discuss the issue, being less laden with condensational symbols (such as "life" versus "choice"). For the debate to survive beyond the afterglow of *Webster* it is important for interest groups to find new definitions of the issue.

Abortion Policy in the States Following Casey
and the 1992 Presidential Elections

Casey, the Court's latest pronouncement on abortion, reaffirmed the central tenets of *Roe,* while upholding most provisions of Pennsylvania's 1989 Abortion Control Act. At present, abortion regulations that do not create an "undue burden" standard are constitutionally acceptable. As the December 1992 Supreme Court decision to refuse to hear an appeal in *Ada* indicates, laws previously passed in Guam, Louisiana, and Utah appear to create an undue burden and would not be constitutional.

The Court's greatest impact will be to force lower federal courts to untangle what constitutes an "undue burden." Under the new standard, an abortion regulation (such as the waiting period) may not present a prima facie "undue burden," but in practice, may thwart a woman's access to abortion substantially, thus creating an undue burden. At present, federal courts have permitted Mississippi to implement an informed consent law with a 24-hour waiting period; in December 1992, the Supreme Court refused to hear an appeal in this case (*Barnes v. Moore,* 970 F.2d. 12 [1992]). Injunctions against a host of other informed consent statutes and waiting periods currently are being reopened in federal court. In short, the announcement of the new standard means that many previously settled questions of law will be re-examined in light of *Casey.*

Casey is likely to have the greatest impact on codifier and acquiescer states where legislators have waited for clearer signals from the Court to enact abortion restrictions. Supporter states probably will continue to pass broad abortion-rights laws that codify *Roe* (e.g., Connecticut), rather than rely on the Court to do so. Challengers may try to implement laws enacted previously, but creating new test laws is problematic; the most novel Pennsylvania regulation—spousal notification—failed to meet the undue burden standard. The road for challengers is less clear pending the decision of national antiabortion organizations to settle on a new strategy.

The election of President Clinton, who courted the abortion-rights community, signals an important change in abortion politics. In the short term, the abortion debate will focus more heavily on Congress, especially with regard to the disposition of the Freedom of Choice Act (FOCA). Originally proposed to codify the principles of *Roe* by federal statute, the initiative lost steam in the summer of 1992 as the *Casey* decision failed to mobilize abortion-rights supporters. Democratic leaders, sensing they did not have sufficient votes to pass an unamended bill, did not bring FOCA before the 102nd Congress.

Despite Clinton's support of FOCA and the gain of seats in Congress for pro-choice organizations, the legislation's fate is far from certain. Some abortion-rights organizations, notably the National Organization for Women, are unwilling to support an amended FOCA (one that would allow states to write parental involvement statutes and informed consent statutes, for instance). If FOCA passes, it faces an almost certain legal challenge by state legislatures wishing to defy its dictates. Hence, federal courts will rely on statutory, rather than constitutional, principles to interpret abortion law.

Antiabortion organizations are facing the chilliest environment in Washington, DC, in 12 years. Their attempt to get a majority of the Supreme Court to overturn *Roe* appears to have fallen one vote short. Many decisions supporting abortion access that passed Congress failed to become law because of vetoes by Presidents Reagan and Bush. With Clinton in the

White House, abortion policy will change significantly. As a result, states should become even more important forums for an antiabortion community seeking safe haven in a hostile sea. Convincing state legislators that abortion regulations are supported by the public and are reasonable and rational public policy will likely be easier in state capitols than in Washington, DC, at least in the near future.

Conclusion

States have played and continue to play an important role in abortion policy making during the post-*Roe* era. Often dismissed as inconsequential actors in light of *Roe,* state legislatures vigorously debated abortion regulations, institutionalized their approaches to policy making, and served as sounding boards for antiabortion organizations who found the federal courts and Congress difficult venues in which to secure victories. In short, states were not "paper tigers," but significant participants in making abortion policy. After *Webster,* states began to play a pronounced role, though they generally followed the policy-making approach developed during the 1973-1989 period. In view of the Court's holding in *Casey,* and a Congress and White House now controlled by forces more sympathetic to pro-choice organizations, states should continue to be the level of government where the antiabortion message can be most easily advanced.

Studying state abortion policy making after 1973 also has important theoretical implications for public policy. Although the most widely watched events regarding abortion policy after *Roe* occurred in Washington, DC, groups opposed to abortion were working in several venues, especially state legislatures. Organizations desire more hospitable terrain when seeking to push an issue definition; in the case of abortion, we cannot begin to understand the demise of *Roe* and the current chaos surrounding U.S. abortion policy without determining the role state legislatures (especially in challenger states) played in undermining that decision. If state legislatures had not continued to press the issue, the Court would not have been forced to square the *Roe* ruling with a large number of state regulatory schemes.

Finally, state legislatures have played a significant role in redefining the abortion issue by making it more technical. For the most part, lawmakers did not spend time debating the "life" versus "choice" question after 1973. They were forced to address specific regulatory proposals that limited, but did not outlaw, abortion. As a result, abortion continued to be discussed, but in a more technical, policy-oriented vein, rather than one in which emotion was the dominant theme.

The institutional venue, scope of conflict, and institutional context concepts all have significant import for the analysis of abortion policy in the 1990s. The story of abortion politics cannot be understood without acknowledging the different forums it has been debated in during the past 20 years. The institutional venue notion developed by Baumgartner and Jones (1991) is critical to understanding why this seemingly unresolvable conundrum continues to bedevil policymakers. While doors may be more tightly shut in Washington, DC, it is likely that state legislatures will continue to promote the pro-life perspective. Antiabortion entrepreneurs are certain to bring their agenda items to state legislatures. Furthermore, the Christian Coalition's stealth campaign was successful in electing more antiabortion state legislators, perhaps tipping the balance of power toward the pro-life perspective in several states (Rubin 1992).

The scope of conflict should expand during the 1990s as well. Clinton's victory was a major shock to the interest group system; antiabortion organizations are already witnessing a growth in membership, much as Goggin's framework would predict. While the focus of this analysis has been on the state legislature as a forum for the expansion of the scope of conflict, antiabortion organizations are likely to use outsider, rather than insider, tactics to bring attention to their perspective on the abortion debate. The activities of militant pro-life groups such as Operation Rescue are on the rise, and the Arizona affiliate of the insider-oriented National Right to Life Committee has decided to use the broadcast media to publicize the names of doctors who perform abortions (Rubin 1992).

The institutional context at the state level will continue to be dominated by pluralistic bargaining. Unlike the zero-sum battle emerging over FOCA, state-level abortion organizations have every incentive to compromise. Abortion-rights organizations have every incentive to make abortion legislation more palatable, if they cannot defeat it outright, because *Casey's* legacy is that many abortion restrictions will withstand constitutional scrutiny. The decrease in abortions performed after Mississippi implemented its 24-hour waiting period (Denniston 1992) should spur pro-life organizations to lobby for restrictions validated in *Casey*. The effects of even a 24-hour waiting period should find pro-life organizations willing to compromise, lest no legislation be passed.

In sum, abortion politics at the state level will be even more important to study during the 1990s. Understanding state-level abortion politics requires an appreciation of the role subnational jurisdictions played in expanding the scope of conflict, promoting pluralistic bargaining, and providing a forum for the antiabortion movement. The present balance of power concerning abortion only accentuates the significance of these concepts.

Abortion Laws/Resolutions Enacted, 1973-1989

State	A	B	C	D	E	F	G	H	I	J	K	L	M	N	O	P	Q	R	S	Total
AL						X			X											2
AK																				0
AZ	X	X	X	X			X		X		X	X								8
AR		X	X		X							X								4
CA	X	X	X						X		X									5
CO								X												1
CT																				0
DE				X	X	X			X											4
FL	X	X	X	X	X			X			X		X							8
GA	X		X	X	X		X	X				X		X						8
HI													X							1
ID	X		X		X	X		X	X		X			X	X	X				10
IL	X	X	X	X	X		X		X	X	X	X	X	X		X		X	X	15
IN	X	X	X				X		X		X	X		X	X					9
IA	X		X	X					X											4
KS	X																			1
KY	X	X	X	X	X	X			X	X	X		X	X		X	X			13
LA	X	X	X	X	X	X	X	X	X	X		X		X						12
ME	X				X						X	X	X		X					6
MD	X				X				X				X							4
MA	X	X	X	X	X	X		X	X	X	X				X					11
MI	X	X							X											3
MN	X	X	X	X	X		X	X	X				X			X	X			11
MS							X		X				X							3
MO	X	X	X	X	X	X			X	X	X			X	X	X	X			13

continued

State	A	B	C	D	E	F	G	H	I	J	K	L	M	N	O	P	Q	R	S	Total
MT	X	X	X				X			X	X	X								7
NB	X	X	X	X	X					X	X	X				X				9
NV	X		X	X	X	X		X		X	X	X								9
NH				X																1
NJ	X			X	X		X													4
NM		X		X			X													3
NY			X	X										X						3
NC	X							X	X											3
ND	X	X	X	X	X	X	X	X	X	X	X		X	X	X	X	X			16
OH	X	X		X				X			X									5
OK	X	X	X	X	X	X							X							7
OR																				0
PA	X	X	X	X	X	X		X	X	X	X		X	X	X	X				14
RI	X	X		X	X	X		X	X			X				X				9
SC	X		X																	2
SD	X	X	X	X	X	X		X	X											8
TN	X	X	X	X	X	X		X	X	X	X		X							11
TX	X		X	X																3
UT	X	X	X	X	X	X	X		X	X	X	X	X	X	X					14
VT								X												1
VA	X		X	X				X					X							5
WA			X																	1
WV				X						X										2
WI	X		X	X	X					X										5
WY	X	X	X	X				X	X				X							7

Legend

A. *Conscience Clauses* (35 states). These clauses permit medical personnel and, in some cases, institutions to refuse to perform abortions without fear of retribution. Most clauses were the initial reactions states took in response to *Roe*. Clauses passed with little resistance in state legislatures, though pro-choice periodicals argued that the laws (especially those allowing institutions to refuse to perform abortions) were an attempt to limit *Roe's* effect.

B. *Fetal Experimentation* (23 states). Antiabortion partisans argue that such laws are necessary to protect fetuses born alive during abortions from being used for experimental purposes. Laws also prohibit experimentation prior to an abortion. Even though these laws never were subject to legal challenge, some members of the biomedical community are concerned about the scope of such legislation.

C. *Post-Viability Requirements* (29 states). *Roe* permits states to write regulations following viability. It did not specify when viability is attained (though it suggests that this occurs around the 28th week of pregnancy). States typically allow post-viability abortions only when necessary to save the mother's life or to preserve her health. Controversy arose not from the instances in which abortions were to be permitted, but from when viability occurred. When state legislatures established a standard point of viability (generally based upon gestation length), the Court struck down these laws, arguing that viability was a medical concept to be determined by physicians, not judges or legislators (see especially *Colautti v. Franklin* 439 U.S. 379 [1979]).

D. *Post-Viability Standard of Care* (29 states). These laws outline the mandates physicians must follow when performing post-viability abortions. In general, they require the presence of a second physician during the abortion whose sole purpose is to attempt to save the life of the fetus. Furthermore, the physician performing the abortion is to use the method most likely to preserve the life and health of the fetus. Legal challenges have been successful when the Court has determined that such statuses provide more protection for the fetus than for the woman (see *Thornburgh v. American College of Obstetricians and Gynecologists* 476 U.S. 747 [1986]).

E. *Memorials to Congress* (25 states). Most resolutions ask Congress to send a human life amendment to the states for approval; some memorials register sentiment against *Roe* without calling for a constitutional corrective. Especially popular in the years immediately following *Roe*, the memorial's purpose was to pressure Congress to propose a constitutional amendment outlawing abortion.

F. Call for a Constitutional Convention (19 states). Antiabortion groups, frustrated by the lack of congressional action on a human life amendment, went on the offensive in state legislatures in the mid-1970s. Their goal was to garner support for an Article V constitutional convention on the abortion issue or, fearing the effects of a constitutional convention, force Congress to send such an amendment to the states. The effort largely was abandoned after 1980, a casualty of the internecine battle within the National Right to Life Committee and some state affiliates.

G. Feticide (9 states). Citing *Roe,* some state Supreme Courts (among them Minnesota's) declared that a fetus was not a person, hence, charges could not be brought against an individual for killing a fetus intentionally. To rectify this situation, antiabortion groups proposed feticide laws, making it a crime to injure or kill a fetus. Although both pro-choice and pro-life groups support penalties for those who injure or kill a fetus, pro-choice advocates vehemently oppose legislation that imparts personhood status to the fetus (which ultimately may assist in outlawing abortion). Instead, pro-choice groups prefer legislation that renders fetal injury or death to be a crime against the mother.

H. Fetal Disposal (11 states). Antiabortion advocates have brought allegations in several states that abortion clinics dispose of fetal remains in garbage dumpsters. Such charges have prompted state legislatures to write statutes requiring humane and sanitary disposal of fetal remains. Opponents argue that laws requiring the cremation or burial of fetuses grant personhood status to fetal tissue. Several cities (notably Dallas and Milwaukee) have adopted fetal disposal ordinances; many have debated the topic.

I. Public Funding (25 states). A common response by federal and state lawmakers immediately following *Roe* was to restrict the use of public funds for indigent women seeking abortions. In a series of cases culminating in *Harris v. McRae* (448 U.S. 297 [1980]), the Supreme Court upheld state and federal restrictions on the use of public funds for abortion. Most states, following the lead of Congress, made public funds available for abortion only when necessary to save the mother's life. In general, the decision to continue or to restrict funding was made by state welfare departments in accordance with federal guidelines. A number of states, however, fund abortions under state court order, most notably California.

The Appendix includes only those states where a funding decision was made by the legislature. While a majority of these legislatures opted to codify federal restrictions, some states selected a more expansive route and allowed funds to be used in cases of rape, incest, and gross fetal abnormality.

J. Informed Consent (17 states). These statutes require the physician to inform the woman of numerous details about the abortion procedure and her pregnancy. Requirements vary, but the woman generally must be informed of the gestational age of the fetus she is about to abort, its physiological and anatomical characteristics, possible medical complications, and that public assistance is available to help her carry the pregnancy to term. Such statutes were held constitutionally infirm in *Akron v. Akron Reproductive Health Center* 462 U.S. 416 (1983) and *Thornburgh v. American College of Obstetricians and Gynecologists* 476 U.S. 747 (1986).

K. Parental Consent (17 states). Such laws require minors to obtain the consent of their parents prior to securing an abortion. Blanket parental consent laws were struck down by the Supreme Court in *Planned Parenthood v. Danforth* 428 U.S. 52 (1976). States were instructed in *Danforth, Bellotti v. Baird,* 428 U.S. 132 (1976), and *Bellotti v. Baird,* 443 U.S. 622 (1979) to protect the privacy rights of "mature" minors. In response to these decisions, states began writing judicial bypass provisions into parental consent statutes; in such schemes, the minor either tells her parents or secures a ruling from a court that she is mature enough to make the decision to abort on her own. Although many states wrote parental consent provisions into their early post-*Roe* abortion statutes, the Appendix shows only those states that passed such laws subsequent to *Danforth* and *Bellotti.* Many of these statutes are not enforced due to constitutional infirmities.

L. Parental Notification (18 states). Here the minor is required only to notify her parents of her intent to abort, rather than to secure their consent. Such legislation generally has been enacted with a judicial bypass mechanism. Many of these statutes have injunctions issued against them.

M. Spousal Notification (7 states). Numerous states required spousal consent prior to performing an abortion in their early post-*Roe* statutes; the Court struck down these provisions in *Danforth.* Several states have since incorporated notification provisions into abortion statutes, though most attempts have been deemed unconstitutional (the U.S. Supreme Court has not ruled on this question).

N. Second-Trimester Hospitalization Requirements (17 states). With *Roe,* states were given the ability to regulate abortions in the interest of maternal health during the second trimester. Second-trimester abortions are considerably more complicated procedures than those performed during the first trimester; consequently, some states required that second-trimester abortions take place in hospitals. Hospital abortions cost more than those done in clinics, but improvements in abortion techniques made second-trimester procedures safe in ambulatory settings by the early 1980s. In *Akron,* the Court declared that hospitalization requirements were no longer reasonably related to maternal health, thus unconstitutional.

O. Wrongful Life/Wrongful Birth (8 states). This legislation prevents lawsuits whereby a person argues that he or she should not have been born (wrongful life) or parents allege that, had they been informed correctly, they would have had an abortion (wrongful birth). While banning wrongful life suits has not generated great controversy, abortion proponents often believe that proscribing wrongful birth suits permits antiabortion physicians from recommending tests, such as amniocentesis (which may detect a fetal abnormality), that a woman may have undergone had she known of their existence. A challenge to the Minnesota law was upheld by the state's Supreme Court (*Hickman v. Group Health Plan, Inc.*, 396 N.W.2d 10 [1986]).

P. Insurance Restrictions (10 states). These laws allow companies to offer insurance policies that include maternity benefits, but not coverage for abortions. Antiabortion groups have sought legislation to allow health maintenance organizations to refuse coverage for abortion services.

Q. Public Facilities (4 states). These statutes prohibit the use of public facilities for performing abortions. Such statutes were upheld in *Webster*.

R. Fetal Pain (1 state). After release of the antiabortion film, *The Silent Scream* (in which a fetus is alleged to feel pain during an abortion), state legislatures entertained bills requiring physicians to inform women undergoing post-viability abortions that the fetus feels pain and anesthesia is available to alleviate such pain. Abortion proponents argue that the fetus does not feel pain and that the sole purpose of this legislation is to increase abortion fees. The American College of Obstetricians and Gynecologists finds no scientific evidence to support the fetal pain claims of antiabortion groups.

S. Gender Selection (1 state). With the development of chorionic villus sampling, the sex of the fetus can be determined as early as 9 weeks into pregnancy. Amniocentesis also can determine fetal sex, but at a later period in pregnancy. Both of these tests, however, are principally designed to detect serious genetic abnormalities. According to newspaper accounts, some women have had abortions based not upon the presence of any fetal defect, but upon the gender of the fetus such tests have revealed. Except when associated with a genetic disorder, Illinois has banned gender-based abortions.

SOURCES: For 1973-1980, *Family Planning/Population Reporter;* for 1981-1989, "State Legislative Record—Fertility-Related Bills and laws," published by the Alan Guttmacher institute, Washington, DC.

11

Abortion Opinion and Policy in the American States

MALCOLM L. GOGGIN

CHRISTOPHER WLEZIEN

The recent Supreme Court decisions in *Webster* and *Casey* have effectively given states permission to pass more restrictive antiabortion laws, as long as these restrictions do not have "the purpose or effect of placing a substantial obstacle in the path of a woman seeking an abortion of a nonviable fetus" (*Casey,* at 82). As a result of *Webster* and *Casey,* as well as the Court's refusal to hear an appeal of a statute criminalizing abortion in the territory of Guam, the fate of abortion policy now is significantly more in the hands of state politicians. These developments highlight the importance of understanding the relationship between state abortion policy, on the one hand, and other state-level variables, especially sentiment toward abortion among those who live and vote in the state, on the other hand.

Empirical research shows that states differ in terms of the ideological dispositions of the people who live there, and that the orientation of policies in states tends to follow those ideological dispositions (Wright, Erikson, and McIver 1987). Simply, the more conservative the opinion of the people in the state the more conservative the policies of that state, and vice versa. And, because it would seem that pressure for restrictive abortion laws varies considerably from state to state, it is likely that abortion policies in the states reflect this variation in public preferences as well.

A number of recent studies have attempted to account for the differences in the restrictiveness of states' abortion statutes, using various individual-, group-, and system-level variables, including political and socioeconomic

AUTHORS' NOTE: We wish to thank Kathleen Knight for helpful comments on this chapter. Deborah A. Orth, Wanda Seguin, and Jung-Ki Kim also assisted with the data.

characteristics of the states (e.g., Strickland and Whicker 1990a; Hansen 1990; Goggin and Kim 1992; and chapters in Part III of this volume).[1] However, none of these studies systematically addresses the connection between public preferences about abortion and abortion policy in the states. Invariably, the complaint from researchers is that a reliable measure of state-by-state attitudes toward abortion does not exist (e.g., Chapter 13).

Goggin and Kim (1992) explicitly redress this imbalance in a very recent study that relies on a November 1990 *CBS/New York Times* exit poll of 64,029 adults in 42 states, with an average of 1,524 respondents per state. In addition to various questions about the attributes of the respondent, the *CBS/New York Times* survey asked about abortion preferences, specifically whether abortion should "be legal in all circumstances," "legal in some circumstances," or "not legal in any circumstances." With these data and measures of state abortion policy in hand, Goggin and Kim (1992) develop and estimate a two-stage model of state abortion policy. Their analysis indicates that state abortion policy does follow state public preferences, although the effect of abortion opinion is mediated by the preferences of the state political actors that make abortion policy, namely, governors and legislators.[2] Ultimately, there is representation of state public preferences in abortion policy, so that in states where the public wants significant restrictions on the availability of abortion it generally gets many restrictions (see also Chapter 12).

Goggin and Kim's findings are consistent with the considerable literature that generally corroborates a linkage between public preferences and public policy (e.g., Weissberg 1976; Monroe 1979; Page and Shapiro 1983, 1992; Wright, Erikson, and McIver 1987). Although it is fairly clear from this research that policymakers are responsive to public preferences, it is not clear whether the public is itself attentive and responsive to policy behavior, that is, whether the public adjusts its preferences for more policy activity in response to what policymakers do. This issue is not a trivial one, for the representational linkage hinges on the *adjustment* of public preferences for policy activity; otherwise, politicians would lack the incentive to represent what the public wants (Wlezien 1992).

Wlezien's (1992) recent research examines the interrelationship between public preferences and policy, in the context of federal defense spending.[3] That research indicates that in the defense budget-opinion domain there is both representation of public preferences in policy and "feedback" of policy on those preferences: When the public wants more spending on defense it gets more, and when it gets more it doesn't want as much more. In effect, the public behaves like a thermostat, where a departure from the favored policy temperature produces a signal to adjust policy accordingly and, once sufficiently adjusted, the signal stops (Wlezien 1992:1).

There also is a suggestion of this dynamic in the abortion context (Wlezien and Goggin 1993). Wlezien and Goggin's analysis of national abortion opinion during the 1980s indicates that the public became increasingly more supportive of keeping abortion legal "as it is now" in response to court cases and Supreme Court nominations and confirmations that challenged the abortion status quo. Although absolute preferences about the legality of abortion remained substantially unchanged *in the aggregate* during the 1980s (Stimson 1991:82-84; Page and Shapiro 1992:105-6; Cook, Jelen, and Wilcox 1992a:37; also see Chapter 3), it appears as though the public perceived a shift in national abortion policy toward more restricted access and became less supportive of further restrictions on the availability of abortion. But, is it the case that *state* public preferences for more (or less) restrictive abortion policy follow *state* abortion policy itself? In other words, do state "publics" themselves behave like thermostats with respect to abortion policy?

This chapter effectively extends the work of Wlezien and Goggin (1993) to abortion preferences in the American states. Specifically, a model of state abortion opinion and policy is developed that relates *absolute state preferences,* or what members of the public say they want with respect to abortion policy; *state abortion policy;* the collection of abortion statutes, rules, and regulations that dictate the terms under which a woman can legally seek an abortion in the state; and *relative state preferences,* or what people say they want relative to existing abortion policy. The connections specified in the model are examined empirically, at a single point in time, relying on various recent *CBS/New York Times* polls and a measure of abortion policy restrictiveness. The analysis strongly suggests that state publics do indeed adjust their relative preferences in response to policy output.

A Model of State Abortion Opinion

Although we do know that state policymakers are responsive to state absolute preferences about abortion policy (Goggin and Kim 1992), we do not know whether state publics are themselves attentive and responsive to what state policymakers actually do. Specifically, it is not clear whether state publics adjust their relative preferences for abortion policy—those preferences for more policy activity than is currently in place—in response to state policy itself. These relative preferences result from individuals' comparisons of their absolute preferences with their perceptions of the state policy status quo, and may differ from absolute preferences over time because policy itself (or the perception of policy) changes. As abortion policy in a state becomes more restrictive, for example, attentive individuals may be less likely to support further restrictions on abortion. Although

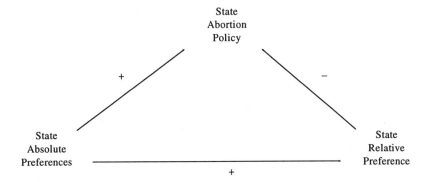

Figure 11.1. A Model of State Abortion Opinion and Policy

their absolute preferences remain unchanged, individuals may become more supportive of the abortion status quo. It follows (Wlezien 1992) that, when taken as aggregates of individuals, state publics may behave like thermostats, adjusting their relative preferences for restrictions on abortion in response to state policy behavior.

This thermostatic model of state public preferences implies a dynamic relationship between preferences and policy over time. But the model also suggests a cross-sectional pattern of relationships: In those states in which abortion policy is more (less) restrictive than the public wants, the public is expected to be less (more) supportive of further restrictions on the availability of abortion. The set of relationships relating state absolute preferences, state abortion policy, and state relative preferences is depicted in Figure 11.1. As is implied by the thermostatic model, state relative preferences are hypothesized to be positively related to state absolute preferences, and negatively related to policy itself.[4]

Ultimately, a dynamic model of relative state abortion opinion would (have to) take the national context into account. In this sense, as individuals perceive a shift in (or threat to) national abortion policy, they may be less likely to support further restrictions on the availability of abortion, regardless of state policy (Wlezien and Goggin 1993). Because the model described above is applied to cross-sectional data in the analyses that follow, it does not explicitly incorporate national factors; that is, at any point in time national political forces are a constant across states.

Data

In order to assess the foregoing model of abortion opinion empirically, it is necessary to create measures of three variables: the absolute state preference, state abortion policy, and the relative state preference. It is to these measures that the discussion turns next.

State Absolute Preference

The state absolute preference is operationalized as the mean state voter opinion about the legality of abortion. The data are drawn from the November 1990 *CBS/New York Times* exit poll of voters in 42 states.[5] The number of respondents per state ranges from 787 to 3,313. The exact wording of the abortion question is as follows: "Which of these statements comes CLOSEST to your view about abortion? (1) It should be legal in all circumstances; (2) It should be legal only in some circumstances; or (3) It should not be legal in any circumstances." The mean response for each state is computed, where 1 = legal in all circumstances (the abortion-rights position), 2 = legal only in some circumstances, and 3 = not legal in any circumstances (the fetal-rights position). Hence, a state with a mean score at or near "1" would be a state where the average voter prefers no restrictions on access to abortion (a pro-choice state) whereas a state with a mean score at or near "3" would be a state where the average voter prefers to re-criminalize abortion (a right-to-life state). The higher the score, the higher the level of support either for placing restrictions on access to abortion or for making abortion illegal.

State Abortion Policy

The restrictiveness of abortion policy in each state is operationalized as the accumulation of a series of authoritative decisions in each state limiting access to abortions. In other words, we use the abortion laws that were written between 1973 and 1988 (summarized by Halva-Neubauer 1989b; see also Chapters 10 and 13) plus new restrictions that were added between 1988 and November 1989, based on data from the Council of State Governments (1990). The states and the individual provisions in their statutes and regulations, together with the measure of state absolute preference, are reported in Table 11.1. Each of the attributes, if present, is given a value of "1," and a restrictiveness index is calculated for each state by summing the abortion laws that apply in the state. The variable ranges from 1 in Alaska, Connecticut, Oregon, and Vermont (the least restrictive states) to 18 in Missouri (the most restrictive state).

State Relative Preference

Following Wlezien and Goggin (1993), the state relative preference for abortion policy is based on the *CBS/New York Times* abortion item that

(text continued on page 197)

Table 11.1 Aggregate Abortion Policy and Absolute Abortion Preferences by State

STATE	A	B	C	D	E	F	G	H	I	J	K	L	M	N	O	P	Q	R	S	T	U	V	W	X	TOTAL	PREF.
ALABAMA				1				1	1																3	1.97
ALASKA								1	1																2	
ARIZONA	1	1	1	1		1		1	1							1									8	1.76
ARKANSAS		1	1		1			1	1														1		6	1.99
CALIFORNIA	1	1	1					1	1																5	1.56
COLORADO								1	1																2	1.68
CONNECTICUT								1																	1	1.63
DELAWARE			1	1	1			1	1	1															6	1.72
FLORIDA	1	1	1	1	1			1	1		1	1													9	1.68
GEORGIA	1		1	1	1		1	1	1		1		1												9	1.81
HAWAII								1				1													2	1.69
IDAHO	1		1		1	1		1	1	1		1	1	1							1				11	1.81
ILLINOIS	1	1	1	1	1		1	1	1	1	1	1		1		1	1					1	1		16	1.74
INDIANA	1	1	1		1			1		1		1	1												8	1.91
IOWA	1		1	1				1																	4	1.87
KANSAS	1							1																	2	1.85
KENTUCKY	1	1	1	1	1	1		1	1	1	1	1		1	1							1	1		15	2.08
LOUISIANA	1	1	1	1	1	1		1	1	1	1		1					1		1	1	1			15	
MAINE	1				1			1	1	1			1												6	1.65
MARYLAND	1				1			1		1															4	1.67
MASSACHUSETTS	1	1	1	1	1	1		1	1	1	1			1					1						12	1.66
MICHIGAN	1	1						1																	3	1.83
MINNESOTA	1	1	1	1	1		1	1	1		1		1	1					1						12	1.82
MISSISSIPPI						1		1	1		1														4	
MISSOURI	1	1	1	1	1	1		1	1	1		1	1	1	1			1	1	1	1		1		18	
MONTANA	1	1	1			1		1	1	1		1											1		9	1.89
NEBRASKA	1	1	1	1	1			1	1	1			1										1		10	1.96
NEVADA	1		1	1	1	1		1	1	1	1	1							1						11	1.78
NEW HAMPSHIRE				1				1																	2	1.68
NEW JERSEY	1		1	1				1																	4	1.78
NEW MEXICO		1		1			1	1	1																5	1.86
NEW YORK		1	1					1					1					1							5	1.66
NORTH CAROLINA	1							1										1							3	1.86
NORTH DAKOTA	1		1	1	1	1	1	1	1	1	1	1	1	1	1	1		1						1	17	
OHIO	1	1		1				1	1																5	1.76
OKLAHOMA	1	1	1	1	1	1		1				1							1						9	1.85
OREGON								1																	1	1.57
PENNSYLVANIA	1	1	1	1	1	1		1	1	1	1		1	1	1	1						1	1	1	17	1.85
RHODE ISLAND	1	1		1	1	1		1	1	1	1		1												10	1.76
SOUTH CAROLINA	1		1					1		1									1						5	1.89
SOUTH DAKOTA	1	1	1	1	1	1		1	1	1												1	1		11	2.08
TENNESSEE	1	1	1	1	1	1		1	1	1			1						1						11	1.93
TEXAS	1		1	1				1																	4	1.82
UTAH	1	1	1	1	1	1	1	1	1	1	1	1	1						1						14	
VERMONT						1																			1	1.62
VIRGINIA	1		1	1				1				1													5	

continued

Table 11.1 Continued

STATE	A	B	C	D	E	F	G	H	I	J	K	L	M	N	O	P	Q	R	S	T	U	V	W	X	TOTAL	PREF.
WASHINGTON				1				1	1																3	
WEST VIRGINIA			1					1	1																3	2.01
WISCONSIN	1		1	1	1			1																	5	1.85
WYOMING	1	1	1	1			1	1		1															7	1.87

LEGEND TO INDIVIDUAL PROVISIONS A THROUGH X:

A: conscience clauses
B: fetal experimentation
C: post-viability requirements
D: post-viability standard of care
E: memoriala to congress
F: call for constitutional convention
G: feticide
H: fetal disposal
I: public funding to save life of woman, or in cases of rape, incest,
  or deformed fetus, or for medically necessary abortions
J: informed consent
K: parental consent or parental notification
L: spousal notification
M: 2nd trimester hospitalization requirements
N: wrongful life wrongful birth
O: insurance restrictions
P: prohibit use of public facilities
Q: fetal pain
R: prohibit gender selection
S: prohibit abortion counselling
T: prohibit involvement of public employee
U: require viability tests
V: viability assumed from 18 to 24 weeks
W: would make abortion illegal if Roe vs. Wade overturned
X: preamble protection of fetus

SOURCE: State policy index adapted from Glen Halva-Neubauer, "The Reversal
of Roe: A View from the States." Paper presented at the 1989 Annual Meeting
of the American Political Science Association, Atlanta; and Council of
Governments, "Status of Abortion Laws." State Government News (1990):16-17.

NOTE: Aggregate state absolute preference based on data from the November,
1990, *CBS/NYT* exit poll. See text for question wording.

asks about keeping abortion legal "as it is now." The question wording is: "Should abortion be legal as it is now, or legal only in such cases as rape, incest, or to save the life of the mother, or should it not be permitted at all?" The state relative preference is operationalized as the mean response to series of two separate abortion surveys conducted in May and August 1989. There were 2,548 in the entire sample and the average number of voters polled per state was 64.[6]

A state's preference for the abortion status quo is operationalized by computing a mean response for the state, where 1 = legal as it is now, 2 = legal only in such cases as rape, incest, or to save the life of the mother, and 3 = not be permitted at all. Hence, a state with a mean score at or near "1" would be a state where the average voter prefers the abortion status quo, whereas a state with a mean score at or near "3" would be a state where the average voter prefers to re-criminalize abortion. In effect, the higher the score, the higher the level of support for placing additional restrictions on access to abortion.

It should be made clear that the measure of relative preferences does not perfectly capture public support for more (less) restrictions on the availability of abortion, that is, because the survey item used to construct the measure asks about absolute preferences in addition to support for keeping abortion legal "as it is now." Although the measure is imperfect, it is based on the best available information about individuals' relative preferences. And, Wlezien and Goggin's (1993) research suggests that the measure provides at a least a rough indication of those preferences.[7]

Absolute Preferences, Abortion Policy, and Relative Preferences in the States

The model portrayed in Figure 11.1 implies a set of connections relating state absolute preferences, state abortion policy, and state relative preferences. The primary connection between state absolute preferences and abortion policy already has been documented in other research, as discussed above. It nevertheless is useful to show the relationship between the two variables; accordingly, the two variables are depicted graphically in Figure 11.2. The pattern in Figure 11.2 indicates a positive, although only modest, relationship ($r = 27$) between state absolute preferences and state abortion policy; the higher the state absolute preference—the more the public in a state supports restrictions on the availability of abortion—the higher the number of restrictions in place, and vice versa. It appears that there is some representation of state absolute preferences about abortion in actual abortion policy, perhaps indirectly through the preferences of political actors.

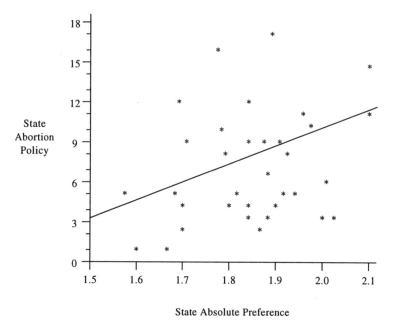

State Absolute Preference

Figure 11.2. State Absolute Preferences and Abortion Policy

Although there is representation of state absolute preferences in abortion policy, is it the case that the public perceives and reacts to policy in its relative preferences? That is, do state publics actually adjust their preferences for more policy activity in accordance with what policymakers actually do? Before explicitly addressing the issue of feedback, it is necessary to consider the relationship between the measures of state absolute and relative preferences, which was described in Figure 11.1. These two variables are plotted in Figure 11.3.

It is clear from the figure that absolute and relative state preferences are closely related ($r = .69$). Those states that are most supportive of fully legalized abortion also are strongly supportive of keeping abortion legal "as it is now," and vice versa. There still is considerable variation in relative preferences that is unaccounted for by absolute preferences (see Figure 11.3). Indeed, there are some very "conservative" states that are fairly supportive of the abortion status quo; that is, their relative preferences are much lower than their absolute preferences. And there are some very "liberal" states that are more supportive of further restrictions on the availability of abortion than their absolute preferences would imply.

There is reason to suspect that the unexplained variation in relative preferences is at least partially due to policy itself. For example, although

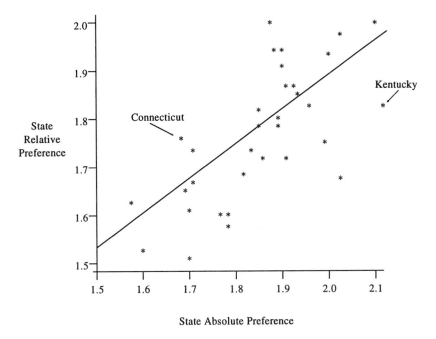

State Relative Preference

State Absolute Preference

Figure 11.3. State Absolute and Relative Preferences

the public in Kentucky generally favors restrictions on the availability of abortion, a very large number of restrictions (15) are in place, and the public is not very supportive of further restrictions (see Figure 11.3). Conversely, although the public in Connecticut is not very supportive of restrictions on abortion, there is but a single restriction in place in that state, and the public is more supportive of additional restrictions on the availability of abortion than the absolute preference implies. These examples suggest that abortion policy feeds back on state relative preferences, that the public's support for abortion "as it is now" in the states results from individuals' comparisons of their absolute preferences with their perceptions of state policy itself.

In order to rigorously assess this feedback of state abortion policy on public support for the abortion status quo, it is necessary to estimate a model of relative state preferences. To begin with, an equation is estimated that only contains state absolute preferences, the results of which are reported in Table 11.2. The equation summarizes the relationship illustrated in Figure 11.3, indicating that state relative preferences are substantially structured by state absolute preferences. And, when the measure of state abortion policy is added to the model (see the second equation in

Table 11.2 State Relative Abortion Preferences Regressions

Intercept	.50**	.45*	.44*
	(.24)	(.23)	(.24)
State Absolute Abortion Preference	.69***	.74***	.74***
	(.13)	(.13)	(.13)
State Abortion Policy	—	−.006	—
		(.004)	
State Abortion Policy (Dichotomous)	—	—	−.06*
			(.03)
R^2	.48	.51	.52
Adjusted R^2	.46	.48	.49
$N = 33$			

NOTES: The numbers in parentheses are standard errors.
The variables are defined as follows:
State Absolute Abortion Preference = the mean state response to the *CBS/New York Times* Exit Poll item about the general legality of abortion (see Table 11.1).
State Abortion Policy = the number of abortion laws that apply in each state (from Table 11.1).
State Abortion Policy (Dichotomous) = 1 for states in which more than nine of the abortion laws apply; 0 otherwise.
*** $p < .01$; ** $p < .05$; * $p < .10$ (2-tailed)

Table 11.2), there is some suggestion that the state relative preferences do reflect policy together with absolute preferences. The coefficient for the measure of state abortion policy is appropriately (negatively) signed, implying that in those states in which many (few) restrictions on abortion apply the public is less (more) supportive of further restrictions on abortion, that is, when controlling for state absolute preferences. In addition, when the measure of state abortion policy is added to the model, the estimated parameter for the state absolute preference is larger (statistically indistinguishable from "1") and the explained variance is slightly higher than in the first equation. However, it is difficult to credit the relationship, since the parameter relating state abortion policy and relative preferences just misses conventional levels of statistical significance.

It is possible that the measure of state abortion policy does not readily distinguish the degree of restrictiveness of abortion policy across states. In this sense, the measure is constructed by adding together the number of restrictions on abortion that apply in each state, reflecting the assumption that restrictions are equal in their severity. But, the actual severity of the restrictions may differ qualitatively, implying that an additive measure is inappropriate. In lieu of a measure of state abortion policy restrictiveness that distinguishes the degree of severity of the various laws, state policy restrictiveness may be approximated by merely separating those states in which many restrictions on abortion apply from those in which few apply.

Accordingly, a dichotomous measure of state abortion policy was created that takes the value "1" in those states in which more than nine of the abortion restrictions apply, and "0" otherwise.

When substituted for the original measure in the analysis (see the third equation in Table 11.2), the dichotomous measure of state abortion policy is shown to be a reliable influence on state relative preferences. In those states in which abortion policy is more (less) restrictive than the public wants, the public generally is less (more) supportive of further restrictions on the availability of abortion. It appears, therefore, that state "publics" are attentive and responsive to abortion policy, and adjust their preferences for more policy activity in accordance with what policymakers actually do.

Conclusion

Recent Supreme Court decisions have shifted the political landscape and put states in the spotlight of the abortion issue. Because states have been given considerable leeway in adopting their own abortion laws, policies have also come to differ from state to state, with some states adopting much more restrictive abortion laws than others. Empirical research has shown that the restrictiveness of state abortion policy follows state abortion opinion. Even though it is fairly clear from this research that state policymakers are (at least effectively) responsive to public preferences about abortion policy, it is not clear whether state "publics" are attentive and responsive to policy behavior itself, whether they adjust their preferences for more policy activity in response to what policymakers do. In other words, do state publics effectively behave like thermostats with respect to abortion policy?

In this chapter, a thermostatic model of state public preferences about abortion was developed and then assessed empirically. According to the model, the state relative preference (state public support for current abortion policy) reflects the state absolute preference for abortion policy taken together with policy itself. In effect, the state relative preference represents the (state) aggregate of individuals' comparisons of their absolute preferences with state policy. And the analysis suggests that state publics do react thermostatically: In those states in which abortion policy is more (less) restrictive than the public wants, the public generally is less (more) supportive of further restrictions on the availability of abortion. Ultimately, it appears that state publics are attentive and responsive to abortion policy, adjusting their preference for more policy activity in accordance with what policymakers actually do.

Notes

1. Strickland and Whicker (1990a:12-13), for example, conclude that compared to socio-economic factors, political variables "have little impact" on state restrictiveness toward abortion. Hansen (1990:13), on the other hand, finds that political history, state ideology, and political culture are positively correlated with the state's propensity to support feminist policies, including making abortion services accessible to women who want them.

2. Note that Goggin and Kim's (1992) analysis indicates that system-level socioeconomic variables are important, but indirectly through their influence on state abortion preferences.

3. Although there is much recent literature that addresses aggregate public opinion, only a few studies explicitly focus on opinion about policy (Page, Shapiro, and Dempsey, 1987; Page and Shapiro, 1992). Both of these studies are suggestive about the feedback of policy on public preferences, particularly Page and Shapiro's (1992) analysis of public support for troop withdrawals during the Vietnam War. Their analysis indicates that as troop withdrawals increased public opposition to the rate of troop withdrawal decreased, although the relationship is fairly unreliable (Page and Shapiro, 1992:239).

4. In effect, if there is no representation of state absolute preferences in state abortion policy—if policy is equally restrictive across states—state relative preferences are expected to be dictated by state absolute preferences. If representation is perfect, however, relative preferences are expected to be a constant across states, where all states are equally, strongly supportive of the abortion status quo.

5. States not included are Alaska, Louisiana, Mississippi, Missouri, North Dakota, Utah, Virginia, and Washington.

6. Because of unacceptably low sample sizes, the following states were excluded from the analysis: Delaware, Hawaii, Idaho, Maine, Nevada, New Hampshire, New Mexico, North Dakota, Vermont, and Wyoming. Thus, only 33 states remain for which there are measures of both absolute (see Note 5) and relative preferences.

It should be noted that the measure of state relative preferences is based on information that is slightly more dated (by about a year) than the exit poll used to construct the measure of state absolute preferences. This slight difference may not be very significant, because absolute preferences about abortion remain largely unchanged over time, as was discussed above (also see Chapter 3). What may be most important, therefore, is that the measures of state relative preferences and state abortion policy are based on information collected at the same point in time, 1989.

7. As noted above, Wlezien and Goggin (1993) show that although absolute public preferences about abortion under various hypothetical circumstances remained fairly stable through the 1980s, the national public generally became more supportive of policy "as it is now" leading up to the *Webster* decision, in close correspondence with court activities as reported in various mass media.

12

Public Opinion, Interest Groups,
and Public Policy Making

Abortion Policy in the American States

JEFFREY E. COHEN

CHARLES BARRILLEAUX

Perhaps the most contentious issue in American politics for the past 20 years has been abortion (Franklin and Kosaki 1989). For most of that period, abortion politics has been contested in a judicial venue (Cook, Jelen, and Wilcox 1992a:5-10; Tribe 1990). Pro-life, antiabortion advocates have hoped to overturn the *Roe v. Wade* Supreme Court decision of 1973, which legalized abortion, with another judicial pronouncement. To effect such a strategy, pro-life adherents have aimed to influence presidential politics in hopes that the president would restructure the Supreme Court and the federal judiciary by appointing jurists who also hold pro-life attitudes.

With the election of Ronald Reagan in 1980, a pro-life president assumed office. By the end of the decade, the judicial strategy seemed to have paid off. In 1989, the Supreme Court issued the *Webster v. Reproductive Health Services* decision, which observers interpreted as inviting "state legislatures to rewrite abortion laws, which will then be subject to judicial review" (Cook et al. 1992a:3). This decision was followed with *Planned Parenthood of Southeastern Pennsylvania v. Casey,* a decision

AUTHORS' NOTE: An earlier version of this chapter was presented at the 1992 meeting of the American Political Science Association, Chicago, September 3-6, 1992. We would like to thank Burdette Loomis for his comments on another draft of this chapter, and the editor, Malcolm L. Goggin, for useful comments in the preparation of this chapter.

that seemed to affirm the right of states to impose further restrictions on abortion access, even though the Court agreed with Planned Parenthood that spousal notification, required under Pennsylvania law, was unduly restrictive. These two decisions changed the abortion policy venue from one that only involved the federal judiciary to one in which state legislative politicians, as well as federal jurists, would participate.

This chapter addresses two issues. The first is an attempt to assess the possible impact of the *Webster* and *Casey* decisions on state-level abortion policy making. What will the state legislatures do? Will they restrict abortion access heavily, as many claim, or will the states refrain from altering the status quo that the *Roe* decision created? Moreover, what factors about state politics might affect the policy course that the states travel?

Our second concern is more theoretical. One characteristic of the abortion debate is that the public, though uncomfortable with abortion, generally supports access to abortion services. In contrast, the interest group system seems more slanted against abortion. Thus abortion represents a case of public opinion clashing with interest groups. We raise the timeless question, When public opinion and interest groups collide, who wins?

Abortion Policy and Public Opinion in the States

A huge literature now exists on trends and determinants of attitudes towards abortion (Cook et al. 1992a; Page and Shapiro 1992). We need not review much of that literature, as our concern is with the impact of the distribution of opinion on policy, not the determinants of that opinion. Several points about opinion toward abortion stand out for this analysis. Pro-choice sentiment is more common among the mass public than is opposition toward abortion. Yet a significant fraction of the populace is somewhat ambivalent, wanting to keep access to abortion legal, but regulating that access. These patterns have been quite stable since the late 1970s (Page and Shapiro 1992:63-64, 105-110).

In particular, nearly 40% of the public will allow abortion for any reason.[1] This total increases for special circumstances. If the mother's health is endangered nearly 90% would support abortion, and around 80% would allow abortion for rape or birth defect reasons. However, support declines for other reasons, such as low income (about 45% support), single mothers (about 40% support), and birth control (about 40%). And about 10%-15% of the public would never allow abortion for any reason (see Stanley and Niemi 1990:33). Because public support for abortion changes so radically depending on the reason, one must be very cautious to match the public opinion reading to the policy under investigation.

In the November 1990 *Washington Post Exit Poll,* 9,444 voters from 41 states and the District of Columbia were queried on their attitudes toward abortion. This unique and large data set becomes our public opinion data base.[2] However, it poses two problems. One relates to the missing states, the other to the question that was posed to voters.

Nine states are absent: Alaska, Idaho, Louisiana, Mississippi, Missouri, North Dakota, Utah, Virginia, and Washington. A few potential biases may occur because of their absence. Smaller western states are overrepresented among the absentees, while northeastern and New England states are underrepresented. And it appears that more conservative states are over-represented. Only Washington, Alaska, and perhaps Virginia,[3] may hold pro-choice-leaning positions on abortion. To check to see if the missing states may cause a sampling bias problem, we regressed a dummy variable for whether or not the state was included in the *Post* sample on a host of variables reported later in this chapter. No significant differences were detected between the states included and excluded from the *Post* survey.[4]

The text of the *Post* question reads: "Which of these statements comes closest to your view about abortion? (1) It should be legal in all circum-stances; (2) It should be legal only in some circumstances; or (3) It should not be legal in any circumstances." The limitation of this question is that it does not raise the further issue of which circumstances are legitimate to those in the middle category. Thus this question will be inappropriate to use to study the vast array of regulatory policies that the states have implemented (e.g., parental and/or spousal notification, funding restric-tions, waiting period).

State opinion on abortion is highly variable. Figure 12.1 plots the distribution. We estimate mean state abortion opinion relying on the formula that Wright, Erikson, and McIver (1985, 1987) used to create their mean ideology and partisanship measures. We multiply percentage anti-abortion attitudes by −1, the middle category (allow abortion in some circumstances) by 0, and pro-abortion opinion by 1. Thus we take advan-tage of the stability and hardness of the opinions of those on the extremes, while eliminating the more fluid middle category from consideration. This opinion index represents the relative advantage of the pro-choice versus pro-life opinion holders in a state.

The average state shows a 19.14% net opinion favoring the pro-choice position. Around this average is great variability ranging from 10% net pro-life to 44% net pro-choice. Moreover, the series is highly reliable, in part because of the strong variance. We compute a reliability coefficient by dividing the average sample variance for each state cross-section by the variance for the series itself, and subtracting that fraction from 1.[5] Dividing 9,444 by 42 gives us an average *n* of 225. The series variance is

			Indiana		
			Iowa	Arizona	
			Montana	Colorado	Michigan
			New Mexico	Delaware	Minnesota
			North Carolina	Florida	Nevada
			Oklahoma	Georgia	New Hampshire
			Pennsylvania	Hawaii	New Jersey	California
		Alabama	South Carolina	Illinois	New York	Connecticut
		Arkansas	Tennessee	Kansas	Ohio	Maine
Kentucky	Nebraska	Wisconsin	Maryland	Rhode Island	Oregon
South Dakota	West Virginia	Wyoming	Massachusetts	Texas	Vermont
Pro-Life	**Even**	**Majority**	**Landslide**		**Consensus**

Figure 12.1. Distribution of State Public Opinion on Abortion

SOURCE: Calculated from *Washington State Exit Poll,* November 1990
NOTES: Definitions: Pro-Life = Greater than net 5% pro-life; Even = Net less than +/- 5% pro-life or pro-choice; Majority = Net 5%-15% pro-choice; Landslide = Net 16%-35% pro-choice; Consensus = Net greater than 36% pro-choice (see text for further details on these calculations)

175.55, and we assume a high error variance of 8.5% for samples of $n = 225$. We obtain a reliability of .95.

Interest Groups and Abortion

Not only is abortion a salient, charged issue to the public, but it is one with intense interest group activism, as well. Few issues of the day can equal the mobilization and intensity of interest groups associated with the abortion debate. The 1990 *Congressional Quarterly Washington Information Directory* (Congressional Quarterly 1990) identifies 11 interest groups as primarily concerned with abortion. In a comprehensive study of abortion political action committees (PACs), Wilcox (1989b) counts 85 such organizations contributing money to candidates for office from 1978-1984. In detailed studies, Hershey (1986) documents the mobilization of abortion interest groups into the congressional election arena. Moreover, interest groups on both sides of the issue fought heavily to influence presidential nomination choices to the Supreme Court. Some have even made the abortion issue their litmus test for supporting/opposing federal judicial nominations (Medoff 1989).

Pro-life forces within the interest group system seem more strongly poised for action than the pro-choice groups, biasing the interest group system toward the pro-life side. Of the 85 PACs located by Wilcox (1989b), 81 are pro-life, 4 are pro-choice, and the pro-life PACs contributed more money from 1980-1984 than the pro-choice forces: $1,032,494 (53%) to $914,874 (47%). However, a comparison of PAC receipts, a better indicator of available resources, shows a stronger tilt toward the pro-life coalition ($5,224,346 to $2,431,822): pro-life PACs took in about 68% of abortion PAC related monies.

Measuring attributes of state interest group systems has proved difficult (see, e.g., Gray and Lowery 1990; but see Goggin and Kim 1992 for an example as applied to the abortion case). We assume that the greater the resources at the disposal of an interest group, potentially the greater impact it may have on policy making. Resources come in many varieties, from campaign contributions to information. Moreover, we must take into account the comparative resource advantages of pro-life and pro-choice interests in the states. Theories of countervailing power of interest groups suggest that the presence of two comparable but opposed interests may cancel out each other's impact, producing a policy impasse if no other policy motivating factor is at work.

Because data concerning specific state-level interest groups are hard to come by (see the effort by Goggin and Kim 1992), we rely on the core resource of an interest, whether it is organized and possesses an existing organization structure. We determine this by establishing whether or not the two major abortion adversaries, the National Abortion Rights Action League (NARAL) and the National Right to Life Committee, have state or local organizational affiliates. Thus, we generate two dummy variables, one for each side, of whether or not such an organization is present. We used the *Encyclopedia of Associations* to determine existence.

However, because our true concern is the net advantage of one side of the debate over the other, we subtract the NARAL dummy from the Right to Life one. We hypothesize that when both possess such state organizations their net impact will be the same as if neither was so organized, a suggestion consistent with countervailing power theories of interest group organization and competition. If the resulting variable takes on a value of one (+1), the pro-life side is advantaged, and the pro-choice side is advantaged if the variable's value is negative one (−1).

There exists considerable variation in this variable. Pro-choice advantages are shown by 11 states (26.8%), 9 (22.0%) display pro-life, and 21 (51.2%) reveal no net advantage. Also, the correlation between abortion attitudes and interest group advantage is not statistically significant ($r =$ .13). In some states aggregate opinion and the interest group system reinforce each other. In others, neither element is poised strongly in favor of one side or the other. In a third set, opinion and interests appear opposed. Thus all three logical possibilities are represented.

The Dependent Variable: Abortion Policy in the States

Our public opinion measure severely limits which policy can be investigated. None of the many state regulatory policies are viable candidates because public opinion in support or opposition varies so widely depending upon the reason or regulation. We are thus restricted to a policy that relates to the dimension that the *Post* question taps into: whether abortion should be legal or illegal.

One type of state policy fits this condition well, whether or not the state has passed legislation calling for a constitutional amendment to ban abortion. (Data on state actions vis-à-vis the amendment ban are presented in Stanley and Niemi 1990:18-19). Of our sample of 41 states, 15 (34.1%) have passed the banning amendment and 27 (65.85%) have not.[6] The list of states supporting the banning amendment include notably conservative states (Wyoming, North Dakota, Alabama) as well as some of the most liberally inclined states in the nation (Massachusetts, Rhode Island, Pennsylvania). Similarly, some states that are conventionally considered liberal have not accepted the amendment (New York), while states often thought conservative have also refused to enact the amending proposition (North Carolina). As other studies have shown, abortion does not cleanly relate to the division between liberals and conservatives (e.g., Berkman and O'Connor 1992).

However, this policy does cause us some potential problems. State action on the Constitutional amendment ban ceased by the early 1980s, after Ronald Reagan was elected and indicated a willingness to appoint pro-life justices to the Supreme Court. The pro-life movement turned its political strategy away from the states in general and toward the overthrow of *Roe v. Wade*.

The problem that arises is that our predictor variables, public opinion and interest groups, are collected at a time point after state action ceased, causing us potential causality problems. However, as public opinion has been so stable, especially for the strong pro-life and pro-choice opinion holders, the *Post* measure should be a relatively valid measure of extreme state opinion during the period of state policy action. Our measure is associated with categorical indicators of two state abortion policy measures, whether a state requires parental consent for minors seeking abortions ($\chi^2 = 5.53$, $p < .05$, $\gamma = .72$) and whether a state funds abortions for

Medicaid enrollees ($\chi^2 = 4.58$, $p < .05$, $\gamma = .60$), that are contemporaneous with our opinion data.

Interest groups have not been as stable as opinion. We attempted to ameliorate this problem by collecting interest group data as close to the policy period as possible (mid-1980s), but the interest group world is still notably dynamic. However, we may use this to our advantage. The impact of this measurement error of the interest group world should weaken the impact of interest groups in our statistical analysis, providing us with conservative estimates of interest group impact, compared to the more precise impact from public opinion.

An Initial Examination:
Is Abortion Policy a Function of Ideology,
Partisanship, or Abortion Demand?

Many studies of policy making have focused on the influence of political parties, partisanship, and ideological leanings on public policy (for a good review, see Jackson and Kingdon 1992). Demand for policy has also been used as an explanation for policy outcomes. We initially address the question of whether this abortion policy is a function of partisanship, ideology, and/or demand. Past research indicates that abortion policies may not relate to these conventional policy factors, especially partisanship and ideology (Nice 1988), but studies have found an association between public demand for abortion and abortion policy stances of a state's senators (Medoff 1989). We use the following equation to test the partisanship-ideology-demand perspective:

Abortion Policy = Constant + State Partisanship
+ State Ideology + State Party Competitiveness
+ State Abortion Use.

The state partisanship and ideology variables come from Wright et al. (1985), party competition from Bibby, Cotter, Gibson, and Huckshorn (1990:66), and abortion use is defined as the 1985 abortion rate per 1,000 (*Statistical Abstract of the United States* 1990). As the Wright et al. data do not contain figures for Hawaii, we run the equation on the remaining 49 states. The dependent variable is dichotomous; we estimate the equation with probit regression.

Results are presented in Table 12.1. None of the variables proves a potent predictor of state action on the proposed amendment to ban abortion, and the equation as a whole is unimpressive. The percentage correctly

Table 12.1 Partisan, Ideological, and Demand Impacts on State Abortion Policy

Variable	b	SE	t
Constant	-2.04	1.23	-1.65
Ideology	4.85	3.54	1.37
Partisanship	2.42	2.86	0.84
Party Competition	2.31	2.03	1.14
Abortion Use	-0.005	0.03	-0.16
Base	65%		
% Correct	65%		
Log Likelihood			
initial	-25.90		
convergence	-23.97		
n	40		

NOTE: Hawaii is excluded because the Wright, Erikson, and McIver (1985) ideology and partisanship measures do not present data on Hawaii.

predicted does not improve over the baseline and the log likelihood barely improves.

These results indicate, as has other research, that abortion policy is a function of neither state partisan forces nor citizen ideology. This stands in stark contrast to Wright et al. (1987) who found strong relationships between state liberal opinion and some state policies. However, the policies that they looked at reasonably relate to the liberal-conservative dimension. Abortion does not seem to. Moreover, abortion policy is not a function of abortion use. That is, policymakers are neither responding to the demand for abortion as indicated in use rates—in contrast to what Medoff (1989) finds—nor are they reacting to use rates.

Abortion Policy as a Function of Public Opinion and Interest Group Influence

The above analysis suggests that state abortion policy is not related to normal partisan divisions or ideological orientations. In addition, it seems unrelated to the demand for abortion services (abortion use rates) or reactions to those rates. In this section we estimate the impact of state public opinion on abortion and the mobilization of the interest group system on state action on the constitutional amendment to ban abortion. Throughout, we have been suggesting that abortion policy is a function of those two factors. We test these ideas with the following equation:

Table 12.2   Probit Results of Public Opinion and Interest Groups Effects on State Passage of the Constitutional Amendment to Ban Abortion

Variable	b	SE	t
Constant	.34	.42	0.81
Public Opinion	.044	.020	2.16
Interest Group	.898	.358	2.51
Baseline	65.85		
% Correct	75.61		
Improvement	9.7%		
Log Likelihood			
initial	−28.42		
convergence	−19.72		
n	41		

Abortion Policy = Constant + Mean State Opinion on Abortion
+ Net Interest Group Mobilization.

Table 12.2 presents the results of the probit estimation of our two variables on abortion policy. The results speak clearly. Both interest groups and public opinion significantly affect state action on the abortion banning amendment, and the signs for the variables are in the expected directions. When either public opinion or the interest group system leans pro-life, states are more likely to pass the constitutional amendment.

Further, addition of the partisan, ideological, and abortion use variables, singularly or in any combination, has no effect on these results. None of those variables reaches statistical significance, nor does their inclusion affect the impact of the public opinion and interest group variables. We added an indirect measure of the interest group system to the equation: state antiabortion religiosity (measured by summing the percentage of the state's Catholics, Southern Baptists, and Mormons). Still, only the direct measures of public opinion and interest groups affect state abortion policy. The indirect measure of the interest group climate fails to reach statistical significance and does not affect the performance of the direct opinion and interest variables. Hence, the impact of direct measure of opinion and interest groups does not appear to be spurious.

Moreover, the model is quite robust. It improves over the baseline by nearly 10% (from 65.85 to 75.61), which represents a proportionate reduction of error of 28.6%. Plus, the log likelihood ratio is improved upon from an initial value of −28.42 to a convergence value of −19.72, a proportional

Table 12.3 Probabilities of State Passage of the Constitutional Amendment to Ban
Abortion

Public Opinion*	Interest Groups		
	net for	even	net against
10% net for	.90	.67	.32
even	.82	.50	.18
10% net against	.68	.33	.09
20% net against	.49	.19	.04
44% net against	.15	.03	.00

NOTE: *10% net for is the maximum for, 19.14% net against is the mean, 44% net against is the maximum
against.

change of 30.6%. These are statistically significant improvements over
merely knowing the distribution of accepting/non-accepting states (the
baseline). However, as probit coefficients (labeled b in the tables) cannot
be interpreted intuitively, we convert them into probabilities to calculate
the impact of the two predictor variables under varying conditions.

Table 12.3 presents results of the probability analysis. The even-even
cell provides us with the probability of passage when neither interest
groups nor public opinion leans in either direction, that is, when both are
evenly divided. Here, the probability of passage is .5. This can serve as a
baseline from which to compare the effects of interest groups and public
opinion under varying conditions.

By reading across the second (even) row, we can estimate the effect of
interest group impact when public opinion is evenly divided on the abortion issue. The probability of passage rises to .82 when pro-life groups
possess a net advantage in the state. Alternatively, the probability drops to
.18 when pro-choice forces have an organizational advantage. As this
variable is measured symmetrically, we produce a symmetric effect. This
is crude measurement, but it tells us that when public opinion is divided
(or uninformed) on an issue, interest groups have a strong probability of
carrying the day. If opinion is divided, interest groups that are organiza-
tionally advantaged seem able to prevail on policy outcomes, a not too
surprising finding.

The center column contains estimates of the impact of public opinion
leanings when interest group resources either cancel out or are not present
(the latter seems an unlikely prospect on most issues). If opinion leans
toward passage by 10%, the true maximum observed in these data, the
probability of passage is .67, a change of .17 from the base. Alternately,
if opinion shifts in the opposite direction by 10%, the probability of

passage declines to .33. The average opinion split across the states, however, was nearly a 20% advantage for pro-choice opinions over pro-life ones. Here the probability of passage dims to .19. And when the pro-choice opinion advantage reaches its maximum of 44%, the probability of passage of the abortion banning amendment nearly extinguishes at .03.

Clearly, both interest groups and public opinion can affect policy outcomes when their opposite number is evenly divided (or nonorganized). But this finding is far from compelling. More interesting are situations when opinion and interests clash, situations that many observers feel to be quite common. Aside from the abortion issue, it is thought to exist on issues of gun control, busing, and affirmative action, to name only some of the more well-publicized issues. Thus we ask: Can interest groups block popular impact on public policy? What are the limits to interest group frustration of popular control over public policy? The probabilities in Table 12.3 offer us some answers based upon this abortion example.

For instance, assume pro-choice interest groups hold the advantage, but public opinion favoring banning abortion is at its maximum level, 10% net (the uppermost left cell). The probability of passage is only .32. When opinion is only mildly in favor of the banning amendment, but interests are mobilized against banning abortion, interests win. The same is true when opinion is mildly against banning abortion, again at the 10% net rate, but interest groups for banning abortion hold the advantage.

It seems reasonable to find that interest groups should prevail when public opinion is only narrowly positioned on one side of an issue. We caution here that we have no data on the relative strength of interest group resources, only whether organized interests face no opposition. This is probably a relatively extreme situation. It does not tell us if highly endowed interests are more influential than less endowed interests when neither face opposing interest groups. Thus there is a bluntness to our discussion.

What happens in the "typical" case, when a state's opinion is at the national average (about a 20% net advantage against banning abortion), but interest groups for banning abortion hold the advantage. The probability of passage hovers at .49—matters are too close to call. Of interest here is the fact that opinion is at landslide proportions favoring the legality of abortion, but active interests favoring banning abortions can render the political outcome indeterminant. This finding helps explain the great degree of political insecurity among pro-choice advocates. Even when strong public support for their position exists, interest group opposition may prevail.

Only when opinion moves even more decidedly into the pro-choice column, at consensus levels, can opinion easily defeat organized interests.

We see this when opinion reaches its maximum value, 40% against the ban. When such an opinion distribution faces organized interest group opposition, the public can expect to win 85% of the time. Strongly felt public consensus is, however, probably rare in politics.

To summarize, when opinion is narrowly decided on an issue or leans slightly in one direction, interest groups in opposition may prevail. And, even when opinion is at landslide proportions, interest groups may still win about half of the time. Only when opinion is nearly consensual will public opinion consistently defeat organized interests.

Policy Implications:
A Simulation Projected Onto the Post-*Webster* Age

Can we use the above results to say anything about the future of abortion policy in the United States? We need to make several assumptions about the political world and these data before we can offer any predictions.

First, let us assume that the conservative majority on the Supreme Court will almost certainly open the door to increasing state regulation of abortion, as it has already done in *Webster* and *Casey*.[7] Second, we need to distinguish between two types of abortion policies, those that regulate access (such as parental and spousal notification and public financing of abortion) and those that prohibit abortion. As we stated above, our data can only speak to the latter issue.

Third, we must assume that all of the data used above are relatively faithful representations of the structure and preferences of state politics on abortions in the post-*Webster* age. As noted above, that is probably the case for the public opinion data but less likely for the other variables, interest group mobilization and state legislative action to ban abortion through the constitutional amendment procedure.

It is likely, as most theory suggests, that the interest group world is highly dynamic, and the interest group configurations described in this study will not exist in the near future. Mobilization often stimulates mobilization. Moreover, changes in the makeup of the state houses and executive mansions, after years of heated controversy and changes in personnel, may mean that the state policy variable used here only weakly resembles current and future state policy actions. Still, these data may be useful in what they tell us about possible future state policy actions and about the factors that affect the course of state policy on abortion.

Calculations of the likelihood of banning abortion are based on the probability estimates presented above. The results of the simulation indicate that 5 states will most likely ban abortions (Alabama, Iowa, Kentucky,

Nebraska, and South Dakota); 5 others are too close to call with a 50% chance of banning abortions (Arkansas, Delaware, Kansas, New Jersey, and Rhode Island). The simulation predicts that the remaining 30 states in the sample examined here will not take action to ban abortion.

Inspection of the two columns on Table 12.4 reveals why this is the case: Either public opinion is at consensual pro-choice levels, which can offset the appearance of pro-life interest groups that are unchallenged by pro-choice interest groups; or a slightly less strong but still positive public opinion distribution is matched against a divided interest group world. In this second case, public opinion will influence public policy because opposing interest groups cancel out each other's impact on the policy-making process.

These results are much more optimistic than the report by the National Abortion Rights Action League (1989). That report, based on a survey of the states, the general tendencies of the state legislature, prior or pending state action on abortion, and the public positions of the leading state executives, was decidedly more pessimistic about future access to abortion services. The NARAL report found only 5 states where both the governor and both houses of the legislature supported abortion rights, whereas 15 showed all three opposing abortion. The remaining 30 states had some combination consisting of both support and opposition to abortion access.

There are several limitations to the NARAL report. First, it is a partisan document to be used to stimulate pro-choice activity. Thus the report is purposely pessimistic. For instance, the report makes little mention of the strong public support for some type of abortion access, and it underestimates the impact that opinion may have on policy making. Instead it sees pro-life interest groups as extremely potent and successful in influencing policy. However, were the report rosier, it might demobilize political activity in favor of the pro-choice stance.

Second, the report assumes that the attitudes of public officials directly and totally translate into public policy. The report does not recognize that politicians may be symbolically positioning on the issue. That is, some politicians may voice opposition to abortion, with little intention of implementing such policies. Thus politicians may point to the support of the pro-life movement, while also pointing to the fact that action against abortion access has not be forthcoming. In a zero sum game like abortion, where support for one side alienates the other side, the life of political leaders becomes decidedly more complex and uncertain. Thus we need to be more cautious in our reading of political leaders' policy preferences from their public statements.

Still, the results of the simulation are open to criticism. The timeliness and dynamic quality of some of the data used may greatly affect the

Table 12.4 Predictions of State Activity on Banning Abortions if *Roe v. Wade* is Overturned

	Public Opinion Distribution	Interest Group Distribution	Predicted Policy
Alabama	Even	Anti	Ban
Arizona	Landslide	Pro	
Arkansas	Even	Even	Ban .5
California	Consensus	Even	
Colorado	Landslide	Pro	
Connecticut	Consensus	Pro	
Delaware	Landslide	Anti	Ban .5
Florida	Landslide	Even	
Georgia	Landslide	Even	
Hawaii	Landslide	Even	
Illinois	Landslide	Even	
Indiana	Majority	Even	
Iowa	Majority	Anti	Ban
Kansas	Landslide	Anti	Ban .5
Kentucky	Anti	Anti	Ban
Maine	Consensus	Anti	
Maryland	Landslide	Even	
Massachusetts	Landslide	Even	
Michigan	Landslide	Even	
Minnesota	Landslide	Pro	
Montana	Majority	Pro	
Nebraska	Even	Anti	Ban
Nevada	Landslide	Even	
New Hampshire	Landslide	Pro	
New Jersey	Landslide	Anti	Ban .5
New Mexico	Majority	Even	
New York	Landslide	Even	
North Carolina	Majority	Pro	
Ohio	Landslide	Even	
Oklahoma	Majority	Pro	
Oregon	Consensus	Pro	
Pennsylvania	Majority	Even	
Rhode Island	Landslide	Anti	Ban .5
South Carolina	Majority	Even	
South Dakota	Anti	Even	Ban
Tennessee	Majority	Even	
Texas	Landslide	Even	
Vermont	Consensus	Even	
West Virginia	Even	Pro	
Wisconsin	Majority	Even	
Wyoming	Majority	Pro	

NOTE: Variable Definitions:
1. Public Opinion Distribution: *Anti* = Greater than net 5% pro-life (never allowing abortion to be legal); *Even* = Net less than + or − 5% pro-life or pro-choice; *Majority* = Net 5%-15% pro-choice (always allow abortion); *Landslide* = Net 16%-35% pro-choice; *Consensus* = Net 36%+ pro-choice.
2. Interest Group Distribution: *Anti* = only pro-life abortion group present; *Even* = either both pro-life and pro-choice groups present, or neither present; *Pro* = only pro-choice group present.

stability of the simulation results. It is plausible that the configuration of the interest group system may differ markedly in the 1990s from what we found in the mid- to late 1980s. Moreover, although we believe that public opinion is relatively stable on this issue, the possibility exists for opinion conversion. With the change in the political venue from the Court to the state setting, abortion may become more entangled with party and electoral forces, which may stimulate a realignment in public opinion on the issue. However, we believe that the symbolic and deep-seated nature of this issue strongly mitigates against such a possibility. Still, the policy debate may be redefined in such a way as to make the use of the proxy dependent variable, past state action on the constitutional amendment to ban abortion, invalid. Lastly, the simulation, because of data limitations on the opinion variable, cannot address the question of whether less sweeping but still restrictive abortion laws will be passed.

Conclusions

In this conclusion we address the two themes that motivated this chapter, abortion policy in the states in the post-*Webster*, post-*Casey* era, and the relative impact of public opinion and interest groups on policy making.

On the policy level, we witness great change as well as stability. The most important changes that the post-*Webster*, post-*Casey* era should bring concerns the venue of political activity. The judiciary no longer stands alone in policy making on this issue. Elected politicians, especially at the state levels, through recent Court decisions can now actively make abortion policy. This may change the terms of debate from one of constitutional and legal argumentation to one of campaign rhetoric, symbolic posturing, and partisan debate.

However, our results also indicate that not much may change substantively. General abortion access will likely be provided in most of the states; only a handful may try to outlaw abortion, as is currently the case in Utah and Louisiana. And another subset will probably try to restrict access. Although our simulation results are subject to several criticisms, as noted above, one reason stands out to explain the likely substantive stability. The main characters in the abortion policy arena—public opinion and interest groups—have not altered their general positions or strength in the political system. Moreover, as some research indicates, the Court is sensitive to the political environment. Thus the types of decisions that emerge from the judiciary may not differ radically from those that other politicians make on an issue such as abortion, which is not very technical, and where deep-seated emotions affect peoples thinking, and the policy system is in a high level of political mobilization. All politicians may similarly feel these strong pressures.

The recent election of Bill Clinton to the Presidency may also limit the degree of policy change. First of all, Clinton has publicly supported the pro-choice alternative, the first time in 12 years that a pro-choice advocate has occupied the White House. Any vacancies that occur on the Supreme Court, or throughout the federal judiciary, are thus likely to filled with pro-choice jurists, reversing the trend of the Reagan-Bush era. While this may not reverse the position of the Court on abortion policy, it may indicate at least a temporary halt in the Court's shift from the pro-choice *Roe* decision toward the more restrictive decisions of recent years.

With the Court no longer a secure bastion of pro-life sentiment, pro-life advocates in the states may scale back their attacks on abortion, offering more modest restrictions, lest they take the chance that a more liberal judiciary will overturn their more extreme efforts. Also, pro-life proponents may revive the constitutional amendment route to reverse the *Roe* decision, a strategy, that if successful, would insulate abortion policy from the tides of presidential elections. Thus the strategy device of nearly 20 years ago may reemerge.

Several important theoretical points also emerge from this study. Policy making is responsive to both public opinion and interest groups. More important, though, is that we are able to specify the conditions under which public opinion and interest groups influence policy making.

First, public opinion on the issue must be unambiguous. Here we define *clarity* in terms of net leanings of opinion in the mass public. The closer the public is to an even split on an issue, the less likely that it will influence policy making. Factors other than opinion may also affect clarity, for instance public understanding, knowledge, and information levels. But clarity in communicating to political leaders is an important prerequisite for public influence over public policy.

This point, while seemingly obvious, bears further scrutiny. Some studies of public opinion's influence on policy making cast the public as an undifferentiated mass (e.g., Denzau and Munger 1986). Results herein suggest that we pay particular attention to the distribution of opinion in the mass public, the number of people holding particular positions.

We also detected policy responsiveness to interest groups. Like the findings for public opinion, the net leanings of the contending interest groups were important in assessing interest group influence. Thus the point about clarity, again defined in consensual terms, is critical. The more unified the interest group system, the more impact it will have on policy making. An evenly divided interest group environment may erode any influence that interests may have, as the resources of competing interests cancel each others impact. Such a result is consistent with theories of countervailing power and Madison's *Federalist 10* prescription that pitting ambition against ambition is a hearty defense against factional (interest group) capture of government.

Yet the analysis presented above is not without some limitations. Future research along these lines requires that we refine our measurement of interest group resources. Here we employed just two criteria. The first was whether the interest possessed an organizational presence, providing us with an indication of permanence, organization, and sustained activity, which are the organizational foundations of interest resources and influence. The second criterion looked at the relative balance among competing sides. We need, especially along the first dimension, to account for differentials in organization resources like staffing, budgets, expertise, and so forth. Moreover, we need to assess the credibility, legitimacy, and public acceptance of an interest's activation in a particular issue arena. It is quite likely that wealthy interests, for instance oil lobbies, are less effective than their organizational resource base would predict because of a poor public image. Further, we need to extend the design across a broader array of issues.

What about our motivating question: Can interest groups block the public in the policy-making process? The answer is "sometimes," and the sometimes uncovered in this case study resonate well with the biases that Madison and the Federalists structured into our constitutional system.

The relative impact of public opinion and interest groups is in part dependent on the distribution of public opinion. We can categorize four different distributions of public opinion: divided, simple majoritarian, landslide majoritarian, and consensual. As our measures of interest group mobilization are cruder, we can only speak of the interest group system as being either divided or united. How do these four categories of public opinion distributions stack up against united interest groups?

Interest groups appear relatively successful in the first three levels, from divided opinion to landslide majoritarian. Specifically, when opinion is divided or possesses only simple majorities, united interest groups will usually prevail. Even when opinion leans in one direction at landslide proportions, united interest groups will prevail approximately half of the time. Only when public opinion is consensually united will it consistently defeat united opposition from interest groups. And this is as Madison would have it.

Checks and balances structure political and power relationships under American-styled constitutionalism. They not only affect political institutions, but also those who try to influence those institutions, such as the public and interest groups. Still, the system is designed to check public opinion somewhat more than interest groups, as our results also indicate.

Federalist 10 not only cautioned against the evils of faction, but suggested that majority factions were the most dangerous, as they could overwhelm minority factions through votes. Thus, although competitive ambition would cure the mischiefs of minority faction, structural impediments to majority rule faction were interposed into the constitutional structure. Hence, we find political arrangements that attempt to insulate some decision makers from direct popular influence: the president originally was not elected, Supreme Court justices are appointed and serve for life, amending the Constitution requires huge Congressional majorities or state action, Senators attain office through state legislative action. Moreover, minority protections were implemented into the Constitution through the Bill of Rights and the reserved power clause. Although majority rule is allowed under the Constitution, its role is highly restricted and circumscribed.

Only when the public speaks uniformly and consensually in support of a policy direction can the system be mobilized easily and swiftly to accord with public preferences. Again, we see the limits of majoritarianism inherent in our constitutional structure. But, insofar as the interest group system may be biased toward the upper and advantaged classes, public policy may be skewed toward their advantage as well. Little wonder that the public feels that interest groups may have too much influence in the political system. It may be the case.

Notes

1. The figures cited in this paragraph are taken from the Gallup Poll and the General Social Survey (GSS). The Gallup question was posed annually by the Gallup organization from the mid-1960s to 1973. From 1973 onward, the General Social Survey of the National Opinion Research Center at the University of Chicago included the Gallup Poll questions. Complete texts of the question and responses broken down by year are reported in Stanley and Niemi 1990, p. 33. Both the Gallup Poll and the GSS are nationwide surveys of the mass public.

2. Our use of these exit poll data are based upon pioneering work by Robert Erikson, Gerald Wright, and John McIver, who use exit polls from *The New York Times* to investigate state public opinion attributes, like partisanship, ideology, and culture; see Erikson, McIver, and Wright (1987), Erikson, Wright, and McIver (1989), and Wright et al. (1985, 1987). See also Goggin 1992 and Chapter 11 in this volume for other uses of exit polls to study abortion politics.

3. Although Virginia is usually considered a conservative state, Douglas Wilder, a black Democrat, was able to win the 1990 governorship, in part by injecting the contest with the abortion-rights issue, and thereby steering it away from a racially divisive contest. Hence, at least on abortion, we may circumspectly presume Virginians are somewhat more pro-choice.

4. Another procedure would be to use the opinion distributions of states neighboring those absent from the sample to create distributions for the missing states. However, as Erikson, McIver, and Wright (1987) demonstrate, each state's opinion structure, after controlling for factors such as demographics and economics, is still unique. That is, state residence affects

the opinion of its residents. Thus creating these spatially interpolated opinion distributions would involve some measurement error, something that we have tried to avoid by using directly observed, not inferred, opinions.

5. Here we assume that each sampled state has the same number of respondents. The *Post* survey report did not indicate state specific totals and we were unable to retrieve at this time the raw data from the *Post* to calculate these figures. However, using the average as we have done here should only trivially affect the reliability coefficient. If the averaging procedure has any effect, it is to depress the true reliability. In addition, we were conservative in assigning an error variance, which also has the effect of suppressing the computed reliability coefficient. Our interest here is not so much in computing a precise reliability value, but rather determining if the series can be thought of as generally reliable.

6. This compares with 19 (38%) states that have passed the amendment and 31 (62%) that have not. Thus our sample of states closely resembles that entire set of 50 states in its propensity to adopt the amendment.

7. However, the election of Bill Clinton to the presidency in 1993 may alter the makeup of the Court as Clinton, an avowed supporter of abortion rights, is able to make appointments to the Court.

13

Differences in Public Policies Toward Abortion

Electoral and Policy Context

SUSAN B. HANSEN

Ever since the Supreme Court's *Webster* decision (July 1989), public and media attention has focused on interstate differences in access to abortion. Following every new Supreme Court action, graphs or maps highlighting state differences in abortion policies appear in the mass media. Public opinion, political culture, religious composition, mobilization by pro- or anti-choice groups, availability of medical services, and legislative or gubernatorial leadership have all been examined to explain state differences in abortion restrictions (Halva-Neubauer 1989a; Hansen 1980; Medoff 1988, 1989; other chapters in this book).

Although women are most directly affected by laws and policies pertaining to abortion, mobilization by women themselves has received little attention in the growing published literature on state abortion policy. As Luker (1984) and Ginsburg (1989) have shown, the 1973 *Roe v. Wade* decision galvanized both anti- and pro-choice forces at the grass roots, with women active in both camps. Since *Roe,* women have become increasingly prominent in the labor force and the electorate, and have become much more visible in state capitals, as lobbyists, legislators, cabinet members, or holders of statewide executive or judicial office. Has such activity made any difference for state abortion policy? This analysis will show that the proportion of women in state legislatures has indeed had such an effect, in part reflecting political and social circumstances that favor the election of women in certain states. Although not all elected women are feminists, pro-choice, or even concerned with the abortion issue, restrictions on abortion are less likely to be enacted or implemented in states where more women hold legislative office.

Funding restrictions, however, are somewhat more likely in states where more women hold executive positions. Yet, despite prohibitions against Medicaid funding for abortions in all but a few states, abortion rates have declined little if at all. And the multitude of other restrictions adopted since *Roe* have likewise had little impact. Does mobilization by women have anything to do with the lack of relationship between policy enactment and policy outcomes?

In order to answer such questions, I will first describe six possible indicators of mobilization by women, and test the functional form of the relationship between the strongest indicator (the proportion of women in the state legislature) and several measures of state policies affecting women. But because women legislators remain a distinct minority in all states, alternative explanations for abortion policy must be considered as well. A two-stage least squares analysis finds that state political culture and policy history affect both abortion policy and the rate at which women are elected to public office. Finally, I will examine the impact of abortion restrictions on abortion rates, changes in those rates, and reliance on out-of-state abortion providers. Neither legal restrictions, funding cutbacks, nor violence directed at clinics produced any declines in actual abortion rates in the 1980s. Both symbolic politics and countermobilization by women are suggested as reasons why abortion restrictions have so little effect.

State Differences in Abortion: How Much and Why?

Nearly two decades after *Roe v. Wade,* the American states still exhibit sharp contrasts in abortion rates. Rates as of 1988 ranged from 145 per 1,000 women of childbearing age (the standard demographic rate) in Washington, DC, and 45.9 in California, to only 5.1 per 1,000 women in Wyoming (Table 13.1).[1] In Table 13.1, states that (as of 1988) still funded most Medicaid abortions are marked with an asterisk. Most such states had relatively high abortion rates, although there are several exceptions. West Virginia, a poor rural state with few medical facilities, is the only state funding Medicaid abortions that has a low rate. And despite Medoff's (1988) prediction, the cutoff of funding for Medicaid abortions did *not* lead to the decline he expected in abortion rates.

The total number of abortions has remained constant at the national level (about 1.5 million yearly) throughout the 1980s. Abortion rates have declined only very slightly, despite evidence of increased sexual activity by teenagers; these modest declines have been attributed to increased use of contraception.[2] But most nonfunding states have had low rates ever

Table 13.1 Abortion Rates by State per 1,000 Women Age 15-44, 1988

*District of Columbia	145.9	Pennsylvania	18.9
*California	45.9	Tennessee	18.9
*New York	43.3	Alabama	18.7
*Hawaii	43.0	Alaska	18.2
Nevada	40.3	Minnesota	18.2
Delaware	35.7	Nebraska	17.7
*New Jersey	35.1	New Hampshire	17.5
Florida	31.5	South Carolina	16.7
*Connecticut	31.2	Montana	16.5
Rhode Island	30.6	Missouri	16.4
*Massachusetts	30.2	Louisiana	16.3
Arizona	28.8	Maine	16.2
*Maryland	28.6	Oklahoma	16.2
Michigan	28.5	Wisconsin	16.0
*Washington	27.6	North Dakota	14.9
Illinois	26.4	Iowa	14.6
*Vermont	25.8	Kentucky	13.0
*North Carolina	25.4	Utah	12.8
Texas	24.8	Indiana	11.9
*Oregon	23.9	Arkansas	11.6
Virginia	23.7	Mississippi	8.4
*Georgia	23.5	Indiana	8.2
*Colorado	22.4	*West Virginia	7.5
Ohio	21.0	South Dakota	5.7
Kansas	20.1	Wyoming	5.1
New Mexico	19.1		

NOTE: * State funds Medicaid abortions.

since abortion was legalized after *Roe*. In fact, abortion rates as of 1976 are strongly associated with 1988 abortion rates ($R = .87$), although states with low rates in 1976 experienced the fastest growth in rates between 1976 and 1988. We have, then, a great deal of public controversy about limiting access to abortion, but little evidence of change in private behavior. Two immediate questions emerge: If abortion has indeed been made so much more difficult and expensive, why have rates not dropped? Further, if abortion restrictions have so little effect, why are they being proposed or adopted in such large numbers by so many states?

Part of the answer, of course, is that a few states (including those that account for a large proportion of abortions performed) have used legislation, referenda, constitutional provisions, or court interpretations of their own Equal Rights Amendments or right-to-privacy statutes in order to guarantee access to abortion services (Boling 1991; Coglianese 1991;

Kincaid 1988). Elsewhere, highly restrictive legislation has been passed, but is on hold pending legal appeals; the *Casey* restrictions (upheld by the Supreme Court in 1992) have yet to be implemented in Pennsylvania.[3] Other states are actively debating the issue, although as recent studies of the Ohio and Missouri legislatures demonstrate, elected officials sometimes prefer to avoid this controversial topic altogether (Cates 1991; Richard 1991b).

Which states are most likely to restrict abortion? Following every new Supreme Court action, graphs or maps highlighting state differences in abortion policies appear in the mass media. Public opinion, political culture, religious composition, mobilization by pro- or anti-choice groups, availability of medical services, and legislative or gubernatorial leadership all help account for state differences in abortion restrictions, based on regression models (Albritton and Wetstein 1991; Goggin and Kim 1992; Hansen 1980; Medoff 1988, 1989), case studies (Halva-Neubauer 1989a), or simulation (Chapter 12, this volume).

One might anticipate that generally liberal states would be less likely to restrict abortion, whether or not they elected many women. Some states (such as Minnesota and California) have strongly favored equal rights for women and have adopted many policies from the feminist political agenda. Other states (such as Mississippi, which never formally ratified the Nineteenth Amendment) have done little in these respects. Yet states that are quite liberal by most indicators have not always favored specific policies affecting women's rights. Minnesota, a pioneer in comparable worth policies, has passed several laws restricting access to abortions, including a rigorous parental notification law.[4] New York, usually a staunchly liberal state, failed in a 1980 referendum to ratify a state ERA. Illinois was the only northern industrial state that did not ratify the federal ERA. Conversely, Texas, a generally conservative state, was an early ratifier of the ERA and now has a feminist governor (Ann Richards) and several female big-city mayors. Pennsylvania is an interesting anomaly: Despite a state ERA, polls indicating public support for abortion rights and legal reforms in areas such as battering and child support, the state recently adopted some of the most restrictive abortion laws in the United States and has consistently ranked very low (46th out of 50 in 1990) in its proportion of female state legislators.

In other words, we cannot assume a priori that general support for women's rights will predict either abortion legislation or other feminist policies.[5] Abortion is a highly controversial issue affecting deeply held political and religious values, and the politics thereof may thus differ in important respects from policies more amenable to compromise and incrementalism (Luker 1984; Tribe 1990). Further, recent Gallup polls have shown that public opinion is strongly in favor of many restrictions on abortion (parental or spousal consent, a waiting period, mandated counseling concerning abortion risks and alternatives), although opposition to a total ban on abortion remains strong (Hugick 1992). In such a context, symbolic restrictions with little policy impact may well result, unless *Roe* is overturned altogether (as now seems unlikely under Bill Clinton's Presidency and his likely Supreme Court appointees).

Accounting for State Differences in Abortion Policies

The abortion controversy is more one of values than of economics. Although abortion *rates* are higher in wealthier, urbanized states with greater access to medical care (Hansen 1980), abortion *policies* are likely to reflect political factors (ideology, public opinion, the number and strength of state interest groups, religious and demographic composition of the electorate and of state government). The issue here is whether women, as workers, elected officials, or lobbyists, have any impact over and above other factors affecting abortion policy.

Mobilization

Political mobilization by women themselves has increased considerably since 1973. One potential indicator of women's political influence is the proportion of women in the labor force, which varied in 1988 from a low of 39% in West Virginia to more than 70% in California (*Statistical Abstract of the U.S.* 1991). Working women are more likely to be aware of public policies affecting their interests and are usually in a better position to mobilize on their own behalf than women who are homemakers, students, or retired (Anderson 1975; Hansen, Franz, and Netemeyer-Mays 1976; Sapiro 1991). Medoff (1988) found a significant positive relationship between the proportion of white-collar women in a state's labor force and the probability of a pro-choice vote by the state's U.S. Senators.

On the average, 18% of state legislators are now women, and many women have been elected to statewide office (e.g., governor, lieutenant governor, attorney general, judge).[6] Other studies (Darcy, Welch, and Clark 1987; Hill 1982; Mezey 1978) have noted that women in public office tend to be somewhat more liberal than their male peers. A major 1989 study by the Rutgers Center for American Women and Politics (CAWP) found that 75% of female state legislators, compared with 61% of their male counterparts, were against banning abortion (Center for American Women and Politics [CAWP] 1991); women legislators, regardless of party, were more likely than their male counterparts to focus on women's issues. Berkman and O'Connor (Chapter 15, this volume) and Goggin and Kim (1992) also observed a negative association between the proportion of women state legislators and adoption of abortion restrictions, although the regression coefficients they reported were modest and assumed linear relationships.

A high proportion of women holding statewide office (governor, secretary of state, etc.) should indicate greater support for policies favorable to women's equal rights, as Leader (1977) found for the 1970s. Although women are a distinct minority in all state governments, the proportion of women in public office varies considerably across states and has increased steadily since the 1970s.

A fourth potential indicator of political mobilization by women is the representation of women's concerns by interest groups in the states. Women's PACs have been growing in number and influence (Kleeman 1983). Gray and Lowery (1989) have developed measures for 1975 and 1980 of women's groups as a proportion of total state registered lobbyists, and have provided me with their data. I also have data on membership by state from the National Abortion Rights Action League (NARAL).[7] These indicators, though not ideal, should permit interstate comparisons of lobbying efforts by women. It is more difficult to obtain cross-state indicators of mobilization by anti-choice groups such as the Concerned Women of America; as will be described below, religious membership figures will be used as a surrogate indicator of organized opposition to abortion rights.

A final indicator of mobilization by women is the presence of a statewide commission on the status of women, which Evans and Nelson (1989) found to be important for adoption of comparable worth policies. As Sapiro (1981) cautions, however, such commissions are usually broad based, and may function more as agenda-setters and forums for discussion than as advocacy groups on behalf of either feminist or anti-feminist positions.

It would be simplistic to assume that the impact of female mobilization on women's policy issue is linear, increasing in direct proportion to the number of women elected. Karnig and Welch (1980) found that a threshold of about 20% was necessary before black officials could exert a measurable impact upon urban policy; women in only a few states have reached that level of representation in state legislatures. If a "threshold effect" holds for women as it does for blacks, token representation will have few policy consequences. New Hampshire merits special consideration; it has the highest proportion of women, but its large, part-time, volunteer legislature is hardly typical.

Increased representation by women officeholders may lead to *decreased* support for women's rights. As Darcy et al. (1987) note, while women have usually been more liberal than their male colleagues in Congress and in state legislatures, these differences have diminished over time, for several reasons. At least before 1992's "Year of the Woman," many women found it more difficult to get elected if they advocated feminist causes (Carroll 1984). The election of feminist or liberal women may encourage more conservative women to run (and both parties to nominate female candidates). As women elected officials learn the ropes and advance to positions of power, they may become more like their male colleagues in orientation (Kirkpatrick 1974; see also Genovese 1993). Carroll and Taylor (1989:19) found evidence of a "critical point somewhere near the 25% mark where women become such a sizeable minority that individual women legislators no longer feel as strong a personal responsibility to represent women as they do when women are a smaller minority." We might thus anticipate a curvilinear relationship—less support for equality and abortion rights at the highest and lowest levels of representation by women, more support in the middle range.

Political Values, Ideology, and Political Culture

States described as generally liberal in ideology, policy, or voting patterns should be most supportive of women's rights and access to abortion services. Ideally, state opinion polls or referenda results could be consulted to estimate public support for women's rights and abortion, but high-quality statewide surveys are seldom available, and only a few states have had initiatives or referenda on abortion issues. However, Albritton and Wetstein (1991) found that state averages of "pro-choice" responses to pooled ICPSR questions on abortion (1980-1988) ranged from 19% in Kentucky and Louisiana to 64% in Washington State; these state averages will be used here.[8]

States described as "moralistic" in political culture tend to favor a large role for the public sector and equality of access for all groups in society (Kincaid 1982; Kincaid and Lieske 1991). Such states tend to elect proportionately more women to public office (Hill 1981), and should be most supportive of policies involving equal rights for women. However, as Halva-Neubauer (1991) notes, the abortion issue is likely to be a conflictual one in a moralistic culture, which values both personal freedom and willingness to regulate in the interests of the commonwealth or a vulnerable class (the fetus). He thus describes an active pro-life movement and numerous abortion restrictions in Minnesota, a state with an otherwise strongly democratic and liberal tradition.

Organized Interests Favoring or Opposing Abortion

The abortion issue is of great concern to many groups other than women's rights advocates. Early feminist successes (the *Roe* decision,

Congressional approval of ERA) led to countermobilization by conservative groups such as the Eagle Forum (Conover and Gray 1983). Much of this has had a strong religious base. Fundamentalist Christians and Mormons were active in efforts to defeat ERA (Mansbridge 1986); the Roman Catholic Church strongly opposes abortion. Earlier research on state abortion rates (Hansen 1980) found that dominance of a state by one of these religious groups helped to explain low abortion rates; Louisiana and Utah were cases in point. But in cosmopolitan urban states, religious and secular groups tended to counterbalance one another. Thus, even though New York has proportionately more Catholics than Louisiana, New York has liberal abortion policies. These same patterns of balance or dominance by religious interests should continue to affect support for women's rights and abortion in more recent years.[9]

Countermobilization can work for pro-choice groups as well. States that enacted abortion restrictions after *Webster* or that have experienced a high degree of abortion-related violence experienced a greater increase in membership in NARAL between 1987 and 1990. The *Webster* decision was also a spur to organized efforts by pro-choice groups; nationally, NARAL membership more than doubled within a year after *Webster,* and the 1989 elections of Governors James Florio in New Jersey and Douglas Wilder in Virginia were widely attributed to negative popular reaction to *Webster* (see Chapter 8, this volume).

Earlier research (Hansen 1980) found that the number of abortion providers in a state was a strong predictor of high abortion rates.[10] Many doctors are concerned with the health risks to women from illegal abortions, and the American Medical Association opposed the "gag rule" because of concerns about liability and infringement on doctors' professional judgment. Abortion providers also have an economic interest in maintaining abortion access, and doctors and hospitals have well-developed lobbying connections in state capitals. In this analysis, the percentage of a state's hospitals performing abortions will be used to indicate the strength of medical lobbying on behalf of abortion access.

Historical Trends in State Politics and Policy

Even if a zero-order relationship between current abortion policics and mobilization by women could be established, this need not imply any causal relationship. Scholars writing on representation (Achen 1978; Pitkin 1967) tell us that demographic representation ("standing for") is no guarantee of representation of interests ("acting for"). Considerable feminist legislation was enacted in the late 1960s and early 1970s when women held a very small proportion of state offices. Divorce reform, state-level abortion liberalization before *Roe*, most state ERAs, and ratification of the federal ERA in 33 states, all occurred before 1976, when women occupied less than 4% of state legislative seats. Current patterns of political mobilization may have less impact on policies affecting women than historical trends in culture and public opinion.

Consider some historical precedents: Married Women's Property Rights laws in the 1840s were enacted long before suffrage and when the feminist movement had barely begun (Simon and Danziger 1991); there was more federal support (via the Sheppard-Towner Act) for child care and women's health in the 1920s than is the case today, when many more women vote and hold office (Stetson 1991). The major civil rights laws of the 1960s were enacted before many blacks held public office, although the use of mass protest was an effective alternative political strategy for blacks (Carmines and Stimson 1989).

What accounted for these early policy successes for women? One might argue than the first few women elected to state or federal office were effective far beyond their numbers; Frances Perkins, Jeannette Rankin, Margaret Chase Smith, Martha Griffiths, and Shirley Chisholm all had well-honed political skills. But Diamond (1977) and Kirkpatrick (1974) found that women's issues were not a priority for female state legislators of the early 1970s, and that few if any women held leadership positions. A more plausible explanation is that other groups in society were supportive of women's rights, particularly during the 1960s when civil rights was a popular cause. Women in public office would have sought alliances with such groups to support their own limited numbers. As Luker (1984) documents, support for liberalization of abortion came from doctors, lawyers, and mainline Protestant and Jewish clergy as well as from feminists (both male and female) and from mass-membership groups such as Planned Parenthood and the ACLU.

If these patterns persist, factors such as union membership, percentage blacks in the state legislature or the population, pro-choice opinions held by male legislators, and a moralistic political culture may carry as much or more weight than current mobilization by women themselves. Fundamental aspects of political culture and politics could lead both to the election of women to public office and to support for women's rights by other interest groups; current mobilization by women themselves would have little independent impact on either abortion rights or other policies affecting women. Both organizational inertia and the continuation of patterns of interest group pressures can account for this stability over time, despite recent legislative and judicial furor over abortion restrictions. But political action by women may still provide some protection against erosion of earlier policy gains.

We have, then, four different hypotheses to account for the enactment of state policies affecting abortion and women's rights:

H1. Support for abortion access and women's rights is a function of liberal ideology, public opinion, and moralist political culture. These factors may encourage the election of women to public office, but mobilization by women has little independent impact.

H2. Abortion access is a function of the influence of organized state groups (Mormons, Catholics, Protestant fundamentalists, doctors, abortion providers, the ACLU) with strong moral or economic interests in abortion policies. States where other liberal groups (unions, blacks, Democrats outside the South) are strong should also be pro-choice.

H3. Mobilization by women, as elected officials, lobbyists, or in the labor force, promotes feminist policies. The impact may be linear, curvilinear, or may show a threshold effect, and persists despite controls for other factors.

H4. Early support for women's rights predicts later support. Likewise, states that restricted abortion in the 1970s continue to do so. Current efforts by women themselves show little independent impact.

Measures and Methodology

Dependent Variables

Three indices of state abortion policy will be used in this chapter. The first is a *Congressional Quarterly* (CQ) index of recent abortion restrictions, reported in Biskupic (1989) from data gathered by the Alan Guttmacher Institute; the index is a summary measure of the number of restrictions a state had adopted by 1989.[11] A second index has been compiled by Glen Halva-Neubauer (1990), and is a count of the total number of abortion restrictions and resolutions adopted by state between 1973 and 1989. This ranges from 0 (Alaska, Connecticut, and Oregon) to 16 (North Dakota), and provides a broad gauge of total legislative activity directed against abortion.

A third indicator of abortion restrictions is a 4-point scale based on the 1988 status of state funding of Medicaid abortions. States scored 1 funded all Medicaid abortions; states coded 2 did so under court order (usually while other litigation affecting abortion funding was pending). States coded 3 funded abortions only in cases of rape or incest; states coded 4 funded Medicaid abortions only if the life of the mother was at stake (based on information in Reid 1989). This index shows correlations of .48 with the Halva-Neubauer index, but −.13 with the CQ index of restrictions; many more states restrict funding than impose other limitations. Scores for all states on each of these measures are shown in the Appendix to this chapter. In a later section of this chapter, all three measures will be used to test for the impact of abortion restrictions on actual abortion rates as of 1988.

Independent Variables

Mobilization by Women. The Center for American Women and Politics at Rutgers University has collected statistics on women officeholders for many years. I will use their data for both current and past women state legislators (percentage of total) and for women elected to statewide executive office. Other measures include women as a percentage of a state's labor force, NARAL membership per capita, and lobbyists for women as a percentage of total state registered lobbyists (as previously described). Finally, states with a public commission on women were coded 1, otherwise 0 (based on Evans and Nelson 1989:180).

Groups Opposing Abortion. No good measures of countermobilization by women are currently available; pro-life and conservative groups such as the Eagle Forum or the Concerned Women of America do not release state membership figures. The percentage Roman Catholic and Mormon of a state's population will be used to indicate organized efforts to restrict access to abortion (based on Johnson and Quinn 1974). States with a traditional political culture orientation (based on Elazar's [1972] index) are also expected to favor abortion restrictions.

Groups Supporting Abortion. The proportion of state hospitals performing abortions (Tatalovich and Daynes 1989) will be used as an indicator of mobilization of the medical community on behalf of abortion rights. It is true that in recent years, many more abortions have been performed in clinical, nonhospital settings, but data on abortion clinics are not available for all states. However, the number of state hospitals and clinics offering abortion services shows a very close statistical relationship ($r = .95$).[12] The proportion of union members in a state's labor force (as of 1982, the latest available state data) will be used as an indicator of organization on behalf of liberal policies; the proportion of black population and black state elected officials as of 1986 will be used for the same purpose (all three are from the *Statistical Abstract of the U.S.*).

Current and Historical Policies Affecting Women. Klingman and Lammers (1984) have developed a general policy liberalism scale based on state policies adopted by the early 1970s. Their scale (inverted here so that high values indicate liberal policies) includes support for the ERA, and is thus a logical indicator of state policies favoring equality and autonomy for women. Earlier state abortion restrictions (1973-1976) will be based on a comprehensive index constructed by Johnson and Bond (1980).

A summary index of state policies affecting women has been developed by the National Organization for Women (NOW). The Legal Defense and Education Fund of NOW has recently published *The State-By-State Guide to Women's Legal Rights* (NOW Legal Defense and Education Fund and Cherow-O'Leary 1987). This represents an ambitious attempt to classify state policy toward women along several dimensions including home and family, education, employment, and women in the criminal justice system. The index scores range from 6 (Alabama, South Carolina) to 36 (Washington) out of a possible 64; high scores represent greater state commitment to women's legal rights (at least in NOW's view) as of the mid-1980s.[13]

Mass and Elite Opinion. Wright, Erikson, and McIver's (1985) operationalization of liberal ideology (based on survey data) will be used to predict current abortion policy, as will ICPSR state estimates of prochoice public opinion in the 1980s (as described above). The American Civil Liberties Union's Reproductive Rights Project has coded state Congressional delegation voting on a series of abortion measures, and this will be used to indicate attitudes toward abortion rights held by state political elites.[14] Ideally, some indicator of liberal values and abortion opinion based on state legislative voting would be used, but no comparable measures are available across states; the ACLU index will be used on the assumption that state legislators and members of Congress in a given state tend to be recruited from a similar applicant pool and share many values.[15]

Time series data would be ideal to disentangle some of the causal relationships (countermobilization, impact of earlier abortion restrictions) suggested here. But reliable yearly measures are not available either for abortion restrictions or for other measures of state politics or policy. However, the use of a cluster of measures from the early 1970s in a two-stage least squares analysis will permit inferences concerning the historical context of current abortion rates and restrictions.

Before turning to the regression models used to test for the relative impact of the factors hypothesized to affect state abortion policies, let us consider the functional form of the various indicators of mobilization by women.

Mobilization by Women and State Policies on Abortion

Several possible indicators of mobilization by women and of policy and opinion liberalism have been described; because of multicollinearity and

Table 13.2 Mobilization by Women, Public Opinion, Policy Liberalism, and Abortion Restrictions, 1973-1988

	Pearson Correlations			
	H-N Index	C-Q Index	Funding Limits	NOW Index
Mobilization by Women				
% women in state legislature, 1980-1988	−.29	−.26	−.21	.37
% women in labor force, 1986	−.14	−.33	−.05	.18
Women's lobbyists as % total	−.12	−.09	−.04	−.32
Public commission on women	.08	.18	−.25	.14
No. of women in state exec., 1988	.05	.01	.33	−.14
NARAL membership	−.06	.07	−.38	.38
Political Values				
% pro-choice (ICPSR)	−.41	−.30	−.56	.52
Congressional vote on abortion (ACLU)	.06	−.02	−.09	.17
Liberal ideology	−.24	−.06	−.46	.57
Political culture = moralist	−.08	.15	.00	.43
% union members	−.00	.11	−.15	.46
% Catholics	.11	.12	−.15	.46
% Mormons	−.27	.30	.12	−.02
Liberal Policies				
General policy liberalism	.15	−.16	−.40	.77
Welfare $ per capita	−.14	.07	−.43	.63
NOW index of women's rights policies	−.15	.06	−.66	—

an N limited to 50, not all of these can be used in a single regression equation. Let us therefore first consider zero-order relationships and test for curvilinear or threshold effects.

Table 13.2 displays Pearson correlations between these indicators, our three abortion indices (Halva-Neubauer, *Congressional Quarterly,* funding limits), and the NOW index. As predicted above, the proportion of women in state legislators consistently indicates a negative association with abortion restrictions or funding limits. But the number of women holding statewide elective office has the opposite effect, and is inversely related to the proportion of women legislators. Why? Because urban, industrialized states with professional legislatures are less likely than many smaller, rural states to elect women to statewide office such as governor or lieutenant governor, treasurer, or secretary of state. Small, rural, or Southern states are also more likely to have a divided executive authority. Women in such statewide offices are therefore more likely to be Republican and/or conservative.[16]

States with high proportions of working women have significantly fewer abortion restrictions, but only marginally lower funding limits. These states are more urbanized, with a different economic profile than the rural and heavy-manufacturing states with fewer women in the work force (although measures of these economic factors showed no relationship to abortion legislation). Public commissions on women are associated with lower limits on funding, but also (weakly) with other abortion restrictions; the proportion of women's lobbying groups, as predicted, makes little difference because of the diverse aims of such lobbyists. States with lower limits on abortion funding also have higher per capita membership in NARAL (unfortunately, earlier NARAL membership is not available to test whether such membership has had any policy impact).

The liberal ideology and ICPSR public opinion measures show fairly strong correlations with state abortion restrictions in the predicted (negative) direction, but both are positively associated with the NOW index. However, neither the political culture scale nor Congressional voting (ACLU coding) show any association with state abortion policy.[17] Surprisingly, the proportions of Catholics or Mormons show little (zero-order) relationship to abortion limitations. States with high proportions of union members are less likely to limit Medicaid funding of abortions, but otherwise neither race nor unionization bear much relationship to abortion policy.

General policy liberalism, welfare spending, and the NOW index are negatively related to abortion funding limits but not to other abortion restrictions. Liberal ideology, union membership, welfare spending, and general policy liberalism are strongly associated with the NOW index. Funding limits as well seem to partake of features associated with liberal/conservative policy dimensions, but as suggested above neither ideology nor general support for women's rights necessarily predict state policies on abortion. The proportion of women legislators (averaged for the 1980s) emerges as the most consistent (as well as the most logical for policy enactment) indicator of mobilization by women across all these policies. NARAL membership is associated with both the NOW index and lower funding limits on abortion, but bears little relationship to other abortion restrictions.

Consider now the functional form of the relationship between the proportion of female legislators, 1988, and our four policy measures. A breakdown of four levels of women's representation in state legislatures will be used to test for linear, curvilinear, or "threshold" relationships (Table 13.3). There is little evidence of departure from a linear trend for abortion funding, the CQ index of restrictions on abortion, or the NOW index if all 50 states are used; support for more feminist policies is a linear function of the proportion of women in state legislatures.

Table 13.3 Abortion Restrictions, Women's Rights Legislation, and Percentage
Women in State Legislature, 1988[a]

N of Abortion Restrictions (range 1-16): Halva-Neubauer Index, 1973-1989		Correlation With % Women in Legislature
% women:		
1%-10%	6.33	−.285
11%-17%	6.43	
18%-21%	6.63	
Over 21%	3.73	
N of abortion restrictions (range 1-5): CQ index, 1990		
% women		
1%-10%	1.40	−.336
11%-17%	1.19	
18%-21%	1.13	
Over 21%	.55	
Limits on abortion funding (range 1-4)		
% women:		
1%-10%	3.53	−.223
11%-17%	3.31	
18%-21%	3.00	
Over 21%	2.82	
NOW index of women's rights legislation (range 1-36)		
% women:		
1%-10%	16.27	−.373
11%-17%	20.38	
18%-21%	23.75	
Over 21%	23.27	

NOTE: a. 1%-10%: AL, AR, KY, LA, MS, NJ, NM, NY, PA, SC, TN, TX, UT, VA
11%-17%: CA, DE, GA, IN, IA, MI, MN, MO, MT, NC, ND, NV, OH, OK, OR, RI, WV
18-21%: AK, FL, IL, KS, MA, MD, NE, SD
Over 21%: AZ, CT, CO, HA, ID, ME, NH, VT, WA, WI, WY

The Halva-Neubauer index does provide evidence for a threshold effect: high levels of effort to restrict abortion until women average more than 20% of the legislature, then a sharp drop. This index has a greater range than the others and thus may pick up such effects more easily. But it also includes non-binding "resolutions" restricting abortion. As Berkman and O'Connor (Chapter 15 in this volume) found, female legislators, despite their minority status, are more effective at blocking actual legal restrictions rather than symbolic attempts to limit women's choices. But no evidence of a curvilinear relationship is found, even including New Hampshire, whose large, low-paid, part-time legislature has for many years attracted by far the highest proportion of women of any state legislature (33% in 1988). There was also no evidence of curvilinearity in the relationship between feminist policies and the proportion of lobbyists representing women's groups.

Testing Hypotheses Concerning
Adoption of Abortion Restrictions

Let us now predict state scores on abortion restrictions and funding limitations, using women in the legislature to indicate mobilization by women (the percentage will be squared for the Halva-Neubauer prediction equation to model the nonlinear threshold relationship [Studenmund and Cassidy 1987]). Other factors hypothesized to influence state policy concerning abortion (history of abortion restrictions, earlier policy liberalism, other legislation on women's rights [the NOW index], the proportion of hospitals performing abortions, percentage Catholic and Mormon) were initially selected on the basis of the zero-order relationships within each of the four theoretical categories and excluded from subsequent runs if t tests indicated that they failed to contribute to the variance explained. Other hypothesized indicators (percentage blacks or union members, welfare spending, the ACLU index) failed to meet minimum standards for inclusion in the prediction equations.

To check for multicollinearity, separate equations were run predicting each potential independent variable as a function of all of the others. Tests for multicollinearity among the independent variables found two potential problems. The Elazar 8-point scale was strongly associated with Klingman-Lammers measure of policy liberalism, but if equations including these measures were run separately, general policy liberalism showed the highest t and F values. Also, public support for abortion rights was closely associated with the proportion of women in the legislature. Again, equations including the latter measure alone showed stronger coefficients and higher R^2 values. Interestingly, public opinion on abortion showed *no* relationship ($R = -.02$) to the ACLU indicator of voting on abortion by a state's Congressional delegation. On this issue, it appears that women legislators are more closely attuned ($R = .45$) to popular preferences.

The results of this regression analysis are displayed in Table 13.4. Abortion restrictions (CQ index) are significantly more numerous in states that also restricted abortion access before 1976. The percentage of women in the state legislature is significantly associated with fewer abortion

Table 13.4 State Passage of Abortion Restrictions and Women's Rights Legislation, 1973-1988

| | Abortion Restrictions | | | | Funding Limits | | NOW Index | |
| | H-N INDEX | | CQ INDEX | | | | | |
	b	t	b	t	b	t	b	t
% Women in State Legis.[a]	−.005	−2.15*	−.045	−2.25*	—	—	—	—
% Catholic	.100	2.57*	.027	2.34*	—	—	—	—
% Mormon	.110	2.37*	—	—	—	—	—	—
% Public Favoring Abortion Rights	—	—	—	—	—	—	.150	1.77
NOW Index	—	—	.068	2.78*	−.111	−5.46**	—	—
% Hospitals Performing Abortions	−.100	−3.85**	—	—	−.027	−4.98**	—	—
General policy liberalism	—	—	.046	2.81*	−.031	−2.79**	−.38	−6.56**
1970s abortion restrictions	—	—	.043	3.19**	.018	1.69	—	—
Constant	8.46	6.98*	−1.69	−1.73	7.00	10.53*	24.29	6.08*
R^2	.41		.45		.69		.61	
Adj. R^2	.36		.38		.67		.60	
F	7.76		7.06		24.21		37.75	

NOTE: * significant at .05 level; ** significant at .01 level.
a. Squared for H-N Index equation.

restrictions, but shows no relationship to funding limits or scores on the NOW index. As anticipated, fewer restrictions or limits on abortion funding are found in states where a high percentage of hospitals perform abortions. Once other factors were controlled, the proportion of Catholics and of Mormons are associated with more restrictions (significantly more, based on the Halva-Neubauer index).

The NOW index of women's legal rights shows no significant relationship with any of these indicators except general policy liberalism (although there is a modest relationship with pro-choice public opinion). State concern with women's legal rights overall is clearly higher in states considered liberal on other dimensions. The NOW index is in fact associated with *more* abortion restrictions (CQ index), but funding limitations are sharply lower in states that provide other policies favoring equal rights for women. Although these results provide some support for the impact of mobilization by women on abortion restrictions, funding limits prove to be more likely in more liberal states (although as noted above, with little if any impact).

55

55

Table 13.5 State Abortion Rates, 1988, and Abortion Rate Change, 1976-1988

	Abortion Rate, 1988		Abortion Rate Change, 1976-1988		% Abortions Out of State, 1988	
	b	t	b	t	b	t
% hospital providers	.218	3.60	.006	1.10	−.109	−.93
Abortion violence	.058	.67	−.030	−.41	−4.038	−2.54
Abortion restrictions	.48	.73	.026	.45	−.62	−.48
Funding limits	1.56	1.81	−.12	−1.65	−1.93	−1.16
Social welfare spending per capita	−2.17	−.36	−.22	−.43	−14.11	−1.21
% urban	.003	1.01	.0005	1.80	.005	.74
Predicted 1976 abortion rate	.478	2.49	−.056	−3.40	−.361	−.97
% abortions out of state	−.369	−4.70	−.004	−.68	—	—
Constant	4.39	.72	1.58	3.01	36.73	3.50
R^2	.81		.31		.33	
Adjusted R^2	.78		.18		.22	
F	22.55		2.32		2.99	

As a further test of the robustness of these results, several factors that have been postulated to increase the proportion of women in state legislatures (political culture, legislative professionalism, rural rather than urban residence, proportion of women in the labor force) were considered in relation to abortion policy. But as Darcy et al. (1987:46-48) note, these factors have never explained much of the variance in the proportion of women legislators elected[18] and none of them proved to be stronger predictors of abortion policy than did the proportion of women in state legislatures. States that elected more women in the 1970s continue to do so; the proportion of women elected in 1975 is the single best predictor (R = .78) of the proportion of women elected in 1988. It is these states that have been least likely to further restrict abortion access.

The Impact of State Politics Upon Abortion Rates

Finally, let us consider the impact of current state politics and policies on state abortion rates, 1988; the change in those rates since 1976; and the percentage of out-of-state abortions in 1988 (Table 13.5). There is a strong positive association between abortion rates over time (R = .87 between the 1976 and 1988 rates). In order to test for the importance of political and policy history, I first predicted 1976 abortion rates on the basis of political and social indicators from the early 1970s.[19] This predicted value, which accounted for 71% of the variance in 1976 rates, was then included in the equations estimating 1988 rates. This methodology is analogous to two-stage least squares regression, and preserves degrees of freedom while introducing an historical dimension into cross-sectional analysis.

Turning now to current state policies, according to Henshaw and Van Vort (1990) the availability of abortion services is the strongest predictor of current abortion rates in a state (as Hansen 1980 found for the 1970s). The percentage of state hospitals performing abortions (as described above) will also be used to indicate service availability.

In recent years violence against abortion clinics has escalated; such violence may restrict access to abortion both by closing clinics and by intimidation of patients. In this analysis, the extent of violence against a state's abortion providers is estimated based on a map for 1977-1989 prepared by the National Abortion Federation. States are coded 2 (major violence), 1 (isolated or attempted violence), or 0 (no incidents reported).

In the United States as a whole, 6% of all abortions are performed outside a women's state of residence. In some instances, a high out-of-state rate may result from restrictions on in-state abortion services. In other cases, women may prefer to use medical facilities in a metropolitan area outside their home state; thus many Maryland women receive abortions in Washington, DC, despite Maryland's liberal abortion policies. The relationship between state abortion restrictions and the number of out-of-state abortions (based on Henshaw and Van Vort 1990) also is presented in Table 13.5.

As Table 13.5 indicates, even when other factors were controlled, 1976 abortion rates were good predictors of 1988 rates. Also, the lower the 1976 rates, the greater the increase in abortion rates between 1976 and 1988. But 1976 abortion rates had little impact on the current proportion of abortions performed out of state.

Next consider the impact of abortion restrictions and funding limitations on abortion rates. In part because most clinic violence has been conducted in states where many abortions are performed, there is a positive regression coefficient between violence and abortion rates. But while abortion violence is associated with a marginally lower rate of increase in abortions performed within a state, states with a high degree of abortion-related violence have lower proportions of abortions performed out of state. As Johnson and Bond (1980) found for the 1970s, abortion restrictions have very little impact upon rates, rate increases, or the proportion of out-of-state abortions. But funding limits are associated with a modestly lower rate of increase in abortions in recent years.

States with high levels of spending on welfare experience somewhat lower abortion rates and slower rates of increase in rates, as well as fewer out-of-state abortions. The coefficients are not statistically significant at the usual .05 level, but the signs are opposite those that Johnson and Bond (1980) found for the 1970s. In the 1980s generous welfare services have apparently been more effective than abortion restrictions in reducing rates. But recent cuts in welfare benefits and tighter restrictions on eligibility may ultimately result in higher abortion rates.

As previous studies have shown, abortion rates are largely a function of urbanization and the availability of medical services. Women from more rural states are more likely to seek abortion services elsewhere: The highest proportions of out-of-state abortions are found in Wyoming (56%), Kentucky (30%), and West Virginia (28%). But states with a high proportion of out-of-state abortions do have significantly lower abortion rates. Limiting the number of providers may indeed reduce the abortion rate within a state. As Henshaw and Van Vort (1990) note, the death or retirement of a single doctor in a rural state may drastically reduce the availability of abortions, as occurred in South Dakota between 1985 and 1988. The number of abortion providers nationwide has fallen 11% since 1982; in rural areas, the decline was 26%. But because most of the decline occurred in states that already had few providers and low abortion rates, the impact on overall access to abortion has been minimal. Also, pro-choice groups have made vigorous efforts to maintain access to abortion services for rural women, either by bringing doctors in or by providing transportation for women to other states.

The equations in Table 13.5 do a good job of accounting for current abortion rates (nearly 80% of the variance explained), but do less well in accounting for changes in rates and the proportion of out-of-state abortions. In part, this is because these changes are not large and are often due to idiosyncratic factors; closure or lack of data from a single facility can make a big difference in a small rural state. Most of the states with large residuals (Nevada, Wyoming, West Virginia, Utah, Colorado, Vermont) fit this description. The single exception is Pennsylvania; although usually classified as industrialized and urban, it also has a high proportion of rural residents and limited access to medical facilities in rural counties. Although its strongly pro-life legislature and governor have enacted a series of restrictive abortion policies (Halva-Neubauer 1989a), the most restrictive of these have been enjoined by the courts. But proximity to New York also accounts for Pennsylvania's relatively low abortion rate, because 90% of its out-of-state abortions are performed in that state (Kochanek 1990).

Despite changes in both legislation and demographics (fewer women of childbearing age, more teenage pregnancies), U.S. abortion rates remained stable throughout the 1980s. Most women who want abortions are still able to obtain them, although travel is costly and leads to greater health risks for late-term abortions. Despite the political furor that they have caused, neither violence, restrictions, nor funding limitations produced much decline in abortion rates in the 1980s. Certainly many more restrictions have been enacted since *Webster,* and in the absence of more recent data on abortions by state we cannot yet assess their impact. But on the basis of this analysis one would anticipate that their effects would be minimal and could even be counterbalanced by the recessionary conditions and cuts in welfare or family planning of the past three years.

Conclusion

The proportion of women elected to state legislatures has increased considerably since *Roe.* By no means are all female legislators feminist or pro-choice in orientation, and certainly many male legislators have been staunch supporters of abortion rights, in Congress as well as in the states. Nevertheless, it is the proportion of women in state legislatures, rather than other indicators of support either for liberal policies or for women's rights in general, that emerges as a consistent predictor of the continuation of abortion access guaranteed by *Roe.* Ironically, if the Supreme Court does act to overturn *Roe* and returns the abortion question to the states, women's rights may fare better in many states than in a federal judiciary now dominated by conservative Reagan and Bush appointees.

The results reported here have some good news and some bad news for advocates of a feminist political agenda for the American states. The good news is that electing more women to state legislatures reduces the number of abortion restrictions adopted, and that efforts to limit access to abortion to date have been largely ineffective. States with high abortion rates in the 1970s continue to perform most abortions. Efforts to restrict funding or access have been concentrated in more conservative and rural states, which have traditionally had low abortion rates, and even there have had little impact. Many rural women do seek abortions in neighboring states, but the cost and inconvenience must be balanced against the higher quality of medical care from more experienced providers and the anonymity available in metropolitan areas. Recent reports from Mississippi (Applebome 1992) have described harassment of Mississippi women, their families, and employers during the recently imposed 24-hour waiting period; such harassment may well cause more women to seek abortions further from home, at considerable financial and emotional cost.

The bad news is that mobilization by women has shown little independent impact upon the enactment of policies supportive of equal rights for women. States supporting feminist policies today did so in the early

1970s as well. Conversely, states that enacted abortion restrictions in the 1970s tend to have fewer women state legislators today, and these states account for a large proportion of the many restrictions proposed since *Webster*. A generally liberal polity and political culture in a state leads both to the election of more women and to the enactment of feminist policies. States with a high proportion of black legislators have enacted fewer abortion restrictions; strong labor states score higher on the NOW index. Alliances with such traditionally liberal groups would appear to be advantageous for backers of feminist policies.

The possibility remains, however, that mobilization by women may limit the erosion of public commitment to feminist policies. To date, states that increased the proportion of women in state legislatures between 1975 and 1992 have enacted fewer abortion restrictions ($r = -.08$) or funding limitations ($r = -.27$). And states with many abortion restrictions or anti-abortion violence have also seen sharp increases in NARAL membership. In Pennsylvania, an "overground railroad" with funding from church and abortion-rights advocacy groups has already been set up to help women circumvent the *Casey* restrictions when and if they are imposed. In order to test these patterns more fully, more data are needed on changes over time and on countermobilization efforts by conservative and right-to-life groups.

This research has also raised some questions about the relationship between policy outputs (actions by governments) and outcomes (effects on society). Much of the debate over abortion, as Luker (1984) and Conover and Gray (1983) have argued, concerns the symbolic position of women and families in American politics. The enactment of restrictions on abortion represents a public commitment to traditional religious and social values and gender roles; the election of women to public office represents at least some degree of public support of feminist values and of expanded options for women. But if the European experience is any guide, and as this analysis has suggested, spending more on welfare and family planning is more likely to lead to actual reductions in abortion rates.[20]

Despite the media hype about 1992 as "The Year of the Woman," women are still a distinct minority at all levels of state government. And many factors other than mobilization by women continue to influence abortion legislation. Budget difficulties and soaring Medicaid costs at both state and federal levels will make increases in welfare or family planning funds hard to come by. Unless the recent anti-incumbency mood and distrust of "politics as usual" produces sharp increases in the number of women elected to state office, many more symbolic restrictions on abortion are likely to be debated. The outcome of the abortion debate will continue to depend, like Tennessee Williams's Blanche Dubois, on "the kindness of strangers."

Notes

1. Abortion data by state is collected by the Alan Guttmacher Institute and reported periodically in their journal, *Family Planning Perspectives.* These figures do not include abortions (about 100,000 yearly, or 6.5%) performed in doctors' offices, but do include abortions performed on out-of-state residents.

2. The Abortion Surveillance Unit was disbanded under President Bush, and no state-by-state abortion statistics have been published since 1988. The National Center for Health Statistics (1991:3) does note a modest increase in the birth rate among teenagers, but attributes this to increased sexual activity rather than to abortion restrictions. Missouri noted an increased number of abortions after *Webster* and Minnesota found only minor yearly fluctuations during the 1980s resulting from a parental notification law. Pennsylvania, by contrast, did experience a 22% decline in abortions during the 1980s even though none of its restrictive laws have yet taken effect because of legal appeals (statistics supplied to me by the Missouri, Minnesota, and Pennsylvania state health departments).

3. Legally, the *Casey* decision overturned an injunction issued by U.S. District Judge Daniel H. Huyett, III. But it is up to Judge Huyett (who is pro-choice) to determine when and how to lift the injunction. He is currently awaiting evidence that each of Pennsylvania's 67 counties has enacted appropriate regulations to ensure the privacy of both women and their physicians under the newly mandated reporting procedures; this could well be a lengthy process (Slobodzian 1993).

4. In competitive states with divided legislatures, the role of the governor and party leaders can be crucial. Halva-Neubauer (1991) found that the election of the first pro-choice governor since 1973 (Arne Carlson) in Minnesota in 1990 had considerable policy impact despite that state's well-organized and powerful pro-life lobby.

5. The roots of the second women's movement in the civil rights movement of the 1960s has, to some, meant a lack of support for women as mothers or caregivers. See Young (1990) for an extended discussion of the conflict within feminism over "equality" versus "difference" as either a viable goal or a manageable policy focus.

6. Data on women elected to public office in the United States are collected annually by the Center for the American Women and Politics (CAWP) at Rutgers University, and published in their annual Fact Sheets from the National Information Bank on Women in Public Office. Figures cited here are from 1988.

7. Data on NARAL membership in 1987 and 1990 was supplied by Robert Bingaman, NARAL's national field director. These data represent national memberships only; state affiliates in many states have additional members. NARAL membership per capita was used for this analysis.

8. Each state's score is the percentage of respondents favoring "abortion on demand," averaged across National Election Study data for 1980-1988 ($N = 9,193$). Albritton and Wetstein assigned states with small Ns (less than 40) the regional mean score (note 5, p. 13). Still, the national sample cannot be interpreted as representative of the population of any particular state. See Goggin and Kim (1992) for use of exit polls to describe state opinion on abortion.

9. Studies of public opinion studies have consistently found that Catholics are in fact no less pro-choice than most Protestants. But as Goggin and Kim (1992) show, organized interests (including church lobbyists) have had a more direct impact upon abortion restrictions than has public opinion.

10. Clinics are more numerous in metropolitan areas where hospitals are also located. As Henshaw and Van Vort (1990) note, abortions in rural areas tend to be performed in hospitals, and 93% of nonmetropolitan counties lack an abortion provider. The number of clinics could

not be used for this statistical analysis because Henshaw and Van Vort did not report numbers for nine states in order to protect confidentiality of sources.

11. The specific restrictions include parental notification, tests for fetal viability, Constitutional protection of fetal right to life, prohibition of abortion in public facilities or by public employees, and limits on abortion counseling. The index ranged from 0 to 5; not surprisingly, Louisiana and Missouri receive the highest scores. No attempt was made to determine the current legal status of these requirements, given the fast-changing pace of legal appeals and stays issued for state abortion laws. The ACLU's bimonthly *Reproductive Rights Newsletter* is the best source for tracking ongoing policy changes.

12. Rosenberg (1991) argues that creation of abortion clinics, not *Roe v. Wade,* led to a rise in abortion rates. But such an analysis ignores the role of legalization in enabling abortion clinics to emerge as economically viable units. Abortion rates after *Roe* did increase considerably and did become much more widely dispersed across states (Hansen 1980).

13. This index has not been published previously, but issued as a press release when the NOW/Cherow-O'Leary book was published in 1987. The index appears to have considerable face validity; Southern states generally rank low, while Northeastern and Midwestern states (many of those coded by Elazar as "moralistic") rank high. Washington and Massachusetts received the highest scores (36 and 35 out of a possible 64).

14. *Reproductive Rights Update,* Dec. 15, 1989, Special Edition No. 2, pp. 7-21. Each state's score was the percentage of votes agreeing with the ACLU's position on seven pieces of abortion legislation, expressed as a percentage of the total possible votes in a state Congressional delegation (ignoring ties and absences). Scores ranged from 0 (several small rural states) to 64% (in Massachusetts).

15. This assumption has become more valid in recent years given the "Congressionalization" of state legislatures described by Salmore and Salmore (1993).

16. As of 1988, according to CAWP, women held 41 (13%) of 322 statewide elective offices: 28 states had no women holding such offices; 20 had one; 8 had two. Breakdowns of the dependent variables found marginally higher scores in states with one executive-branch woman rather than two or none, but the differences were too small to indicate either statistical or political significance.

17. Elazar's eight-level political culture index cannot be assumed to be linear, but correlations with dummy variables for traditionalistic, moralistic, or individualistic categories also showed no relationship with abortion restrictions. "Moralistic" states, however, do score considerably higher on the NOW index of women's rights policies, as do states with high scores on general policy liberalism.

18. The hypothesized predictors of the election of women legislators explained only 30% of the variance for the 1970s and 40% for the 1980s. Goggin and Kim's (1992) analysis found that political culture accounted for most of the variance in the proportion of women elected to the lower house of state legislatures. The proportion of women legislators as of 1975 also showed a close association with the proportion in 1988 ($R = .78$).

19. The prediction equation for 1976 was as follows:

5.266 * (1976 hospitals performing abortions)

−.392 * (1975 % of female legislators)

−.077 * (1975 union members)

+.618 * pre-1973 abortion legalized (0 = no, 1 = yes)

+.133 * political culture index

+.037 * % women in the labor force

−.119 * Johnson/Bond index of abortion restrictions, 1976

+.111 * general policy liberalism (Klingman-Lammers index)

+.106 % percent Catholic, 1971

−7.494 (constant)

20. State expenditures (from state funds) for family planning is another potential indicator of abortion rates, but because of multicollinearity with state welfare spending per capita could not be included in these equations.

APPENDIX

State Scores on Abortion
and Women's Rights Indices

	Halva-Neubauer Index 1973-1989	CQ Index 1980-1988	Funding Limits	NOW Index of Women's Rights Laws
Alabama	2	1	4	6
Alaska	0	1	1	32
Arizona	8	2	4	12
Arkansas	4	2	4	11
California	5	1	2	25
Colorado	1	0	4	22
Connecticut	0	1	1	31
Delaware	4	0	4	13
Florida	8	0	4	18
Georgia	8	0	4	10
Hawaii	1	1	1	27
Idaho	10	0	4	23
Illinois	15	1	4	24
Indiana	9	2	4	18
Iowa	4	0	4	24
Kansas	1	0	3	11
Kentucky	13	2	4	16
Louisiana	12	4	4	20
Maine	6	0	4	20
Maryland	4	1	1	30
Massachusetts	11	3	2	35
Michigan	3	0	4	31

continued

	Halva-Neubauer Index 1973-1989	CQ Index 1980-1988	Funding Limits	NOW Index of Women's Rights Laws
Minnesota	11	1	4	27
Mississippi	3	0	4	8
Missouri	13	4	4	18
Montana	7	1	4	23
Nebraska	9	2	4	20
Nevada	9	1	4	8
New Hampshire	1	0	4	18
New Jersey	4	1	2	30
New Mexico	3	0	4	18
New York	3	2	1	33
North Carolina	3	2	1	25
North Dakota	16	3	4	16
Ohio	5	0	4	18
Oklahoma	7	1	4	14
Oregon	0	1	2	26
Pennsylvania	14	3	3	20
Rhode Island	9	1	4	20
South Carolina	2	2	4	6
South Dakota	8	1	4	20
Tennessee	11	1	4	16
Texas	3	0	4	14
Utah	14	2	4	18
Vermont	1	1	1	20
Virginia	5	0	3	14
Washington	1	1	1	36
West Virginia	2	2	1	22
Wisconsin	5	0	3	32
Wyoming	7	0	4	15

14

Abortion Politics and Abortion Funding Policy

KENNETH J. MEIER

DEBORAH R. McFARLANE

Abortion became legal across the United States in January 1973 when the U.S. Supreme Court handed down *Roe v. Wade* and *Doe v. Bolton*. In those decisions, the Court held that a woman's right to choose abortion was constitutionally protected as a part of her right to privacy. These decisions prohibited state governments from interfering with abortion during the first trimester of pregnancy, but states were permitted to enact laws necessary to protect the health of pregnant women during the second and third trimesters. When the fetus reached the point of viability (roughly at the end of the second trimester), states were permitted to restrict or prohibit abortions, "except where it is necessary, in the appropriate medical judgement, for the preservation of the life or health of the mother" (*Roe v. Wade* 410 US 113 [1973] at 165).

Roe v. Wade established the right of a woman to choose abortion but did not mandate access to abortion. The question remained whether public programs established to provide low-income persons access to medical services would also fund abortions for the poor. Throughout the 1970s, Congress and the federal courts debated this issue. In 1980, the Supreme Court ruled in *Harris v. McRae* that the federal and state governments could exclude coverage of abortions from Medicaid, the joint federal-state program that funds medical services for many poor Americans (Gold 1990:8).

The federal government first prohibited the use of federal Medicaid funds for abortion in 1977. As a result, policies regarding funding abortions for low-income women have devolved to state governments. Given the wide discretion permitted by the Court, that state policies have varied

Table 14.1 Abortion Policy and Number of Abortions Funded

State	1985 Policy	1985 Number	1987 Policy	1987 Number	1990 Policy	1990 Number
Alabama	3	10	3	7	3	5
Alaska	1	NA	1	300	1	626
Arizona	3	0	3	0	3	2
Arkansas	3	2	3	2	3	0
California	2	84,000	2	77,000	2	88,153
Colorado	1	947	4	4	4	3
Connecticut	2	NA	2	2,950	2	NA
Delaware	3	3	3	3	3	4
Florida	3	1	3	56	3	0
Georgia	3	0	3	5	3	0
Hawaii	1	1,800	1	NA	1	1,155
Idaho	3	6	3	2	3	0
Illinois	3	6	3	2	3	6
Indiana	3	1	3	0	3	1
Iowa	4	20	4	10	4	13
Kansas	3	0	3	1	3	4
Kentucky	3	0	3	0	3	6
Louisiana	3	0	3	5	3	0
Maine	3	7	3	NA	3	3
Maryland	1	3,484	1	2,642	1	3,550
Massachusetts	2	7,497	2	5,800	2	NA
Michigan	1	20,620	2	20,000	3	4
Minnesota	4	4	4	2	4	6
Mississippi	3	NA	3	0	3	0
Missouri	3	0	3	0	3	0
Montana	3	NA	3	1	3	1
Nebraska	3	1	3	0	3	3
Nevada	3	1	3	0	3	0
New Hampshire	3	0	3	0	3	0
New Jersey	2	9,891	2	10,422	2	12,016
New Mexico	3	0	3	1	3	90
New York	1	43,000	1	53,495	1	43,500
North Carolina	1	6,576	1	4,205	1	1,925
North Dakota	3	0	3	0	3	0
Ohio	3	306	3	0	3	0
Oklahoma	3	0	3	0	3	0
Oregon	1	1,602	1	1,376	1	2,748
Pennsylvania	4	0	4	478	4	96
Rhode Island	3	0	3	0	3	0

continued

Table 14.1 Continued

State	1985 Policy	1985 Number	1987 Policy	1987 Number	1990 Policy	1990 Number
South Carolina	3	3	3	8	3	10
South Dakota	3	0	3	0	3	0
Tennessee	3	20	3	4	3	6
Texas	3	11	3	199	3	6
Utah	3	0	3	0	3	0
Vermont	2	183	2	266	2	362
Virginia	4	48	4	62	4	86
Washington	1	4,025	1	5,093	1	7,584
West Virginia	1	458	1	419	1	602
Wisconsin	4	0	4	NA	4	6
Wyoming	4	NA	4	0	4	0

considerably is not surprising. As of January 1991, 30 states and the District of Columbia did not provide public funding for abortions unless the woman's life was in danger; and 8 states provided public funding in certain additional though very limited circumstances, such as when the pregnancy resulted from reported rape or incest. Most or all abortions for Medicaid-eligible women were funded by 12 states (NARAL Foundation 1991:v).

The variation in state policies toward funding abortions has produced wide differences in the number of state-funded abortions (see Table 14.1) For example, California funded 88,153 abortions in 1990 whereas Illinois funded only 3. A more standardized measure of funded abortion levels, the funded abortion rate (the number of funded abortions per 1,000 female population aged 15-44) also reveals the broad range of state practices (see Table 14.2). In 1990, New York funded 10.24 abortions per 1,000 women aged 15-44, but Wisconsin funded only .005. The funded abortion ratio (the number of funded abortions per 1,000 live births), a second indicator of abortion access, also differs across the states. Among the 32 states that funded at least one abortion in 1990, the funded abortion ratio ranged from .012 in Indiana to 159.366 in California.

This research examines the determinants of state policies toward funding abortions and analyzes differences in the outputs of these policies. Determinants of state decisions to fund abortions and factors that determine how many abortions states actually fund are each important issues. They assume even more importance in light of two recent Supreme Court decisions, *Webster v. Reproductive Health Services* (1989) and *Planned*

Table 14.2 Funded Abortion Rates and Ratios

State	Funded Abortion Rate			Funded Abortion Ratio		
	1985	1987	1990	1985	1987	1990
Alabama	0.010	0.007	0.005	0.167	0.117	0.082
Alaska	NA	2.309	4.767	NA	25.692	55.734
Arizona	0.000	0.000	0.002	0.000	0.000	0.030
Arkansas	0.004	0.004	0.000	0.057	0.058	0.000
California	13.230	11.518	12.980	178.363	152.956	159.366
Colorado	1.120	0.005	0.004	17.180	0.074	0.056
Connecticut	NA	3.875	NA	NA	62.845	NA
Delaware	0.020	0.019	0.025	0.312	0.303	0.384
Florida	0.000	0.022	0.000	0.006	0.320	0.000
Georgia	0.000	0.003	0.000	0.000	0.049	0.000
Hawaii	7.048	NA	4.446	98.323	NA	60.646
Idaho	0.025	0.009	0.000	0.342	0.126	0.000
Illinois	0.002	0.001	0.002	0.033	0.011	0.032
Indiana	0.001	0.000	0.001	0.012	0.000	0.012
Iowa	0.030	0.016	0.020	0.485	0.264	0.341
Kansas	0.000	0.002	0.007	0.000	0.026	0.103
Kentucky	0.000	0.000	0.007	0.000	0.000	0.118
Louisiana	0.000	0.005	0.000	0.000	0.068	0.000
Maine	0.026	NA	0.011	0.414	NA	0.175
Maryland	3.179	2.334	3.108	51.224	36.419	46.854
Massachusetts	5.449	4.012	0.000	91.695	68.677	0.000
Michigan	9.191	8.942	0.002	149.398	142.270	0.029
Minnesota	0.004	0.002	0.006	0.059	0.031	0.090
Mississippi	0.000	0.000	0.000	0.000	0.000	0.000
Missouri	NA	0.000	0.000	NA	0.000	0.000
Montana	NA	0.005	0.005	NA	0.082	0.086
Nebraska	0.003	0.000	0.008	0.039	0.000	0.125
Nevada	0.004	0.000	0.000	0.065	0.000	0.000
New Hampshire	0.000	0.000	0.000	0.000	0.000	0.000
New Jersey	5.661	5.722	6.600	93.695	91.931	102.035
New Mexico	0.000	0.003	0.252	0.000	0.037	3.332
New York	10.446	12.560	10.238	165.726	196.587	154.997
North Carolina	4.348	2.704	1.231	73.560	45.164	19.728
North Dakota	0.000	0.000	0.000	0.000	0.000	0.000
Ohio	0.119	0.000	0.000	1.907	0.000	0.000
Oklahoma	0.000	0.000	0.000	0.000	0.000	0.000
Oregon	2.346	2.087	4.115	40.571	35.558	68.611
Pennsylvania	0.000	0.174	0.035	0.000	2.939	0.580
Rhode Island	0.000	0.000	0.000	0.000	0.000	0.000
South Carolina	0.004	0.010	0.012	0.058	0.152	0.181

continued

Table 14.2 Continued

State	Funded Abortion Rate			Funded Abortion Ratio		
	1985	1987	1990	1985	1987	1990
South Dakota	0.000	0.000	0.000	0.000	0.000	0.000
Tennessee	0.017	0.003	0.005	0.300	0.059	0.085
Texas	0.003	0.049	0.001	0.036	0.659	0.020
Utah	0.000	0.000	0.000	0.000	0.000	0.000
Vermont	1.398	1.939	2.609	22.773	32.718	44.631
Virginia	0.034	0.042	0.058	0.558	0.686	0.923
Washington	3.637	4.591	6.705	57.312	72.384	104.603
West Virginia	1.008	0.953	1.381	18.979	18.684	27.557
Wisconsin	0.000	NA	0.005	0.000	NA	0.085
Wyoming	NA	0.000	0.000	NA	0.000	0.000

Parenthood of Southeastern Pennsylvania v. Casey (1992), each of which granted the states additional discretion in determining abortion policy.

The abortion controversy, therefore, has moved even more substantially back to the states. States can not only decide whether to fund abortions for poor women and whether to intervene in the decision of a minor to have an abortion, but they can also regulate the use of public facilities for abortion as well as require physicians to perform specified tests to determine viability before performing an abortion (Alan Guttmacher Institute 1989; NARAL Foundation 1991:v). States can require a waiting period from the time a woman requests an abortion and when she may have the procedure. States may also require parental consent for minors seeking abortion (Alan Guttmacher Institute 1992a). Although this research focuses on state abortion policies implemented before the *Casey* decision, our findings should offer insights into current state abortion politics.

Abortion and State Politics

Because state governments have been restricted from intervening in abortion policy, there was little literature on abortion at the state level before the publication of this volume. Hansen's (1980) seminal article examined abortion politics at both the national and the state levels. Her most recent state-level data were from 1976, however, before Medicaid funding restrictions were permitted. A recent descriptive assessment by Halva-Neubauer (1990) categorizes state attempts to restrict abortion after the *Roe* decision. The result is an interesting dependent variable, but no analysis is done on it. Some economic research has assessed the demand for abortions (Medoff 1988) and the probability of passing a constitutional amendment (Gohmann and Ohsfeldt 1990; Medoff 1989).

The limited research on state abortion policies means that the general state policy literature needs to provide the framework for this study. A recent effort to examine the content of state abortion policies from 1973 to 1989 takes a similar approach (see Goggin and Kim 1992). In a recent essay, Hwang and Gray (1991:278) argue that state policies can be grouped into two types—redistributive policies and developmental policies. A substantial literature supports the proposition that redistributive policies are determined primarily by political and governmental forces (interest groups and political parties, for example) while developmental policies are determined by socioeconomic forces (e.g., industrialization and affluence).

Despite the general consensus on these two broad clusters of state policy, a third policy type exists at the state level—morality policy. State governments have a long tradition of enacting policies that are driven by concerns with morality (see Gusfield 1963). Included among such policies are the regulation of alcohol, gambling, drug use, Sunday closing, and, we think, abortion politics. State morality policies have a different set of determinants; they result from the competition of religious and citizen groups within a defined political and policy environment (see Meier and Johnson 1990; Morgan and Meier 1980). The major determinants of morality politics are citizen groups, political forces, and the demand for the "immoral" good.

Abortion funding policy is not a pure morality issue; it also involves paying for abortions for low-income women. In this sense it is a redistributive issue. The combination of a redistributive issue with morality concerns suggests a type of politics that combines aspects of both policy areas.[1] From morality politics, determinants such as religious/interest groups, demand for abortion services, and the political environment (related policies) should influence abortion funding. From redistributive politics, partisan forces and political ideology should play a strong role.

These general determinants are also influenced by the nature of the abortion issue. Gormley (1986:599-600) argues that an issue's salience and complexity determine the actors most likely to have the greatest impact on the pertinent public policy. A salient issue is one that affects a large number of people in a significant way. A complex issue requires specialized knowledge and training to address the factual questions (Gormley 1986:599-600; Meier 1988:30).

Abortion is a highly salient public issue; that is, it is characterized by intense conflict of a broad scope.[2] *Roe v. Wade* divided the country into "two uncompromising camps." The pro-choice forces have aimed to protect the policy of legal abortion, and the pro-life forces have been determined to overturn *Roe v. Wade,* either by reversal or by constitutional amendment (Sheeran 1987:1). Abortion policies have been the subject of elections, referenda, protest marches, and even violence.

Although emotionally charged, abortion, as it is presently discussed in the policy arena, is not a complex public issue.[3] Abortion concerns human reproduction, and "in matters of giving birth and raising children, we all have opinions and we are all instant experts" (Rosoff 1990:61). Similarly, in defining human life and personhood nearly everyone has strong beliefs. The abortion issue is salient because there are conflicting and deep-seated views about these issues within American society. By stressing a right to privacy or a right to life, both sides of the debate have framed the issue as noncomplex, so as to exploit its salience.

Each combination of salience and complexity produces a different policy scenario. Issues that are salient but not complex are debated in "hearing room politics" (Gormley 1986). In this policy scenario, issues receive an open airing by politicians, citizens' groups, and journalists. Highly salient issues of low complexity are made to order for politicians. Salience raises the rewards for acting, that is, politicians can generate political support for doing so. If the issue is not complex, it will be much easier to explain to constituents (Meier 1988:66).

Citizens' groups are also influential in areas of high salience and low complexity. Salience aids organizational efforts. Groups can appeal to values held dear by many citizens (see Gamson 1968). Complexity, on the other hand, is a formidable barrier to effective citizen participation. In complex issue areas only those with access to relevant policy knowledge can participate effectively (Sabatier 1988).

Media coverage of salient public policy issues of low complexity is usually accurate and understandable (Gormley 1986:604). Unlike other scenarios, bureaucrats and specialized interests (e.g., physicians) are not free to do as they please regarding salient issues of low complexity. Journalists, politicians, and citizens' groups will be watching their activities here. In short, the policy characteristics of abortion policy also suggest that politicians and citizens (through interest groups) will have major impacts in determining policy. Bureaucrats who dominate complex issues will have less of an impact.

Although citizens' groups often play a major role in hearing room politics, the policies that emerge from this scenario may not represent the interests of all sectors of society. Most low-income persons do not belong to citizens' groups or otherwise participate in politics; therefore, their views may not be aired in the hearing room. Indeed, the major pathology of hearing room politics is that the concomitant democratic politics affect only the more affluent members of the political community (Gormley 1986). Within this framework for public policy, it is noteworthy that one of government's major restrictions, limiting funding for abortions, affects only low-income women.

The salience of the abortion issue also has a partisan dimension. Although the Democratic party has consistently endorsed a pro-choice position, many members of its traditional New Deal coalition are pro-life (e.g., Catholics). Republican politicians, until recently, have generally staked out a pro-life position to attract votes from Democratic identifiers. Democrats, more recently, have stressed their pro-choice position to attract Republican identifiers who support access to abortion. Abortion, as a result, has become a major, cross-cutting electoral issue.

Based on the characteristics of abortion funding (i.e., being a morality/redistributive issue that is salient but not complex), four sets of independent variables will be used to examine policy: the presence of citizen/advocacy groups, the strength of political forces, the demand for abortion, and the influence of related public policies. Given the hearing room scenario, we expect that both advocacy groups and political forces will contribute significantly to state abortion policies and policy outputs.

Data, Measurement, and Hypotheses

Dependent Variables

State policies on funding abortions generally fall into three groups. First, several states pay for abortions for all women who are covered by Medicaid; these states are termed "voluntary-unrestrictive." Second, state courts in several states have ruled that the state must cover abortions for Medicaid-eligible women if the state also covers pregnancies; these states are termed "court order-unrestrictive." Third, all other states prohibit the use of public funds for abortions for Medicaid-eligible women unless the life of the mother is in danger or some similarly restrictive policy.[4] Our measure is a 2-point scale coded "1" if the state is unrestrictive (voluntarily or not) and "0" if the state prohibits funding abortion for Medicaid-eligible women.[5]

Two other dependent variables will be used to assess the impact of state funding policies for abortions for low-income women. The first, the funded abortion rate, is the number of funded abortions per 1,000 women between the ages of 15 and 44. The second, the funded abortion ratio, is the number of abortions funded per 1,000 live births.[6] Because both variables are highly skewed, a log transformation of each was used in the regression analysis.[7]

Independent Variables

Advocacy groups exist on both sides of the abortion question. Perhaps the most visible pro-choice advocate is the National Abortion Rights Action League (NARAL). Our measure of NARAL strength (obtained directly from the organization) is the number of members in the state per 1,000 population. Pro-life groups were unresponsive to requests for state membership information. As a result, two surrogates will be used for pro-life strength: the percentage of the state population that is Catholic and the percentage of the population that belongs to Christian fundamentalist churches.[8] Both groups are associated with right-to-life activities. The Catholic Church in particular has been extremely active; all 180 U.S. dioceses operate separate offices for right-to-life activities (Moore 1989:912). *We expect that NARAL membership will be inversely related to the restrictiveness of state policies toward abortion funding and directly related to the rates and ratios of publicly funded abortions. Similarly, we expect the percentages of the population who belong to Catholic or fundamentalist Christian churches to be directly related to the restrictiveness of state policies regarding abortion funding and inversely related to funded abortion rates and ratios.*

Four *political variables* are included as independent variables: Democrats, party competition, conservatives, and New Deal liberalism. The Democrats measure is simply the percentage of Democrats in both houses of the state legislature for the decade of the 1980s; for Minnesota with its nonpartisan legislature, the distribution of the partisan vote for members of Congress was used instead.[9] *Given the platforms for each major political party, we expect that the greater the percentage of Democrats, the less restrictive the state's policy toward funding abortions, and the higher the states' funded abortion rates and ratios.*

Political scientists generally hypothesize that greater party competition increases public expenditures because political parties try to create or expand programs (especially redistributive programs) to satisfy voters. In an area as controversial as abortion, however, one may expect a reversal of this relationship (see Colby and Baker 1988). With less party competition (or issue salience), elected officials are more likely to allow the professional judgment of public health officials or bureaucrats to determine policies. We perceive that party competition during the 1980s has led to restriction on abortion funding. Party competition was calculated in the traditional way by subtracting 50 from the percentage Democratic, taking the absolute value of this figure and subtracting it from 100 (see Bibby, Cotter, Gibson, and Huckshorn 1990). *We hypothesize that the greater the party competition, the more restrictive would be state policies for funding abortion.*

Consequently, we expect that the greater the party competition within a state, the lower the state's funded abortion rate and ratio.

Two ideology measures are used. The measures are designed to tap conservative strength and the ability to appeal to traditional (i.e., New Deal) Democrats on the abortion issue. Conservative strength is a measure of state electoral conservatism developed by Holbrook (1984) that is the sum of conservative coalition scores for all members of Congress from a state. New Deal liberalism is a measure developed by Rosenstone (1983) to measure how well state policies fit the New Deal social welfare liberalism mold (see Holbrook-Provow and Poe 1987). New Deal liberalism is a measure of economic liberalism rather than social liberalism. It should be associated with the susceptibility of New Deal Democrats to the abortion issue. *We expect that states' conservative strength and New Deal liberalism will be directly related to the restrictiveness of state policies toward abortion funding. Consequently, we expect that conservative strength and New Deal Liberalism will be inversely related to state funded abortion rates and ratios.*

Demand for abortions is measured by a series of demographic surrogates that are related to abortion rates in the general population. Four measures are used: Percentage urbanization, percentage of females in the labor force, percentage of black population, and percentage of Hispanic population.[10] Henshaw and Silverman's (1988:162) assessment of abortion patients showed that nonwhite women, Hispanic women, employed women, and women living in urban areas were more likely to have had an abortion in 1987. *We expect that each of these variables will be inversely related to the restrictiveness of state policies toward funding abortions. Similarly, we expect that the percentage of black women, Hispanic women, employed women, and urban women will each be directly related to funded abortion rates and ratios.*

Related policies are also expected to influence abortion funding policy. Funded abortions are only a minuscule percentage of state health care budgets. In areas where few resources are expended, Hofferbert and Urice (1985) argue that states will adopt policies similar to other related policies. These related policies create a policy environment that frames the policy issue under consideration. Two policy areas are directly related to abortion funding—welfare and family planning.

Medicaid generosity, our measure of welfare policy, is a factor measure developed by Colby and Baker (1988) to assess state Medicaid programs in terms of benefits provided and population covered. Medicaid generosity should reflect a commitment to redistributive policy. *We expect that the generosity of the state Medicaid program is inversely related to the restrictiveness of state policy toward funding abortions. Similarly, we expect that the generosity of the state's Medicaid program is directly related to its funded abortion rate and ratio.*

Family planning policy is measured by the per capita expenditures from all public sources for family planning (see McFarlane 1989). If family planning programs are successful, the number of unplanned pregnancies should decline. With a decline in unplanned pregnancies, the demand for abortion should also drop. To allow sufficient time for family planning programs to have an impact on funded abortions, this variable was lagged by 2 years. A well-funded family planning program could be perceived as an alternative to funding abortions. *Because family planning services can reduce the demand for abortion, we expect that public funding for family planning may be inversely related to abortion funding and the funded abortion rate and ratio.*

Findings

We have specified several hypotheses where the independent variables are likely to overlap. Collinearity may be a problem. To avoid the problems of collinearity, models were reestimated after deleting statistically insignificant variables. Only the final model will be presented here.

Table 14.3 presents the results of the logit analysis to predict which states will fund abortions. Many of the independent variables presented above are not directly related to abortion funding policy. In fact, with only four variables—percentage Catholic, NARAL membership, party competition, and conservatives—state policies can be accurately predicted. The model correctly predicts 49 states in 1990, 47 in 1987, and 47 in 1985. The incorrectly predicted states are North Carolina in all 3 years, Michigan in 1985 and 1987, Colorado in 1985, and Maine in 1987.

Abortion funding policy is clearly a function of citizen groups and political forces, exactly what one would expect in a highly salient but noncomplex policy area. Table 14.3 also presents impact coefficients that are essentially the change in probability of funding abortions for a one standard deviation change in the independent variable holding all other independent variables constant at the mean. These coefficients show that NARAL membership is the strongest single determinant of abortion funding policy. The other three forces are relatively equal in 1990 but this represents an increased impact of party competition over the coefficients for 1987 and 1985.

Table 14.4 examines the determinants of the number of abortions funded per 1,000 women age 15-44. To the independent variables we have added a dummy variable coded "1" if the state funded abortions in that year and

Table 14.3 Determinants of State Abortion Funding Policy: Logit Coefficients

Dependent Variable = Abortion Funding Policy—Dummy Variable

Independent Variables	1990	Impact	1987	Impact	1985	Impact
Advocacy Groups						
Percentage	−.259	.47	−.157	.41	−.192	.54
Catholic	(.120)*		(.071)*		(.086)*	
NARAL	7.003	.81	3.799	.57	4.294	.65
Membership	(2.942)*		(1.305)*		(1.427)*	
Political Forces						
Party	−.268	.51	.118	.29	−.115	.30
Competition	(.138)**		(.065)**		(.066)**	
Conservative	−.104	.55	−.068	.50	−.073	.56
Coalition	(.047)		(.027)*		(.029)*	
Model Chi Square	42.53		35.40		37.97	
Percentage Correctly						
Predicted	98.0		94.0		94.0	
Proportionate						
Reduction in Error	92.3		78.6		78.6	

NOTE: * $p < .05$; ** $p < .10$.

"0" if it did not.[11] Both regression models perform well, explaining 76% of the variation in 1985, 87% in 1987, and 93% in 1990.

Although the major influence on the abortion funding rate is current funding policy, several other factors also influence the rate. In all 3 years, demand variables are important; percentage black and percentage Hispanic are both positively related to abortion funding rates. Once the policy to fund abortions is established, demand for abortions becomes a factor even though demand has no impact on adopting a policy.

Although political forces have a strong influence on the decision of whether or not to fund abortions, they also have some direct impacts on the funded abortion rate. In all 3 years, New Deal Liberalism is negatively related to the funded rate; party competition is positively correlated with the funded rate in 1985, an unexpected relationship. Striking in their absence of impacts are the interest group variables. Only percentage Catholic, and only for 1990, is related to funding policy. A reasonable conclusion from this table is that interest group forces have little impact on the funded abortion rate. A modest relationship between related policies and the funded rate exists. In 1987, the funded abortion rate is negatively associated with family planning expenditures.

Table 14.4 Determinants of Funded Abortion Rate

Dependent Variable = Logged Funded Abortions per 1,000 Women 15-44

Independent	1985		1987		1990	
Variables	*Slope*	*s.e.*	*Slope*	*s.e.*	*Slope*	*s.e.*
Advocacy Groups						
Percentage						
Catholic	—	—	—	—	−.0022	.0016**
Political Forces						
Party						
Competition	—	—	.0063	.0019*	—	—
New Deal						
Liberalism	−.0959	.0354*	−.0681	.0281*	−.0955	.0243*
Demand for Abortions						
Percentage						
Black	.0086	.0034*	.0140	.0031*	.0040	.0017*
Percentage						
Hispanic	.0070	.0037**	.0058	.0028*	.0077	.0019*
Related Policy Forces						
Family Planning	—	—	−.0672	.0348**	—	—
Abortion Funding						
Policy	.5588	.0625*	.6174	.0483*	.6430	.0366*
R^2	.76		.87		.93	
Adjusted R^2	.74		.85		.93	
F	36.45		46.58		113.19	

NOTE: * $p < .05$; ** $p < .10$.

Table 14.5 presents the determinants of the funded abortion ratio (number of funded abortions per 1,000 live births). The results of Table 14.5 are generally similar to those in Table 14.4. Abortion funding policy is the major determinant of the funding ratio. Need factors continue to play a modest role with significant impacts for black population and, for one year, urbanization (1987) and for two years, Hispanic population (1987 and 1990). Of the interest group and political forces, only New Deal liberalism has a consistent negative impact on funding. Party competition again has an unexpected positive impact in 1987, but only for 1987. In 1990 NARAL membership is positively related to the funding ratio. The models predict very well, explaining 81% of the variation in 1985, 97% of the variation in 1987, and 98% in 1990.

The relationships of party competition to abortion funding policies and funded abortion rates merits discussion. Party competition is negatively related to the decision to fund abortions but positively correlated with the

Table 14.5 Determinants of Funded Abortion Ratio

Dependent Variable = Logged Funded Abortions per 1,000 Live Births

Independent	1985		1987		1990	
Variables	Slope	s.e.	Slope	s.e.	Slope	s.e.
Advocacy Groups						
NARAL						
Membership	—	—	—	—	.0896	.0369*
Political Forces						
Party						
Competition	—	—	.0048	.0020*	—	—
New Deal						
Liberalism	−.1308	.0714**	−.0690	.0293*	−.0561	.0248*
Demand for Abortions						
Urbanization	—	—	.0024	.0010*	—	—
Percentage						
Black	.0123	.0068**	.0104	.0032*	.0037	.0022**
Percentage						
Hispanic	—	—	.0059	.0030**	.0123	.0025*
Related Policy Forces						
Abortion						
Funding Policy	1.4450	.1256*	1.6285	.0507*	1.6058	.0520*
R^2	.81		.97		.98	
Adjusted R^2	.80		.97		.98	
F	64.38		265.50		403.76	

NOTE: * $p < .05$; ** $p < .10$.

number of abortions funded. One explanation for this is that abortion funding policy is a combination of a morality issue and a redistributive issue. As a morality issue, competitive political systems should influence politicians to avoid funding abortions, as discussed earlier in the chapter. Once abortion is funded, however, the number of abortions funded is influenced by the responsiveness of the political system to "have nots." This finding is consistent with the long-held theory that competitive party systems benefit the poor and the minorities. After passage, therefore, abortion funding should be considered a welfare issue rather than a morality issue.

The Implications of This Study for Post-*Casey* Policies

Because abortion funding policies were one of the few policy areas that states were permitted to control prior to *Webster*, state policies have generally been fairly stable in this area. The results of the logit analysis for 1990, however, can be used to predict states that are likely to change their policies. The model assigns each state a probability of funding abortions. Such predictions are often highly accurate. In 1985 and 1987 the models predicted Michigan should not fund abortions even though the state did. By 1990, Michigan eliminated its funding policy. The dramatic impact of changing policy can be seen in Table 14.1. Michigan went from funding 20,000 abortions a year to funding 4. According to these models, the state most likely to change in policy is North Carolina. The model predicts that North Carolina has only a .025 probability of funding abortions yet fund them it does. An examination of Table 14.1 suggests that efforts to cut back the number of funded abortions in North Carolina have already occurred. In 1990 the state funded only about one-third the number of abortions that it funded in 1985.

Two other states that fund appear to be somewhat likely to change policies. New York and West Virginia both have a .67 predicted probability of funding abortions; the only other state with a probability of less than .8 is New Jersey with .77. Nonfunding states with the highest probability of funding are Maine (.19) and Virginia (.41). These predicted probabilities suggest that a few states, but only a few, may change their funding policies in the near future.

As mentioned earlier, two recent Supreme Court decisions have expanded abortion policy options available to the states. In the *Webster* decision, the Court upheld the Missouri ban on the use of public facilities for performing abortions not necessary to save the woman's life (Alan Guttmacher Institute 1989). This provision indicates that states may interpret the ban on public facilities quite broadly. In this case, the facility under litigation was the Truman Medical Center, which was considered publicly owned because it was situated on leased public land. If this definition were expanded to include *any* connection with government, then this ruling could be used to prohibit nearly all private hospitals from providing abortions. Indeed, only a very few health facilities have *no* fiscal connection with government.

The *Webster* decision also upheld a state's prerogative to require specific medical tests to determine the viability of fetuses at 20 weeks gestation. Here the plurality said that the law did not require physicians to perform all tests in every case, but simply to perform tests that "are useful in making subsidiary findings as to viability" (Alan Guttmacher Institute 1989). Because fetuses are not viable at 20 weeks gestation, this provision may serve as a precedent for states to dictate the practice of medicine, especially in the case of abortion (Alan Guttmacher Institute 1989).

The 1992 *Casey* decision did reaffirm the essential holding of *Roe v. Wade:* "that prior to fetal viability, a woman has the constitutional right to obtain an abortion. . . . At the same time, however, the Court discarded *Roe*'s trimester framework that severely limited the states' power to regulate abortion in the early stages of pregnancy" (Alan Guttmacher Institute 1992a). Instead, the Court, adopted a more lenient and vague standard, the "undue burden."

In *Casey,* the Court defined the "undue burden" standard as a policy that "has the purpose or effect of placing a substantial obstacle in the path of a woman seeking an abortion of a nonviable fetus." Under the "undue burden" standard, the Court upheld a 24-hour waiting period for abortion, and a requirement that abortion providers give patients a considerable amount of nonmedical information, as well as a parental consent provision. It is noteworthy that just a few years ago the very same restrictions were struck down by the Supreme Court as being contrary to the *Roe v. Wade* decision (Alan Guttmacher Institute 1992a).

These cases have established new parameters for state abortion policies. Obviously, states' options for restricting abortions have increased substantially. Prior to *Webster* states could exercise discretion in abortion policy only through funding or parental consent requirements. The next section explains that the same dynamics of state abortion politics, as revealed by our findings, are likely to continue under expanded state policy options.

Conclusion

Although *Roe v. Wade* and *Doe v. Bolton* established a woman's right to choose abortion, these judicial decisions did not mandate access to abortion. In 1977 Congress prohibited the use of federal funds for abortion. A 1980 Supreme Court ruling permitted the states to exclude coverage of abortion from their Medicaid programs. Given such wide discretion, it is not surprising that state policies toward funding abortions have varied greatly.

Our findings regarding state policies are consistent with a policy that combines morality with redistribution in a hearing room scenario. State policies were, in large part, responses to the strength of advocacy groups and political forces in the state. Particularly striking were the countervailing influences of the Catholic population and the NARAL membership. In spite of the importance of political forces, the politics of this issue did not follow political party affiliations. The findings were more consistent with the notion that conservative politicians were using the issue to appeal to New Deal liberals (economic liberals but social conservatives).

The determinants of the policy outputs measured here, the funded abortion rate and the funded abortion ratio, differed from those that determined the type of state policy implemented. State policy was the strongest predictor; other factors that contributed to these policy impacts were New Deal Liberalism and demand for abortion. Urbanization measures not only abortion demand, but also the accessibility of abortion providers. Abortion services are much more available in urban areas; indeed, abortion providers are located in only 10% of nonmetropolitan counties in the United States.[12] Although nonwhites are substantially more opposed to abortion than whites (Franklin and Kosaki 1989:758), nonwhites experience a much higher incidence of abortion (Henshaw and Silverman 1988:162). The relationship here thus likely reflects increased demand.

What appears to be happening is that policy (whether or not to fund) is set in the political environment. Once policy is set, however, politics ceases to be a major direct factor; policy and need determine outputs. Such a pattern is consistent for a policy as it moves from a political to a bureaucratic environment. Once authorized to fund abortions, bureaucrats will attempt to match funding with need.

The hearing room scenario of state abortion politics is likely to continue. In the context of late 20th century American society, abortion can be considered an inherently salient issue (Franklin and Kosaki 1989:768). Both sides of the debate continue to cast abortion as a noncomplex issue so as to appeal to popular opinion. Pro-choice supporters focus on government intrusions into private decisions, and pro-life supporters focus on popular restrictions (e.g., gender selection abortions) (Halva-Neubauer 1990:41). Notably absent from many forums is any discussion of unwanted fertility and the demonstrated contribution of family planning to reducing the demand for abortion (Jones, Forrest, Henshaw, and Torres 1989:53-62).

Given the hearing room scenario, both advocacy groups and political forces will continue to play important roles. It is unlikely that these political forces will be organized along party lines. We have already pointed out that the abortion issue has been a cross-cutting issue for the Democrats in the 1980s. This issue promises to divide the Republicans as well. The core constituencies of the Republican party are religious conservatives and prosperous suburbanites. "No issue is better able to drive these groups apart than abortion" (Schneider 1989:2).

One of the most interesting questions that remains concerns what the impact of advocacy groups will be. Our analysis of abortion funding from 1985 to 1990 showed pronounced effects from advocacy groups on both sides of this issue. The pro-life forces have been well organized for well over a decade. Many analysts believe that *Webster* made it easier to mobilize pro-choice forces (Halva-Neubauer 1990:27; Woliver 1990:2); if so, even more recent developments such as *Casey* should facilitate this mobilization. To a large extent, then, the development and implementation of state abortion policies may be a function of the organization of pro-choice opinion.

The results of this research should be informative for the future of abortion politics in the United States. At the present time, allowable restrictions on abortion affect poor women more than women who are not poor. Requirements that abortions be performed in hospitals or that viability tests be conducted increase the cost of abortion, which disproportionately affects low-income women. Waiting periods, allowed by the "undue burden" standard established in *Casey,* also will increase costs, especially for women who have to travel long distances to obtain abortions.

For upper and middle-class women, on the other hand, only a complete ban on abortion throughout the United States is likely to limit their access to abortion (Luker 1984), and such a scenario is unlikely, especially given the Clinton election. Even though the new Administration is pro-choice, it is unlikely that President Clinton will push to rescind the Hyde amendment in the near future. The burden of abortion restrictions, therefore, will be on the poor; and the politics is likely to form a pattern similar to that revealed here.

Notes

1. Goggin (1993:note 20) correctly notes that abortion policies have elements of redistributive, regulatory, and distributive policies. Our study examines only one aspect of abortion policy, that of funding abortions for poor women. Such policies are classically redistributive similar to other welfare policies; the moral dimension of this welfare policy makes a different sort of redistributive policy.

2. Not all scholars of abortion perceive it to be a conflictual issue. In Chapter 3, Wetstein portrays abortion as a relatively stable issue with most of the population clustered in the middle rather than on the extremes. The intensity of opinions held by those on the extremes and the role the issue has played in elections and mass demonstrations, however, makes an argument about lack of conflict difficult to maintain.

3. Abortion is, in fact, a fairly complex issue. The literature on abortion suggests that it raises all sorts of issues that result in endless philosophical debate. Public policy disputes, however, avoid this controversy and frame the issue in terms of right to life on one side and right to choice on the other (see Luker 1984). The result is an issue that is perceived to be not complex.

4. Some states include rape or incest as reasons for Medicaid funding of abortions, but so few abortions are performed for these reasons that this restriction can be viewed as identical to the mother's life restriction. A more elaborate classification of funding policy can be found in Weiner and Bernhardt (1990).

5. Abortion policy data for 1900 are from Gold and Daley (1991), for 1987 are from Gold and Guardado (1988:231), and for 1985 are from Gold and Macias (1986).

6. The source of these data is listed in the previous note. The number of women between the ages of 15 and 44 was calculated by the authors by taking the number of women reported

by age in the 1980 *Census of Population.* These population figures were then aged to get the appropriate year (e.g., 1985, 1987, 1990) and further adjusted to account for migration to the state. The data on live births were taken from the U.S. Department of Health and Human Services, *Vital Statistics of the United States* (Hyattsville, MD). Births in 1990 were estimated by using 1988 births. All data can be obtained by contacting the authors.

7. The rate and ratio measures all had standard deviations twice the size of their respective means. All measures had a large positive skew. To avoid problems with states that funded no abortions, a constant of 1 was added to each rate and ratio before the log transformation was made.

8. Data on church membership were taken from Bernard Quinn et al., *Churches and Church Membership in the United States,* Glenmary Research Center, Atlanta, 1980. The following churches were identified as Protestant fundamentalist: Churches of God, Mormons, Churches of Christ, Church of the Nazarene, Mennonites, Conservative Baptist Association, Missouri Synod Lutherans, Pentecostal Free Will Baptists, Pentecostal Holiness, the Salvation Army, Seventh Day Adventists, Southern Baptists, and Wisconsin Synod Lutherans.

9. Data on partisanship are taken from the U.S. Bureau of the Census, *Statistical Abstract of the United States: 1990* (110th ed.), Washington, DC: 1990 and earlier editions.

10. All data are from the 1980 *Census of Population.*

11. States that fund abortions voluntarily are no different in terms of the number funded from states that fund them under court order.

12. In 1985, only 32,000 abortions—2% of the national total—were performed in non-metropolitan counties (Gold 1990:25-26).

15

Do Women Legislators Matter?
Female Legislators and State Abortion Policy

MICHAEL B. BERKMAN

ROBERT E. O'CONNOR

Although the number of female members of state legislatures more than doubled during the 1980s, women still fill only about 17% of state legislative seats. Although we have some ideas about why state legislatures underrepresent women generally, and why there are differences in the level of female representation across states, we know much less about whether the presence of female legislators makes a difference in state policy outputs. We address this question through an analysis of the impact of women state legislators on state abortion legislation.

Women Legislators and Public Policy

If the presence of large numbers of women in state legislatures does affect policy, we should see it in state abortion policies. In contrast to male representatives' emphasis on economic and business concerns, women representatives have traditionally placed a higher priority on social and family issues (Diamond 1977; Kirkpatrick 1974; Thomas and Welch 1991; Werner 1968). Thomas (1991) finds that, where women legislators have organized a formal caucus or account for a relatively high proportion of the legislature, they are more likely to introduce and to be successful in passing women's, children's and family legislation. Abortion is a social and family issue, and it is an issue where men and women legislators differ. Women legislators are significantly more pro-choice than their male counterparts (Darcy et al. 1987; Hill 1982; Johnson and Carroll 1978; Leader 1977; Stanwick and Kleeman 1983; Welch 1985).[1] If women legislators do matter, we should detect it in abortion policy.

We begin with Thomas's (1991) hypothesis: We expect to find that where women constitute a significant number in the legislature, they will affect abortion legislation. For reasons we describe below, we also expect that the presence of women Democrats will be more important than women legislators generally. We broaden Thomas's approach, however, in looking for influence in other ways than introducing and passing bills. A focus on the amount of legislation introduced and passed by women and with their support may ignore committees, the key locus of legislative activity. Committees provide a place for legislative minorities to exercise power disproportionate to their numbers in the chamber. Therefore, an emphasis on committees may demonstrate how women can influence this policy area despite their relative lack of representation. Women may be influential not because they pass legislation, but because they are able to block bills they oppose.

The analysis proceeds in two parts. First, for two dimensions of abortion policy, we test Thomas's (1991) general finding that the presence of women legislators, after a threshold is reached, is important. To establish that women have an independent effect on abortion policy, we must first address the interstate variation in policy accounted for by factors such as partisanship, ideology, and interest group strength. This section addresses whether the number of women in a legislature and the number of women Democrats explain state abortion decisions after other likely explanatory factors are held constant. We then shift our focus from policy outputs to the policy process. Through an analysis of the fate of post-*Webster* (*Webster v. Reproductive Health Services,* 109 S. Ct. 3040 [1990]) bills, we pay particular attention to the role of women in committees that block abortion bills. We modify our questions in this section and explore whether the presence of women on key committees, even if there are few women in a legislature, has a significant impact on the fate of abortion bills.

Dimensions of State Abortion Policies

In the 1973 *Roe v. Wade* (410 U.S. 113 [1973]) decision, the Court ruled that, during the first trimester, the state has no right to interfere because abortion has almost no medical risk. During the second trimester, a state can regulate to further its compelling state interest in maternal health. During the third trimester, the state may regulate additionally consistent with its interest in potential life. Although the *Roe* decision did establish a right to first-trimester abortions, the decision left the door open for substantial interstate variation on issues such as funding, parental notification, and other regulatory areas (see, e.g., Halva-Neubauer 1990; Rodman, Sarvis, and Bonar 1987; Rubin 1987; Staggenborg 1991; Tribe 1990). The 1989 *Webster* decision characterized "the right to abortion as a lesser liberty interest rather than a fundamental right" and "appeared to signal that the Court would approve limitations on abortions" (Mezey 1992:262).

Two areas in which the courts have allowed a significant amount of state discretion have been for regulations requiring parental consent and public funding of abortions.[2] We look first at whether funding and parental consent are part of one policy dimension or two distinct dimensions of state abortion policy. If it is the latter, we may find that women legislators' influence is different for each. Parental consent may be seen as largely a symbolic issue, and therefore important only to the most committed advocates[3], whereas public funding is seen as a social welfare issue that directly affects the availability of abortions for poor women. If this is so, we would expect women legislators to be an important factor in a state's decision to enact liberal parental consent laws. In contrast, public funding for abortions would be expected in states with liberal public policies, but the number of women legislators would have no independent impact.

As Condit (1990) has argued, the abortion debate is often symbolic. Parental notification measures may provide a significant symbolic message that the state is promoting traditional family values. Donovan (1990) reports that both pro-life and pro-choice lobby groups agree that parental consent measures do not greatly reduce the number of minors seeking abortions. The openness of state court systems to minors seeking abortions will largely shape the extent to which these measures actually do restrict abortions. Although lobby groups in particular will see parental consent as a step toward restricting abortions, many people see the issue as dealing with parental authority, control, and responsibility. This explains why a substantial number of pro-choice political leaders—including Governors Florio and Wilder who emphasized their support for abortion rights in their successful 1989 campaigns—see no inconsistency in also favoring some sort of parental involvement in minors' abortion decisions.

We find strong evidence to suggest that these are two different dimensions of state abortion policy. We constructed scales for both parental consent and funding policies.[4] The pro-choice position (funding abortions, not having parental notification requirements) is coded positively throughout the chapter. The Pearson correlation coefficient between the pro-choice position on abortion funding and the pro-choice position on parental notification requirements is .37. Although states that fund abortions for poor women are more likely also to permit minors to have abortions

without involving their parents, the relationship is not so strong that
abortion funding and parental notification are essentially two manifesta-
tions of the same policy.

Women, Public Opinion, Democratic Party Control, and Abortion Policy

Klingman and Lammers (1984) have identified a single factor that
underlies most state policies. If abortion policies are consistent with a
state's general policy liberalism or conservatism, there is little room for
women legislators to exercise special influence. In fact, states with overall
liberal policies are more likely to fund abortions, as expected, but the
relationship between general policy liberalism and parental notification is
much weaker. The Pearson correlation coefficient between funding abortions for poor women and the Klingman-Lammers general liberalism
measure is .52, whereas the correlation coefficient for parental notification
is only .22. Thus abortion funding appears to be part of the same general
dimension as other state social welfare policies. The parental notification
issue is less aligned with other state policies.

Erikson, Wright, and McIver (1989) have found that most state policies
can be explained by public opinion and Democratic party control, and we
would therefore expect that these factors explain abortion funding decisions as well. A simple correlation between their state opinion conservatism measure (Wright et al. 1985) and the Klingman-Lammers policy
measure is .66, which demonstrates the explanatory power of their sensitive opinion measures. Although attitudes toward abortion do not have the
same "mood" swings as do other political attitudes (Stimson 1991), we
still hypothesize that state abortion policies will reflect the general ideological climate in the state. We test the general Wright et al. (1985) model
with each of our two measures of state abortion policy through multiple
regression analysis. Democratic party control should be especially important to differences among states in regard to both types of abortion policies
because national parties have adopted sharply different positions on the
abortion issue (Rovner 1991), as have many of the state parties (NARAL
Foundation 1991). We hypothesize that Democratic party strength in the
legislature will be likely to produce pro-choice policies.[5]

Besides the Wright et al. (1985) measure of state opinion conservatism,
for public opinion we use other measures that may more succinctly capture
attitudes toward abortion. We expect that more specific measures that
involve intensity may be more significant (see, e.g., Wilcox and Jelen
1990). The literature suggests three variables that may act as accurate

measures of intense state opinion toward abortion. Religious beliefs correlate with positions on the abortion issue (Himmelstein 1986; Jelen 1988a). We expect to find that states whose citizens are predominantly affiliated with pro-life churches are more likely to have pro-life policies. We examined data for members of three pro-life churches, but include only membership in the Roman Catholic Church in the analysis that follows.[6] The pro-life position of the Catholic Church is well known, and we expect that the impact of large numbers of Roman Catholics in some states will influence them toward more pro-life policies. We use the percentage of Roman Catholics who are church members rather than who merely identify themselves as Catholics because, we believe, it better captures those who have intense pro-life attitudes.

States with many professional women should have more pro-choice policies than states with fewer women pursuing careers outside of the home. Kristin Luker (1984) has argued that the abortion debate is so passionate because it is for many women a symbolic referendum on the value of motherhood (see also Fried 1988 and Ginsburg 1989). She found that pro-choice women typically possess an education that provides career opportunities. These women see motherhood as an option, a private choice. On the other hand, women who lack career resources typically want to see motherhood recognized as the most important role for women. They are more likely to support pro-life policies. Our measure is the proportion of professional women in the adult female population.

We also include the proportion of a state's population who are members of NARAL as a measure of intensity of support for the pro-choice position.[7] Interest group membership can be interpreted as a measure of intensity of public opinion as well as an indication of interest group strength. We expect that high NARAL membership in states reflects more intense pro-choice sentiment.

The additional public opinion intensity measures significantly improve the ability of the Wright et al. (1985) model to explain state abortion funding policies. Column 1 in Table 15.1 presents unstandardized coefficients from the regression of both state abortion measures on their conservatism measure and Democratic party control. This simple model offers no explanation for parental notification policies (R^2 = .03), but a fair amount for funding policies (R^2 = .27). Adding the additional public opinion measures improves the funding equation to the extent that we can explain more than half of the variance among states (column 2). Interestingly, when these intensity measures are added, their measure is no longer significant: States with a greater percentage of Roman Catholics have less liberal funding policies and those with a larger proportion of NARAL members, along with Democratic control of the legislature, have more liberal funding policies. (Because of their high correlation with one another,

Table 15.1 Models of State Public Funding and Parental Notification Policies

Dependent Variable	Independent Variables	1	2	3	4	5
Funding Abortions	Democratic Strength	.13 (1.03)	.86 (.96)	2.03** (.92)	2.03* (1.16)	2.01** (.92)
	Conservatism	−.01*** (.00)	−.00 (.002)			
	Roman Catholics		−.02*** (.008)	−.02** (.01)	−.02** (.008)	−.02** (.007)
	NARAL Membership		1.83*** (.38)	1.76*** (.27)	1.75*** (.27)	1.74*** (.27)
	Professional Women		−16.56 (12.30)			
	Number of female legislators (logged)			−.14 (.59)		
	Number of female Democratic legislators (logged)				.02 (.65)	−.045 (.54)
	Number of female Republican legislators (logged)				−.05 (.93)	
	Referendum Option					−.091 (.28)
	R^2	.27	.57	.55	.54	.55
	Adjusted R^2	.23	.52	.51	.49	.50
Parental Notification	Democratic Strength	−.53 (.83)	−.42 (.96)	.91 (.85)	.28 (1.06)	−.23 (.80)
	Conservatism	−.001 (.11)	.00 (.00)			
	Roman Catholics		−.01 (.008)	−.01 (.01)	−.01 (.007)	−.01 (.006)
	NARAL Membership		.32** (.25)	.33 (.25)	.32 (.25)	.30 (.24)
	Professional Women		−10.60 (12.28)			
	Number of female legislators (logged)			1.11** (.55)		
	Number of female Democratic legislators (logged)				1.22** (.6)	1.10** (.47)
	Number of female Republican legislators (logged)				−.06 (.53)	
	Referendum Option					−.54** (.25)
	R^2	.03	.14	.16	.17	.26
	Adjusted R^2	−.02	.03	.08	.07	.17

NOTE: Entries are unstandardized regression coefficients. Number of cases is 47. Numbers in parentheses are standard errors.
* .10 level of significance; ** .05 level of significance; *** .01 level of significance.

professional women and NARAL membership are not both significant when included in the same equation.)

It would appear that there is little room for women legislators to make much difference in funding policies once these other factors are taken into account. But the story for parental consent is markedly different and suggests that on this policy dimension we should expect women legislators to matter. The R^2 for the second notification measure is .14, and only NARAL membership is significant. This is consistent with our expectation that funding is one of a bundle of social welfare policies, but that parental notification would be important only to the most committed advocates.

Women and Symbolic Politics

Several analysts have found that female legislators are more likely to favor pro-choice policies than are male legislators. Continuing increases in female representation in most state legislatures (Rule 1990) may be providing a sufficiently large critical mass in many legislatures for the perspectives of female legislators to have influence (Kanter 1977; Saint-Germain 1989; Thomas 1991). Following Thomas, we expect that the relationship between women in the legislature and abortion policy will not be strictly linear: Each additional woman up to a certain point is more important than each additional woman once a threshold, or critical mass point, has been reached. We model this relationship by logging the number of women in the legislature.

We are also interested in whether there are differences among Republican and Democratic women legislators. Democratic women legislators were found in a survey by the Center for the American Women and Politics at Rutgers University to be more pro-choice than other Democrats and both male and female Republicans, whereas female Republicans were more pro-choice than male Republicans.[8] We include measures of both the number of Republican women in the legislature and Democratic women, and following the logic above, log both. By retaining Democratic party strength in the equation, we control for the independent effects of party support and can evaluate whether women Democrats are, as this survey would suggest, especially committed to the abortion issue. We expect that women Democrats, the most pro-choice among all legislators, will show their strength on the parental notification measure because they are least likely to see it as inconsequential and to view it instead as a step toward restricting abortions.

We also expect that the existence of a referendum option in a state will influence abortion policy, especially regarding parental notification. Sigelman,

Lowery, and Smith (1983) have found that, for tax cutting measures, states that provide referenda options are particularly likely to address symbolic concerns that are often ignored in state legislatures. Parental notification, a popular idea,[9] may be the type of symbolic policy that is difficult for pro-choice legislators to defeat in states that provide a referendum option.

Both measures of state abortion policy are regressed on the logged number of women legislators and the logged number of women Democratic legislators in columns 3 and 4 of Table 15.1. The expected difference between the two dependent variables is confirmed. For parental notification the presence of greater numbers of women legislators has a significant impact on state abortion policies. The greater the number of women, the more likely the state will not require parental notification. The results are even stronger when we consider women Democrats. There appears to be no significant effect on parental notification legislation from the presence of women Republican legislators, but the presence of women Democrats explains far more variation across states than measures of Democratic party strength or the several measures of state public opinion.

In the final column of Table 15.1, referendum is included in a full model for both dependent variables, although we now exclude women Republicans. We find that funding and parental notification can each be explained by different factors. For parental notification, the existence of a referendum option has a strong negative impact: A state with a referendum moves down a full half point on the 3-point scale. This supports the idea that this is a symbolic issue. Parental notification is probably not, however, seen as merely symbolic by women legislators. The presence of large numbers of Democrats or even female legislators will not affect a state's parental consent laws to the extent that female Democratic legislators will. For them, this is an important issue on which they have significant impact.[10]

Committees and Abortion Legislation

Female legislators are disproportionately pro-choice, but we find no evidence that they have had an impact on decisions to fund abortions. Public funding of abortions appears to follow traditional liberal/conservative, welfare state lines: Liberal states with Democratic legislatures will support the use of state funds for abortions. Women's impact appears significant, other than through membership in NARAL, only on the parental notification legislation. But women legislators can also play a role, even where there are very few of them, through their ability to block legislation by choosing strategic committee assignments. We can see this through an analysis of legislative activity after the 1989 *Webster* decision.

Table 15.2 Legislative Activity on Post-*Webster* Pro-Choice and Pro-Life Abortion Bills

Stage in Legislative Process	Pro-Life					Pro-Choice		Total
	Restric- tions	User Obstruc- tions	Parental Notifi- cation	Provides Obstacles	Cut Funding	Promote Privacy	Ease Access	
Introduced	114	56	59	49	66	47	34	425
Not killed in committee	17	7	7	3	7	8	3	52
Died in House Committee	54	26	30	32	36	28	19	25
Died in Senate Committee	39	18	18	11	21	9	9	125
Died in both committees	4	5	4	3	2	2	3	23
Passed House floor	10	6	4	2	5	5	2	34
Passed Senate floor	9	4	6	3	5	5	3	35
Governor vetoed	2	1	1	1	0	1	0	6
Enacted	4	3	1	1	3	3	1	16

NOTE: Entries are the number of bills introduced.

Post-*Webster* Bills

The *Webster* decision of July 3, 1989 "was perceived as an invitation to state legislatures to enact new laws restricting access to abortion" (Mezey 1992:262). Responding to the *Webster* decision, state legislators introduced more than 400 abortion-related bills in the 40 state legislatures that were still in session in July 1989 or met in 1990. These bills provide an opportunity to assess the ability of women legislators to block pro-life legislation at the committee level.

The flurry of legislative activity after *Webster* was not a flurry of lawmaking. In the initial post-*Webster* period of 1989 and 1990, state legislators introduced 425 bills, of which 344 were pro-life and 81 pro-choice.[11] Only 16 of these bills became laws, 12 pro-life and 4 pro-choice. Table 15.2 summarizes the fate of the bills. Only 4% of the 425 bills that were introduced became laws in 1989 or 1990. Not unexpectedly, the vast majority (88%) of the bills died in committee. Only 7% of the bills died on the floor and 1% were vetoed.

Women and the Fate of Post-*Webster* Bills

Our research question remains the same as it was in our analysis of funding and parental notification policies: Do women legislators matter?

Table 15.3 Female Legislators' Representation on State Legislative Committees That Blocked Pro-Life Legislation, 1989-1990

	House Committees	Senate Committees
Democrats	1.40 (1.37)	1.21 (0.97)
	N = 36	N = 29
Republicans	.86 (0.66)	1.29 (1.28)
	N = 32	N = 24

NOTE: Entries are ratios of the percentage of women for each party on committees that blocked pro-life legislation divided by percentage of women for each party in chamber. Numbers in parentheses are standard deviations. N is the number of states.

Traditionally, women legislators have served on health and welfare committees. Although the jurisdiction of these committees varies both across chambers and across states, women legislators' presence on these committees has long placed them in a position to influence abortion policies (Diamond 1977; Thomas and Welch 1991).[12] The likely placement of women on health and welfare committees, along with the propensity for female legislators to favor the pro-choice position, may be convenient for other legislators who do not want to vote on the abortion issue (Halva-Neubauer 1990; Richard 1991a). Leaders have the option of assigning abortion bills to disproportionately female committees in the expectation that those committees will bury the bills. We hypothesize first that committees with jurisdiction over abortion will have a larger percentage of women than the chamber at large. Second, if Democratic women are a key to pro-choice policy outputs, we should see a higher proportion of these women than Republican women gravitating to committees that deal with abortion where they will be in position to block pro-life legislation.

To test these hypotheses, we use the ratio of women that compares the percentage of women for each party on the committee with the proportion of women for each party in the full chamber: A score of 1 for Democrats on a given committee would indicate that there is no difference between the proportion of Democratic women on that committee and the proportion of Democratic women in the chamber.[13] We use this measure instead of the simple proportion of women on committees because we are particularly interested in committees that overrepresent women: Only in this way can we tell if women have disproportionate influence, within the chamber, on abortion committees.[14] We use these measures in Table 15.3 for house and senate committees that blocked at least one pro-life bill, whatever the name and overall jurisdiction of the committee. For each state, we take the average ratio, computed separately for Democrats and Republicans, for all committees that blocked such bills. The unit of analysis in Table 15.3, therefore, is the state. Most action occurs in lower chambers, so our N of cases is higher for this category.

Overall, committees in both chambers that blocked pro-life bills had a disproportionate number of women Democrats. In the 36 state houses that blocked at least one pro-life bill after *Webster,* women Democrats occupied 40% more of their party's seats on these blocking committees than women Democrats occupied for all Democratic seats in the lower chamber. The story of Republican women, however, is mixed. The ratio of women Republicans on blocking committees to all women Republicans in the house is less than 1. This seems consistent to us with the findings of the regression analysis above that women Republicans in state legislatures have not effectively promoted either pro-choice or pro-life legislation.

The difference between house and senate Republican women is quite striking. Lower house committees that blocked pro-life legislation had 14% fewer Republican women than the lower houses as a whole, but senate committees that blocked pro-life bills overrepresented Republican women. We do not attribute this difference between senate and house Republican women to sampling error (despite the relatively large standard deviations) because we report data for the full population of all committees that dealt with abortion bills. We expect that the difference may be a consequence of the larger jurisdiction of senate committees compared with house committees, meaning that house committees are more likely to deal with abortion and not other types of legislation. A Republican woman senator uninterested in the abortion issue would have a more difficult time avoiding service on a committee that dealt with abortion. Because lower houses were more active on abortion legislation (see Table 15.2), it seems more significant to us that these committees underrepresented Republican women and dramatically overrepresented Democratic women.

Importance of Women in Pro-Life States

Perhaps women serve disproportionately on committees that deal with the abortion issue in states where there is little support for pro-life legislation. Women may be effective in killing pro-life bills in states where such bills have little chance. Halva-Neubauer (1990) developed a measure of post-*Roe* policy approaches that allows us to examine this argument. The typology of states ranges from supporters (states that support *Roe),* acquiescers (few attempts to regulate abortion since 1973), codifiers (states that regulated abortions as permitted by the courts), to challengers (states hostile to the *Roe* decision). This measure is related to the amount

Table 15.4 Ratio of Women on Committees That Block Pro-Life Legislation to Women in Chamber, for Supporters and Other States

Halva-Neubauer State Type	House Democrats	House Republicans	Senate Democrats	Senate Republicans
Challengers, codifiers, and acquiescers	1.58 (1.44) $N = 29$	.80 (.64) $N = 25$	1.19 (1.02) $N = 25$	1.42 (1.30) $N = 21$
Supporter	.65 (.64) $N = 7$	1.08 (1.08) $N = 7$	1.39 (.53) $N = 3$	.38 (.67) $N = 3$

SOURCE: Halva-Neubauer state types were taken from Halva-Neubauer (1990).
NOTE: Entries are mean ratio scores. Numbers in parentheses are standard deviations. N is the number of states.

of activity in the 1989-1990 period as the challenger, acquiescer, and codifier states had an average of nine pro-life bills introduced, whereas, in the supporter states, the mean number of bills introduced was less than six. If female legislators matter, they would play a major role in challenger, codifier, and acquiescer states, but no disproportionate role in supporter states. Further, we expect Democratic women to play the largest role: In challenger, codifier, and acquiescer states Democratic women should be more likely to serve on committees that kill pro-life bills.

We find support for these hypotheses in the lower chambers in Table 15.4. In states with a real threat to pass pro-life legislation, house committees that killed pro-life legislation had 58% more women Democratic legislators than the chamber at large. In supporter states, where there is no apparent threat to pro-choice forces, there is little reason to suspect women would be especially involved in blocking them. There are, in these states, 35% fewer women Democrats on the committees than in the chamber. For house Republicans, however, just the opposite is true. The findings for senate Republican women, when considered along with those reported in Table 15.3, suggest that there may be important differences between senate and house Republican women.

Importance of Women in States With Few Female Legislators

Committees that blocked pro-life legislation had a greater proportion of women than in the chamber at large, and Democratic women were especially prominent in those states most likely to pose a threat to *Roe*. But we

Table 15.5 Ratio of Women Legislators on Committees That Block Pro-Life Abortion Bills in Legislatures With Low, Medium, and High Numbers of Women, by Party

Number of Women in Chamber	House		Senate	
	Democrats	Republicans	Democrats	Republicans
Low	1.73 (2.32)	.88 (.99)	.92 (1.36)	.44 (.53)
	N = 11	N = 8	N = 9	N = 6
Medium	1.35 (.62)	.85 (.51)	1.39 (.73)	2.28 (1.36)
	N = 20	N = 19	N = 12	N = 10
High	.85 (.63)	.89 (.68)	1.27 (.79)	.69 (.61)
	N = 5	N = 5	N = 8	N = 8

NOTE: Entries are the mean ratio of women on committees that blocked pro-life legislation to women in chamber. Numbers in parentheses are standard deviations. N is the number of states.

have not yet seen how women in legislatures with few women might have used committees to pursue pro-choice objectives that might be obfuscated within the larger chamber. Because legislatures with few women are most likely to be in challenger states in the Halva-Neubauer (1990) typology, the assignment of pro-life bills to committees with disproportionate female representation may have been particularly significant to pro-choice blocking strategies. If pro-life bills would have support on the floor, their committee assignments are critical, and there is reason to expect women concerned with the abortion issue would seek to serve on these committees.

In Table 15.5, the ratio of women on committees that blocked pro-life legislation is broken down by the number of women in the legislature. Our hypothesis finds strong support for house Democratic women. The highest ratio of women on a committee to women in the chamber is found for women Democrats in states with the least number of women; the lowest ratio is found in states with the highest number of women. The comparison with house Republican women is striking: Most Republican women in the lower chambers had not been seeking a significant role in abortion policy. The conclusion is that, in those states with the greatest likelihood of passing pro-life legislation (and the fewest women), Democratic women were likely to be found on those committees that had been blocking pro-life bills.[15]

Abortion Policy After *Planned Parenthood v. Casey*

The 1992 Supreme Court decision in *Planned Parenthood of Southeastern Pennsylvania v. Casey* (91-744 [1992]) affirmed the *Webster* decision

Table 15.6 Mean State Predicted Values of Parental Notification Scale and Abortion Funding Scale for Post-*Webster* Abortion Legislation

	Parental Notification	*Funding Abortions*
Pro-Life Legislation		
Passed Both Chambers	−.18 (1.00)	−.02 (.03)
	N = 9	*N* = 9
Did not Pass Both	.16 (1.07)	.12 (1.12)
	N = 36	*N* = 36
Pro-Choice Legislation		
Passed Both Chambers	.84 (1.11)	.33 (.99)
	N = 4	*N* = 4
Did not Pass Both	.39 (.86)	.17 (1.02)
	N = 26	*N* = 26

NOTE: Entries are mean standardized predicted values. Numbers in parentheses are standard deviations. *N* is the number of states.

by permitting states to pass laws restricting abortions so long as they do not pose an "undue burden" on women seeking abortions. More cases will follow and the Court may eventually overturn the *Roe* framework, upheld in *Casey* by a single vote. As many state legislators have been awaiting the *Casey* decision we may a expect a burst of state legislative activity on abortion. Based on the findings of this chapter, what is likely to happen?

To address this question we return to our earlier analysis to estimate the potential of states to pass further abortion restrictions. Although some states would further restrict abortions, we suspect that most states would change their current policies only slightly. When the *Webster* decision broadened the opportunities for states to regulate abortions more extensively, only 16 bills passed in 1989 and 1990—and 4 of these were pro-choice. Most state legislatures could have erected more barriers for women seeking abortions, but chose not to act. We find that our earlier equations well predict the states that passed these measures, and, based on the estimates developed above, we expect few further changes.

From the equations in column 5 of Table 15.1, we calculate predicted values for both dependent variables for each state. These values are standardized estimates of the scales for abortion funding and parental notification. If the equations are good predictors of legislative activity after *Webster,* we should find that states that passed pro-life legislation in the post-*Webster* period would have negative scores on each of these scales; states that did not pass this type of legislation or passed pro-choice legislation should have positive scores. Positive and negative scores indicate that a state is above or below the mean on each of these abortion scales.

For each state included in Table 15.1, we average the predicted values on both scales for pro-life and pro-choice bills that passed both chambers or did not pass both chambers.[16] This is a test that must be interpreted carefully because of the low number of bills that actually passed. The results are quite encouraging for our model, however. On pro-life legislation, states have an average predicted value of less than zero on both dimensions for bills that passed both chambers, and greater than zero for bills that did not. On pro-choice legislation states have positive values for legislation that passed and values greater than these for those that did not pass (although these are positive values).

The differences between the two scales are interesting and, we think, speak to the importance of women Democratic legislators, who are weighted more heavily in the parental notification equation. The parental notification predicted values are extremely high—nearly one standard deviation above the mean—for states that pass pro-choice legislation. The value is significantly lower than that for the funding variable for pro-life legislation that passed both chambers. Although differences between the values on these tables are often small, they are consistent with our expectations and findings in the rest of the article. Our conclusion is that although both equations predict legislative activity after *Webster* well, the parental notification equation offers a better model for explaining the range of restrictions permitted by *Webster*. And perhaps most important, the tendency of states high on the parental notification scale to pass pro-choice legislation indicates that states with large numbers of women Democrats (but not necessarily large numbers of Democrats) are the most opposed to the pro-life position.

Given the equations above, there should not be dramatic shifts in most state policies either as a consequence of *Casey* or if *Roe* were overturned. The variables for abortion policy are unlikely to shift dramatically in a pro-life direction. Public opinion (particularly as measured by NARAL membership), Democratic party strength, the number of female Democratic legislators, and the absence of a referendum option are predictive of different pro-choice policies. There is no national trend toward non-referendum states adding referenda. Public opinion regarding abortion has been stable for years (Niemi, Mueller, and Smith 1989). The threat posed by *Casey* should help NARAL recruit more members as abortion rights would be threatened. The number of Democratic female legislators has been rising consistently. The idea of term limits for state legislators, if adopted, should open more opportunities for women to win seats.[17] Only the variable of Democratic party strength seems at all to have the possibility of moving in the pro-life direction. It will likely take a resurgence of the Republican party in the states to increase the likelihood of pro-life bills being enacted.

Notes

1. The abortion debate includes struggles over terminology as each side attempts to frame the issue. We adopt the "pro-life" and "pro-choice" labels because these are terms used by the largest interest groups to define themselves (Rubin 1991).

2. In two 1977 cases, *Beal v. Doe* (432 U.S. 438 [1977]) and *Maher v. Roe* (432 U.S. 464 [1977]), the Court ruled that states do not have to fund abortions for poor women under the Medicaid program. In 1980, in *Harris v. McRae* (100 S. Ct. 2671 [1980]), the Court upheld the constitutionality of the Hyde amendment, which barred any state from using Medicaid funds to pay for any abortion "except where the life of the mother would be endangered if the fetus were carried to term." Although the federal government funds few abortions, no court has denied the right of a state to spend its own money to fund abortions.

In the *Bellotti v. Baird* (443 U. S. 622[1979]) decision, the Court threw out a Missouri law that required parental consent, but wrote that the law would have been constitutional if it had provided a judicial bypass for minors unable to secure parental consent. Recent cases have focused on notification as well as consent. In the *Hodgson* (*Hodgson v. Minnesota* 110 S. Ct. 2926 [1990]) decision, the Court upheld a Minnesota statute that required two-parent notification, but included a judicial bypass. On the same day, in *Ohio v. Akron Center for Reproductive Health* (110 S. Ct. 2972 [1990]), the Court upheld a law that required one-parent notification, again with a judicial bypass.

3. Donovan (1990) argues that committed advocates on the abortion issue admit that parental notification is mostly symbolic, but still devote considerable resources to influencing public policy on the issue. Both sides are concerned that their opponents will use the issue to win broad support and to establish precedents.

4. The source of the data in this section is the NARAL Foundation (1991:183-84). This manuscript also serves as our source for information on all of the bills introduced in 1989 and 1990 in the post-*Webster* period. Twenty-four states require parental consent for a minor to obtain an abortion, the most conservative policy; 11 states require parental notification, but not consent; and 15 states have no laws mandating parental involvement in abortion decisions. Thirty states have the same conservative policy of not funding abortions except when the life of the mother is in danger. Five states fund abortions in cases either of rape or incest, or fetal deformity (but not both). Three states fund abortions in cases both of rape or incest, or fetal deformity. Twelve states fund abortions in all or most circumstances. The parental-consent and notification measures goes from 1 (consent required) to 3 (no requirements). Funding goes from 1 (funding only to save the life of the mother) to 4 (funding under all or most circumstances).

5. Our measure of Democratic party strength is computed by dividing the total number of Democrats in both the lower and upper chambers of the legislature by the size of the legislature. It ranges from .00 for a Republican-dominated legislature to 1.00 for a totally Democratic state legislature.

6. The data are church membership for Roman Catholics, Latter Day Saints, and Lutheran Missouri Synod—the largest denominations with explicitly pro-life positions, identified through documents and phone calls to national headquarters. The source of numbers of adherents is Quinn et al. (1982).

7. We were unable to obtain membership figures for the National Right-to-Life Committee.

8. The survey was released on June 10, 1989, in a press release titled "Gender Gap Found in Legislative Support for Abortion." It reported the results of a national survey of state legislators conducted in 1988.

9. For a summary of public opinion on parental notification and state legislative activity, see Donovan (1990).

10. The press release cited in Note 8 reported that 67% of Democratic women legislators opposed parental consent requirements. Only 42% of Democratic men, 45% of Republican women, and 26% of Republic men also opposed parental consent.

11. The description of these bills came from the NARAL Foundation (1991). For the 40 legislatures that were in session, we coded all of the bills that seemed to us clearly pro-life or pro-choice in their intentions and substantively affected either the availability, terms, or funding of abortions. The pro-life bills would have restricted abortions (e.g., eliminating second-trimester abortions), increased obstacles for women (e.g., waiting periods), required parental notification or consent, increased regulations with which providers would have to comply, or cut back on funding. The pro-choice bills either would have enhanced the privacy granted women choosing abortions or eased access to the abortion option. Almost all of the bills listed in the NARAL book fell into one of the seven categories. Most of the bills we excluded provided for drug testing for pregnant women, penalties for drug use by pregnant women, regulated the use of fetal tissues, or were largely symbolic, such as those calling for constitutional amendments.

12. Of the abortion bills introduced in the House after *Webster*, 41% died in Health and Welfare Committees, followed by Judiciary committees, where 27% died. In the Senate, these values were 53% and 28%, respectively.

13. Data on committee assignments were collected for the first committee each of our 425 bills passed and the final committee in which it died for each chamber. Each bill, therefore, could have committee data for up to four committees. The roster for the committees was found in either the state's 1989 "Blue Book" or by calling the appropriate legislature. We determined gender by the name if obvious, by picture where possible, and by asking when gender was still unclear to us.

14. There is also a very high correlation between the proportion of women on committees and the proportion, or the number, in the chamber at large.

15. The difference in means between Democratic house women in states with a medium number of women and states with a high number of women is significant at the .08 level, using a one-tail *t* test; between house Democratic women in chambers with a low number of women and a high number of women .05; and, for Republican senate women in medium states and high states .00. The other differences are not significant at levels below .15 as we might expect with such small *N*s and standard deviations so easily affected by one outlying state.

16. We exclude from the pro-life bills those that restrict funding or require parental notification. States already with parental notification requirements cannot be expected to pass more stringent laws on this dimension of abortion policy because of *Webster*. Similarly, the *Webster* decision is irrelevant for state abortion funding policies. Further, we use the less stringent test of comparing bills that pass both chambers rather than those signed by the governor because we believe the results of equations shown in Table 15.1 best predict legislative activity.

17. As our findings suggest, however, the election of more Republican women might operate in either direction. As Lee Atwater noted in his call for a "big tent" for the national party on the abortion issue, the repeal of *Roe* threatens to expose a cleavage in the party.

Conclusion

The Future of the New Politics of Abortion

MALCOLM L. GOGGIN

The framework for understanding the "new" politics of abortion that was offered in the Introduction yielded a number of questions for research that have been addressed in the 15 chapters that followed. Hopefully, these chapters not only provide a timely assessment of the abortion controversy but also portend what abortion policy and politics is likely to be like, now that *Casey* has been settled and now that, for the first time since 1980, the executive and legislative branches of government seem to agree on the fundamentals of a national abortion policy. Drawing on my own research and the research of others that has been presented in this volume, this concluding chapter addresses questions that were raised in the Introduction. It also analyzes recent Supreme Court decisions and the Clinton victory and their implications for understanding the future of the new politics of abortion.

What Is the Basis of Conflict?

Abortion is a simple "either/or" issue for some, but it is clearly a complex, multidimensional issue for many others. When conflict is over moral principles, abortion is a relatively "easy" issue, with abortion-rights supporters justifying their position with the argument that they have a moral obligation to the living, citing the Due Process Clause of the Fourteenth Amendment of the U.S. Constitution. Fetal-rights champions counter that their obligation is to protect the interests of the yet unborn, and add that because no absolute right to privacy can be found in the U.S.

Constitution, that right need not be guaranteed. Yet when the controversy is over specific policies like informed consent, parental consent, the use of abortion as a form of birth control, or the use of taxpayers' money to pay for abortions, then abortion becomes much more complex.

For the many people who treat a woman's decision to have an abortion as essentially a private decision that should be beyond government control, but are willing to accept reasonable limits, the issue is not "easy." These people in the middle of the two extremes find neither unrestricted access to abortion nor an outright ban acceptable. And this is where the conflict arises. As Ellen M. Dran and James R. Bowers make clear in their analysis of public attitudes toward adoption as an alternative to abortion, *policy* choices are often hard.

Several authors of chapters in this book have identified and discussed one or more of the bases of abortion conflict that were highlighted in the Introduction. Conflict has been explained in terms of underlying differences in individual values and variations in personal perspective, interests, and motives that are tied to differences in age, race, or worldviews, including political and social goals and agendas.

For one, underlying values are multidimensional: The structure of abortion attitudes consists of individual attitudes about what is the proper relationship between rulers and ruled, maintenance of the family unit, the parameters of parental authority, and welfare spending (Goggin 1993:note 6). These and other underlying values are also frequently in conflict. As demonstrated in the survey of SUNY, Stony Brook college students conducted by Frauke Schnell, high levels of conflict can decrease the strength with which abortion attitudes are held, and, consequently, reduce the potential for these attitudes to translate into political action.[1]

Second, beliefs, opinions, perceptions, interests, and motives vary by subgroup, for example, according to socioeconomic status, age, or race, and these demographic differences often contribute to conflict over the issue of abortion. Take the case of young whites. Younger whites' support for elective abortion has waned in recent years, and there is no clear answer as to why. Cook, Jelen, and Wilcox offer one plausible answer: The youngest cohorts have grown so accustomed to the availability of legal abortion that they have taken it for granted; they do not perceive a credible threat to access to abortion. Because their life experiences differ from their elders'—they have not lived through the era when access to abortion was not protected—younger people are more likely to accept abortion restrictions.

Conflicting perceptions and motives among leaders within the abortion-rights and fetal-rights movements have also been well documented (e.g., Eisenstein 1984; Gelb 1989; Klatch 1987; Luker 1984). For example, among abortion-rights activists, there is considerable conflict between "radicals" and "reformists" (Gelb 1989). And as one can see from the results of James L. Guth and colleagues' survey of elites that is reported in Chapter 2, among evangelical activists who are part of the fetal-rights movement, conflict arises between those who prefer strict limits on abortion (fundamentalists and charismatics) and other evangelical leaders who are somewhat more willing to compromise. Another source of conflict among the leadership of the fetal-rights movement may be religious prejudice, be it anti-Catholic or anti-Protestant.[2]

How Is Conflict Likely to Be Resolved?

Much of the research reported in chapters in this volume has focused not on the structural basis of conflict but on the ways in which the seemingly irreconcilable differences between the two sides of the abortion controversy can be resolved. How is a conflict that is premised on competing claims, with each side arguing that its claim has greater legitimacy, likely to be settled? Is abortion policy making a classic case of ideological bargaining, or is it more pluralistic than ideological?

My response to these queries is similar to the one suggested in answer to the question of whether abortion is an easy or a hard issue: It depends upon what aspect of abortion is being debated. When the debate is over the core moral dimension of abortion, then policy making is likely to look more like the ideological bargaining process that was described in the section on institutional context in the Introduction to this volume. But if the issue that is being debated is more subtle, for example, when funding for abortions of poor women is being discussed or when restrictions on abortion access for the so-called soft reasons like birth control, sex selection, or for the convenience of the woman are being considered, then the institutional context is likely to be more consensual, and thus more pluralistic. Let us now turn to a brief discussion of policy-making style in the context of one institution, the state political system.

How Is State Abortion Policy Likely to Be Made?

As Glen A. Halva-Neubauer's historical analysis of state abortion policy making in Chapter 10 makes clear, for the past 20 years, rather than engaging in philosophical discussion of core issues like "life" or "liberty" (Tribe 1990), state legislators have devoted a great deal of attention to debating "technical" questions about the advisability and legality of abortion restrictions. Other theoretical research on legislative behavior in the

U.S. Congress has suggested that when debate is steered toward "fact" and away from "value" questions, the search, estimation, and choice behavior that we associate with the act of legislating is likely to be more pluralistic than ideological (Goggin 1988; Goggin, Bowman, Lester, and O'Toole 1990; Chapter 7 in this volume). But how has the scope of the conflict over abortion policy been affected by this emphasis on technical questions?

To the extent that *either* of the two protagonists directs its appeals to absolute, core values, it will have difficulty attracting and mobilizing those members of the public who hold the more ambivalent "restrictiveness" position, that is, who prefer neither abortion on demand nor a return to criminalization, but are willing to accept some sort of restriction on access. Despite the murder of Dr. David Gunn, a service provider in Pensacola, FL, by a pro-life zealot in March 1993, there is already some evidence of this softening of positions by groups such as NARAL and National Right to Life.[3] The movement that is most successful at this will be in the best position to gain substantially more supporters.

In June 1992, few would have predicted that the newly constituted Reagan-Bush Court would refuse to overturn *Roe* at its first opportunity, or that Bill Clinton would defeat George Bush, the incumbent right-to-life president. These shifts in the political landscape make it unlikely that *Roe* will be overturned in the near future. What this illustrates is the volatility of this *political* issue and the changing fortunes of the protagonists. Volatility has its effects, and it to this subject that we now turn. The remainder of this chapter assesses the ways in which the *Casey* decision and the Clinton victory are likely to affect abortion policy and politics in the near future.

What Are the Implications of *Casey* and the Clinton Victory?

In *Casey,* a deeply divided Supreme Court reasserted its position that a woman's access to abortion prior to fetal viability is protected by the Constitution.[4] Furthermore, states were given latitude to limit that access, but only to the extent that restrictions do not constitute a substantial obstacle to access. Much of what states do in the near future will undoubtedly be directed at defining the limits of this "undue burden" principle. And, as Kenneth J. Meier and Deborah R. McFarlane point out in Chapter 14, if there are further state restrictions, they are likely to be at the margin.

During the 1992 presidential campaign, candidate Clinton promised his supporters that he would: Rescind the "gag" rule; lift a ban on funding for fetal tissue research; ask the Food and Drug Administration to look into the feasibility of importing RU-486; lift the ban on providing abortion services in military hospitals; appoint pro-choice judges when vacancies occurred; and, in general, find ways of making abortion more accessible.[5] He made good on the first four of these promises on his first day in office.

What a Clinton election victory over Bush also did was remove a major obstacle—the Presidential veto—to codifying *Roe v. Wade.* On the first day after 12 years of divided government, Senate majority leader George Mitchell (D-Maine) promised to pass the Freedom of Choice Act; and pro-choice members of Congress were busy promoting bills that would prevent fetal-rights groups like Operation Rescue from shutting down abortion clinics.

This did not sit well with right-to-life groups, who have already used the Clinton victory to increase membership. On the 20th anniversary of *Roe v. Wade,* right-to-life forces were already invoking the threat posed by a pro-choice Clinton administration in order to expand the scope of the conflict, thus hoping to build a majority coalition by drawing more supporters to their side.

From a tactical point of view, supporters of either the fetal-rights or abortion-rights position would do well to soften their image, thus avoiding strident appeals to absolute values. Because fetal-rights groups now find themselves in the unenviable position of "outsiders" once again (Goggin 1992), they need to get more of the uncommitted involved in the fray over abortion. One way to accomplish this is to compromise by supporting public funding for alternatives to abortion, for example, adoption, or by supporting legislation that would provide more funds for sex education, or family planning services as a means to *prevent* unwanted pregnancies, thus obviating the need for many abortions. Pro-choice supporters, on the other hand, would do well to elect more women and more blacks to the state legislature. For, according to Susan B. Hansen's research, it is the proportion of women in the state legislature that serves as the best predictor of continued support for abortion rights (see also Chapter 15, this volume); and states with a high proportion of black legislators tend to pass fewer restrictions on access to abortion services.

The unexpected shocks of Conservative Justices Souter, Kennedy, and O'Connor siding with liberal Justices Stevens and Blackmun to resist pressure from antifeminists and the Christian Right to overturn *Roe v. Wade* in the *Casey* decision and Bill Clinton's surprising upset victory over George Bush have already altered the status quo. These developments have put fetal-rights organizations on the defensive and served as a catalyst to expand the scope of conflict; and pro-life mobilization may have stimulated pro-choice advocates to take steps to contain the scope of conflict. Whether conflict will be resolved through pluralistic or ideological bargaining will depend, in large part, upon which particular aspect of abortion is under consideration. Can it be that post-*Webster* abortion politics is looking increasingly like the politics of abortion in the immediate post-*Roe* period?

Notes

1. What Schnell and others have made clear is that the *strength* as well as direction of attitudes must be taken into account; one must also make clear which preferences—relative or absolute—are being measured. On this point, see Wlezien and Goggin 1993, and Chapter 11 in this volume.

2. Compared to sentiment about abortion among mass publics, the attitudes of activists are more intense, and victories of the fetal-rights groups to redefine *Roe* over the past two decades testify to the power of an intense minority.

3. NARAL has shown a recent interest in shifting their emphasis away from "choice" toward adopting public policies that prevent unwanted pregnancy and even exploring the adoption option. Pro-life forces may have to moderate their demands for further restrictions in light of the Court's recent ruling in *Casey*.

4. Confirmation battles for new appointments to the Supreme Court, which seems to be in mo mood to confront *Roe* directly, will be contentious.

5. This would mean encouraging the establishment of abortion clinics in many of the 83% of the counties that do not now provide abortion services.

References

Abelson, Robert P. 1988. Conviction. *American Psychologist* 43:267-75.

Abramson, Paul. 1976. Generational change and the decline in party identification in America 1952-1974. *American Political Science Review* 70:469-78.

Achen, Christopher. 1978. Measuring representation. *American Journal of Political Science* 22:475-510.

Ada v. Guam Society of Obstetricians/Gynecologists. 962 F.2d 1366 (1992).

Akron v. Akron Center for Reproductive Health. 462 U.S. 416 (1983).

The Alan Guttmacher Institute. 1974. A review of state abortion laws enacted since January 1973. Pp. 88-93 in *Family Planning/Population Reporter* (October). Washington, DC: Alan Guttmacher Institute.

The Alan Guttmacher Institute. 1989. The Court edges away from *Roe v. Wade. Family Planning Perspectives* 21:184-187.

The Alan Guttmacher Institute. 1990. Looking ahead to 1990—Opportunities and Obstacles. *Washington Memo* (January 31).

The Alan Guttmacher Institute. 1992a. Bare Court majority reaffirms *Roe,* but standard for reviewing state laws is relaxed. *Washington Memo* (July 2) WM11:1-2.

The Alan Guttmacher Institute. 1992b. *State Reproductive Health Monitor* (September). Washington, DC: Alan Guttmacher Institute.

Albritton, Robert B., and Matthew F. Wetstein. 1991. Determinants of abortion use in the American states. Paper presented at the annual meeting of the Midwest Political Science Association, Chicago.

Allport, Gordon W. 1954. *The nature of prejudice.* Menlo Park, CA: Addison-Wesley.

Anderson, Kristi. 1975. Working women and political participation, 1952-1972. *American Journal of Political Science* 19:439-54.

Apple, R. W., Jr. 1989. Limits on abortion seem less likely. *The New York Times* (National Edition.) September 29, pp. 1, 8.

Applebome, Peter. 1992. Mississippi law fails to reduce abortion strife; 24-hour waiting period offers look at future. *The New York Times,* October 13, pp. A8, A14.

Arney, William Ray, and William H. Trescher. 1976. Trends in attitudes toward abortion, 1972-1975. *Family Planning Perspectives* 8:117-24.

Arterton, F. Christopher. 1978. Campaign organizations confront the media. In *Race for the presidency,* edited by James D. Barber. Englewood Cliffs, NJ: Prentice-Hall.

Asher, Herbert B. 1983. *Causal modeling.* Sage University Paper Series on Quantitative Applications in the Social Sciences, series no. 07-003. Beverly Hills, CA: Sage.

Attitudes on abortion little changed since Supreme Court's 1973 ruling. 1989. *Gallup Report* No. 281:16-23.

Baker, Donald. 1989. Abortion debate heats up Va. gubernatorial race. *The Washington Post* July 8, p. B5.

Baker, Ross K., Laurily K. Epstein, and Rodney D. Forth. 1981. Matters of life and death: Social, political, and religious correlates of attitudes about abortion. *American Politics Quarterly* 9:89-102.

Balch, Burke. 1989. NRLC proposes a post-Webster state legislative program. *National Right to Life News,* October 19, pp. 6-7.

Barber, James David. 1978. *Race for the Presidency.* Englewood Cliffs, NJ: Prentice-Hall.

Barnartt, Sharon N., and Richard J. Harris. 1982. Recent changes in predictors of abortion attitudes. *Sociology and Social Research* 66:320-34.

Barnes v. Moore. 920 F.2d. 12 (1992).

Baumgartner, Frank R., and Bryan D. Jones. 1991. Agenda dynamics and policy subsystems. *Journal of Politics* 53:1044-74.

Beal v. Doe. 432 U.S. 438 (1977).

Bellotti v. Baird. 428 U.S. 132 (1976).

Bellotti v. Baird. 443 U.S. 622 (1979).

Benson, Peter, and Dorothy Williams. 1982. *Religion on Capitol Hill.* San Francisco: Harper & Row.

Berkman, Michael B., and Robert O'Connor. 1992. The determinants of state abortion policies: A post-Webster analysis. Paper presented at the annual meeting of the Midwest Political Science Association, Chicago, April.

Bernstein, Robert A., and William W. Anthony. 1974. The ABM issue in the Senate, 1968-1970: The importance of ideology. *American Political Science Review* 68:1198-1206.

Bibby, John F., Cornelius P. Cotter, James L. Gibson, and Robert J. Huckshorn. 1990. Parties in state politics. Pp. 85-122 in *Politics in the American states,* 5th ed., edited by Virginia Gray, Herbert Jacobs, and Robert B. Albritton. Boston: Little, Brown.

Bishop, George W., Robert W. Oldendick, and Alfred J. Tuchfarber. 1985. The importance of replicating a failure to replicate: Order effects on abortion items. *Public Opinion Quarterly* 49:105-14.

Bishop, Nadean. 1979. Abortion: The controversial choice. In *Women: A feminist perspective,* edited by Jo Freeman. Palo Alto, CA: Mayfield.

Biskupic, Joan. 1989. New limits on abortion rights are upheld by 5-4 majority. *Congressional Quarterly Weekly Report* 47:1698-1700.

Biskupic, Joan. 1992. Pennsylvania case portends new attack on abortion. *Congressional Quarterly Weekly Report* 50 (January 25):167-71.

Blake, Judith. 1971. Abortion and public opinion: The 1960-1970 decade. *Science* 171, 12:540-49.

Blake, Judith, and Jorge H. del Pinal. 1980. Predicting polar attitudes toward abortion in the United States. In *Abortion parley,* edited by J. T. Burtchaell. Kansas City, KS: Andrews & McMeel.

Blank, Robert H. 1978. *Regional diversity of political values: Idaho political cultures.* Washington, DC: University Press of America.

Boling, Patricia. 1991. Talking about abortion rights in a post-*Roe* world. Paper presented at the annual meeting of the American Political Science Association, Washington, DC, August 29-September 1.

Boloton, S. 1982. Views from the post-feminist generation. *The New York Times Magazine,* October, pp. 2, 5-7, 9-11.

Boneparth, Ellen, ed. 1982. *Women, power and policy.* Elmsford, NY: Pergamon.

Brudney, Jeffrey, and Gary W. Copeland. 1984. Evangelicals as a political force: Reagan and the 1980 religious vote. *Social Science Quarterly* 65:1072-79.

Butler, David, and Donald Stokes. 1969. *Political change in Britain.* New York: St. Martin's.

Carmines, Edward G., and James A. Stimson. 1980. The two faces of issue voting. *American Political Science Review* 74:78-91.

Carmines, Edward, and James Stimson. 1989. *Issue Evolution: Race and the Arenas of American Politics.* Princeton, NJ: Princeton University Press.

Carroll, Susan J. 1984. Women candidates and support for women's issues: Closet feminists. *Western Political Quarterly* 37:307-23.

Carroll, Susan J., and Ella Taylor. 1989. Gender differences in policy priorities of U.S. state legislators. Paper presented at the annual meeting of the American Political Science Association. Atlanta, GA, August.

Carlson, Margaret. 1990. Abortion's hardest cases. *Time,* 36 (July 9): 22-26.

Casey, Gregory. 1984. Intensive analysis of a "single" issue: Attitudes on abortion. *Political Methodology* 97-124.

Cates, Nancy. 1991. A change of heart: Abortion in the Missouri General Assembly. John F. Kennedy School of Government, case analysis #1007.

CBS/New York Times Surveys. 1989-1991.

Center for American Women in Politics. 1991. *Reshaping the agenda: Women in state legislatures.* New Brunswick, NJ: Rutgers University, Eagleton Institute of Politics.

Chressanthis, G. A., K. S. Gilbert, and P. W. Grimes 1991. Ideology, constituent interests, and senatorial voting: The case of abortion. *Social Science Quarterly* 72:588-600.

Church, George J. 1989. Five political hot spots. *Time,* July 17, p. 64.

Citrin, Jack. 1974. Comment: The political relevance of trust in government. *American Political Science Review* 68:973-88.

Clausen, Aage. 1973. *How congressmen decide: A policy focus.* New York: St. Martin's.

Coglianese, Cary. 1991. After the federal retreat: State constitutional protection of abortion rights. Paper presented at the annual meeting of the Midwest Political Science Association. Chicago. April.

Colby, David C., and David G. Baker. 1988. State policy responses to the AIDS epidemic. *Publius: The Journal of Federalism* 18:113-30.

Collie, Melissa. 1985. Voting behavior in legislatures. Pp. 471-518 in *Handbook of legislative research* (by Gerhard Loewenberg), edited by Samuel C. Patterson and Malcolm E. Jewell. Cambridge, MA: Harvard University Press.

Combs, Michael W., and Susan Welch. 1982. Blacks, whites, and attitudes toward abortion. *Public Opinion Quarterly* 46:510-20.

Condit, Celeste M. 1990. *Decoding abortion rhetoric: Communicating social change.* Urbana: University of Illinois Press.

Congressional Quarterly. 1990. *Congressional Quarterly Washington information directory.* Washington, DC: CQ Press.

Conover, Pamela Johnston, and Stanley Feldman. 1986. Religion, morality and politics. Paper presented at the annual meeting of the American Political Science Association, Washington, DC, August.

Conover, Pamela Johnston, and Virginia Gray. 1983. *Feminism and the New Right: Conflict over the American family.* New York: Praeger.

Converse, Philip E. 1964. The nature of mass belief systems in mass publics. Pp. 206-61 in *Ideology and discontent,* edited by David E. Apter. Glencoe, IL: Free Press.

Converse, Philip E. 1970. Attitudes and nonattitudes: The continuation of a dialogue. Pp. 168-89 in *The quantitative analysis of social problems,* edited by D. Apter. Reading, MA: Addison-Wesley.

Converse, Philip E., and Gregory B. Markus. 1979. Plus ça change . . . : The new CPS election study panel. *American Political Science Review* 73:32-49.

Cook, Elizabeth. 1993. The generations of feminism. Pp. 57-66 in *Women and politics: Outsiders or insiders,* edited by Lois Duke. Englewood Cliffs, NJ: Prentice-Hall.

Cook, Elizabeth Adell, Ted G. Jelen, and Clyde Wilcox. 1991. Generations and abortion attitudes. Paper presented at the Annual Meeting of the Midwest Political Science Association, Chicago.

Cook, Elizabeth Adell, Ted G. Jelen, and Clyde Wilcox. 1992a. *Between two absolutes: Public opinion and the politics of abortion.* Boulder, CO: Westview.

Cook, Elizabeth, Ted G. Jelen, and Clyde Wilcox. 1992b. *Choice vs. life: Public attitudes toward legal abortion.* Boulder, CO: Westview.

Council of State Governments. 1990. Status of abortion laws. *State Government News,* pp. 16-17.

Dahl, Robert A. 1956. *A preface to democratic theory.* Chicago: University of Chicago Press.

Danielsen, A. L., and P. H. Rubin 1977. An empirical investigation of voting on energy issues. *Public Choice* 31:119-42.

Darcy, Robert, Susan Welch, and Janet Clark. 1987. *Women, elections, and representation.* New York: Longman.

Davis, James A., and Tom W. Smith. 1990. *General Social Surveys, 1972-1990* (machine readable data file). Chicago: National Opinion Research Center, producer, 1990; Storrs, CT: The Roper Center for Public Opinion Research, University of Connecticut, distributor. One data file (26,265 logical records) and one codebook (909 pages).

Davis, James Alen, and Tom W. Smith. 1972-1991. General Social Surveys: 1972-1991. [Codebook and machine-readable datafile.]

Davis, James A., and Tom W. Smith. 1984. *The General Social Surveys, 1972-1984: Cumulative codebook.* Chicago: National Opinion Research Corporation.

Daynes, Byron W., and Raymond Tatalovich. 1984. Religious influence and congressional voting on abortion. *Journal for the Scientific Study of Religion* 23:197-200.

Daynes, Byron W., and Raymond Tatalovich. 1992. Presidential politics and abortion, 1972-1988. *Presidential Studies Quarterly* 22:545-61.

Decker, Cathleen. 1989. Abortion and gender frame governor race. *Los Angeles Times,* September 3, p. A3.

Decker, Cathleen. 1990. Wilson should quiz Souter on abortion issue, Feinstein says. *Los Angeles Times,* August 8, p. A3.

Deitch, Cynthia H. 1983. Ideology and opposition to abortion: Trends in public opinion, 1972-1980. *Alternative Lifestyles* 6:6-26.

Denniston, Lyle. 1992. Supreme court upholds Miss. abortion-wait law. *Commercial Appeal* (Memphis, TN, newspaper), December 8, p. A1.

Denzau, Arthur T., and Michael C. Munger. 1986. Legislators and interest groups: How unorganized interests get represented. *American Political Science Review* 80:89-106.

Diamond, Irene. 1977. *Sex roles in the state house.* New Haven, CT: Yale University Press.

Diamond, Irene, and N. Hartsock. 1981. Beyond interests in politics: A comment on Virginia Sapiro's "When are interests interesting? The problem of political representation of women." *American Political Science Review* 75:717-21.

Dionne, E. J. 1990. *Why Americans hate politics.* New York: Simon & Schuster.

Dodson, Debra L. 1989. Are parties gender-neutral? Paper presented at the 1989 annual meeting of the Midwest Political Science Association, Chicago.

Dodson, Debra L., and Lauren D. Burnbauer, with Katherine E. Kleeman. 1990a. *Election 1989: The abortion issue in New Jersey and Virginia.* New Brunswick, NJ: Eagleton Institute of Politics.

Dodson, Debra L., and Lauren D. Burnbauer. 1990b. Issue voting in the post-*Webster* era. Paper presented at the annual meeting of the American Political Science Association, San Francisco.

Donovan, Beth. 1990. Campaigns grow complicated over parental notification. *Congressional Quarterly Weekly Report* 28:1573-75.

Ebaugh, Helen Rose Fuchs, and C. Allen Haney. 1980. Shifts in abortion attitudes: 1972-1978. *Journal of Marriage and the Family* 42:491-99.

Ebaugh, Helen Rose Fuchs, and C. Allen Haney. 1985. Abortion attitudes in the United States: Continuities and discontinuities. Pp. 163-77 in *Perspectives on abortion,* edited by Paul Sachdev. Metuchen, NJ: Scarecrow Press.

Eccles, M. E. 1978. Abortion: How members voted in 1977. *Congressional Quarterly Weekly Report* 36:258-67.

Eckberg, Douglas Lee. 1988. The physician's anti-abortion campaign and the social bases of moral reform participation. *Social Forces* 67:378-88.

Eisenstein, Zillah R. 1984. *Feminism and sexual equality: Crisis in liberal America.* New York: Monthly Review Press.

Eisenstein, Zillah R. 1988. *The female body and the law.* Berkeley: University of California Press.

Elazar, Daniel. 1972. *American federalism: A view from the states,* 2nd ed. New York: Thomas Y. Crowell.

Elder, Charles D., and Roger W. Cobb. 1983. *The political uses of symbols.* New York: Longman.

Epstein, Lee, and Joseph F. Kobylka. 1992. *The Supreme Court & legal change: Abortion and the death penalty.* Chapel Hill: University of North Carolina Press.

Erikson, Robert S., John P. McIver, and Gerald C. Wright. 1987. State political culture and public opinion. *American Political Science Review* 81:797-814.

Erikson, Robert S., Gerald C. Wright, and John P. McIver. 1989. Political parties, public opinion, and state policy in the United States. *American Political Science Review* 83:729-50.

Evans, Sara M., and Barbara J. Nelson. 1989. *Wage justice: Comparable worth and the paradox of technocratic reform.* Chicago: University of Chicago Press.

Falik, Marilyn. 1983. *Ideology and abortion policy politics.* Landmark Dissertations in Women's Studies Series, edited by A. Baxter. New York: Praeger.

Fazio, Russell, Martha C. Powell, and Paul M. Herr. 1983. Toward a process model of the attitude-behavior relationship: Accessing one's attitude object. *Journal of Personality and Social Psychology* 44:723-35.

Fazio, Russell, and Mark P. Zanna. 1981. Direct experience and attitude-behavior consistency. Pp. 164-81 in *Advances in experimental social psychology,* Vol. 14, edited by L. Berkowitz. New York: Academic Press.

Feldman, Stanley. 1983. Economic individualism and American public opinion. *American Politics Quarterly* 11:3-29.

Feldman, Stanley. 1988. Structure and consistency in public opinion: The role of core beliefs and values. *American Journal of Political Science* 32:416-40.

Feldman, Stanley. 1989. Moral values and social order. Paper presented at the annual meeting of the International Society of Political Psychology, Tel Aviv, Israel.

Findlay, Barbara Agrasti. 1985. Correlates of abortion attitudes and implications for change. In *Perspectives on abortion,* edited by Paul Sachder. Metuchen, NJ: Scarecrow Press.

Fiorina, Morris. 1981. *Retrospective voting in American national elections.* New Haven, CT: Yale University Press.

Franklin, Charles H., and Liane C. Kosaki. 1989. Republican schoolmaster: The U.S. Supreme Court, public opinion, and abortion. *American Political Science Review* 83:751-71.

Freeman, Jo, ed. 1979. *Women, a feminist perspective,* 2nd ed. Palo Alto, CA: Mayfield.

Fried, Amy. 1988. Abortion politics as symbolic politics: An investigation into belief systems. *Social Science Quarterly* 69:137-54.

Fried, Marlene Gerber, ed. 1990. *From abortion to reproductive freedom: Transforming the movement.* Boston: South End Press.

Frohock, Fred M. 1983. *Abortion: A case study in law and morals.* Westport, CT: Greenwood Press.

Gallup Poll Monthly. 1991. No. 305 (February), 32.

Gallup, George, and Frank Newport. 1990. Americans shift toward pro-choice position. *Gallup Poll Monthly* No. 295:2-4.

Gamson, William A. 1968. *Power and discontent.* Homewood, IL: Dorsey Press.

Gelb, Joyce. 1989. *Feminism and politics: A comparative perspective.* Berkeley: University of California Press.

Gelb, Joyce, and Marian Palley. 1987. *Women and public policies,* 2nd ed. Princeton, NJ: Princeton University Press.

Genovese, Michael A., ed. 1993. *Women as national leaders.* Newbury Park, CA: Sage.

Gilens, M. 1988. Gender and support for Reagan: A comprehensive model of presidential approval. *American Journal of Political Science* 32:19-49.

Ginsburg, Faye D. 1989. *Contested lives: The abortion debate in an American community.* Berkeley: University of California Press.

Glazer, Sarah. 1987. Abortion policy. *Editorial Research Reports* October 16, 1987: 534-47.

Goggin, Malcolm L. 1984. The ideological content of presidential messages: The message-tailoring hypothesis revisited. *American Politics Quarterly* 12:361-84.

Goggin, Malcolm L. 1988. Policy redesign: A concept and its empirical referents. Paper presented at the annual meeting of the Western Political Science Association Meeting, San Francisco.

Goggin, Malcolm L. 1992. The tactical choices of abortion interest groups. Paper presented at annual meeting of the Midwest Political Science Association, Chicago, April.

Goggin, Malcolm L. 1993. Understanding the new politics of abortion: A framework and agenda for research. *American Politics Quarterly* 21:4-30.

Goggin, Malcolm L., and Jung-Ki Kim. 1992. Interest groups, public opinion, and abortion policy in the American States. Paper presented at the annual meeting of the Western Political Science Association, San Francisco, March.

Goggin, Malcolm L., and Christopher Wlezien. 1991. Interest groups and the socialization of conflict. Paper presented at the 1991 annual meeting of the Midwest Political Science Association, Chicago.

Goggin, Malcolm L., and Christopher Wlezien. 1992. Interest groups and the dynamics of abortion politics. In *Perspectives on American and Texas politics,* 2nd ed., edited by Donald S. Lutz and Kent L. Tedin. Dubuque, IA: Kendall/Hunt.

Goggin, Malcolm L., Ann O'M. Bowman, James Lester, and Laurence O'Toole, Jr. 1990. *Implementation theory and practice: Toward a third generation.* Glenview, IL: Scott, Foresman.

Gohmann, Stephan F., and Robert L. Ohsfeldt. 1990. Predicting state abortion legislation from U.S. Senate votes. *Policy Studies Review* 9:749-65.

Gold, Rachel B., and Daniel Daley. 1991. Public funding of contraceptive, sterilization, and abortion services, fiscal year 1990. *Family Planning Perspectives* 23:204-11.

Gold, Rachel Benson. 1990. *Abortion and women's health: A turning point for America?* New York and Washington, DC: The Alan Guttmacher Institute.

Gold, Rachel Benson, and Sandra Guardado. 1988. Public funding of family planning, sterilization and abortion services. *Family Planning Perspectives* 20:228-33.

Gold, Rachel Benson, and Jennifer Macias. 1986. Public funding of contraceptive, sterilization, and abortion services, 1985. *Family Planning Perspectives* 18:259-64.

Goldenberg, Edie, and Michael Traugott. 1984. *Campaigning for Congress*. Washington, DC:
CQ Press.

Gordon, Linda. 1977. *Woman's body, woman's right: A social history of birth control in
America*. Harmondsworth, UK: Penguin.

Gormley, William T. 1986. Regulatory issues in a federal system. *Polity* 18:595-620.

Granberg, Donald. 1978. Pro-life or reflection of conservative ideology? An analysis of
opposition to legalized abortion. *Sociology and Social Research* 62:414-29.

Granberg, Donald. 1982. The abortion activists. Comparison of pro-choice and pro-life
activists. *Population and Environment* 5:75-94.

Granberg, Donald. 1985. The United States Senate votes to uphold *Roe versus Wade*.
Population Research and Policy Review 4:115-31.

Granberg, Donald. 1987. The abortion issue in the 1984 elections. *Family Planning Perspectives* 19:59-62.

Granberg, Donald, and James Burlison. 1983. The abortion issue in the 1980 elections.
Family Planning Perspectives 15:231-38.

Granberg, Donald, and Beth Wellman Granberg. 1981. Abortion attitudes, 1965-1980:
Trends and determinants. *Family Planning Perspectives* 12:250-61.

Granberg, Donald, and Beth Wellman Granberg. 1985. Social bases of support and opposition
to legalized abortion. In *Perspectives on abortion*, edited by Paul Sachdev. London:
Scarecrow Press.

Grandolfo, Jane, and Mike Hailey. 1990. Richards cites abortion as key issue. *The Houston
Post*, April 12, pp. A1, A18.

Gray, Virginia, and David Lowery. 1989. The corporatist foundations of state industrial
policy. *American Political Science Review* 88:109-31.

Gray, Virginia, and David Lowery. 1990. The deep structure of state interest group systems
I: Interest group system density. Paper presented at the annual meeting of the American
Political Science Association. San Francisco, September.

Greenstone, J. David, and Paul E. Peterson. 1973. *Race and authority in urban politics:
Community participation and the war on poverty*. New York: Russell Sage.

Gurin, Patricia. 1985. Women's gender consciousness. *Public Opinion Quarterly* 49:143-63.

Gusfield, Joseph R. 1963. *Symbolic crusade*. Urbana: University of Illinois Press.

Guth, James, and John Green. 1990. Politics in a new key: Religiosity and participation
among political activists. *Western Political Quarterly* 43:153-79.

Hale, Jon. 1987. The scribes of Texas: Newspaper coverage of the 1984 U.S. Senate
campaign. In *Campaigns in the news: Mass media and congressional elections*, edited by
Jan Vermeer. Westport, CT: Greenwood Press.

Hall, Elaine J., and Myra Marx Ferree. 1986. Race differences in abortion attitudes. *Public
Opinion Quarterly* 50:193-207.

Halva-Neubauer, Glen. 1989a. Success of the anti-abortion agenda in state legislatures:
Lessons from Virginia, Pennsylvania, and Minnesota. Paper presented at the annual
meeting of the Midwest Political Science Association, Chicago, April.

Halva-Neubauer, Glen. 1989b. The reversal of Roe: A view from the states. Paper presented
at the annual meeting of the American Political Science Association, Atlanta.

Halva-Neubauer, Glen. 1990. Abortion policy in the post-*Webster* age. *Publius: The Journal
of Federalism* 20:27-44.

Halva-Neubauer, Glen. 1991. Abortion policymaking in the post-*Webster* age: The case of
Minnesota. Paper presented at the annual meetings of the Midwest Political Science
Association. Chicago, April.

Halva-Neubauer, Glen. 1992. Legislative agenda setting in the states: The case of abortion policy. Ph.D. diss., University of Minnesota.

Hansen, Susan B. 1980. State implementation of Supreme Court decisions: Abortion rates since *Roe v. Wade. Journal of Politics* 42:372-95.

Hansen, Susan B. 1990. State differences in public policies toward women: A test of three hypotheses. Paper presented at the annual meeting of the American Political Science Association, San Francisco.

Hansen, Susan B., Linda M. Franz, and Margaret Netemeyer-Mays. 1976. Women's political participation and policy preferences. *Social Science Quarterly* 54:576-90.

Harris, Richard J., and Edgar W. Mills. 1985. Religion, values and attitudes toward abortion. *Journal for the Scientific Study of Religion* 24:119-36.

Harris v. McRae. 448 U.S. 297 (1980).

Hartz, Louis. 1955. *The liberal tradition in America.* New York: Harcourt Brace Jovanovich.

Henshaw, Stanley K., and J. Silverman. 1988. The characteristics and prior contraceptive use of U.S. abortion patients. *Family Planning Perspectives* 20:158-68.

Henshaw, Stanley K., and Jennifer Van Vort. 1990. Abortion services in the United States, 1987 and 1988. *Family Planning Perspectives* 22:102-8, 142.

Hershey, Marjorie Random. 1986. Direct action and the abortion issue: The political participation of single issue groups. Pp. 27-45 in *Interest group politics,* edited by Allan J. Cigler and Burdett A. Loomis. Washington, DC: CQ Press.

Hertel, Bradley R., and Michael Hughes. 1987. Religious affiliation, attendance, and support for "pro-family" issues in the United States. *Social Forces* 65:858-82.

Hertzke, Allen. 1988. *Representing God in Washington: The role of religious lobbyists in the American polity.* Knoxville: University of Tennessee Press.

Hill, David B. 1981. Political culture and female political representation. *Journal of Politics* 43:159-68.

Hill, David B. 1982. Women state legislators and party voting on the ERA. *Social Science Quarterly* 63:318-26.

Himmelstein, Jerome. 1986. The social basis of antifeminism. *Journal for the Scientific Study of Religion* 25:1-15.

Himmelstein, Jerome. 1990. *To the right: The transformation of American conservatism.* Berkeley: University of California Press.

Hodgson v. Minnesota. 648 F. Suppl. 756, 764 (D. Minn. 1986).

Hofferbert, Richard I., and John K. Urice. 1985. Small scale policy. *American Journal of Political Science* 29:308-29.

Hofstaedter, Richard. 1972. *The American political tradition.* New York: New Vintage Edition.

Holbrook, Thomas M. 1984. Economics and presidential elections: The view from the states. (unpublished paper, University of Iowa).

Holbrook-Provow, Thomas M., and Steven C. Poe. 1987. Measuring state political ideology. *American Politics Quarterly* 15:399-416.

Howell, Susan E., and James M. Vanderleeuw. 1990. Economic effects on state governors. *American Politics Quarterly* 18:158-67.

Hugick, Larry. 1992. Abortion: Public support grows for *Roe v. Wade Gallup Poll Monthly* No. 316 (January):5-9.

Hunter, James D. 1983. *American evangelicalism: Conservative religion and the quandary of modernity.* New Brunswick, NJ: Rutgers University Press.

Hunter, James D. 1987. *Evangelicalism: The coming generation.* Chicago: University of Chicago Press.

Hurwitz, Jon. 1986. Issue perceptions and legislative decision-making. *American Politics Quarterly* 14:150-85.

Hwang, Sung-Don, and Virginia Gray. 1991. External limits and internal determinants of state public policy. *Western Political Quarterly* 44:277-99.

Inglehart, Ronald. 1977. *The silent revolution: Changing values and political styles among Western publics.* Princeton, NJ: Princeton University Press.

Inglehart, Ronald. 1990. *Culture shift in advanced industrial society.* Princeton, NJ: Princeton University Press.

Jackson, John E., and John W. Kingdon. 1992. Ideology, interest group scores, and legislative votes. *American Journal of Political Science* 36:805-23.

Jackson, John E., and Maris A. Vinovskis. 1983. Public opinion, elections, and the "single-issue" issue. Pp. 64-81 in *The abortion debate and the American system,* edited by Gilbert Stein. Washington, DC: Brookings Institution.

Jacobson, M. 1981. You say potato and I say potato: Attitudes toward feminism as a function of its subject-selected labels. *Sex Roles* 7:349-54.

Jelen, Ted. 1984a. Candidate ambiguity and the clarity of citizen's perceptions. *Texas Journal of Political Studies* 6:23-29.

Jelen, Ted G. 1984b. Religion and political civility: The coming generation of American evangelicals. *Review of Religious Research* 25:220-31.

Jelen, Ted. 1984c. Respect for life, sexual morality, and opposition to abortion. *Review of Religious Research* 25:220-31.

Jelen, Ted G. 1988a. Changes in the attitudinal correlations of opposition to abortion, 1977-1985. *Journal for the Scientific Study of Religion* 27:211-28.

Jelen, Ted. 1988b. The effects of gender role stereotypes on political attitudes. *Social Science Journal* 25:353-65.

Jelen, Ted. 1989. Biblical literalism and inerrancy: Does the difference make a difference? *Sociological Analysis* 51.

Jelen, Ted. 1991. *The politicization of religious beliefs.* New York: Praeger.

Jennings, Kent, and Richard Niemi. 1981. *Generations and politics.* Princeton, NJ: Princeton University Press.

Jewell, Malcolm E. 1981. Editor's introduction: The state of U.S. state legislative research. *Legislative Studies Quarterly* 6:1-25.

Jewell, Malcolm E., and David M. Olson. 1987. *American state political parties and elections,* 3rd ed. Homewood, IL: Dorsey Press.

Johnson, Stephen D., Joseph B. Tamney, and Ronald Burton. 1990. The abortion controversy: Conflicting beliefs and values in American society. Paper presented at the Annual Meeting of the American Political Science Association, San Francisco, August.

Johnson, Blair T., and Alice H. Eagly. 1989. Effects of involvement on persuasion: A meta-analysis. *Psychological Bulletin* 106:290-314.

Johnson, Charles A., and Jon R. Bond. 1980. Coercive and noncoercive abortion deterrence policies. Pp. 185-207 in *Policy implementation: Penalties or incentives?* edited by J. Brigham and D. W. Brown. Beverly Hills, CA: Sage.

Johnson, Douglas, and Bernard Quinn. 1974. *Churches and church membership in the United States.* Washington, DC: Glenmary Research Center.

Johnson, Marilyn, and Susan Carroll. 1978. Statistical report: Profile of women holding public office, 1977. In *Women in public office: A biographical directory and statistical analysis,* edited by Kathy A. Stanwick and Marilyn Johnson. Metuchen, NJ: Scarecrow Press.

Jones, E. F., J. D. Forrest, S. K. Henshaw, and A. Torres. 1989. *Pregnancy, contraception, & family planning services in industrialized countries.* New Haven, CT: Yale University Press.

Jöreskog, Karl G., and Dag Sörbom. 1986. *LISREL VI.* User's guide, 4th ed. Mooresville, IN: Scientific Software.

Joslyn, Richard. 1984. *Mass media and elections.* Reading, MA: Addison-Wesley.

Kanter, Rosabeth M. 1977. Some effects of proportion on group life: Skewed sex ratios and response to token women. *American Journal of Sociology* 82:965-90.

Karnig, Albert, and Susan Welch. 1980. *Black representation and urban policy.* Chicago: University of Chicago Press.

Katz, Irwin, Joyce Wackenhut, and R. Glen Hass. 1986. Racial ambivalence, value duality and behavior. Pp. 35-60 in *Prejudice, discrimination, and racism,* edited by J. F. Dovidio and S. L. Gaertner. New York: Academic Press.

Keefe, William, and Morris Ogul. 1989. *The American legislative process,* 7th ed. Englewood Cliffs, NJ: Prentice-Hall.

Kellstedt, Lyman, and Corwin Smidt. 1991. Measuring fundamentalism: An analysis of different operational strategies. *Journal for the Scientific Study of Religion* 30:259-78.

Kerr, Peter. 1989. Second debate in New Jersey turns nasty. *The New York Times,* October 12, sec. B.

Key, V. O. 1961. *Public opinion and American democracy.* New York: Knopf.

Keyes, Edward, with Randall K. Miller. 1989. *The Court vs. Congress; Prayer, busing, and abortion.* Durham, NC: Duke University Press.

Kincaid, John. 1982. *Political culture, public policy and the American states.* Philadelphia: ISHI Press.

Kincaid, John. 1988. State court protection of individual rights under state constitutions: The new judicial federalism. *Journal of State Government* 61:164-69.

Kincaid, John, and Joel Lieske. 1991. Political subcultures of the American states: State-of-the-art and agenda for research. Paper presented at the annual meeting of the American Political Science Association, Washington, DC, September.

Kinder, Donald R. 1983. Diversity and complexity in American public opinion. Pp. 389-425 in *Political science: The state of the discipline,* edited by Ada W. Finifter. Washington, DC: American Political Science Association.

King, Gary. 1990. When not to use R-squared. *The Political Methodologist* 3:Fall.

Kirkpatrick, Jeane. 1974. *Political women.* New York: Basic Books.

Klatch, Rebecca E. 1987. *Women of the new right.* Philadelphia: Temple University Press.

Kleeman, Katherine E. 1983. *Women's PAC's.* New Brunswick, NJ: Center for American Women and Politics.

Klein, Ethel. 1984. *Gender politics.* Cambridge, MA: Harvard University Press.

Klingman, David, and William W. Lammers. 1984. The "general policy liberalism" factor in American state politics. *American Journal of Political Science* 28:598-610.

Kluckhohn, Clyde. 1965. Values and value-orientations in the theory of action. Pp. 388-433 in *Toward a general theory of action,* edited by T. Parsons and E. A. Shils. New York: Harper & Row.

Kochanek, Kenneth. 1990. Induced terminations of pregnancy: Reporting states, 1987. *Monthly Vital Statistics Report* 38:9 (supplement), 1-3.

Komarovsky, A. 1985. *Women in college.* New York: Basic Books.

Krosnick, Jon A. 1988. The role of attitude importance in social evaluation: A study of policy preferences, presidential candidate evaluations, and voting behavior. *Journal of Personality and Social Psychology* 55:196-210.

Krosnick, Jon A. 1989. Attitude importance and attitude accessibility. *Personality and Social Psychology Bulletin* 15:297-308.

Krosnick, Jon A. 1991. The stability of political preferences: Comparisons of symbolic and nonsymbolic attitudes. *American Journal of Political Science* 35:547-76.

Leader, Sheila Gilbert. 1977. The policy impact of elected women officials. Pp. 265-84 in *The impact of the electoral process,* edited by Louis Maisel and Joseph Cooper. Beverly Hills, CA: Sage.

Leege, David, and Michael Welch. 1989. Religious roots of political orientations: Variations among American Catholic parishioners. *The Journal of Politics* 51:137-62.

Legge, Jerome. 1983. The determinants of attitudes toward abortion in the American electorate. *Western Political Quarterly* 36:479-90.

Legge, Jerome S. 1987. Abortion as a policy issue: Attitudes of the mass public. *Women & Politics* 7:63-82.

Leippe, Mark R., and Richard E. Elkin. 1987. When motives clash: Issue involvement, and response involvements as determinants of persuasion. *Journal of Personality and Social Psychology* 52:269-78.

Levitin, Teresa. 1973. Values. In *Measures of social psychological attitudes,* edited by J. P. Robinson and P. R. Shaver. Ann Arbor: Institute for Social Research, University of Michigan.

Liberman, Akiva, and Shelly Chaiken. 1991. Value conflict and thought-induced attitude change. *Journal of Experimental Social Psychology* 27:203-16.

Lindsay, J. M. 1990. Parochialism, policy, and constituency constraints: Congressional voting on strategic weapons systems. *American Journal of Political Science* 34:936-60.

Lipset, Seymour Martin, and Earl Raab. 1970. *The politics of unreason: Right-wing extremism in America, 1790-1970.* New York: Harper & Row.

Long, J. Scott. 1983a. *Confirmatory factor analysis.* Sage University Paper Series on Quantitative Applications in the Social Sciences, series no. 07-033. Beverly Hills, CA: Sage.

Long, J. Scott. 1983b. *Covariance structure models: An introduction to LISREL.* Sage University Paper Series on Quantitative Applications in the Social Sciences, series no. 07-034. Beverly Hills, CA: Sage.

Lotstra, Hans. 1985. *Abortion: The Catholic debate in America.* New York: Irvington Publishers.

Lowi, T. J. 1988. Foreword: New dimensions in policy and politics. Pp. x-xxi in *Social regulatory policy: Moral controversies in American politics,* edited by Raymond Tatalovich and Byron W. Daynes. Boulder, CO: Westview.

Lowi, Theodore. 1964. American business, public policy, case studies, and political theory. *World Politics* 16:667-715.

Luker, Kristin. 1984. *Abortion and the politics of motherhood.* Berkeley: University of California Press.

Luker, Kristin. 1985. Abortion and the meaning of life. Pp. 25-45 in *Abortion: Understanding differences,* edited by S. Callahan and D. Callahan. New York: Plenum.

MacKinnon, Katherine. 1987. *Feminism unmodified.* Cambridge, UK: Cambridge University Press.

Maher v. Roe. 432 U.S. 464 (1977).

Mannheim, Karl. 1972. The problem of generations. In *The new pilgrims,* edited by Philip Altbach and Robert Laufer. New York: David McKay.

Mansbridge, Jane. 1986. *Why we lost the ERA.* Chicago: University of Chicago Press.

Marcus, Ruth. 1989. Justice Dept. urges workers to adopt. *The Washington Post,* November 3, A3.

Marsden, George. 1980. *Fundamentalism and American culture.* New York: Oxford University Press.

Matthews, Donald, and James Stimson. 1975. *Yeas and nays: Normal decision-making in the U.S. House of Representatives.* New York: John Wiley.

McCormick, J. M. 1985. Congressional voting on the nuclear freeze resolutions. *American Politics Quarterly* 13:122-36.

McCormick, J. M., and M. Black. 1983. Ideology and voting on the Panama Canal treaties. *Legislative Studies Quarterly* 8:45-63.

McCulloch, Anne, and Jack Reinward. 1988. The Mormon influence on Idaho's politics: A rethinking of Elazar's political culture model. Paper presented at the annual meeting of the Pacific Northwest Political Science Association, Portland, OR, November.

McCutcheon, Allen L. 1987. Sexual morality, pro-life values, and attitudes toward abortion. *Sociological Methods and Research* 16:256-75.

McFarlane, Deborah R. 1989. Testing the statutory coherence hypothesis: The implementation of federal family planning policy in the states. *Administration and Society* 20:395-422.

McGuire, William J. 1969. The nature of attitudes and attitude change. In *The handbook of social psychology,* Vol. 3, edited by G. Lindzey and E. Aronson. Reading, MA: Addison-Wesley.

McGuire, William J. 1985. Attitudes and attitude change. Pp. 233-346 in *The handbook of social psychology,* Vol. 2, edited by G. Lindzey and E. Aronson. New York: Random House.

McIntosh, William, Letitia T. Alston, and Jon P. Alston. 1979. The differential impact of religious preference and church attendance on attitudes toward abortion. *Review of Religious Research* 20:195-213.

McIntosh, William A., and Jon P. Alston. 1977. Acceptance of abortion among white Catholics and protestants, 1962 and 1975. *Journal for the Scientific Study of Religion* 16:295-303.

Medoff, Marshall H. 1988. An economic analysis of the demand for abortions. *Economic Inquiry* 26:353-59.

Medoff, Marshall H. 1989. Constituents, ideology, and the demand for abortion legislation. *Public Choice* 60:185-91.

Meier, Kenneth J. 1988. *The political economy of regulation: The case of insurance.* Albany: SUNY Press.

Meier, Kenneth J., and Cathy Johnson. 1990. The politics of demon rum. *American Politics Quarterly* 18:404-29.

Melina, Lois. 1989. Liberating birthparents from shame. *Adopted Child* 8:4.

Merton, Andrew H. 1981. *Enemies of choice: The right-to-life movement and its threat to abortion.* Boston: Beacon Press.

Meyer, Donald. 1987. *Sex and power: The rise of women in America, Russia, Sweden, and Italy.* Middletown, CT: Wesleyan University Press.

Mezey, Susan Gluck. 1978. Support for women's rights policy: An analysis of local politicians. *American Politics Quarterly* 6:485-97.

Mezey, Susan Gluck. 1992. *In pursuit of equality: Women, public policy, and the federal courts.* New York: St. Martin's.

Mileti, Dennis S., and Larry D. Barnett. 1972. Nine demographic factors and their relationship to attitudes toward abortion legalization. *Social Biology* 19:43-50.

Miller, Arthur, Anne Hildreth, and Grace Simmons. 1986. The political implications of gender group consciousness. Paper presented at the annual meeting of the Midwest Political Science Association, Chicago.

Miller, Arthur, and Martin Wattenberg. 1984. Politics from the pulpit: Religiosity and the 1980 elections. *Public Opinion Quarterly* 48:301-7.

Moe v. Secretary of Administration and Finance. 417 N.E.2d 387 (1981).

Moen, Matthew. 1989. *The Christian right and Congress.* Tuscaloosa: University of Alabama Press.

Moen, Peggy. 1974. Abortion regulatory laws can serve pro-life interests. *The Wanderer,* May 16, p. 9.

Moncrief, Gary F. 1987. Idaho: The interests of sectionalism. Pp. 67-74 in *Interest group politics in the American west,* edited by Ronald Hrebenar and Clive Thomas. Salt Lake City: University of Utah Press.

Monroe, Alan. 1979. Consistency between constituency preferences and national policy decisions. *American Politics Quarterly* 7:3-19.

Moore, W. John. 1989. Lobbying the court. *The National Journal* 22:908-13.

Morgan, David R., and Kenneth J. Meier. 1980. Politics and morality: The effect of religion on referenda voting. *Social Science Quarterly* 61:144-48.

Morriss, Frank. 1974. A look at Nebraska's "catholic" abortion law. *The Wanderer,* June 20, p. 5.

Moyer, W. 1973. House voting on defense: An ideological explanation. In *Military force and American society,* edited by B. Russett and A. Stephens. New York: Harper & Row.

Mueller, Keith J. 1986. An analysis of congressional health policy voting in the 1970s. *Journal of Health Politics, Policy and Law* 11:117-35.

Muldoon, Maureen. 1991. *The abortion debate in the United States and Canada: A source book.* New York: Garland.

The NARAL Foundation. 1991. *Who decides? A state-by-state review of abortion rights.* Washington, DC: National Abortion Rights Action League.

NOW Legal Defense and Education Fund and Renee Cherow-O'Leary. 1987. *The state-by-state guide to women's legal rights.* New York: McGraw-Hill.

National Abortion Rights Action League. 1979. Are "pro-lifers" anti-social?. *NARAL Newsletter* (March):6-7.

National Abortion Rights Action League. 1989. *Who decides? A state by state review of abortion rights in America.* Washington, DC: National Abortion Rights Action League.

National Association for Repeal of Abortion Laws. 1973. Letter from Lana Clarke Phelan, Carol Greitzer, Lawrence Lader, and Lee Gidding to NARAL members. April 5.

National Center for Health Statistics. 1991. *Monthly Vital Statistics Report* 40:8 (supplement). December 12. Atlanta: Centers for Disease Control.

Nice, David C. 1988. Abortion clinic bombings as political violence. *American Journal of Political Science* 32:178-95.

Nicholson, Jeanne Bell, and Debra W. Stewart. 1978. The Supreme Court, abortion policy, and state response: A preliminary analysis. *Publius: The Journal of Federalism* 8:159-78.

Nie, Norman H., Sidney Verba, and John R. Petrocik. 1979. *The changing American voter.* Cambridge, MA: Harvard University Press.

Niemi, Richard G., John Mueller, and Tom W. Smith. 1989. *Trends in public opinion: A compendium of survey data.* Westport, CT: Greenwood Press.

Norusis, Marija J. 1990. *SPSS advanced statistics users guide.* Chicago: SPSS Inc.

Nye, Mary Alice. 1991. The U.S. Senate and civil rights roll call votes. *Western Political Quarterly* 44:971-86.

O'Hara, Thomas. 1990. Pennsylvania Catholics and the Abortion Control Act of 1989. Paper presented at the annual meeting of the American Political Science Association, San Francisco, August.

Okin, Susan. 1989. *Justice, gender and the family.* New York: Basic Books.

O'Steen, David N., and Darla St. Martin. 1985. Legislating life. Pp. 100-25 in *Arresting abortion: Practical ways to save unborn children,* edited by John Whitehead. Westchester, IL: Crossway Books.

Ostrom, Thomas M., and Thomas C. Brock. 1968. A cognitive model of attitudinal involvement. In *Theories of cognitive consistency: A sourcebook,* edited by R. P. Abelson and E. Aronson. Hillsdale, NJ: Lawrence Erlbaum.

Outshoorn, Joyce. 1986. The rules of the game: Abortion politics in the Netherlands. In *The new politics of abortion,* edited by Joni Lovenduski and Joyce Outshoorn. London: Sage.

Overby, L. Marvin. 1991. Assessing constituency influence: Congressional voting on the nuclear freeze, 1982-83. *Legislative Studies Quarterly* 16:297-312.

Page, Benjamin, and Robert Shapiro. 1983. Effects of public opinion on policy. *American Political Science Review* 77:175-90.

Page, Benjamin I., and Robert Y. Shapiro. 1992. *The rational public: Fifty years of trends in American policy preferences.* Chicago: University of Chicago Press.

Page, Benjamin I., Robert Y. Shapiro, and Glenn R. Dempsey. 1987. What moves public opinion? *American Political Science Review* 81:23-43.

Paige, Connie. 1983. *The right to lifers.* New York: Summit Books.

Patterson, Thomas. 1980. *The mass media election: How Americans choose their president.* New York: Praeger.

Peltzman, Sam. 1984. Constituent interest and congressional voting. *Journal of Law and Economics* 27:181-210.

Petchesky, Rosalind Pollack. 1984. *Abortion and woman's choice: The state, sexuality, and reproductive freedom.* New York: Longman.

Peterson, Karen K., and Jeffrey E. Dutton. 1975. Centrality, extremity, intensity: Neglected variables in research on attitude-behavior consistency. *Social Forces* 54:393-414.

Piereson, James E. 1977. Sources of candidate success in gubernatorial elections, 1910-1970. *Journal of Politics* 39:939-58.

Pitkin, Hanna Fenichel. 1967. *The concept of representation.* Berkeley: University of California Press.

Planned Parenthood Association of Kansas City v. Ashcroft. 462 U.S. 476 (1983).

Planned Parenthood of Central Missouri v. Danforth. 428 U.S. 52 (1976).

Planned Parenthood of Southeastern Pennsylvania v. Casey. 112 S.Ct 2791 (1992).

Plutzer, Eric. 1988. Work life, family life, and women's support of feminism. *American Sociological Review* 53:640-49.

Poole, Keith T. 1988. Recent developments in analytical models of voting in the U.S. Congress. *Legislative Studies Quarterly* 13:117-33.

Poole, Keith T., and R. Steven Daniels. 1985. Ideology, party, and voting in the U.S. Congress, 1959-1980. *American Political Science Review* 79:373-98.

Powell-Griner, Eve, and Katherine Trent. 1987. Sociodemographic determinants of abortion in the United States. *Demography* 24:553-61.

Quinn, Bernard, Herman Anderson, Martin Bradley, Paul Goetting, and Peggy Shriver. 1982. *Churches and church membership in the United States.* Atlanta, GA: Glenmary Research Center.

Raden, David. 1985. Strength-related attitude dimensions. *Social Psychology Quarterly* 48:312-30.

Ransford, H. Edward, and Jon Miller. 1983. Race, sex, and feminist outlooks. *American Sociological Review* 48:46-59.

Regan, Dennis T., and Russell Fazio. 1977. On the consistency between attitudes and behavior. A look to the method of attitude formation. *Journal of Experimental Psychology* 13:28-45.

Reid, T. R. 1989. Patchwork pattern of abortion rules. *The Washington Post,* April 17, A1, A8.

Renzetti, C. 1987. New wave or second stage? Attitudes of college women toward feminism. *Sex Roles* 16:265-77.

Rice, Charles. 1974. Some tough decisions for the pro-life movement. *The Wanderer,* August 22, p. 4.

Richard, Patricia Bayer. 1991a. Abortion policy in a changing political environment. Paper presented at the annual meeting of the American Political Science Association, Washington.

Richard, Patricia Bayer. 1991b. They'd rather it would go away: Ohio legislators and abortion policy. Paper presented at the annual meeting of the Midwest Political Science Association. Chicago, April.

Roberts, Raequel. 1990. Abortion no longer hot campaign topic. *The Houston Post,* October 26, pp. A1, A13.

Rodman, Hyman, Betty Sarvis, and Joy Walker Bonar. 1987. *The abortion question.* New York: Columbia University Press.

Roe v. Wade. 410 U.S. 113 (1973).

Rokeach, Milton. 1968. *Beliefs, attitudes, and values.* San Francisco: Jossey-Bass.

Rokeach, Milton. 1973. *The nature of human values.* New York: Free Press.

Rosenberg, Gerald N. 1991. *The hollow hope: Can courts bring about social change?* Chicago: University of Chicago Press.

Rosenblatt, Roger. 1992. *Life itself: Abortion in the American mind.* New York: Random House.

Rosenstone, Steven J. 1983. *Forecasting presidential elections.* New Haven, CT: Yale University Press.

Rosoff, Jeannie I. 1990. Afterword: A turning point? Pp. 61-66 in *Abortion and women's health: A turning point for America?* edited by Rachel B. Gold. New York and Washington, DC: The Alan Guttmacher Institute.

Rossi, Alice S., and Bhavani Sitaraman. 1988. Abortion in context: Historical trends and future changes. *Family Planning Perspectives* 20:273-81.

Rothenberg, Stuart, and Frank Newport. 1984. *The evangelical voter.* Washington, DC: Free Congress Research and Education Foundation.

Rovner, Julie. 1991. "Pro-Life" Democrats break ranks, lie low. *Congressional Quarterly Weekly Report* 49:3640-44.

Rubin, Alissa. 1991. Interest groups and abortion politics in the post-*Webster* era. In *Interest group politics,* 3rd ed., edited by Allan J. Cigler and Burdett A. Loomis. Washington, DC: Congressional Quarterly.

Rubin, Alissa. 1992. The abortions [sic] wars are far from over. *The Washington Post* (National Weekly Edition), December 21-27, p. 25.

Rubin, Eva R. 1987. *Abortion, politics, and the courts: Roe v. Wade and its aftermath,* rev. ed. Westport, CT: Greenwood Press.

Rule, Wilma. 1990. Why more women are state legislators. *Western Political Quarterly* 43:437-48.

Russett, Bruce. 1970. *What price vigilance: The burden of national defense.* New Haven, CT: Yale University Press.

Rust v. Sullivan. 110 S. Ct. 2559 (1990).

Sabatier, Paul A. 1988. An advocacy coalition framework of policy change and the role of policy-oriented learning therein. *Policy Sciences* 21:129-68.

Saint-Germain, Michelle. 1989. Does their difference make a difference? The impact of women on public policy in the Arizona legislature. *Social Science Quarterly* 70:956-68.

Salmore, Barbara G., and Stephen A. Salmore. 1993. The transformation of state electoral politics. Pp. 51-78 in *The state of the states,* 2nd ed., edited by Carl E. Van Horn. Washington, DC: CQ Press.

Sample, John, and Rex Warland. 1973. Attitudes and the prediction of behavior. *Social Forces* 51:292-304.

Sapiro, Virginia. 1980. News from the front: Intersex and intergenerational conflict over the status of women. *Western Political Quarterly* 33:260-77.

Sapiro, Virginia. 1981. Research frontier essay: When are interests interesting? The problem of political representation of women. *American Political Science Review* 75:701-16.

Sapiro, Virginia. 1983. *The political integration of women.* Urbana: University of Illinois Press.

Sapiro, Virginia. 1991. Feminism: A generation later. Pp. 10-22 in *American feminism: New issues for a mature movement,* edited by Janet K. Boles. ANNALS of the American Academy of Political and Social Science, 515.

Schattschneider, E. E. 1960. *The semi-sovereign people.* New York: Holt, Rinehart & Winston.

Schneider, Jerrold E. 1979. *Ideological coalitions in Congress.* Westport, CT: Greenwood Press.

Schneider, William. 1989. Abortion: Trouble for the GOP. *Public Opinion* 12:2, 59-60.

Schuler, Marsha. 1990. Most like Roemer but not legislature. *Morning Advocate* (Baton Rouge newspaper), September 23, pp. 1A, 9A.

Schuman, Howard, and Stanley Presser. 1981. *Questions and answers in attitude surveys: Experiments on question form, wording and context.* New York: Academic Press.

Schwartz, Herman. 1988. *Packing the courts: The conservative campaign to rewrite the Constitution.* New York: Scribner.

Schwartz, Shalom H. 1978. Temporal instability as a moderator of the attitude-behavior relationship. *Journal of Personality and Social Psychology* 36:715-24.

Scott, Jacqueline. 1989. Conflicting beliefs about abortion: Legal approval and moral doubt. *Social Psychology Quarterly* 52:319-26.

Scott, Jacqueline, and Howard Schuman. 1988. Attitude strength and social action in the abortion dispute. *American Sociological Review* 53:785-93.

Sears, David O. 1986. College Sophomores in the laboratory: Influence of a narrow data base on social psychology's view of human nature. *Journal of Personality and Social Psychology* 51:515-30.

Sears, David O., and Leonie Huddy. 1988. On the origins of the political disunity of women in politics. In *Women in 20th century American politics,* edited by P. Gurin and L. Tilly. New York: Russell Sage.

Segal, Jeffrey A., Charles M. Cameron, and Albert D. Cover. 1992. A spatial model of roll call voting: Senators, constituents, presidents, and interest groups in supreme court confirmations. *American Journal of Political Science* 36:96-121.

Sheeran, Patrick J. 1987. *Women, society, the state, and abortion: A structuralist analysis.* New York: Praeger.

Sherif, Muzafar, and Howard Cantril. 1947. *The psychology of ego-involvement.* New York: John Wiley.

Sigelman, Lee, David Lowery, and Roland Smith. 1983. The tax revolt: A comparative state analysis. *Western Political Quarterly* 36:30-51.

Silberman, Jonathan I., and Garey C. Durden. 1976. Determining legislative preferences on the minimum wage: An economic approach. *Journal of Political Economy* 84:317-29.

Simon, Rita J., and Gloria Danziger. 1991. *The women's movement in America: Successes, disappointments, and aspirations.* New York: Praeger.

Sivacek, John, and William D. Crano. 1982. Vested interest as a moderator of attitude-behavior consistency. *Journal of Personality and Social Psychology* 43:210-21.

Skerry, Peter. 1978. The class conflict over abortion. *Public Interest* 52:69-84.

Slobodzian, Joseph. 1993. Judge stays on abortion lawsuit. *Philadelphia Inquirer,* February 3, pp. B1, B7.

Smidt, Corwin. 1988. Evangelicals within contemporary American politics. *Western Political Quarterly* 41:601-20.

Smidt, Corwin. 1992. Evangelicals and American politics: 1976-1988. In *No longer exiles: The religious new right in American politics,* edited by Martin Cromartie. Washington, DC: Ethics and Public Policy Center.

Smith, Eric R. A. N. 1989. *The unchanging American voter.* Berkeley: University of California Press.

Smith, Steven T. 1981. The consistency and ideological structure of U.S. Senate voting alignments, 1957-1976. *American Journal of Political Science* 25:780-95.

Smith, T. Alexander. 1975. *The comparative policy process.* Santa Barbara, CA: ABC-Clio.

Staggenborg, Suzanne. 1987. Life-style preference and social movement recruitment: Illustrations from the abortion conflict. *Social Science Quarterly* 68:779-97.

Staggenborg, Suzanne. 1991. *The pro-choice movement: Organization and activism in the abortion conflict.* New York: Oxford University Press.

Stanley, Harold W., and Richard G. Niemi. 1990. *Vital statistics on American politics,* 2nd ed. Washington, DC: CQ Press.

Stanwick, Kathy A., and Katherine E. Kleeman. 1983. *Women make a difference.* New Brunswick, NJ: Center for American Women and Politics.

Statistical abstract of the United States. Annual editions. Washington, DC: Government Printing Office.

Stetson, Dorothy. 1991. *Women's rights in the U.S.A.* Belmont, CA: Wadsworth.

Stimson, James. 1991. *Public opinion in America: Moods, cycles and swings.* Boulder, CO: Westview.

Strickland, Ruth Ann, and Marcia Lynn Whicker. 1986. Banning abortion: An analysis of senate votes on a bimodal issue. *Women & Politics* 6:41-56.

Strickland, Ruth Ann, and Marcia Lynn Whicker. 1990a. Indicators of state restrictiveness toward abortion. Paper presented at the Annual Meeting of the Southwestern Political Science Association, Ft. Worth, March.

Strickland, Ruth Ann, and Marcia L. Whicker. 1990b. Political and socio-economic indicators of state restrictiveness toward abortion. Paper presented at the annual meeting of the American Political Science Association, San Francisco, August.

Studenmund, A. H., and Henry J. Cassidy. 1987. *Using econometrics: A practical guide.* Boston: Little, Brown.

Suchman, Edward A. 1950. The intensity component on attitude and opinion research. Pp. 213-76 in *Measurement and prediction,* edited by S. A. Stouffer. Magnolia, MA: Peter Smith.

Tatalovich, Raymond, and Byron W. Daynes. 1981. *The politics of abortion: A study of community conflict in public policy making.* New York: Praeger.

Tatalovich, Raymond, and Byron W. Daynes. 1988. *Social regulatory policy: Moral controversies in American politics.* Boulder, CO: Westview.

Tatalovich, Raymond, and Byron W. Daynes. 1989. The geographical distribution of U.S. hospitals with abortion facilities. *Family Planning Perspectives* 21:81-84.

Tetlock, Philip E. 1984. Cognitive style and political belief systems in the British House of Commons. *Journal of Personality and Social Psychology* 46:365-75.

Tetlock, Philip E. 1986. A value pluralism model of ideological reasoning. *Journal of Personality and Social Psychology* 50:819-27.

Thomas, Sue. 1991. The impact of women on state legislative policies. *Journal of Politics* 53:958-76.

Thomas, Sue, and Susan Welch. 1991. The impact of gender on activities and priorities of state legislators. *Western Political Quarterly* 44:445-56.

Thornburgh v. American College of Obstetricians and Gynecologists. 476 U.S. 747 (1986).

Thornton, Arland, and Deborah Freedman. 1979. Changes in sex role attitudes of women, 1962-1977. *American Sociological Review* 44:831-42.

Tidmarch, Charles, and Brad Karp. 1983. The missing beat: Press coverage of congressional elections in 8 metro areas. *Congress and the Presidency* W:47-61.

Tidmarch, Charles, Lisa Hyman, and Jill Sorkin. 1984. Press issue agendas in the 1982 congressional and gubernatorial election campaigns. *Journal of Politics* 46:1226-42.

de Tocqueville, Alexis. 1955. *Democracy in America.* New York: Vintage.

Toner, R. 1989. House, in big shift, votes to restore aid for abortions. *The New York Times,* October 12, pp. A1, 10.

Tosini, S. C., and E. Tower. 1987. The textile bill of 1985: The determinants of congressional voting patterns. *Public Choice* 54:19-25.

Traugott, Michael W., and Maris A. Vinovskis. 1980. Abortion and the 1978 congressional elections. *Family Planning Perspectives* 12 (5):238-46.

Tribe, Laurence H. 1990. *Abortion: The clash of absolutes.* New York: Norton.

Vinovskis, Maris A. 1980a. Abortion and the presidential election of 1976: A multivariate analysis of voting behavior. Pp. 184-205 in *The law and politics of abortion,* edited by Carl E. Schneider and Maris A. Vinovskis. Lexington, MA: Lexington.

Vinovskis, Maris A. 1980b. The politics of abortion in the House of Representatives in 1976. Pp. 224-61 in *The law and politics of abortion,* edited by Carl E. Schneider and Maris A. Vinovskis. Lexington, MA: Lexington.

Wald, Kenneth D., and Michael B. Lupfer. 1983. Religion and political attitudes in the urban South. Pp. 84-100 in *Religion and politics in the South: Mass and elite perspectives,* edited by Tod A. Baker. New York: Praeger.

Walsh, Edward J. 1988. *Democracy in the shadows: Citizen mobilization in the wake of the accident at Three Mile Island.* Westport, CT: Greenwood Press.

Webster v. Reproductive Health Services. 109 S. Ct. 3040 (1989).

Weiner, Janet, and Barbara A. Bernhardt. 1990. A survey of state Medicaid policies for coverage of abortion and prenatal diagnostic procedures. *American Journal of Public Health* 80:717-20.

Weissberg, Robert. 1976. *Public opinion and popular government.* Englewood Cliffs, NJ: Prentice-Hall.

Welch, Michael, and David Leege. 1991. Dual reference groups and political orientations: An examination of evangelically oriented Catholics. *American Journal of Political Science* 35:28-56.

Welch, Susan. 1985. Are women more liberal than men in the U.S. Congress? *Legislative Studies Quarterly* 10:125-34.

Werner, Emmy L. 1968. Women in the state legislatures. *Western Political Quarterly* 21:40-50.

Wetstein, Matthew E. 1992a. How stable is stable? Abortion attitudes in the 1972-1976 NES panel study. Paper presented at the annual meeting of the Midwest Association for Public Opinion Research, Chicago, April.

Wetstein, Matthew E. 1992b. A LISREL model of public opinion on abortion. Paper presented at the annual meeting of the Midwest Political Science Association, Chicago, April.

Wilcox, Clyde. 1986a. Evangelicals and fundamentalists in the new Christian right. *Journal for the Scientific Study of Religion* 25:355-63.

Wilcox, Clyde. 1986b. Fundamentalism and politics. *Journal of Politics* 48:1041-51.

Wilcox, Clyde. 1989a. The fundamentalist voter: Politicized religious identity and political attitudes and behavior. *Review of Religious Research* 31:54-67.

Wilcox, Clyde. 1989b. Political action committees and abortion: A longitudinal analysis. *Women & Politics* 9:1-19.

Wilcox, Clyde. 1990. Racial differences in abortion attitudes: Some additional evidence. *Public Opinion Quarterly* 54:248-55.

Wilcox, Clyde. 1992. Race, region, religion, and abortion attitudes. *Sociological Analysis* 53:97-105.

Wilcox, Clyde, and Leopoldo Gomez. 1990. The Christian right and the pro-life movement: An analysis of the sources of political support. *Review of Religious Research* 31:380-89.

Wilcox, Clyde, and Ted G. Jelen. 1990. Evangelicals and political tolerance. *American Politics Quarterly* 18:25-46.

Wilcox, Clyde, Lee Sigelman, and Elizabeth Cook. 1989. Some like it hot: Individual differences in responses to group feeling thermometers. *Public Opinion Quarterly* 53:246-57.

Wills, Garry. 1989. Evangels of abortion. *New York Review of Books* 36 (June 15):15-21.

Wlezien, Christopher B. 1992. The dynamics of representation: Public preferences and budgetary policy for defense. Paper presented at the Annual Meeting of the Midwest Political Science Association, Chicago, April.

Wlezien, Christopher, and Malcolm L. Goggin. 1973. The courts, interest groups, and public opinion about abortion. *Political Behavior* 15.

Woliver, Laura R. 1990. Mobilizing a silent majority: Pro-choice interests after *Webster.* Paper presented at the annual meeting of the American Political Science Association, San Francisco, September.

Woliver, Laura R. 1991. Mobilizing the pro-choice movement in South Carolina. Paper presented at annual meeting of the Midwest Political Science Association, Chicago, April.

World Values Study Group. 1990. The World Values Study, 1981-1983. [Codebook and machine-readable datafile.]

Wright, Gerald C., Robert S. Erikson, and John P. McIver. 1985. Measuring state partisanship and ideology with survey data. *Journal of Politics* 47:469-89.

Wright, Gerald C., Robert S. Erikson, and John P. McIver. 1987. Public opinion and policy liberalism in the American states. *American Journal of Political Science* 31:980-1001.

Wrightsman, L. S. 1973. Measurement of philosophies of human nature. Pp. 603-11 in *Measures of social psychological attitudes,* edited by J. P. Robinson and P. R. Shaver. Ann Arbor: Institute for Social Research, University of Michigan.

Young, Iris Marion. 1990. *Justice and the politics of difference.* Princeton, NJ: Princeton University Press.

Zald, Mayer N., and Bert Useem. 1987. Movements and countermovement interaction: Mobilization, tactics, and state involvement. In *Social movements in an organizational society,* edited by Mayer N. Zald and John D. McCarthy. New Brunswick, NJ: Transaction Books.

Index

Veto, Abortion legislation, 120, 155, 179, 183,
Vinovskis, Maris A., 112, 115
Violence, clinic, 7, 172, 240, 288
Virginia, 171, 220 n.3, 263
   gubernatorial elections in, 137-46, 151,
     152, 171

Waiting period. *See,* Abortion; Notifica-
   tion period
Washington, 171, 179
Washington Post Exit Poll (1990), 205
*Webster v. Reproductive Health Services
   (1989),* xi, 1, 6, 9, 39, 68, 69, 89-90,
   135, 203, 263
   effects of, 9, 143, 146
   impact on state politics, 204
Welch, Susan, 14, 227, 239
West Virginia, 180 n.c, 226, 241, 263
Wetstein, Matthew F., 228
Wetherell, Claire, 132
Whicker, Marcia L., 112
Whites, Abortion attitude of, 79
Wilcox, Clyde, 59, 72, 206, 207
Wilder, Douglas, 135, 140, 145, 146, 179,
   220 n.3, 229, 270

Williams, Clayton, 135, 146-47, 150
Wilson, Pete, 135, 147, 149
Wisconsin, 179, 251
WISH List, 7
Wlezien, Christopher, 61, 191, 192, 194,
   197
Women:
   and career, 13-14, 226, 235, 272
   defined, 12
   democratic legislators, 274-75, 277-
     280, 282
   empowerment of, 12
   gender inequality and, 13-14
   legislators, 14, 127, 226, 234-36, 242
   political mobilization of, 223, 226-27,
     230-37, 242
   political representation of, 14
   Republican legislators, 278
   right to choose, 145
   rights of, 10, 225, 231
   roles of, 11, 73
Women's Issue Scale, 102 n.3
Women's movement cohort, 74, 75
Wright, Gerald C., 209, 271
Wrongful Life/Wrongful Birth, 188 n.O
Wyoming, 208, 241

About the Contributors

Charles Barrilleaux is Associate Professor in the School of Public Administration and Policy and a member of the Policy Sciences Center faculty at Florida State University. His articles have appeared in *American Political Science Review, American Journal of Political Science,* and *Journal of Health Politics, Policy and Law.*

Michael B. Berkman is Assistant Professor of Political Science at The Pennsylvania State University. His book, *The State Roots of National Politics: Congress and the Tax Agenda, 1978-1986* (University of Pittsburgh Press forthcoming), will soon be published.

James R. Bowers is an Assistant Professor of Government at St. John Fisher College. He is author of *Abortion Policy, the Constitution, and John Locke's Liberalism: Can Government Be Both Pro-Choice and Anti-Abortion?* (Paragon forthcoming).

Jeffrey E. Cohen teaches political science at the University of Kansas. His books are *The Politics of the U.S. Cabinet: Representation in the Executive Branch, 1978-1984* (University of Pittsburgh Press 1988) and *The Politics of Telecommunications Regulation: The States and the Divestiture of AT&T* (M. E. Sharpe 1992).

Elizabeth Adell Cook is Visiting Professor in the Department of Government at The American University. She is coauthor of *Between Two Absolutes: Public Opinion and the Politics of Abortion* and coeditor of *The Year* *of the Woman: Myths and Realities.* Her research interests center on gender politics and electoral behavior.

Ellen M. Dran is a Research Associate with the Center for Governmental Studies at Northern Illinois University. She is the director of the Illinois Policy Survey. She has published in *Public Administration Review, Publius,* and *Women & Politics.*

Malcolm L. Goggin is Associate Professor of Political Science at the University of Houston, but he is spending the year in Glasgow, Scotland, as a Fulbright Scholar at the University of Strathclyde. His most recent books include *Policy Design and the Politics of Implementation* (Tennessee 1987) and *Implementation Theory and Practice* (Harper-Collins 1990).

John C. Green is Director of the Ray C. Bliss Institute of Applied Politics and Associate Professor of Political Science at the University of Akron. He has written on campaign finance and religion and politics. Mostly recently he has studied the 1988 Robertson campaign and its aftermath in 1992.

James L. Guth is Professor of Political Science at Furman University, and has published on interest groups, campaign finance, and religion and politics. He is best known for his research on Southern Baptist clergy.

Glen A. Halva-Neubauer is Dana Assistant Professor of Political Science and Director of the Urban Studies program at Furman University. His published work has appeared in *Publius.*

Susan B. Hansen is Associate Professor of Political Science and Director of the Women's Studies Program at the University of Pittsburgh. She is author of *The Politics of Taxation: Revenue Without Representation* (Praeger 1983), and *The Political Economy of State Industrial Policy* (University of Pittsburgh Press forthcoming).

Susan E. Howell is Professor of Political Science and Director of the Survey Research Center at the University of New Orleans. She has published articles in *Public Opinion Quarterly, American Politics Quarterly,* and *Journal of Politics.*

Ted G. Jelen is Professor of Political Science at Illinois Benedictine College. His publications include an edited book of readings titled *Religions and Political Behavior in the United States,* and he is the author of *The Political Mobilization of Religious Beliefs* and coauthor of *Between*

Two Absolutes: Public Opinion and the Politics of Abortion. His current research interests are the politics of abortion, and the status of clergy as political leaders.

Lyman A. Kellstedt is Professor of Political Science at Wheaton College. He has written on evangelical Protestants in the mass public, including measurement issues and partisan realignment.

Deborah R. McFarlane is Associate Professor of Public Administration at the University of New Mexico. Her research has appeared in *Social Science Quarterly, Administration and Society, American Journal of Gynecological Health,* and *Journal of Primary Prevention.*

Kenneth J. Meier is Professor or Political Science at the University of Wisconsin-Milwaukee. His most recent books are *The Politics of Hispanic Education* (SUNY 1991) and *Politics and the Bureaucracy: Policymaking in the Fourth Branch of Government* (Wadsworth 1993).

Gary Moncrief is a Professor of Political Science at Boise State University. He is coeditor of *Changing Patterns in State Legislatures* (University of Michigan Press 1992). His publications have appeared in *Journal of Politics, Legislative Studies Quarterly, Western Political Quarterly,* and *Canadian Journal of Political Science.*

Robert E. O'Connor is Associate Professor of Political Science, a member of the faculty of the Graduate School of Public Policy and Analysis, and an associate faculty member of the Science, Technology, and Society Program—all at The Pennsylvania State University. His articles have appeared in the *American Political Science Review, Legislative Studies Quarterly, American Politics Quarterly,* and *Western Political Quarterly.*

David Schier is a doctoral student in political science at Loyola University of Chicago. He is pursuing dissertation research on the Federal Election Commission.

Frauke Schnell is an Assistant Professor in the Department of Political Science at West Chester State University where she specializes in political psychology and public opinion.

Robert T. Sims is a Research Associate with the Survey Research Center at the University of New Orleans and is currently a doctoral candidate. His interests include political behavior and methodology.

Corwin E. Smidt is Professor of Political Science at Calvin College. He has published on the voting behavior of evangelical Protestants, and is the editor of *Contemporary Evangelical Political Involvement* (University Press of America 1989).

Raymond Tatalovich is a Professor of Political Science at Loyola University of Chicago. Among his coauthored works are *The Politics of Abortion* (Praeger 1981), *Presidential Power in the United States* (Brooks/ Cole 1984), and *Social Regulatory Policy: Moral Controversies in American Politics* (Westview 1988).

Matthew E. Wetstein is a doctoral candidate in political science at Northern Illinois University. He has coauthored articles on Illinois politics in *Illinois Issues.*

Clyde Wilcox is Associate Professor in Government at Georgetown University. He is the author of *God's Warriors: The Christian Right in Twentieth Century America* and coauthor of *Between Two Absolutes: Public Opinion and the Politics of Abortion.* His research interests include religion and politics, gender politics, and campaign financing.

Stephanie L. Witt is an Assistant Professor of Political Science and Public Administration at Boise State University. She is the author of *The Pursuit of Race and Gender Equity in American Academe* (Praeger 1990), and is coauthor of the forthcoming *The Urban West* (Praeger).

Christopher Wlezien is Assistant Professor in the Department of Political Science at the University of Houston. His articles are published in *American Journal of Political Science, Political Behavior,* and *Journal of Politics.*

Marilyn A. Yale recently received her doctorate from the University of Houston and is a first-year professor in the Department of Government at Morehead State University in Morehead, Kentucky. She is currently working on the use of the news media by abortion combatants.

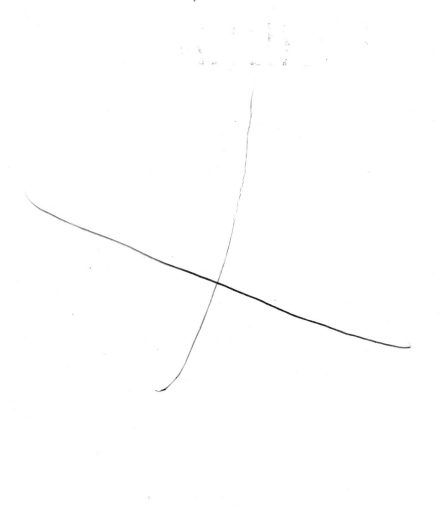